Lidia DiMarco
954 609-2125

MORE THAN
A DREAM

A MYSTERIOUS JOURNEY
TO ANCIENT ISRAEL

BY

BARBARA H. MARTIN

Barbara H. Martin

BARBARA H. MARTIN

ISBN 13:978-0966805482
ISBN: 0-9668054-8-8

Cover design by
Frina Art

Barbara's picture on back cover
By
Jessica Forinash

DEDICATED

To my life-long friend
Rhoda Hux
with gratitude for her love and friendship over the last 40 years
and to
My wonderful friend Delores Chancellor

MY APPRECIATION
for
Katherine Elisabeth Busbee for her tireless help with the back cover
and to
Michael Edward Martin for his many hours of technical support to
make this book possible

This book is a work of fiction. I have tried to depict daily life in Israel according to historical records from many different sources in my extensive research. All names and places, other than the well-known historical facts or people, are the imagination of the author.

I do not pretend to be a historian or an archeologist; so if I have failed to describe some places or events correctly in some areas, please forgive me. I merely wish to present a picture of that era through the eyes of a modern-day atheist Jewish physician, who chooses to rely on science rather than faith in his treacherous, soul-searching journey of self-discovery.

Enjoy the journey.

Chapter 1

Present day Philadelphia.

Thomas Peterson, MD walked out of the surgical suite with a satisfied smile on his face. Another miracle made possible due to his amazing skills and obvious superior talents. On the way out he threw his green face mask and surgical garb into a bin with a practiced motion. He knew he had done well – again. It was a great feeling to be the best; like a high from a powerful drug. Yet just like it, he knew it wouldn't last. A frown crossed his handsome face.

With his six foot, trim, slender body, toned by regular exercise in the gym and self-defense lessons at the club, he presented the perfect picture of a successful professional. His thick, dark, curly hair and intelligent brown eyes were overshadowed by a rather prominent Jewish nose. He walked with confident strides down the long corridor toward the back exit reserved for staff, without bothering to acknowledge anyone on the way. He was one of the youngest Chiefs of Thoracic Surgery in the history of Philadelphia Grace Hospital and that, in his mind, made it unnecessary to bother with the daily amenities toward those he referred to as the lower echelon personnel. He'd had a hard day with several surgeries, preceded by an early staff meeting in the morning, and was ready to call it a day.

It was late afternoon before he stopped his shiny, new, black BMW in front of the three-door garage of his large home. He didn't notice the manicured lawn or the beautifully trimmed hedges lining both sides of the driveway. Melissa would be home fixing dinner. He hated their endless arguments nearly every day, followed by an evening of silence.

Reluctantly, he opened the car door. He wished he had gone to the club to get something to eat and have a drink instead of coming here of all days. It was his birthday today. He was forty-two years old with nothing more to show than being a talented surgeon with a big house and a wife who hated him. How had he and Melissa gotten to this place of mutual dislike?

He entered the kitchen, expecting his wife to be there. Instead, there was a note on the spotlessly clean counter. 'I will be gone till eight. There is food in the fridge.' He stared at the piece of paper and a feeling of utter loneliness came over him. *She forgot my birthday!* It served him right. After all, it was he who had the affair and asked for a divorce. He cringed when he remembered how hurt Melissa was when he told her.

After that came the anger and then the arguments; and in time the silence. No matter how hard he tried to tell her after a while that he had broken off with Jenny, their relationship seemed damaged beyond repair. Melissa had withdrawn into her own world and he did not know how to reach her anymore. She simply did not seem to need him the way she used to. There was a strange calm and even peace that surrounded her he did not understand; and it frustrated him. Unlike surgery, he was no longer in control of their relationship the way he used to be.

His mind went back to the day they met in the hospital cafeteria. She looked so young and beautiful with her thick black hair, dark blue eyes and a figure that even her loose nursing uniform couldn't hide. While filling his coffee cup, his mind went into full gear trying to figure out a way to strike up a conversation that sounded half way casual, when he heard her say,

"Don't you know coffee is bad for your health?" She looked at him with a friendly smile. For the first time since he was five, he didn't know what to say. He shrugged his shoulder in an almost helpless gesture. "I watched you doing surgery yesterday, Dr. Peterson. You are very good, but then I'm sure you already know that." There was a slight tease in her voice.

"I know," he stammered, "I mean, thank you." He looked at her name tag. "I mean, that's nice of you to say, Melissa." He had actually blushed and almost spilled his coffee. "Are you a nurse?" He cringed at his dumb remark, looking at the big RN tag with her name on it.

"I've been assigned to assist in your OR this afternoon, Dr. Peterson. My name is Melissa Brenner." Her smile lit up her face, showing off a row of perfect white teeth.

He finally caught himself and said in his usual professional, crisp tone, "I look forward to working with you, nurse. I guess I will see you then." However, no matter how hard he tried to ignore her, on that day she managed to walk right into his life and his heart.

They started dating not long after and there was no question in his mind, Melissa was the one for him. It didn't matter he was Jewish and she was a Christian. He didn't care, knowing his family would be upset about that fact. Especially his grandmother, who was a devoted Orthodox Jew and would never approve of marrying anyone outside the faith. Adding to that, Melissa's family was equally opposed to the marriage, since her father was a minister. Yet in spite of it, they were married by both, a Rabbi and her father, the minister, nine months later.

That was six years ago. The affair with Jenny had started last year and only lasted for less than six months. While he and Melissa continued to live in the same house, the only time they spoke was by arguing. He spent more and more time at the club and she had her own meetings to go to. He had no idea where or what they were and didn't ask. He had an idea it was some church, but had never bothered to find out.

He sighed as he looked around the empty kitchen and then went to the fridge. He saw the food she had left, but chose a bottle of wine instead, poured a glass and went into the living room. He took his Armani jacket off and flung it carelessly over the couch. With another heavy sigh he sank into the comfortable big chair and took a sip of the wine. It tasted good. He leaned back and closed his eyes. The last thing he felt was an unusual, soothing heaviness spreading gently throughout his body.

In the year 27 A.D. in the land of Israel

He woke up from the bright sunlight bathing his face. A breeze of hot, dry air brushed over him with a gentle wave. He had a hard time focusing for a moment until the braying of a donkey nearby made him sit up with a jolt. Where on earth was he? The strong smell of animals, rotten fruit, fish and sweat assaulted his senses like a hammer. Squinting to block out the sun, he looked around. A real live donkey was standing next to him, tethered to a dilapidated small cart, loaded with a variety of fruit. He had no idea what they were. An old man stood in front of it, sorting out the rotten ones and throwing them on a heap in back of the cart. That explained the smell. He placed the good ones carefully into several woven baskets on a rough bench next to the cart.

On the other side of the narrow dirt path from where he sat, Thomas could see a row of vendors with a variety of merchandise. They were shouting and praising their wares to the few customers at the top of their lungs. One offered olive oil out of big earthen jars, another touted his barley as the best in the land, while the next praised his bundles of wool as coming from sheep good enough for temple offerings. Even white doves were sold to those who wanted to make a sacrifice in the synagogue. A little further down he could smell the fish as it baked in the hot sun with flies humming in droves above. To his left was a stall with baskets filled with figs as well as a variety of cheeses.

Thomas noticed a short, rotund woman with a basket in her hand. Her long, loose-fitting, brownish garb flowed in the gentle breeze behind her. Her face was mostly hidden by a scarf of the same dingy color. There was no doubt about her displeasure as she yelled at one of the vendors in a sharp, biting tongue,

"You dare to offer this worthless garbage to me? Don't you know my mistress will flog me if I so much as get near her with this trash you call pomegranates!" She threw the fruit back on the table and started to walk away.

"Wait, Sarah, I have some over here that will be more to your liking. They have just come in and I was saving them for you." The skinny little merchant reached behind him and produced a bright red, fresh looking fruit and held it out to her. "I offer this to you for your lady at the lowest price ever heard in these parts."

"Hmph, this is a little better, although not as good as I wish. Maybe it might be acceptable to my noble lady," she said, pretending reluctance and doubt as she took three of them, placed them carefully into her basket and then handed him a few coins.

Thomas watched the entire exchange with astonishment. Where was he? And why could he understand everything these people said? He knew they didn't speak English or Hebrew, yet he understood them perfectly. He had heard Aramaic one time in the synagogue at home during a play. This was definitely what it sounded like. Totally confused, he turned to the old man still sorting his fruits.

"Please tell me where I am, Sir. I seem to be lost."

The man stopped for a moment to look at him and then continued with his task as he spoke.

"You are at the market place in Nazareth. Everyone is getting ready for the Shabbat tonight. Are you a stranger from far away to not know this?"

"Yes, I am. What country is this?"

"You are in Israel, of course." The old man stopped and looked at him closely for the first time. "You are dressed strangely. I have never seen such ugly clothes on a man." After that he continued with his task.

Thomas sat back, stunned. How did he get here? He touched his arms and face and stared down at his Armani dress pants and shiny, expensive leather shoes. His tie hung loosely around the collar of his light blue, long-sleeved shirt. What had looked so normal a few minutes ago in his living room at home, now made him feel ridiculously out of place in these humble surroundings. He took out his wallet and stared at his many credit cards and one ten-dollar bill. He looked around again, bewildered and feeling helpless. That's when he saw the large mountain in the distance.

"What mountain is that?" he asked the old man.

"You are indeed a stranger. Everyone knows that is Mt. Tabor," he added with disdain. "Where are you from and how come you speak our language like one born here?"

"I don't know. I am from America."

8

"I can't say I have ever heard of it. Is it from across the waters to the north? Maybe you are one of those barbarians the Romans use as slaves?" He stopped to look at Thomas.

"Have you heard of New York?" Thomas asked.

"I can't say that I have. I have not heard of many places, even in Israel. I was born in Nazareth and it is all I know. Yahweh has given us Jews this land and he will drive the cursed Romans out soon when the Meshiah comes." He leaned over to Thomas in a conspiratorial way and added in a whisper, "Some say He is here now."

"Really, what is his name?" Thomas asked.

"How should I know," the old man said and waved his hand in a dismissive way. "I am not a learned scholar or Rabbi. When the Deliverer of Israel comes, He will let us know." He sighed deeply. "I just wish he would hurry; our people are crying out under this cursed Roman oppression." He looked around nervously, making sure he had not been overheard, as it suddenly dawned on him he was talking to a stranger. "You are not a Roman spy are you?"

"No, I'm not. I am merely a traveler and a stranger and I have no idea where I am."

"I told you this is Nazareth in Galilee."

Thomas leaned back against the stone wall, reeling from the realization, that he was somehow transported back in time to the days of Jesus. He remembered Melissa's grandmother as she made him listen to, what she referred to, as the Gospel. How Jesus came and walked the land of Israel, performing many miracles and proclaiming He was the Messiah. Thomas had not been familiar with the details, but since Melissa insisted they visit Grandma often in the nice retirement home, he got his fill as she told him about the crucifixion and resurrection of this Messiah each time they went. He listened politely, but when she asked him if he wanted to accept Jesus into his heart, he politely declined and dismissed the whole thing as soon as they left. What was funny, his own grandmother made Melissa listen to the Jewish account of the story of the God of Abraham, Isaac and Jacob. Nana, as she was called, made very sure to stress to Melissa that the Jews worship only one God, not three like the Christians. Melissa listened just as politely and like he, never agreed to change her mind.

Thomas recalled his feelings of superiority as he was certain neither grandmother was right. He knew there was no God and felt religion a worthless exercise in futility, emotional hogwash as he called it. He reasoned these were modern times and he was a man of science, who didn't need to believe in fables and old wives tales. Everything in life could be adequately explained through science and without the necessity of faith. Melissa didn't argue with him, but kept her true feelings to herself.

Yet here he was, transported from the year 2016 into the distant past to the land of his ancestors, Israel. There was no way his beloved science could explain what had just happened, no matter how he tried. He felt the hard wall of the small building on his back and watched in stunned silence as the world of ancient history past by him in this tiny, smelly market place in the small town of Nazareth in Galilee.

Chapter 2

"Shalom, you look very strange, Sir." The young boy stood in front of Thomas, looking him over carefully. "I have never seen clothes like that."

Thomas smiled. "I am a stranger here. My name is Thomas, what is yours?"

"I am Saul, but everyone calls me Tiny. As you can see, I am not very tall for my age. My mother tells me, while I am not great in body, I am of a great mind. I know how to read and write and I study the Torah every day. I want to be a great Rabbi someday." He stretched his shoulders upward to appear taller. "I can see you are very tall, but I wish you wouldn't wear such ugly clothes."

"These are all I have. Maybe you can get me some that look better." Thomas stood up and smiled down at the boy.

"Come with me, I know someone who will give you what you need." Tiny stretched out his hand and took his as they walked down the dirt road past the colorful stalls. Thomas was drawn to one with baskets filled with large loaves of barley bread, which emitted the most heavenly smell. Next to it was a vendor of knives, ropes and iron tools. The last stall offered a variety of spices, vegetables and dried herbs, which hung down the front in bundles. Slowly, Tiny led him through the village of Nazareth along narrow alleyways with stairs leading upwards on a slope. The houses along each side were made of uneven stones set in clay mortar with small, high openings for windows and one large one in the front serving as a door. He tried to peak in through some of them to get a glimpse of the small courtyard with stone benches and a blackened top made of stone, apparently used as a cooking area.

A few women were standing by the well, taking turns to draw water from it. A small pool, a little off to the side, enclosed by rocks and set in mortar, was surrounded by several more women washing clothes by beating them on the rocks. Their animated chatter stopped abruptly as Thomas and Tiny drew closer.

Tiny pulled him by the hand as they passed the well in the middle of town.

"He is a stranger from a far-away land and has come to visit us," Tiny shouted to them and others looking down from some of the flat roof tops. "I am taking him to my kinswoman Miriam. He is of our people, a son of Abraham," he said in answer to an old man who wanted to know who the stranger was.

Thomas looked around with a smile and waved to them, but everyone simply stared at him with curious looks of distrust and apprehension.

It must be my clothes, he thought and loosened his tie some more. The heat was stifling and he wiped his forehead with the sleeve of his shirt. He got a glimpse of what seemed to be a synagogue on a hill overlooking the village up ahead.

"How much further to go, Tiny?" he asked with irritation in his voice. He didn't like this dream at all and missed his shiny new BMW for one. *I hate these narrow, filthy dirt roads.*

"We are almost there, Thomas. My kinswoman Miriam will give you clothes her husband Joseph used to wear when he was still alive. He died some years ago."

"Are you sure she will?" He could just imagine Melissa bringing some stranger home for a change of clothes!

"Oh yes, she is a righteous woman who takes care of those who do not have anything. She lives in the house with her relatives, since she is a widow. Her son, who is a carpenter, takes good care of her so she lacks for nothing."

Thomas was embarrassed and aggravated to be counted as one who did not have anything, while an image of his large, luxurious home ran through his mind.

Finally, they arrived at a small house. Thomas looked through the door which led to a tiny courtyard. Since he wasn't sure if the owner of the house might object to him in any way, he remained outside on the street. He peeked through the door and realized the interior of the house was entirely made of stone set in mortar with three rooms, the door openings facing the inner court. He could see a roughly hewn set of steps on the right side leading up to the flat roof and two stone benches lining the walls on two sides. A small cooking area sat on another. Right behind it were two stalls, which held a sheep and two goats in one and a donkey in the other.

"Miriam, I brought a stranger who needs clothes," Tiny said as he ran inside, leaving Thomas waiting out in the street.

"Shalom, please, enter our humble home and allow us to refresh you with whatever you may be in need of." The voice was pleasant and kind. Thomas looked up and saw a small woman in her mid-forties, her face filled with warmth as she motioned for him to come into the courtyard. Her eyes had a lively sparkle in them as she waved him in with a smile. A large, dark, blue scarf draped down to her shoulders, holding her beautiful long, black hair in check. "We do not have much, but whatever it is, we share it with you gladly as our God commands us to do." She motioned again for him to sit on one of the benches. Entering, he had to duck his head to fit through the narrow doorway. Uncertain what to do, he stretched out his hand toward her in greeting. She looked at it in confusion and simply bowed her head gracefully. "I am Miriam, the widow of Joseph, the son of Heli of the house of David."

"I am Thomas, a stranger to these parts. Thank you for your hospitality, Miriam."

"Please be seated and allow me to bring you refreshments after your long journey." She disappeared into the house before he could say anything else.

Thomas looked around the simple surroundings. Everything was made of roughly hewn stone, the benches and the small cooking area in the far corner. Two reddish clay pots stood by the door, filled with water.

"Would you like to wash your hands and feet, Thomas?" Tiny asked when he saw Thomas looking at the water jars. "It will refresh you from your long journey," he added.

Thomas looked at him and made a helpless gesture.

"I have no idea how to do this. Won't you go ahead and show me."

"Do you not wash where you come from, Thomas? It is the law in our land. The Lord God wants us to be clean and so avoid sickness and disease. It is part of the Law of Moses given to us long ago."

"Of course we wash ourselves, Tiny, but we do not have earthen jars in my country."

Tiny shook his head in wonder. "What a strange place you come from. Here, I will show you how to wash your hands and then cleanse your feet from the dust of the road." He poured a little of the water over his hands and rubbed them. Then he took his sandals off, tipped the jar a little and splashed a small amount of water over his bare feet. When he was done, he looked at Thomas' expensive, brown shoes in utter astonishment. "You must take them off after you wash your hands or you cannot cleanse your feet." His amazement grew when he saw Thomas's socks. "Why do you wear clothes on your feet, Thomas? This is very strange. Allow me to take them off for you." He pulled one of the socks off before Thomas could stop him. "I have never seen such clean feet in my life," he said. "No wonder you do not need to wash them. I wouldn't mind having such unusual footwear." He thought for a moment before he went on. "On the other hand, they would be too hot to wear in the sand I imagine. I better find some sandals for you."

"It is a hot day today and you must be thirsty and tired from your long journey." Miriam had returned with cups made of stoneware, filled with wine mixed with water. "Here you are, Thomas. I have brought some bread and goat cheese just in case you are hungry." She put the delicious looking food in front of Thomas, who had taken a seat on one of the cushions along the wall. He did not hesitate to eat since he suddenly realized, he had not had anything since yesterday. He loved the taste of the coarse barley bread and the soft cheese. *All the time Melissa wanted me to eat organic, well, here it is!* He smiled to himself. *If she could see me now,* he thought as he took a sip of the drink and nearly choked. It tasted more like vinegar than wine. He tried hard not to show his dislike since it surely would have offended Miriam. Besides, he had no choice but to drink it since he was really thirsty from the walk.

Miriam stood a little to the side while he ate. "I am sorry my son is not here. He has gone to the synagogue to sit with the religious leaders. He is a wonderful carpenter, but also learned in the Torah and speaks eloquently about the things of God," she said as Thomas took another sip of the sour tasting wine mixture.

"Thank you so much for this drink, Miriam. I was rather thirsty walking all the way from the market. I so appreciate your hospitality." He looked at Tiny next to him and realized the boy could not leave, because it would have been unseemly for Miriam to entertain a man by herself who was not a relative.

"May I ask where you are from, Thomas?" Miriam asked.

"I am not from Israel, but from a country far away."

"Are you not a Jew then?"

"I am an Israelite, but have lived in another part of the world all my life. It is called America."

"How is it you speak our language so well? Your parents must have taught you the ways of our people."

"My grandmother did."

"Is your father a learned man? You sound educated." Miriam said.

"He is a physician at a large center of healing in my country," Thomas said with a slight hesitation. He realized he had to learn to formulate things in a way these uneducated, simple people of this time could understand.

"What brought you back to the land of our people, Thomas?" Miriam's voice was gentle yet curious. "Please forgive my many questions, we don't get too many visitors from far-away lands," she added with an apologetic smile.

"I am also a physician and a healer like my father. My reasons for coming here are not very clear in my mind. Maybe I needed to experience where my roots are," he said, hoping that would satisfy her curiosity.

"I am glad you came, Thomas. Tiny tells me you need clothes." She looked at him with a mischievous twinkle in her large, brown eyes. "I can certainly agree with him. I still have some robes and other garments from my husband Joseph. Since he passed away, I have no need for them any longer." She moved toward the door. "Allow Tiny to keep you company while I fetch them for you," she said and left.

"Tiny, tell me about Miriam's son, the carpenter."

"He is much older than I am and took over his father Joseph's carpentry shop. Yeshua is very kind and has taught me many things about God. He calls Him his Father. Whenever I am around him, I feel good and my heart is at peace. I can't explain it." The boy took a piece of bread and a bit of cheese. "I hope you will stay and meet him when he gets back from the synagogue. He goes there every day when his work is done here. Sometimes the Pharisees argue with him, but he never loses his temper." Tiny giggled as he went on, "but they do. I think he drives them crazy, because he tells them things they don't want to hear or even understand. He really knows the Law of Moses by heart and the Psalms and everything about the prophets. He told them once he did not come to do away with the Law, but he came to fulfill it. They really got mad about that and accused him of heresy. But he just smiled and walked away. He does that when they get really angry with him. They know he is right, but don't want to admit it since he is not a Pharisee." Tiny took another piece of bread and continued.

"Miriam worries about him. She told me, right from the time he was born in Bethlehem, he was different." Before Tiny could go on, Miriam returned with several garments hanging over her arm.

"Here you are. Tiny can show you where you may change into these so that you will not stand out in our village as a stranger." She laid them down next to his cushion. "Take your time and finish your meal. I will go and continue my daily chores." With that she left.

"Tell me more about his birth, Tiny," Thomas said after Miriam was gone. He remembered Melissa's grandmother's tales.

"The way Miriam tells it, she and Joseph had to go to Bethlehem while she was still with child for a census Caesar Augustus had ordered. You see, our families are from the royal line of David, so Joseph and Miriam had to go there to be counted. However, when they got there, her time to deliver came. But there was no room in any of the inns, so Joseph finally found a cave near the town and Miriam gave birth to her son Yeshua." Tiny raised himself up, his cheeks were flushed and with one hand he pushed a strand of his black, curly hair out of his face. "This is where it gets exciting. Miriam tells how shepherds came and knelt down before the little baby and told Miriam and Joseph that an angel had appeared to them, telling them to come and worship at his manger. To this day Miriam doesn't understand all of it, but she knows her son is different and destined for great things."

Thomas listened intently. This was crazy. How could this boy know the story of Christmas? Nothing made any sense. He would have to meet this Yeshua and make sure to debunk this crazy fable. Maybe someone had drugged his wine at the house and he was having hallucinations of some kind. He had always hated Christmas and everything surrounding it. The tinsel, fairytales and gift-giving had never been a part of his life. The worst part was, every year the three-ring circus started earlier. Why not leave the darn tree up all year for heaven's sake? It made him angry that he was confronted with this same legend two thousand years in the past.

"What is wrong, Thomas, are you angry with me?" Tiny touched him on the shoulder. "I didn't mean to upset you." His small face looked worried. "I am certain Miriam told the truth."

"I am absolutely not mad at you, Tiny. I was just thinking about my home and how we have a fable just like this one. Except I don't like it, because it isn't true."

"But Miriam would never lie to us, Thomas. She is the most righteous woman I know and well known in Nazareth for her good deeds and godly behavior. What she told us is true and everyone believes her."

"I am sure they do, Tiny. Everyone seems to believe this unlikely tale at my home as well."

"But you don't?"

"No, I don't. I believe only through science and learning can we explain how things work in life."

"Does that mean you don't believe in *Yahweh*?"

"It does."

"I feel sorry for you, Thomas. How can you not know how our great and mighty God led our people out of Egypt and brought us into this land? How He gave it to our father Abraham as an inheritance and promised him that our people would be as numerous as the stars in heaven. How can you be an Israelite and not believe this? The Meshiah is coming soon and will deliver us from the Romans just like *Yahweh* delivered us from the Egyptians. Everyone is waiting for Him with great anxiety. What is going to happen to you when He comes and you don't believe in Him? You will incur His anger and be condemned for all eternity." Tiny was clearly in a frenzy by now.

"Don't worry about me, Tiny, I'll be ok. I don't think your Meshiah will come any time soon." Thomas patted the boy on the shoulder and got up to change his clothes. *I wish I could tell you that your Meshiah hasn't come even two thousand years from now.*

As he shed his western clothes, Tiny handed him a white loin cloth as an undergarment. It was made from rough material and reached to his knees. After that Tiny unfolded a brown tunic for him to put over it. This was a long piece of material and touched his ankles, sewn up at the sides with openings left for the head and arms. It was to be held together with a long, equally rough rope. Thomas looked for a mirror when he was finished, but of course there wasn't one. *Not exactly Armani,* he thought.

"Now you look like a child of Abraham," Miriam said when she returned. "Tiny will show you how to put on your head covering properly to shield you from the hot sun." She looked at Thomas with approval as she clasped her hands together with a smile. "The hearts of the young maidens will beat faster when they see you."

"I am married, Miriam, back in my country. I have no idea if I will ever see my wife again."

"Is she part of our people, Thomas?"

"No, she is not, but she believes in your Meshiah."

"But he hasn't come yet," Tiny interrupted. "How can she know of Him in a land far away?"

"I can't explain it, but she does," Thomas answered reluctantly.

"Then she is greatly blessed," Miriam said in a quiet voice.

"I think it's time I got on the road, Miriam," Thomas said as he got up. "I have to find a place for the night and then see about some work. Could you tell me where I could find both?"

"I know of a kinsman who is in need of laborers to gather in the barley harvest. I am certain he would be glad to give you shelter and work. His name is David, the son of Aaron of the line of David. He lives a good walk away from here in the town of Cana. As a matter of fact, his son is going to be wed next week. He might need some help with the wedding feast. Tiny will take you to him. There is enough time left in the day for him to make it there and back in time for the start of the Shabbat tonight." She turned to Tiny and handed him another slice of bread and a piece of cheese wrapped in cloth. "Here, this is to sustain you on the way there and back. Let me fill the wineskin with watered wine for the journey. Make sure to let your mother know where you are going before you leave, Tiny," she added.

The noonday sun felt quite hot as they walked northward toward Cana. It was a peaceful scene with rolling hills, dotted with large and small rocks, stretching into the far distance. He could make out a herd of sheep watched by a lonely shepherd in a far-away field of green. Suddenly, a two-wheeled cart, drawn by a donkey, filled with sacks of grain, came towards them from the opposite direction.

"That is another kinsman of ours," Tiny said excitedly. "He is the brother of the groom. Let's ask him how the wedding preparations are going," Tiny shouted and ran towards the cart. "Nathaniel, how good to see you," he yelled long before they were close enough for the other to answer. As soon as the man came into hearing distance, Tiny asked, "Have they finally signed the dowry agreement? I heard it was a difficult time for all."

Thomas fully expected Tiny to be told to mind his own business, but to his surprise the two young men engaged in a long, animated conversation about the year-long haggle over the bride price.

"My father had to pay a lot of dowry after all," Nathanial said. "Naomi is quite a catch for the house of David. She is beautiful, strong in mind and body and shows unusual wisdom for one so young. Besides, she will help my mother in the household, being the one girl among us four brothers. Naomi's father now has to hire a woman from the village to help her mother, and that will be expensive. Also, there is her father's old mother to take care of. They had to take her in when her husband died two seasons ago. And then with the wedding getting close, there is much to do." He pulled on the reins to encourage the donkey to continue his journey. "I have to be on my way. Mother sent me to get some more supplies for the feast in return for the grain. I will be back in time for the last preparations."

"Nathanial, what great timing," Tiny said. "I brought a stranger named Thomas. He is an Israelite, but lives in a distant land. He seeks employment and a place to stay for a while. How fortunate your father is in need of help with all these pressing things going on." He pointed to Thomas. "He comes highly recommended by Miriam. She sent me to show him the way to your father's place." Tiny looked expectantly at Thomas and then at Nathanial. "Surely he was sent by God in your time of need."

"Shalom Thomas, my father will welcome you." He bowed towards Thomas. "I must get on so that I will make it there before sundown and the start of the Shabbat. With that Nathanial flicked the reins sharply and the donkey moved forward reluctantly. "God willing, I will see you both when I get back," he shouted before he was out of earshot.

"Nathanial is the fourth son of his father David and his mother Rebecca. He is a great blessing to them since he is well versed in the buying and selling of goods in spite of his young age." Tiny continued his chatter during the rest of their walk while Thomas listened, nodding his head every now and again. Not used to walking in sandals, he felt his feet starting to hurt. The sandals he had been given had rubbed the spot between the toes on his right foot raw and it was getting quite painful.

"My feet hurt and I am tired. In my country we ride in fancy carts and the roads are much better than this," he said with exasperation in his voice.

"So how come you do not even have water jars at your front door so you can wash as the Lord commands?"

"We don't need them, Tiny, we take showers."

"That is sad, Thomas. What you are saying is, the only time you cleanse yourself in your country is when it rains." He looked at Thomas with concern. "No wonder you seem to complain a lot. My mother does not allow me to do that. She says the Lord our God gives us everything we need for each day and to complain means we tell Him it isn't enough." Tiny smiled at him with an open grin, without judgment or any hint of disapproval.

Thomas shrugged his shoulders in a helpless gesture and walked on, gritting his teeth in pain and frustration. How could he possibly tell Tiny how wealthy he was and what a fabulous house he lived in? He had the sinking feeling no one around here would believe him.

"Here we are," Tiny finally said and pointed to a collection of buildings coming into view in the distance. Even Thomas could tell it was a very large estate. Apparently, Miriam's kinsman was a rich man. "Just around the bend is the village of Cana," Tiny said. "The wedding will be a great affair to which all the people in the town and some from Nazareth will be invited since my kinsman is an important man."

"Can we stop for a minute for me to rest?" Thomas asked, looking at his foot and the bloody spot between his toes. "I think I will take off the footwear the rest of the way, since it really hurts a lot." He waved his hand in a gesture of surrender. "And I'm not complaining. Not much anyway," he added under his breath.

"Rebecca will put a soothing ointment on it as soon as we get there," Tiny said with confidence. "She knows a lot about such things." They had stopped and Thomas sat down by the side of the road and took the sandal off. He examined the wound and knew it was superficial, but without medical attention it could easily get infected in this environment of perpetual sand and dirt. He had no choice but to rely on this woman's treatment and cringed as he longed for his sterile surgical suite back in Philadelphia. Surely he would have to give Rebecca some instructions as to what to do.

"One of your toes is missing!" Tiny shouted as he pointed his finger at his left foot. What happened to it?"

"I was born without it," Thomas said. "It is a genetic flaw in my family. My father had the same thing." Tiny bent down and took a closer look and then straightened up with a worried expression. "Was it hard for your parents to find you a wife, being deformed like that?"

"I wouldn't exactly call it deformed, Tiny," Thomas answered with irritation. "The kind of shoes we wear in my country; no one would ever know." He would never tell Tiny how embarrassed he was as a boy during PE in school and how hard he tried to hide the fact he had only four toes on one foot.

"We really must get going, Thomas," Tiny said, glad to be able to change the subject, since he had noticed Thomas' negative reaction to his comment. "I must get back in time before the start of the Shabbat. Besides, my mother will worry if I don't return in time."

"You haven't told me anything about your family, Tiny," Thomas said, hoping he could delay the inevitable since his sore was really hurting when he tried to put the sandal back on. He felt he had no choice, because the dirt and droppings from the many animals travelling the road would without a doubt lead to a serious infection.

"I am the son of Laban, the metal worker of the house of Samuel. My mother is Rachel, from the town of Capernaum. They live in Nazareth and I have two brothers and three sisters. I am the youngest and the only one left at home. All the others are grown and married with their own place, except my oldest brother Saul who lives with us with his wife Ruth and their three children. He works with my father in the metal shop since father's business will go to him when the time comes." Tiny got up. "We must continue on our way. It is not far to my kinsman's house. Come, Thomas, you can make it, I will help you." He took Thomas's hand and pulled him up.

Chapter 3

Thomas stirred. His entire body ached from lying on the hard straw pallet. With a groan he opened his eyes and squinted into the morning sunlight coming through the loosely woven roof covering. The smell of the two sheep and the four goats tethered to wooden stakes with a rough rope assaulted his nostrils. He looked around when he heard the sound of the donkey relieving himself just four feet away. He was sure some of the spray had found its way onto his clothes. *This cannot be for real, please somebody wake me up!*

It was the second morning he had slept on this hard place imitating a bed; and each day he hoped to find himself back in his luxurious king-size bed back in Philadelphia with Melissa next to him. Melissa. He wondered if she missed him and imagined the police searching for him across the city. His thoughts went to the hospital. Who would have replaced him as Chief while he was missing? Probably Harry Kosack, his arch rival. Thomas knew Harry was itching to fill his spot since he imagined himself a better surgeon. He had overheard him saying as much in the doctor's lounge one day talking to a second year resident. The competition in the field was fierce and Thomas never ceased to feel great pride about having been chosen as Chief of Thoracic Surgery above all the others.

Looking around, as he lay there among a bunch of stinking animals two thousand years in the past, he didn't know whether to cry or laugh. This was ridiculous! Why wasn't he waking up from this nightmare? He groaned. Today was the wedding. His foot had gotten infected just like he knew it would in spite of the ointment Rebecca had put on it the day he arrived. Instead of waiting for it to heal to some degree, he was expected to work as everyone else, after the Shabbat was over. David, the father of the groom had hired him to help prepare the courtyard and the outer area of the house for serving over a hundred guests. The entire village of Cana was invited to the festivities and there was much to be done in the way of setting up tents, cleaning the grounds and getting ready for the big wedding feast.

He could hear scores of women a few feet away in the courtyard and outside in the front of the house. They seemed busy cooking and baking and preparing a great variety of foods and sweets for dessert. This morning, the day of the wedding feast, he watched them arranging platters of figs, pomegranates, pears, cheese and various kinds of delicacies he had no idea what they were. Large baskets filled with round loaves of barley and wheat bread were arranged on the many tables. Thomas cringed at the multitude of flies and insects swarming over the food. Some effort was made by several of the smaller girls to chase them with palm fronds, but with little success. Outside, off to the side of the large courtyard, two large cooking areas made of stones were being heated to cook several lambs, countless fish and two large roasts he imagined were beef. Someone would have to stand all day turning the spits. Thomas hoped he wasn't one of them as the heat would be oppressive enough without the fire added to it.

Large earthen clay jars had been brought in filled with wine. Thomas was put in charge by the master of the house over six stone water jars, held ready for the washing of hands as the guests arrived. He and two others were to stand by the entrance and help each guest wash up before they entered the inner court. Here he was, the chief of surgery of a large hospital, washing people's hands at a wedding! He lay on his straw pallet in total disbelief, until someone yelled at him to get up and start with his assigned chores for the day. He groaned as he tried to put on his sandals. His foot was getting worse and so was his job. Today he was assigned to make sure there were no unsightly messes left from the many animals between the road and the grounds where the tables stood. Grumbling under his breath, he took a broom made of straw, bound with a strand of stalks, and walked toward the road, clearing away any unsightly leftovers. If his friends could see him now! He groaned again. He was shoveling manure!

With resignation he looked down at the dirt, sand and animal feces that covered his injured foot as he went about his job. As a doctor, he understood the danger of infection and even sepsis and death, if he could not keep the wound cleaned. The rough strap of the sandal had cut deep between his toes during the walk from Nazareth. He felt hot and couldn't tell whether it was from the heat of the early sun or from a fever. He stopped for a moment. If all this was a dream, he wished he would wake up right about now. He remembered from psychology 101 in his first year of medical school, the mind does not let anyone die in their own dream, but makes them wake up just before it happens. Maybe he was safe after all. An ironic smile crossed his face as he tried to sort out living in two worlds – one in 2016 and the other in ancient Israel. Nothing made sense and a feeling of helplessness, anger, frustration and confusion swept over him. He had been reduced to the status of a common laborer on the verge of dying, in spite of all his precious medical training. He stood and wiped the perspiration from his forehead and wanted to scream.

"Thomas, I do not pay you a good day's wages for you to stand there and day dream." It was David, the master of the house. "Do not embarrass my kinswoman Miriam by repaying her generosity with laziness. She vouched for you and will be here today. Get to work. There are many more chores to be done until the guests arrive." He hesitated. "Make sure you go by the table set for the laborers and find something to drink and eat when you have finished with your chores," he added with a hint of kindness in his voice.

An hour later, Thomas entered the courtyard and went straight to the *mikvew*, a stone basin filled with clean rainwater. This was used for daily washing by both men and women. Cupping his hands together, he scooped some of the water and splashed it over his foot several times until most of the dirt was gone. He couldn't rub the dirt off because of the pain.

The place where he stayed was a country side manor house, a small distance removed from the village of Cana. It was surrounded by a stone wall with several buildings arranged inside in a u-shape. The main house, built more like a tower, was two stories high with many rooms. The low stables were situated across the way. The large, spacious area in between was made of hard, packed sand. In the middle of it was the *mikvew*. In another area was a crude overhang made of wood and covered with straw. In front of it on the ground was a large, flat stone basin carved from a large, rocky surface with two smaller ones, connected by a small runoff channel at a slightly lower level. It was the wine press. The large basin was designed to be filled with grapes while one or two slaves were used to tread the grapes with their bare feet until the juice flowed down into the two smaller basins in which the residue could settle. From there the juice was poured into clay jars and closed with a mud cork, which had a hole in it to allow the gases of fermentation to escape.

Alongside, underneath an overhang, were two large, flat, round stones with a hole in the middle. They sat on top of another, much larger stone made of basalt. A special donkey was hitched up to make the grinding stone turn. Grinding grain was done daily, just enough to bake the right amount of bread for daily consumption.

The stone-based cooking area in a corner close to the kitchen area inside, had a fire in it. Thomas took his food and went to the covered area where other workers sat, eating their noon meal. It was simple, consisting of a slice of flat barley bread, a helping of crumbly goat cheese and a cup of wine mixed with a lot of water; and dates for dessert. He actually no longer minded the vinegary taste since that is all there was. In silence he ate his simple meal and noticed the others didn't pay any attention to him or look up from their animated conversation.

"I hear Caleb, the bridegroom was wearing splendid clothes when he picked up his betrothed last night at her parents' house in Cana," one of the men said while taking a bite of cheese. "He even wore a crown someone told me. I guess he wants to show off how well to do his father is," he added.

"I wish I could've gone with the procession. The bride's parents are eager for this union and hired someone special to write the blessings they spoke over the couple," another said between bites.

"Naomi will make a beautiful bride," the first man said. "At her young age she will produce many sons and will be a blessing to her husband and her mother-in-law by helping with the household. I heard she is not all that young, fifteen this past season. The parents took so long to decide if the house of David was rich enough for their daughter." There was a murmur of disapproval around the table.

"This is a great house and any woman should feel blessed by the God of Abraham to become its mistress, I say," a woman added, standing by the stove. "Some people are never satisfied with what the Lord gives them. I wish I was the bride; I would have no trouble being the woman of this house."

"The bloom of your youth is somewhat faded, Magdalene, but maybe in the dim light of night you might still do," one of the older men said with a twinkle in his eyes. There was laughter all around as she shook a cooking spoon at him in mock anger. "You are a fine one to talk, Saul. When was the last time you enticed a young maiden to look at you?" She had joined in the laughter.

"I hear Ahab of Nain, the friend of the groom and a distant kinsman, will be the master of ceremony," a young, burly man said. "I did hear him mention to David that he didn't think there will be enough wine, but David wouldn't hear of it," he added between big gulps from his cup. "Magdalene, get me some more of this, it will be a long, hot day." He held it out to her. The woman came over to the place where they were eating with a clay jar resting on her ample hip and proceeded to refill everyone's cup. "There, that should do you fellows. Now get on with it and leave this place so we women can have the space for our cooking," she added good-naturedly. "The day is half over and you haven't done anything yet to earn your keep."

Reluctantly Thomas got up. It was time to start his unenviable task of shoveling manure again. He hobbled toward the road, with his simple broom and a wooden shovel in hand, moaning in pain. It was early afternoon by the time he was done. As he started to limp back to the house, he spotted a group of people walking on the road way in the distance. The first guests were arriving and he better hurry up.

Apparently, as was the custom, the big feast would begin later in the afternoon after the groom had returned home with the bride and the religious ceremony was over. From what he understood, after that the celebration would last for five to seven days. He was sure he would be either dead or at least deathly ill by then with his foot. Not that anyone cared. He felt his forehead. It was definitely hot and he began to shiver. This was not good. It was a real possibility that he could die from this simple, superficial skin sore if it turned into a dangerous, painful major infection.

"It is time to set the tables for the feast, Thomas. It was Jacob, the second oldest son of the house. He was a man in his twenties with dark, curly hair and bushy, thick eyebrows accentuating his strong, square features. Jacob was of medium height and not given to much talk.

"Father said to keep an eye on you. We don't stand for laziness." He normally was in charge of the life-stock. Thomas had never seen him smile as he helped him with the daily chores of cleaning the animal quarters, a covered area close to the main house. It held the donkey, a few goats for milking, some chickens and several sheep as well as several straw pallets for the lowest of the laborers. The rest of the animals were out in the field away from the house.

"I am sorry, Jacob, but my foot is infected and I am in a great deal of pain." Thomas said with slight anger in his voice as he pointed to his swollen toes.

"I thought my mother treated it with ointment. You must have been careless not to keep it clean," he answered as he hurried away.

Thomas stood in front of the house, just outside the door to the courtyard and watched as many servants and neighbors had come to help. Everyone was rushing around in what looked like total confusion in the midst of the last preparation for the wedding feast tonight.

"Thomas, make haste and help with filling the water jars as full as you can. The guests will arrive soon." It was John, the third son. "You will be put in charge to make sure the jars stay filled for the hand washing," he said in a harried voice. Unlike his brother, he was outgoing and friendly, with a slight build and an open, pleasant face. His large, brown eyes sparkled with a keen intelligence and a ready smile made it easy to talk to him. Thomas had no idea what to do first, the tables or the jars.

"Thomas, I see your foot is not doing well. I was hoping mother's ointment would help. I am sorry, it must hurt." He stood in front of him, looking down. "There is nothing more to be done on a day like this. Maybe after things calm down some tomorrow morning, mother can take another look at it. She is quite knowledgeable in the healing arts."

"I am a healer as well, John and this does not look good. My foot needs to be cleansed thoroughly and a bandage applied to the wound to fight the infection," Thomas said.

"That will not be possible today, Thomas," John replied with compassion in his voice. "There are so many preparations yet to be made. I will tell mother and see what she says." He started to walk away.

"Don't bother, Jacob, I know as much if not more than she does; and given the surroundings and the circumstances, there is nothing anyone can do until I have an opportunity to wash the foot and let it rest. But, like you said, I don't think that will be possible today." He smiled at Jacob and turned to help with the water jars, determined to ignore the pain.

They were large stone containers for ceremonial cleansing only and held probably twenty or so gallons each. He was looking for some kind of ladle to use to get the water out. He admired their classic, elegant shape in spite of having been carved of stone to keep things cool instead of the usual clay. He counted six of them and was told he and two other servants would be in charge of keeping them filled and ready at all times during the length of the festivities over the next few days. He was instructed to stand next to them and watch out for guests who felt the need to wash in obedience to the strict laws, which demanded one remain ceremonially clean during the normal, daily activities. It meant he had to stand all day on his foot in the heat of the day, pouring water over their hands and refilling the jars when empty.

Good luck with that, he thought, being sure he would probably pass out. They would carry him to his pallet and he could finally rest and take care of the wound. No one would miss him as he would lay in misery, starving and thirsty until he would wake up before he died from this miserable nightmare. He wiped the drops of sweat from his forehead with a tired gesture.

A lot of guests had arrived, returning from accompanying the bridegroom last night to pick up the bride. The parents of the bride had prepared their own ceremony with prayers from scripture and blessings as they turned over their daughter to her betrothed. The bride then withdrew to a special room with her ten bride's maids while the groom celebrated with music and wine way into the night with his friends. *An old fashioned bachelors party, imagine that.*

There was great excitement among the people who had come as they stood in animated conversation and ready laughter. As Thomas listened to them talk, he realized a wedding was the most important occasion in their life to be celebrated with elaborate festivities that included dancing, drinking and eating for days.

Suddenly, a servant came running through the gate from the outside and up to David.

"Master, there are Roman soldiers outside! They are coming down the driveway!"

"A sudden hush fell over the crowd as the big gate swung open and a group of ten soldiers on horseback rode into the courtyard. The shiny armor over their red tunics gleamed in the sunshine. The leader of the group rode up to David and looked down on him with a steely glare.

"Are you the owner of this house?"

"Shalom, Centurion, I am. How may I help you?" David appeared calm.

"I need water for our horses and wine for my men. I presume you have both?"

"Of course, Sir, you are welcome to rest and take whatever you need." David waved for the servants to bring wine and pointed to the *mikvew*. "There it is, Sir, help yourself to all you need."

The Centurion looked at the crowd of people before he got down from his horse.

"What is going on here? Have we stumbled on an illegal gathering of rebels?"

"No, Sir, my son is getting married today. These are the first guests who have arrived for the festivities this evening."

"I see. This better not be an illegal meeting or I am forced to show what happens when you oppose the Emperor of Rome, Jew." He looked around at each person and then got down. "Let's get these horses taken care of, men."

While the soldiers took the horses to the *mikvew* to allow them to drink, several servants rushed to bring wine. The Centurion looked closely at the crowd and stopped in front of Thomas. "You don't look like a servant. What is your job here?"

"I am hired to clean the grounds so the guests won't step in manure," Thomas said.

"What's the matter, you don't like Romans?" The officer had detected the defiance in Thomas' tone.

"I don't mind them at all, as long as they leave me alone." Thomas raised himself up to his full height and looked down on the Centurion with a forced smile. "Where I come from, soldiers fight in the battle field, not at weddings."

"I knew you weren't a servant. Flavius, arrest this man. I am sure he is a rebel," he shouted.

"Wait, Centurion, I am not a servant, but a physician. I work here because I needed a job and this is all I could find to keep me going until I get to where I am going." Thomas held his stare.

"A physician, hey? Let's see if that's true." He turned and waved to one of the men to come closer. "This is Gaius and he has a nasty boil on his leg. Why don't you fix it, physician?"

"That I can do easily, Sir if you will allow me to get some water, alcohol and a sharp knife." Thomas stepped up to the soldier and looked at the leg. It was indeed a boil and needed to be lanced.

"Lay down on one of the benches," he told the man and pointed under a tree a few feet away. "Get me some clean cloth so I can wrap it when I'm done," he told one of the servants. "I will also need two men to hold this patient down, because what I am about to do is going to hurt."

"My men are trained for battle, physician. They don't need anyone to restrain them for a flea bite like this, isn't that right, Gaius?"

"Yes, Sir. I will be fine. Let's just get it done." The expression on his face did not show near as much confidence as his voice.

It took Thomas only a few minutes to lance the boil, pour wine over it, disinfect it and then wrap it with a clean cloth. "Keep this on for a day or two and pour strong wine into the wound when you take the bandage off until it has healed over. Make sure you keep it clean and you will be alright, soldier," he said and then looked at the Centurion with a smile. "It is done, Sir."

"You really are a physician. What is your name?"

"I am Thomas."

"Well, Thomas, since you have done well and my horses and men have been taken care of, we will continue on our way." He turned to David. "Don't you think it is foolish to have a physician shovel manure? I will never understand you Jews."

The sun was low in the sky when Thomas heard shouts that the bride and groom were coming! He got up carefully so as not to aggravate his foot and slowly hobbled to the water jars. He made it there just before the procession turned into the roadway leading to the house. A colorful, red canopy, held by several servants, was held ready for the bride to walk under. Thomas was stunned by the beautiful white garment she wore, topped off by a magnificent headdress adorned with large, precious stones across her forehead. She was a small girl, looking so very young and vulnerable with her fifteen years. The groom looked to be in his early twenties. They walked slowly toward the house with the many guests lining the way, cheering and waving palm fronts, and throwing flower petals to welcome the pair. The young bride offered a shy smile as she walked with slow, measured steps, making sure her beautiful gown did not get soiled by holding it up with both hands.

The many tables had been set, and were laden with a large variety of food. The air was filled with the smell of roasted lamb served with hot mint sauce, grilled fish and the heavy scent of several large beef roasts cooked to perfection. The fatted calf had definitely been slain for the occasion. The added aroma of freshly baked bread made his mouth water. For dessert there was pear compote made with dried pears boiled in wine and water, together with honey.

Thomas stood ready to scoop out the water for the guests to wash their hands, mindful to avoid putting too much weight on his foot, when he saw Miriam and Tiny walk up to him.

"Shalom, Thomas," Miriam said with a friendly smile. "I am glad my kinsman gave you a job." She looked at him closely. "You don't look well, Thomas. What is wrong?" Her face took on a worried look.

"I have hurt my foot, Miriam, it has gotten infected. There is much pain and I don't know how long I can stand here without fainting." He wiped his forehead again.

"I will let my son Yeshua know about this when he gets here. He will help you," she added and walked on. Tiny had already gone past her to find a place for his mother and Miriam to sit in the women's section.

Thomas was kept busy for the next hour as countless guests stopped to wash their hands. It helped him to ignore the pain to some degree. Caleb of Nain, the master of ceremony and best friend of the groom, stopped by several times to see that he and the two other servants kept the water jars filled at all times.

When everyone was seated, the many servants began to distribute the food among the tables. Three men stood slicing the meat and arranging it on large platters which were then carried by serving women to the different tables.

The women's section on one side of the grounds sounded like a beehive with animated chatter and laughter, while the men's tables were more subdued. But he knew that would change as the evening wore on and the wine flowed freely. Not until the official wedding ceremony was completed, were men and women, as well as the young couple, allowed to sit together in the same area.

Thomas felt weak and exhausted and was ready to sneak back to his pallet, when a group of men entered the courtyard. The groom rose from his seat and hurried over to greet their leader with a friendly kiss on both cheeks. "Shalom kinsman," he shouted. "I was wondering if you and your men were coming. Please, allow me to show you to the water jars so you may freshen up before you sit down." He pointed to where Thomas and the other two servants stood.

"This must be Miriam's son," Thomas said under his breath. He looked at the man who walked toward him. Yeshua had a slight smile on his face. He was of medium height, his slender body covered by a simple, white tunic with a light brown garment over it and held together by a dark rope. He had short, curly brown hair which matched his kind, brown eyes. His lower face was hidden by a cropped, dark beard. Thomas noticed the man's leather sandals were covered in dust when he stood in front of him, holding out both hands.

Thomas stared into the brown, gentle eyes as he poured the water. Before he could say anything, Yeshua bent down and touched his foot with the slightest touch. Without a word he straightened back up, dried his hands on the towel Thomas held out to him and walked away. Thomas lost sight of him as he helped the other men taking their turn at the water jars.

The evening went by fast. After a while he was assigned to the clean-up crew. Platters had to be removed, dishes washed and wine jars carried to the cool of the inside of the house. He was directed to serve guests up on the roof where a slight breeze blew away the heat of the day. As the evening wore on, he was asked to help light the many oil lamps strategically placed in various places. The crowd had become more raucous as the wine helped to loosen tongues.

The feast lasted way into the night, and it was not until after midnight, before the servants were allowed to eat from the leftovers of the feast. When Thomas finally made it to his straw pallet, he didn't remember his head hitting the pallet before a heavy sleep overwhelmed him.

The next morning, he awoke with a start. The donkey brayed in protest, impatient for his food. Thomas squinted into the narrow rays of sunshine peeking through the straw roof. For the first time his body felt rested and without aches and pains from the hard mattress. Pain! He rose up with a jolt and swung his feet to the side and stared at his foot. It didn't hurt anymore. He touched it. All swelling was gone and there was not the first sign anything had been wrong. What in the world! There was no way it could have healed like that overnight, even with the best medicine in Philadelphia. His mind was numb. Nothing made sense anymore. Everything he had ever known, learned or relied on was upside down. This had to be a dream. There was no other way to explain his foot. Although, when the donkey nudged him with his long nose and sent him sprawling across the pallet, it felt quite real. He stretched his arms high above his head as he stepped into the sun. His mind was clear and he felt a fresh sense of wellbeing throughout his body. They were right about dreams. This one was not going to let him die in this strange, backward land after all.

Chapter 4

The many guests had left for their homes after the feast late last night. Thomas looked over the grounds. There would be a lot of cleaning up to do this morning. The crowd of well-wishers would be back by early evening as this was only the third day of the celebrations. He admitted, this crowd knew how to party. The revelries had lasted way into the night again with more song and dance, reading blessings out of the Psalms and the Song of Songs in the yellowish light of countless oil lamps. He had never experienced such religious fervor, not even with his grandmother. These people lived and breathed this Yahweh. What amazed him most was the unanimous expectation by everyone that the Meshiah would come and drive out the Romans.

One of the guests, an old man named Jonah, had stood with him last night and explained in great detail what this Meshiah would do.

"He will be a king and a strong warrior and will gather around him his people, and together we will defeat the Roman scourge once and for all. And then he will set up a kingdom that will last forever. Israel will be the mightiest nation in the world and everyone will worship the Lord God Jehovah." He was so excited, it made his frail little body shake to the point, Thomas was afraid he would keel over with a heart attack.

He smiled. Poor old man, he did not have the heart to tell him that none of this would happen, because two thousand years later, Israel was still fighting for its survival against many nations, who couldn't wait to destroy it. *At least the Romans would be gone.* Here was the proof that all this religious stuff was hogwash, just like he had always thought. He felt sorry for the old man and patted him on the shoulder in a condescending gesture. Jonah stopped shaking abruptly and stared at Thomas with a piercing look.

"You are a stranger in this land and are filled with unbelief. And yet the Lord Jehovah shows me that you will see the Glory of His coming and be touched by Him in a special way. Turn from your doubts and prepare your heart for He will anoint you to take His message into a distant land and time."

A sudden uneasiness came over Thomas and he turned away and pretended to be busy with the water jar. *This was just a dream, he had to remember that, just a dream and nothing else.* As he looked down, trying to hide his embarrassment, his eyes fell on his foot. The infection was gone and so was the pain and neither was there any sign that they had ever been there. Although there was one difference he noticed when he put his sandals on this morning. A thickness of skin had developed between the toes where the sandal strap was that had not been there before. It would not get sore again.

By late afternoon, Thomas watched the crowds return with renewed rejoicing and ready to eat and drink. The bride and groom stood ready to welcome them. Thomas watched the young woman closely. She stood by her new husband with a look of contentment. She seemed happy with him and Thomas had the feeling she would fit in well into her new home. Rebecca, her new mother-in-law, treated her with great affection and warmth from what Thomas could observe. To her she was just another daughter to take care of until the girl had time to fully grow up and then return the favor. He was astounded how young these girls were when they were married off to men they didn't even know. While cleaning up last night, one of the household servants explained things to him when he mentioned his thoughts to her.

"While the parents chose these two to marry, they could have refused if they truly did not care for one another," she told him. "Naomi and Caleb have known each other all their lives. They both belong to the royal line of David and were happy when they were betrothed with the blessing of both parents."

"But do they love each other?" Thomas had asked.

"That comes later. Marriage is not about love, but about obedience to your parents and God's way for providing a secure future, not just for the couple, but for both families. Producing children means the survival of the next generation. It also means in this case, the line of the house of David goes on, because from it the Meshiah will come forth."

Of course we are back to that again, Thomas thought.

As the evening of the third day of the feast progressed, an excited conversation arose among the groom and his father David. They were close to running out of wine. With three more days to go, the supply thought to last for five days was gone! Thomas stood by his water jars and listened to the heated discussion from a distance. He had been here long enough to know this was an embarrassment of colossal proportions for the house of David. It would be spread among Cana, Nazareth and as far as Capernaum that a wealthy house like this had not provided enough wine to last for the duration of the wedding. He could see David was beside himself and ready to rent his clothes, when Miriam walked up to him.

"What is going on, kinsman?" she asked in her gentle voice.

"We are out of wine, Miriam," he answered, his face red with embarrassment. "The shame overwhelms me. How could this have happened?" He threw his hands up in the air in a gesture of utter helplessness. "There is no time to get more before everyone will know of it. The reputation of my house is ruined." He was close to collapse, trembling and weaving in despair.

Miriam turned around and waved toward the table where her son and his men sat. Yeshua got up immediately and joined her.

"They have no more wine," she said, looking at him expectantly.

"Dear woman, why do you involve me?" Yeshua replied. "My time has not yet come." (John 2:2-4) He spoke with quiet authority, yet with great affection as he looked at his mother.

Miriam walked over to where Thomas and the other servants stood. "Do whatever he tells you," she said and pointed at Yeshua who stood behind her. (John 2:5)

There was a moment of tense silence as He stepped toward Thomas and then said to him, "Fill the jars with water." (John 2:7)

Thomas and the other two servants ran to fill the six large jars to the rim while Yeshua waited.

"Now draw some out and take it to the master of the banquet." (John 2:8) With that He turned and walked back to his seat across the other side of the tables and took His place among the men that were with Him.

This is not going to go well, Thomas thought to himself. *These people do not like to drink plain water in the worst of times, least of all at a wedding feast!*

Thomas looked around for the master of ceremony. When he spotted him he dipped his ladle into the water and walked with it as fast as he could over to where the man stood. "...and the master of the banquet tasted the water that had been turned into wine. He did not realize where it had come from, though the servants who had drawn the water knew. Then he called the bridegroom aside and said, "Everyone brings out the choice wine first and then the cheaper wine after the guests have had too much to drink; but you have saved the best till now." (John 2:9-10)

Thomas returned to his water jars and began ladling out the water into the many smaller containers so the serving women could refill the cups of the guests. He wondered why no one was complaining until, when no one was watching, he dipped the ladle into the stone jar and tasted it. To his astonishment it tasted better than the most expensive bottles in his wine collection at home. He chuckled and then mumbled under his breath after he took another sip, "I'm beginning to enjoy this dream after all."

The wedding celebrations went on for another two days. Thomas had no idea how these people had the energy to cook and feed so many on a continuing basis. He looked for Miriam and Yeshua, but they had not returned to the festivities after the incident with the wine.

There was a lot of cleaning up to do and with his foot completely well, Thomas worked hard from morning until sundown. He felt stronger from the daily physical labor and had no trouble sleeping. Even his nose had gotten accustomed to the smell of the animals and he petted the donkey each night before he went to sleep. He had given him the name Igor, a name he remembered from his childhood.

Later that night, he lay on his straw pallet and wondered what he was going to do in the days ahead. He couldn't very well spend his life as a low class laborer. After all, he was a highly trained surgeon! Maybe he could find a doctor and work with him. Imagine the new techniques he could teach these people with his 21st century scientific knowledge! He was getting tired of doing the most menial tasks he never thought he would ever have to do in his life. David had not been impressed when he proved himself to be a physician. How low he had come, from surgeon to servant. Nothing made any sense, not even if this was a dream. He was glad it was, because there was no way he would ever stoop so low in real life, shoveling manure and be a lowly laborer and servant to these simple, uneducated people. What a waste of his superior brains and talents!

There was a nagging thought though, which made him wish he had paid more attention to Melissa's grandmother when she told him about Jesus. Why would he be dreaming about him since he totally rejected him as a religious fable and knew him to be the figment of imagination of some ancient writers? He would have to read the New Testament when he woke up, just to see whether these things had really been recorded in there. How ridiculous, of course they hadn't! He could just imagine how happy Melissa would be if she caught him reading the Bible. He was losing it and it was time he woke up. Instead, he drifted off into a deep sleep.

Igor woke him with his braying at first daylight the next morning after the wedding festival was finally over. It meant another day of chores in this ridiculous dream. He rose with a deep sigh.

"Igor, I'm going to miss you when I finally wake up. You are the only friend I've got here. Everyone else ignores me in this godforsaken place." A sense of depression surrounded him like a cloud and he knew it was time to move on. He stepped out into the open and stretched. On his way over to wash his face in the *mikvew* he noticed John loading up the cart with sacks made of rough fiber filled with barley.

"Come, Thomas, you can help me. I am going to Capernaum today to sell it to a bakery there. After we are done with it, we can break our fast and then hitch up the donkey." He sounded like he was looking forward to the ride and to get away.

"I am ready to move on, John," Thomas said. "Do you think your father can pay me my wages today so I can stay in Capernaum?" he asked.

"I'm sure he won't mind. Although, he might ask you to stay on until all the harvest has been brought in. We could still use your help." John looked at him expectantly.

"I don't think so. I'm ready to seek employment in the field I have been trained in, a healer," Thomas said. "I have been here for eight days and believe I have worked hard."

"That you have, Thomas. My father will pay you well. I will speak to him as soon as we are done here."

It didn't take long until the cart was loaded with seven large sacks of barley. *It will be a heavy load to pull for Igor,* Thomas thought as he ate the simple meal of bread, cheese, a pomegranate and a cup of wine mixture to wash it down. He had learned to like the coarse bread and sharp goat cheese. He even appreciated the wine mixture, because it hid the almost foul taste of the water. He tried not to think about the onslaught of bacteria he put into his body each time he took a sip of it. There was no way his body could fight off the parasites in his intestines in the long run, but amazingly, so far he felt fine.

"Here are your wages, Thomas." It was David. He held out his hand with a few coins in it and Thomas took them. "You have been a good worker and I shall miss you. Come back anytime and I will hire you on again." There was a hint of a smile on his face. "Miriam was right; you are a good man. May the God of Abraham bless you on your journey. Shalom."

Thomas looked at the coins with a frown, trying to ascertain what they were or their value.

"My father gave you eight denarii, Thomas. That is the going rate in Israel. Our God commands that we pay a fair price for a day's labor." It was John.

"Are these Roman coins?" Thomas asked.

"Yes, they are. You can see the hated Emperor's face on them. We are not allowed to make an image of any kind according to the Law of Moses, so this money is an affront to our people. Everything the Romans do is contrary to what our laws say, but until the Meshiah comes and delivers us, we have no choice but to obey those who rule over us with a cruel hand." John's voice was filled with hatred and disgust. He waved Thomas to follow him out of the courtyard. "You can hitch up the donkey while I tell my mother not to worry about me on the trip." He smiled. "She does, you know, as if I was still a child."

A few minutes later, the cart rumbled slowly down the narrow dirt road on the way to Capernaum. From what Thomas gathered, it was a town about 15 miles to the north on the shore of the Sea of Galilee. Igor moved down the one-lane road at a slow pace. They each sat on a sack in the front of the cart, being jostled from one side to the other over the hardened surface of the dirt road. The sand had been trampled down over centuries and had turned the surface as hard as rock, making it an uncomfortable, rough ride. The sun was not yet too hot, but Thomas knew by noon it would be sweltering. He was grateful for the head dress and the rest of the clothes covering his entire body as it kept him from getting sunburned.

"It will be a long ride, Thomas," John said. "Capernaum is about two hours away. Mother packed a few provisions for us and some watered wine." He pointed to a basket filled with a wineskin, some bread, fruit and a handful of dates and figs. "This will last us until we get to the bakery. It belongs to a kinsman of ours and he will put us up for the night. His name is Matthias, the son of Nathanial of the line of David. He bakes bread for some of the upper class connected with Herod's family and seems to do well for himself. At least it's not the Romans he has to please."

"You really don't like those Romans, do you John?" Thomas looked at the young man with a smile. "Are they really that bad or is it because they are not Jewish?"

"You are truly ignorant, Thomas. Have you not heard of the procurator Pontius Pilate who has brutally murdered so many of our people and defiles our laws and customs in Judea and Samaria every day?"

"Is there nothing you can do to get rid of him?" Thomas asked to keep the young man talking.

"Nothing, since he is appointed by Rome and Caesar doesn't care what happens here in Palestine. We are simply a conquered province, far removed from Rome and of no importance."

"I thought we are in Galilee? Where is Palestine?"

"Israel is also called Palestine." He looked at Thomas with consternation. "Let me give you a little lesson about our country since you seem to be quite ignorant about it." He shook the reins a little and urged Igor to hasten the pace as he continued. "When King Herod died some years ago, he left a will that divided our land to be ruled by his three sons. Caesar Augustus had a hand in it as well and made Philipp Tetrarch of the eastern region across the Sea of Galilee which is not really part of our inheritance. Herod Antipas was made king of Perea and Galilee. He rebuilt Sepphoris, his magnificent capitol city, only a short distance from Nazareth on a hill on the plain of Galilee. We stay away from it, because it is built on an ancient burial ground and also because he is not really our king." John spat over the side of the cart in disgust.

"How come you don't want him to be the king?"

"Because he is not of our people, but a despicable Idumean, whose father was put on the throne by the even more despicable Romans to rule our people. He pretends to be one of us, but we know he is merely a puppet of Rome and cares nothing for the Jews."

"Who was the third son of King Herod?" Thomas asked.

"His name was Archelaus. He was given Samaria and Judea in the south. But there was a big revolt. He went to Rome to ask for help when it grew out of control. When they brought him back, he was so brutal to our people that the Romans banished him to Gaul and appointed procurators for the region, of which the current one is Pontius Pilate. This has been so for many years now."

"Is Jerusalem a part of Judea?"

"Of course it is, everybody knows that." John looked at Thomas with astonishment. "You really are an uneducated man aren't you? Did they not teach you the history of our people where you come from?"

"It has been a long time since I went to school, I simply don't remember." Thomas felt embarrassed at his ignorance. How he wished he had gone to the lessons at the synagogue like his grandmother had wanted him to. Since his parents were not practicing Jews, they did not care one way or the other. In essence, he knew very little of the Torah and nothing of the New Testament except that which Melissa's grandmother had shared with him. "Will we see many Roman soldiers in Capernaum?" He asked John.

"Not that many since it is not ruled by the Romans directly, but by Herod Antipas. There is one Roman Garrison led by a Centurion in Capernaum. They are there mostly to guard the tax collections. The ones that stopped by our house are probably part of them. However, Herod gets very upset when he thinks Pontius Pilate, who is in charge of a large Roman presence in Judea, interferes with his rule. Those two don't like each other very much as I understand it, but then who am I to understand our rulers? It is best to stay out of their way and live our lives far away from where they are."

"Your father paid me with Roman coins. Will I be able to use them wherever we go?" Thomas asked.

"Of course, we Jews have our own money, but it is mostly used to buy offerings at the temple. They have money changers there to exchange your Roman coins for our own, because they do not have any graven images on them and therefore are the only ones permitted in the temple. They are minted from silver, bronze or brass at Caesarea.

"There must be something smaller than a dinar?" Thomas asked.

"Of course, it is a copper coin called a putra or a mite. Two denarii make a silver shekel. You can tell it by the face of Tiberius on one side and a seated female figure with the words 'High Priest' on the other."

"How many days can I live on eight denarii?"

"You can stay at an inn for two weeks and still buy enough food to live on," John answered. "Your earnings will give you enough time to find work before they run out."

Surely I will wake up before then, Thomas thought, yet relieved that he would have enough money to last a while.

They drove on, each wrapped in their own thoughts. The sun's rays were beating down on them in full strength by now. It would not be long until they would see the outline of the town of Capernaum.

"My kinsman Yeshua and his disciples will be there by now," John said into the silence. "Maybe we will see him before I have to return tomorrow."

"Tell me about Yeshua, what is he like and what do people think about him?" Thomas asked with sudden interest. "He is different."

"He is." John looked thoughtful. "I don't know why, but I always feel good when I am around him. I can't say that I like the men he has gathered around him though. Some of them are uneducated fishermen. There is even one who is a tax collector. I think Yeshua should have chosen his disciples more carefully."

"Who do you think would be more suitable?" Thomas asked.

"Some of the Pharisees maybe or a rabbi would definitely be better. Even a rich man could come in handy for financial support."

"Would you like to be one of them, John?"

"Oh no, I am definitely not spiritual enough for that sort of life. I am a farmer and a sheepherder, not a religious man." He smiled at Thomas. "But I must say, I feel pretty smart around you, being as ignorant of even the most commonly known things as you are."

"I am considered pretty smart where I come from," Thomas said. "I am a very well respected healer and know how the human body works or how to fix it when sickness strikes."

"So how come you didn't know how to fix your foot when it was so bad?" John said, unconvinced.

"You got me there, John. Where I come from we have medicine for that and it would never have gotten infected," he finally managed to answer.

"How come you didn't bring any of that medicine with you?"

Thomas sighed and could not come up with an answer. "How did my foot get well, John, do you know? It was really bad that evening and the next morning it was completely well. That is impossible."

"Oh, that was Yeshua. He has great healing powers." John leaned toward Thomas. "Did he ever touch your foot at any time?"

"Yes, he did, when he came in at first. I poured water over his hands and then he reached down and touched my foot. It never hurt after that, but I forgot about it until I woke up the next morning, because I was so busy the rest of the evening."

"See, I told you. Yeshua does those things quite frequently. We are all used to it among the family. Since he never talks about it when it happens, we don't say anything either. His mother Miriam knew he would help my father avoid a great embarrassment when we ran out of wine." John smiled at Thomas condescendingly. "I think Yeshua is a much better healer than you are, Thomas, don't you think?"

I can't argue with you there," Thomas answered with a deep sigh. "Do you think he could be the Meshiah, John?"

"Oh no, he would have to be born a king and live in a palace, unless he was a general or the son of a rich, influential family. But he is only an ordinary carpenter from Nazareth. Our people have a saying that nothing good usually comes from Nazareth," he added with a chuckle. The outlines of Capernaum appeared on the horizon as he spoke.

Chapter 5

Thomas stood on the shore of the Sea of Galilee. The surface of the large lake was calm as he looked across to the other side, where mountains lined the horizon. It was early morning and he welcomed the cool breeze coming from the lake. There were several small boats pulled ashore with fishermen cleaning their nets. He could make out their voices, but was unable to understand what they were saying until he stepped closer.

"I'm telling you, Cephas and his brother Andrew left their boats and went with Him. Their father is quite upset," he heard one of the men say.

"Didn't someone say the Rabbi from Nazareth told them to go out and fish some more after they had come back empty the night before?" an old man asked with skepticism in his voice. "There are simply some nights when the fish know we are trying to catch them. No one knows why." He scratched his long beard thoughtfully as he rested from pulling out small, dead fish hung up in the net.

"I'm telling you, Aaron, it is as I said," the first man insisted emphatically. "I was there and saw how they came back with nothing and then on the Rabbi's word went out again and caught so many, we had to help them bring the load in. Cephas let me keep the fish I hauled into my boat, because he couldn't handle them all."

A young man in the group was clearly excited. "Maybe the Rabbi will come back and tell us to go and fish. This morning would be good, because we haven't caught much." He pointed at the few baskets filled with a meager catch. "This is hardly enough to take to market. I have to speak to Cephas next time he is fishing here."

"Don't bother with that," the old man said, "Cephas isn't coming back. He and Andrew are followers of the Rabbi now for good. I told you their father is beside himself. Who is going to do the work now?"

Thomas moved closer to the group.

"Shalom. I am Thomas. Could you tell me where I can find a physician in this town?"

"Are you ill? Because if you are you need to find the Nazarene Rabbi, He is a great healer. Everyone in Capernaum is talking about Him," the young man said. "He is probably at the synagogue talking to the Pharisees right now. They like to argue with Him, but the people love Him, because He has healed many of them over the last few days. He even helped one of our fishermen catch fish," he added with enthusiasm. "Just tell Him you are sick and He will make you well."

"I am not sick, but am looking for work," Thomas said.

"Are you a physician? I have never seen you in these parts before," the old man said before the younger one could answer.

"I am a stranger and yes, I am also a physician and need to find a job," Thomas answered.

"Why not see the Rabbi, He has many men who follow him, maybe he will take you on. But you won't have much to do, because He does all the healing himself," one of the men suggested.

"I would much rather work with a real physician than a religious man," Thomas said with a frown, yet trying not to let his disdain show in front of these simple, uneducated men.

"In that case I know of a Greek who has a place in the city. His name is Lucius and he gets called on by the upper class and by those who are connected with Herod Antipas' household. He must be a smart man to be so honored. The rich always want the very best," he added and spat on the ground.

"Can you tell me where I can find him?" Thomas asked.

"He lives in a large house on the outskirts of Capernaum, close to the villas of the rich. Go to the synagogue and ask, someone will show you the way, because his place of business is close by."

"Thank you." Thomas turned and walked toward the city about two miles west of the Jordan River. On the way he passed several flocks of sheep grazing peacefully among the rocks strewn across the landscape. One of the shepherds, not too far away, sat on a large boulder and took a sip from his wineskin as he watched his charges.

That must be a lonely, boring job, Thomas thought, *to sit and watch a bunch of dumb sheep all day.* Talking about a job, he better find one soon or he would be no better off than the beggars in the streets of Capernaum. He had three denarii left from the eight he had earned in Cana. It was time to seek some sort of employment with this physician named Lucius. He was sure he wouldn't have any trouble getting hired once he demonstrated his superior knowledge of medicine to this so-called doctor.

It took quite a while before he reached the town center. Capernaum was a sizeable town in comparison to Cana or Nazareth. The people called it Kephar Nahum. Unlike the other small villages he had encountered so far, who were steeped in the Jewish faith and spoke Aramaic, he found not only Hellenistic paganism here, but noticed that the official language was Greek. He had seen that a good many people worshiped Greek and Roman gods. By now he had stopped wondering that no matter what language they spoke, it sounded English to him. He chuckled to himself. *This is all Greek to me.*

He knew where the synagogue was and from there had no trouble finding the sign that said "Lucius, The Physician" in a narrow street just a few feet away. Surgical instruments hung over the door of a small building dangling like ornaments. He was astounded that some of them resembled the ones he used in his time. He took a deep breath before entering the narrow doorway. There was no telling what barbaric practices he would find in the place.

"Welcome, Sir." It was a strong, confident voice. It took Thomas a moment to get used to the dim light until he could make out the middle-aged man in the back of the room behind a small table. He could tell immediately he was not Jewish, but a Greek by his clothes. A white tunic over which a blue toga was draped in a graceful Roman-Greco style, which gave him the look of a wealthy man. "I am Lucius, the physician." His smile, together with his small blue eyes, gave his face a kindly look. His brown, wavy hair was cut short in the typical Roman style. His generous middle, tastefully hidden under the folds of his expensive garments, spoke of good food and comfortable living. "How may I serve you kind Sir?" he asked in a professional tone.

"It is rather how I can serve *you*, Lucius. My name is Thomas and I am a physician looking for employment. I was told you might need someone to help you."

"I serve an upper clientele, Thomas, because I am good at what I do. How do I know if you are qualified to assist me?" He looked at Thomas with skepticism as his eyes beheld his simple clothing. He crinkled his nose at their smell. "You do not look like someone who has studied the healing arts in Greece, Rome and Antioch like I have."

"I have studied in a land far from here at a large institute of medical learning for many years. I am a famous physician in my land as you will see if you allow me to demonstrate."

"Where might this great institute be, Thomas?" Lucius asked, raising an eyebrow at the arrogance in his visitor's voice.

"It is called America and lies far away across the sea to the West."

"I have never heard of it and yet I am familiar with the whole world." Lucius sounded more skeptical by the minute.

"If you do not believe me, allow me to prove myself by asking me medical questions or let me accompany you when you visit your patients."

Something in Thomas's tone intrigued the doctor enough to allow this conceited man to prove that he was as good as he claimed to be. Lucius stroked his beard as he studied him carefully. Thomas knew what he was thinking, *He looks intelligent and his Greek sounds like that of an educated man.*

"I will give you a try as my assistant for a day. If you prove helpful I might consider allowing you to clean my instruments and carry my medicine bag. I will pay you a denari for the day if you work diligently."

Wow, I'm really coming up in the medical field. Cleaning instruments and carrying your bag, really?

"That sounds fine. I will not disappoint you, Lucius," Thomas said, realizing he had no choice for now. He would definitely have to show this backward excuse of a doctor his superior knowledge of what modern medicine was all about.

"I was on my way to the house of Claudius, a relative of Herod Antipas. His wife's favorite slave has hurt her arm and is in great pain. They usually don't bother when something happens to slaves, but this one seems to be a special case. Come along, you can show me your knowledge by treating a mere slave and not a human being, in case you mess up."

Thomas could feel his blood pressure rise, but said nothing in order not to blow his chances of keeping his job as he followed Lucius outside. They walked for quite a while to the outskirts of the city until they came to a large estate, hidden behind a high wall. The guard at the door apparently knew Lucius and opened the gate as they approached. Thomas had to duck his head as he walked through into the large courtyard.

Instantly, he felt as if he had entered an oasis of peace and tranquility. The spacious courtyard was shaded by a large sycamore tree to one side with several raised flower beds filled with the most exquisite exotic, colorful greenery along one wall. It was a spacious, two story home with steps leading to the customary flat roof. The floor of the courtyard and the steps to the roof were covered with colorful tiles, probably brought in from Venice. Pictures of Hellenistic gods walking among lush greenery were displayed along the walls as exotic birds rested among them. Thomas was taken in by the vivid, brilliant colors of the paintings and their lifelike style. He felt, if he touched the birds, they would fly away.

A young slave girl led them into the interior of the house with a low bow and a slight wave of her hand.

"The mistress says to come into the study." Thomas was surprised, how relatively cool it was inside. They walked into a luxurious entrance, an imitation of the atrium of a Roman villa. It was lined with Greek columns, statues of various gods and goddesses in the many niches along the hallway. A middle-aged woman in a fine linen dress draped gracefully over one shoulder, rose from her gold colored couch to greet them. Her long, black, luxuriously thick hair hung down to her shoulders. Two gold combs held it away from her face in a graceful style that brought out her fine, aquiline features and large brown eyes. She looked at Thomas with great interest before she turned to Lucius.

"Welcome, Lucius, I am so glad you could come with such speed. I see you brought someone with you."

"Greetings, gracious Lady Diana, it is always a delight to see you. Your beauty is undiminished as always. May the gods grant you a long life," Lucius said as he bowed before her. "This is my assistant Thomas. He says he is a physician, but I am not sure as of yet. I brought him with me on a trial basis and thought he could treat your slave."

Thomas bowed to her and smiled. He had no idea what he was supposed to do or say, so he said nothing and just stood, listening to their conversation.

"What is wrong with your slave, great lady?" Lucius asked.

"Lucretia is extremely ill. She was born into this household and has been my personal attendant since I came into my husband's house so many years ago. I don't think I can do without her."

"What are her symptoms?" Thomas asked.

"She fell on the tile and now screams in pain every time she moves her arm. This has been going on for two days now. It is really annoying, since she is unable to help me dress or do my hair. No one else does it as well as she does."

The Lady Diana sounds much more upset about the inconvenience to herself than the injury of her slave woman, Thomas thought.

"May we see her?" Lucius asked.

"Certainly, I will let Lativia show you to the slave quarters in the back," she said and nodded to a young girl standing at the entrance. "Take these men to Lucretia."

"Yes, mistress," the girl said. She probably was no more than sixteen, with a look of utter servility, bowing in obedience to Lucius and Thomas. "I will show you where she is if you will follow me," she said in a thin little voice.

The surroundings got much plainer as they entered the extension of the house that served as the slave quarters way in the back. There were a great number of rooms with only straw pallets and no other furniture. Most of them did not have openings for windows, just a narrow doorway which allowed for minimal light and air. There was a large yard area outside, with a stove for cooking, an olive press and a water basin filled with rain water. Apparently, the plain courtyard served as the kitchen and eating area for the many slaves. Long stone benches lined the walls without cushions or any other items of general comfort.

Lativia took them to the end of the long hall and stopped in the doorway of one such room. "This is Lucretia's place, master," she whispered and stood aside as they entered.

The interior was stifling hot with no ventilation or much light. It took Thomas a moment to see the pathetic figure of a woman lying on the floor.

"Thomas, I will let you handle this," Lucius said and stepped aside so Thomas could walk in to look at her more closely. "Show me what you can do."

Without hesitation Thomas leaned over the slave.

"Lucretia, my name is Thomas. I am a physician and I am here to help you make your arm well. Will you let me touch it and see what is wrong?"

The woman whimpered and withdrew toward the wall. "It hurts really bad when I move it, master."

"Can we take her outside so I can see what I'm doing?" Thomas asked turning back towards Lucius.

"It is your case, Thomas. You do whatever it is you do, I will simply watch," he said as he stood in the entrance, essentially blocking what little light there was.

"Lucretia, I want you to get up and step outside into the courtyard so I can examine your arm. Come." Thomas held out his hand and she obediently took it with her good hand and raised herself up and followed him. He led her to a bench in the sun and made her lay down on it.

"This is badly swollen, Lucius. They should have called us two days ago when it first happened. It will be more painful to set the bone now." Thomas sounded annoyed.

"Remember, she is only a slave, I am amazed they called us at all," Lucius said.

Thomas turned to Lativia, the little slave girl. "Get me some wine, not the diluted stuff, but the concentrated drink. Fill a wineskin with it and bring it to me right away, together with a cup."

"Yes, master." She ran off down the hall and returned within minutes with both items.

Thomas filled the cup with the wine and held it up to the slave's mouth. He knew the undiluted wine was extremely strong and was never served without mixing water with it first, even in the finest houses. "Here, drink this, all of it." She took a sip and coughed from the strong alcoholic beverage, but dutifully finished it at his urging. He filled the cup two more times and waited for the effect of the wine. Not used to drinking alcohol, the woman's eyes glazed over not too long after and she started to fall asleep. That is when Thomas took her arm and ran his hands over where he figured the break was. *An x-ray machine would be nice.* Since the area was quite swollen, it was hard to locate the exact area of the injury. The woman moaned and tried to move away as he carefully touched the swollen area.

"Get me two strong men, Lativia. We need them to hold her down as I set the bone." The girl ran to do as she was told and came back with two young men. Thomas hoped it was a clean break so that when he pulled her arm in just the right way, the broken bone ends would line up well enough to fuse back together, if he found a splint and wrap it tight around the arm. *Medical school 101.*

"Bring me a piece of clean linen cloth," he ordered Lativia, "not too thick so I can wrap it around her arm. Also, get me a thin, flat wooden board, which I can bind to her arm. Maybe a cutting board would do." She looked at him, unsure what he was talking about and then ran off in the direction of the kitchen. While waiting for her to return, Thomas looked around and took some straw, twisted it tightly into a short piece and turned to Lucretia. "Put this in your mouth and bite on it and don't let it go. What I am going to do next will hurt terribly, but it will make your arm better, do you understand?" he asked her. "If you don't hold still and let me do this, your arm will be crooked and you won't be able to use it anymore. I am sure your mistress will not like that, will she?"

The woman shook her head in fear in spite of being sleepy from the large amount of wine. He motioned for the two men to step closer and showed them how to hold her down so she couldn't move. Then he held her arm gently with both hands. "Remember, it's going to hurt terribly for just a moment and then it will be better. Bite down on the straw. You can scream if you want, but don't let go of the straw in your mouth." Before she had time to nod in agreement he jerked the arm with a sudden, violent twist and felt the broken ends of the bone align into place. She let out a horrible scream and the men had all they could do to hold her down. Thomas laid the arm down gently as her screaming subsided into a continuous whimper. He leaned over and said in a gentle voice, "It's over, Lucretia, it's all done. All I have to do now is use this flat, wooden board and lay it under your arm. Then I will strap it on tight so the bones will grow back together, do you understand?" She nodded. "You have to hold still for just a little while longer. I will try very hard not to hurt you anymore," he added.

Again, she nodded in between sobs, without opening her eyes.

With practiced movements he wrapped the linen around the make-shift cast and tore the end of the cloth in order to make a knot. "That's it, Lucretia. You must keep this on your arm for many days and not use it. With the rest of the linen I will make you a sling for you to put your arm in. You must leave it in there at all times when you are up and around. I will talk to your mistress and tell her that you are not to use your arm at all until I come back to check on you several weeks from now." He smiled and stopped talking. His patient had fallen asleep.

"Thomas, I am impressed. You are indeed a skilled physician," Lucius said on the way back to his office. "I don't think I have ever seen someone fix a broken bone like that before."

"I hope she will keep it still so it can heal completely, without any sign it was ever broken," Thomas said with satisfaction. "It is quite a simple procedure if you know how to pull on the arm correctly so that the two ends of the broken bone line up sufficiently to grow back together."

"Where did you learn such remarkable skills?" Lucius asked with new respect.

"I studied at a great center of medicine in my country called America and have done many such procedures successfully. There we have instruments that allow us to look at the bone without opening up the arm. We also have medicine to put the patient to sleep so that they don't feel any pain while we set it."

"We must sit and discuss some of the things you have learned there, Thomas," Lucius said. "For now, allow me to promote you from cleaning my instruments to a fellow physician. Together, I believe we can do great things." He smiled at Thomas and put his hand on his shoulder. "However, I will retain my more affluent clientele, while I give you the regular local crowd. As a Greek, I am not that fond of them and can relate more to Romans or the people from my country. The Jews simply have no class or style in the finer art of conversation." He smiled before he went on, "also, they have very little money." He stopped and turned to Thomas. "In addition to the one denari per day I offered, you will get to keep whatever they pay you. Is it a deal?"

"That sounds fine with me, Lucius, but first I have to find permanent lodging. Do you know of a place where I can stay that befits my limited income?"

"I have a fine, large house not too far from here. I wouldn't mind if you stayed with me so we can discuss medicine after a day's work is done. You can pay me a small fee for room and board. We will return to my office now and see patients until evening and then you get your belongings and follow me to my home."

Two weeks had gone by. Thomas had settled into the routine of a life as a physician in ancient times with all its limitations and cultural hindrances of the day. Lucius turned out to be a generous host as well as a talented doctor. They spent the evenings in endless medical discussions and comparing the customs and religions of their time. Lucius, a Greek, had been brought up with the Hellenistic gods as well as Roman culture and was perfectly versed in both Greek and Latin. His parents had been well to do in the city of Antioch. As he told Thomas, the city was founded by one of the generals of Alexander the Great centuries ago and rivaled Alexandria as the chief city of the Near East, with its spice trade along the Silk Road and the Persian Royal Road. It was also the main center for Hellenistic Judaism at this time. It was here Lucius had been introduced to Judaism and chose to travel to Israel to learn more about the religion. His father, a prominent man in Antioch, was not pleased with his son's choice of life since he had great plans for him to join him in his lucrative spice trade.

"Have you heard about this new Rabbi in town called Yeshua?" Lucius asked Thomas one day as they were sitting in the fading rays of the setting sun in the courtyard under a large tree.

"I have actually met him," Thomas said, nursing a goblet of wine mixture. "He is a very quiet spoken, gentle man who helped out at a wedding in Cana several weeks ago."

"How so?"

"He turned water into wine." Thomas held up his hand before Lucius could say anything derogatory. "I was there. They put me in charge of the water jugs and I had filled them myself with water. When the wine ran out on the third day, Yeshua came over and, without saying a word, turned it into wine. And it wasn't the cheap stuff either, but the best I've ever tasted." He smiled. "I don't mean to say yours doesn't taste great, Lucius, but that one was better. I have no idea how He did it, all I know is that He did."

"If anyone else told me this, I wouldn't believe them, but if you say it happened, it must be so. I have heard strange tales like that told of Him," Lucius added, "like healing people from leprosy and other incurable ailments."

"He healed my foot," Thomas said quietly. "I had a sore between my toes," pointing to his right foot, "and He touched it, again, without a word spoken, and the next morning it was completely healed. It was infected to the point that I had a fever, combined with pain. As a physician, I know no infection heals that fast, even with medicine from my country," he added.

"How do you explain it?" Lucius asked, intrigued.

"I can't. But then I think this whole thing is a dream anyway and I don't have to," he added with a smile.

"I don't understand."

"Don't worry, I don't either." Thomas shook his head and took another sip of the spiced wine mixture.

"Would you like to go see Him tomorrow?" Lucius asked. "I want to check Him out."

"I have a full schedule tomorrow morning. I'm supposed to go to the house of a man called Simon. He is a fisherman and his mother-in-law is sick with a high fever. They are afraid she might die. Then again, that is in the morning, so we could go in the afternoon and find this Rabbi Yeshua. He probably remembers me from Cana. I know His mother Miriam really well, too."

"You never cease to amaze me, Thomas," Lucius said. "Tomorrow afternoon it is then."

The morning sun was already hot as Thomas made his way to the fisherman's house. He knew with the limited tools available to him, it was unlikely he could do much. *Just one little dose of antibiotic would be nice,* he thought as he entered Simon's house. It was not too far from the center of town and of modest proportions. A young boy opened the door for him as soon as he knocked. They must have been waiting for him.

"Shalom, please enter this house and be welcome," the boy said. "My name is Joseph and I am the nephew of Simon. He has gone to get the Rabbi Yeshua since his mother-in-law is worse and you might not be able to heal her."

"Nothing like having a plan B, Thomas thought and stepped inside the courtyard. There were several women, wringing their hands and weeping as he made his way into the interior of the house. He entered into a small room with a cot against one wall and found a woman in her late forties lying on it, moaning in pain. Thomas walked up to her and placed his hand on her forehead. It was extremely hot. "May I touch your stomach, Mistress?"

She nodded slightly. Thomas pressed in the area where he knew her appendix to be and she cried out in sudden pain. He stepped back. "There is nothing I can do for you. You have an infection inside you. This is very serious and if it gets worse you will die. I am so sorry, but I can't help you." He sounded frustrated. *How easy this would be to cure if he was in his hospital in Philadelphia. Here, the woman will die an agonizing death because of simple appendicitis.* He turned to a woman and a man standing behind him. "Just give her strong wine to drink to ease the pain somewhat and pray to your God if you think that will help." He turned around and walked out of the room, feeling helpless and angry.

Just as he was ready to leave, Simon entered the courtyard with Yeshua and his men. Thomas was startled when the Rabbi looked at him with a knowing smile. He could somehow tell Yeshua knew he did not help the sick woman. Thomas decided to wait and see what happened. He stood a little to the side of the rest of the group of people, when Joseph ran up to him. "The Rabbi wants you to come back into the sick room, Sir."

Thomas hurried back into the house and found Yeshua standing by the bed of Simon's mother-in-law. The other men with him, except for Simon, stood waiting in the hallway. Yeshua looked up at Thomas when he entered the room, then put his hand where the patient's appendix was and closed His eyes as if praying. Then, without another word He walked out. Thomas remained and watched in astonishment as Simon's mother-in-law rose from the bed after a minute without any evidence of pain or discomfort and smiled at him. "I am well. Thanks be to the God of Abraham, Isaac and Jacob, I'm well. The Rabbi Yeshua has healed me." She fastened her eyes on Thomas. "Come, Physician, I will fix a good meal for all of us and we will celebrate." With that she walked out of the room, leaving Thomas standing there in stunned silence and feeling a little guilty and foolish, because he had not done anything to deserve her hospitality.

Chapter 6

"I can't believe it." Thomas had returned to the office and found Lucius sitting behind his desk as usual. "I went to see this patient today," he said and sat down with a heavy sigh. "She had what we call *appendicitis* in my country and was dying for sure, since it was totally inflamed. You see, when that happens, the appendix bursts open and spills poison into the bowel area."

"I understand. So what happened?" Lucius asked.

"This Yeshua came and prayed over her quietly and she was completely healed, got up from her bed and fixed us all a great meal." Thomas rubbed his temples. He felt a headache coming on and continued talking. "We have a fable in my country about this Rabbi. They say he was the Jewish Meshiah and came to save the world." Thomas sighed again, looking confused and frustrated. "I personally never believed it, but millions of people all over the world do."

"How can anyone have heard about Him in your far away country?"

"I can't explain it to you, Lucius, they just do. I can't explain anything about this man or His philosophy and powers. All I know, the Jews are going to reject Him and crucify Him after a while, at least that is what my wife's grandmother told me." The more he talked, the more irritated he became. "I wish this dream was over and I can go home. It's all so confusing."

"You keep talking about a dream, Thomas. You don't look like an apparition to me, but a real man of flesh and blood. Why do you think you are living in a dream?" Lucius asked, puzzled.

"I told you, I can't explain it." Thomas shrugged his shoulders in a gesture of surrender. "There is nothing about this I can explain. I am a smart, educated man of my time and now everything I ever knew and trusted is gone and I am back in the stone age. I can't even cure a simple fever or remove an appendix, since all my medical knowledge is useless without the technology and tools to go with it."

"What is a stone age or technology?" Lucius looked at Thomas with a frown on his face. "You are not making sense, Thomas. Besides, how can time be made of stone?"

"I know, don't pay any attention to me. I am just frustrated about this Rabbi and His power to heal people. How does He do it? Maybe He is an alien from the future." He muttered to himself.

"What is an alien?"

"It is a person from another planet who has come to visit earth." The minute he said it he knew, he would never be able to explain that to

Lucius either.

"You are talking strangely today, Thomas. Maybe another glass of wine will help you relax. Sometimes, the mind does crazy things when we are upset."

"You are right, Lucius, I will. Tomorrow is another day. Can we go see the Rabbi then? I don't think I am up to it today." Thomas put his head in his hands and rubbed his temples. His headache had progressed to a painful throb. Had he ever even been in the 21st Century? It all seemed so far away.

It was two days later before they found the time to look for the Rabbi Yeshua. Thomas would have rather stayed home, but Lucius was anxious to find out more about Him, so he really had no choice but to go along. It was afternoon before they got on the way.

"I have heard He is teaching at a house right here in Capernaum," Lucius said with great excitement. "That is why I came to Israel, to learn more about their beliefs. I know just where the place is. My sources tell me, today many Pharisees and teachers of the law have come from the surrounding villages to hear Him, even from as far as Judea and Jerusalem. There is bound to be a lively discussion between these different religious leaders, which I will enjoy," he added.

"Are you a convert to Judaism then?" Thomas asked.

"No, I am merely interested intellectually. It is an unusual belief system with the worship of only one God. It intrigues me, since it makes a lot more sense than the rest of the world with their many deities. I don't know that much about it, but I have every intention of finding out."

It took them some time before they reached a large crowd in front of a medium-sized home on the other side of Capernaum.

"This is a patient of mine and he will let us in if I can get close enough to let him know," Lucius said, trembling with excitement. "Wait here, I will try to break through the crowd and shout for him when I get to the gate." With that he disappeared into the crowd.

At that moment Thomas heard a commotion behind him and saw several men carrying an obviously paralyzed man on a stretcher. In spite of a lot of shouting and pushing, no one was willing to let them through. After a few more tries, they gave up and disappeared.

Thomas remained at the back of the throng for a long time, until he saw Lucius wave for him to meet him at the gate. With great difficulty he squeezed through the multitude, until he finally reached the doorway.

"Hurry and come in before the people get mad," Lucius said as he pulled him through the opening and into the courtyard. There was barely room for them to stand it was so packed. Thomas saw Yeshua way at the front under the overhang of the tiled roof. He was talking to what appeared to be religious leaders from the way they were dressed. He could not hear what was said, because of the noise of the many people shoving and pushing to get closer. Thomas was getting bored just standing there among the smelly mass of people, when a movement on the roof caught his eyes. Someone was removing the tiles to make a hole in the roof! Before long, he saw the men, still holding the stretcher with the paralytic on it, lowering him down to where Yeshua sat. A hush fell over the crowd. The Rabbi didn't seem to be upset or even surprised. Instead, He looked at the paralyzed man for a moment and then said with a kindly smile,

"Friend, your sins are forgiven." (Luke 5:20)

Thomas could clearly see the frown on the faces of the Pharisees and the teachers, even from way back and knew what they were thinking, "…Who is this fellow who speaks blasphemy? Who can forgive sins but God alone?

Yeshua also knew and asked, "Why are you thinking these things in your heart? Which is easier to say, 'Your sins are forgiven, or to say, 'Get up and walk? But that you may know that the Son of Man has authority on earth to forgive sins…" He said to the paralyzed man, "I tell you, get up, take your mat and go home." Immediately he stood up in front of them, took what he had been lying on and went home praising God." (Luke 5:21-25)

The crowd remained silent for what seemed a long time. Thomas was stunned. He had seen the man up close. In his professional opinion, he was a victim of advanced stage of MS from the short glimpse he had of him. As a physician, the symptoms were obvious. *They can't even cure that in modern times, least of all now,* he thought. And yet, he watched him get up and walk out of there as if nothing had ever been wrong with him. Thomas stood as if glued to his spot. This must be a dream, it had to be. When would he finally wake up from this ridiculous nonsense?

"That was worth going to, don't you think?" Lucius asked on the way home. "I heard some of the things they were arguing with Yeshua about. He trounced them but good. That man is a genius, don't you think, Thomas?"

"It still doesn't explain how He heals people with the most devastating diseases," Thomas said. "As a doctor, please explain it to me, Lucius."

"I watched him, he didn't do anything weird or even out of the ordinary," Lucius said. "He just spoke to the man and the sickness was gone. I looked closely when they lowered him through the roof. He had the wasting disease which no medicine can cure. Although, that part about forgiving his sins was a bit over the top, I must say."

"I don't care about that religious stuff. Let's get back to the paralyzed man. What he suffered from was what we call MS or Multiple Sclerosis," Thomas said. "I have seen many patients with it and at that late stage, there is no cure, even where I come from," he added with a tone of frustration in his voice. "How does this Yeshua do it?"

"Since you know Him, could you ask Him?"

"I sure would like to. Maybe we will get a chance next time we see Him. I might even go back to Nazareth and talk to Miriam and Tiny. Maybe they would know. After all, she is His mother. Surely she can explain to me what or who He really is." Thomas was warming up to the idea. "How would I get to Nazareth? It is too far to walk."

"I have a patient who owns an import business and sends his slaves on trips to different market places in the area to sell his linen cloths. I could ask him if you could accompany one of them when they go to Nazareth."

"Is there a rich man you don't know in this town, Lucius?" Thomas asked with a smile.

"The rich need a doctor as much as the poor," he answered with a twinkle in his eyes. "It's just that they pay more for me to make them feel better than the others."

"How did you get involved with the upper crust of this area?" Thomas asked. "After all, you haven't been here that long to have earned such a great reputation."

"That is quite an interesting story, now that you ask. But let's get into the house and refresh ourselves from this long walk," he said as they entered his courtyard. A boy of about twelve knelt in front of Lucius, untied his sandals and poured water over his hands first and then his bare feet. When he was done, he did the same for Thomas. While the water wasn't cold, it was nevertheless refreshing. Yet Thomas was uncomfortable. He would never get used to the idea of slavery. To think, these poor people would never know freedom or be allowed to have a choice of what they wanted to do with their lives. "Thank you, Servanus," he said to the child when he was done drying off his feet.

"Why do you thank a slave, Thomas? That is simply not done. It spoils them and gives them ideas that they are on our level," Lucius said.

"To me they are," Thomas said and suddenly remembered how terrible he had treated most of the staff at the hospital. He cringed and suddenly realized, he had acted no different toward them than Lucius acted toward his slaves. He decided right then that would definitely change when he got back home, or woke up, or whatever.

"Come, let us sit on a comfortable couch and I will tell you the story of how I became the physician of the rich," Lucius said. They settled down on thick cushions on the floor while a woman brought in a tray with cheese on thin wafers as well as dates and pomegranates cut up in pieces and put it on a low table before them. Thomas had gotten used to eating reclining on the floor, while leaning on one elbow and using his fingers instead of a knife and fork. Lucius was quite the connoisseur and Thomas had learned to appreciate the sumptuous meals served by servants each evening after their work was done.

"I came here a year ago from Antioch like I told you before to study Judaism."

"Why did you come to Capernaum, it is just a small village without importance," Thomas asked.

"You would be surprised. This little town is at the crossroads of our world with the most important trade routes coming from Damascus and Syria going through Galilee on to Egypt. There is an old saying, 'Judea is on the way to nowhere, Galilee is on the way to everywhere.' In other words, the traffic of the world passes through this area. I also knew there were a lot of Roman and Greek traders, who have settled in Galilee, making a lucrative living. And being a physician, I knew I would find a way among them to pay my way.

"It seems you were right," Thomas said with a smile.

"Not long after I opened my practice, I was on my way to a client's home, when a fancy carriage tipped over on the road just ahead of me," Lucius went on. "It had a broken axel, and no matter how hard the slaves tried, they could not get to the man and woman inside to pull them out. Suddenly, I heard a child screaming. That's when I ran over and managed to reach inside and get out a baby trapped in there. It was a little boy, maybe a year old, his face and arms covered with scrapes and bruises. He seemed to be more scared than in pain. I immediately grabbed my bag and covered his bruises with a salve I carry with me, after I ascertained there were no broken bones. I noticed his clothes were of the finest linen interwoven with gold strands. He soon calmed down and stopped crying as I held him in my arms. By the time the couple was able to get out from underneath the carriage, he was sound asleep. Thankfully the man and woman were not hurt. When they realized how I had taken care of the baby, they were very grateful and invited me to visit them the next day to check on the boy.

It turned out, this was none other than Chuza, the head steward of Herod Antipas and his wife Joanna with their grandson. Their gratitude knew no bounds and aside from giving me a great deal of money for my treatment of the boy, they began to recommend me to many of the people in the royal household." Lucius leaned over to refill their wine cups. "From what I hear, since then Joanna has become a follower of this Yeshua and supports him financially as well. Maybe I can ask her what His secret power is."

"You realize Passover is coming up soon," Thomas said. "I would really like to go to Jerusalem and watch the festivities. It was a big deal with my grandmother every year and the whole family had to participate in the Seder, whether we wanted to or not."

"So your family was Jewish?" Lucius asked, surprised. "I thought you did not believe in anything?"

"I don't and neither did my parents. It was my grandmother who clung to the age old customs of Judaism. It is from her I heard the old stories about Moses and the flight out of Egypt to escape slavery under Pharaoh. That is what Passover is all about. This happened about four hundred years ago."

"You must tell me more about this, Thomas. There are so many things I don't understand about these people. All I know, there is no other race I have encountered so fervent about their religion as the Jews." He reached for a piece of lamb, broke some bread and dipped it into the savory sauce. "This is good. My cook is a jewel. I think he is from Egypt brought here by a slave trader. It looks like time has a way of turning things around." He smacked his lips. "Help yourself to this good stuff, Thomas."

"Did you buy him?" Thomas asked.

"Of course I did; how else would I find a cook?" Lucius looked at Thomas and raised his eyebrows slightly. "Sometimes I don't understand you at all. You know so much about medicine, but have no understanding about the most common things of daily life."

"You have no idea," Thomas said with a knowing smile.

"How are we getting to Jerusalem for the Passover, Lucius?" Thomas asked. "From what I can tell, it is too far to walk."

"I have a two-wheeled cart and a donkey for us to use. It will take us three or four days to get there if we don't run across any problems. We can go through Samaria, unlike most of the other pilgrims. The Jews dislike the Samaritans so much, they won't even travel through their region, even if it means walking a much greater distance. Don't ask me what they have against them, I have no idea and I don't care. We on the other hand, can take the straight route and get there before anyone else. That way, we will find lodging in Jerusalem before the thousands of pilgrims inundate the city."

"I must say, I am looking forward to see Jerusalem. It is the city of my ancestors and important to me and to those of us who don't necessarily follow the religion," Thomas said. "My grandmother dreamed of visiting it, but never made it. She would be so pleased to know I am here."

"Passover is next week," Lucius said. "That means we will have to leave four days before that. I will instruct my slaves to prepare the cart and make sure we have enough provisions for the journey there and back."

"Master, forgive me for speaking without having been asked." It was the woman who had brought in the food. She was kneeling before Lucius, waiting to be allowed to go on.

"What is it, Helena?"

"I have lived here in this land since I was born and have traveled the road to Jerusalem several times. If you go through the land of Samaria, you will encounter many robbers on the way, since you will travel alone. It would be much safer if you go where the caravans go along the other side of the Jordan River. They have protection and besides, there are hundreds of travelers looking out for each other." She remained in her kneeling position with her head down almost to the floor. "It is just a suggestion from a worthless slave, master."

"That sounds like a good Idea, Helena," Thomas said before Lucius could get angry with her. "We appreciate your input. You may go." He knew it was not allowed for a slave to speak to the master unless spoken to.

"There you go again, Thomas, treating the slave like she was a human being." Lucius sounded slightly annoyed.

"She is a human being, Lucius. Medically speaking, her body is the same as ours, but I know you already know that. Besides, what she says makes a lot of sense. What good does it do us if we save time, but lose our lives by being waylaid by robbers?"

"Do you realize it adds one third to the trip to take the route around Samaria? That means another day or two. I don't want to do that." Lucius sounded determined. "We are two strong, healthy men and nobody is going to dare attack us. It will be alright, you'll see. Besides, there will be others traveling those roads that are not bound by Jewish traditions."

Chapter 7

The early morning air smelled of spring. Thomas appreciated the hint of a cool breeze when they started on the long, four-day trek toward Jerusalem. A two-wheel cart had been filled with provisions by the slaves, who had worked tirelessly into the night to get everything ready. The little donkey reminded Thomas of Igor. And just like Igor, it had plodded at a steady pace west with the isolated peak of Mt. Tabor coming into view in the distance; and on toward the Plain of Esdraelon in Samaria.

It was on the second day of their journey, when they reached the Valley of Jezreel, they had a magnificent view of the flat, fertile plain stretching out before them. The barley fields waived gently in the wind, ripe for harvest, while the wheat would not be ready until a month later.

"This valley is called Yizre'l, meaning 'God will sow' or May God make fruitful'," Lucius said. "It gives an allusion to the fertility of the area." He turned to Thomas and waved his hand in a sweeping gesture. "It is a land filled with Jewish history as well," he went on. "It is here Gideon's armies defeated the Midianites and Amalekites. And on the slopes of Mt. Gilboa, a little further northwest, Saul and Jonathan were slain. Legend has it that at Megiddo, also to the northwest from here, will be the site where the Jewish God and the evil forces of His enemy will battle at the end of history."

"How do you know all this?" Thomas asked.

"I told you, I am interested in the Jewish religion and have studied its history since I've come here. Yet, while I know a lot about the historical facts, I am not so well versed in the spiritual aspect of their religion. I hope to learn more during this Passover in Jerusalem." They sat on a wooden board at the front of the cart. Lucius held the reins loosely as the donkey didn't need much in the way of direction. It simply followed the ruts in the road at a steady, slow pace.

"Can I ask you a strange question, Lucius?" Thomas asked after a while.

"Sure, what do you want to know?"

"When I talk to you, what language do I speak?"

Lucius looked at Thomas in surprise. "Greek of course. That is what you spoke the first day you came into my office. I have also heard you speak Aramaic fluently when you talk to the slaves and the poor people you treat. You seem to be extremely well versed in several languages."

"I know it sounds crazy, but I have never learned any of those languages."

"Thomas, are you trying to sound humble or something, because if you are, it is not working. Besides, you are not the humble type. As a matter of fact, I am sure you don't mind telling those around you what to do from what I have observed." He chuckled.

Thomas stared straight ahead in silence. All he ever spoke or heard was English since he got here. How then, in god's name was it, what he said came out in different languages? This must be a dream, there was no other explanation possible. But if it was, how did he manage to hear Lucius and all the others he had met during the last few weeks, tell him things he could not possibly know in languages he never learned? None of this made any sense.

Suddenly, the cart hit a hole and he would have fallen onto the road if he hadn't grabbed the wooden sides. When he sat back down, he was astounded at what they called roads here. Most of them were nothing but well used paths with dirt trampled into a solid surface.

Lucius pulled on the reins to slow down the donkey. "Let us pause and rest on the side for a little while. Besides, the donkey has to have something to eat as well. It is noon and we have yet a long way ahead of us." He gently guided the little animal to the side right next to a field of barley. "It's time for a break," he said and jumped off the cart. Before anything else, he took the bit out the donkey's mouth and allowed it to eat the grain on the stalks; and then took a clay jar filled with water and allowed it to drink its fill.

Thomas watched with fascination as Lucius broke off the head of a long stalk, put it between both hands and rubbed them together rapidly. When he opened them, the kernels laid in his palm. After he picked out a few pieces of chaff, he put the kernels into his mouth.

"Won't the owner get upset with us for eating his grain?" Thomas asked.

"I don't think so. How much can one little donkey eat?" He chuckled as he chewed on the grain while rummaging for food on the back of the cart. "It is the custom to allow the poor and travelers like us to eat whatever grows at the edge of the field alongside the road," Lucius said.

Thomas had never seen a grain field. He broke off one of the heads of barley, feeling the long, rough, hair-like strands with his fingers. Imitating Lucius, he rubbed the pods between his palms, picked out the staff and then put the kernels in his mouth. They had a crunchy, rough, earthy taste to them. Thomas liked the aftertaste and continued to eat from a dozen or so stalks.

"They will swell in your stomach, so you have to drink some wine mixture with it," Lucius said and handed him the wineskin. "Let's sit down right here and enjoy our midday meal and allow the donkey to eat his fill and rest."

Before long they had finished eating a good meal of flat bread, cheese and some dates. Just as they were about to stretch out on the ground, they heard voices from around the corner of the field. Three men came into view and stopped, looking at the leftovers of the meal still spread on the grass.

"Look what we have here," the oldest said in a sarcastic tone, "Two Greeks disgracing our soil."

"Good day, gentlemen," Lucius said as he got up with sudden haste. "I am a Greek and my friend is from a land far away called America." He waved his hand toward the food. "Will you not join us in our midday meal? We will share it with you gladly."

"We don't want your food, but we could do with your supplies in the cart and the donkey," the man said as his eyes sized up the treasures in the cart. "Isn't that right, Barabbas?"

"This looks exactly what we were looking for. We don't like Greeks or barbarians from the north." The man had a dark, vicious look on his face and seemed to be the leader of the trio.

"I don't think so guys," Thomas said, getting up slowly and positioning himself between the cart and the men. "I cannot let you do that." He was glad he had taken self-defense classes at the club just for exercise and fun. They might come in handy after all.

The tallest of the three, a young man of no more than sixteen, took his rod and stepped up to Thomas with a threatening gesture.

"So, you really want to fight me, hey?" Thomas said with a grin and went into his self-defense stance. "Come on, let's do this, I can't wait to beat the snot out of you, little boy."

"Thomas, maybe we should just give them what they want," Lucius said in a whisper. "We can always buy more stuff in the next town." He had moved to the other side of the cart, hiding from view of the men.

"Don't you worry, Lucius, I will show these boys what an American cowboy can do," Thomas said in a loud voice. He was itching to try out what he had learned in his class on these crude louts.

"Come on, boys. You want to change your mind before it's too late?"

"You will be sorry you barbarian swine," the younger one shouted as he ran toward Thomas, swinging his thick rod with a pointed end menacingly over his head.

In one lightning quick motion Thomas stepped to the left of the staff. With his weak arm he blocked the staff and grabbed the boy's arm with his strong hand, twisted it to the inside and bringing his attacker to his knees, thereby gaining control of the staff. "Anyone else care to try?

Come on, little boys, let's not be shy."

With a loud, angry roar the other two men charged at Thomas. With a practiced, quick motion he jabbed one of them in the chest with the blunt end of the staff, then swung around and struck the second one named Barabbas on the side of the neck, making him drop like a sack of grain.

Thomas laughed. "I haven't had this much fun in years. Any more ideas about stealing our stuff?" he said with a big grin, totally pleased with himself.

Lucius stood with his mouth open in utter astonishment.

"Thomas, you never cease to amaze me. You are a warrior like I have not seen in the gladiatorial arenas in Greece and Rome!"

"Aw shucks, it was nothing," Thomas grinned as he touched his forehead. "I barely broke a sweat." He looked at the three would-be robbers and held out his hand toward them. "Come on guys, get up, I didn't really hurt you, did I? If I did, you're in luck. I'm a doctor and can make it all better, if you promise not to do it again."

The three men rose slowly, bewildered and shocked at the sudden turn of events. They were not hurt, although Barabbas was still in pain from the blow to his neck. Finally, standing on shaky legs, they looked at Thomas and then at each other and stumbled back in the direction they came from.

"And here I was just getting started, "Thomas said, the grin still on his face. "That was fun, don't you agree, Lucius?"

"I am still in shock. Did they teach you that in medical school?" Lucius stood, still staring at Thomas with an expression of utter astonishment.

"No, it is what I do in my spare time after work. It is my way of exercise and getting rid of stress."

"You saved our lives or at least all our provisions from these robbers. I have heard the name Barabbas. He is a well-known criminal and has been in prison for serious crimes if I'm not mistaken. I think we better continue our journey before we encounter any more like him." Lucius started loading the rest of the food back on the cart. "Do you have any other surprises I don't know about?"

You have no idea, Thomas thought, but didn't answer.

Before long, they were on their way through the lush, rich Plain of Esdraelon, heading toward the hills of Samaria under the shadow of Mount Gerizim and Mount Ebal. The landscape was filled with grain fields waving in the gentle breeze, as well as olive groves and vineyards as far as the eye could see. These were interspersed with green meadows allowing sheep, goats and cattle to graze in small herds. In the distance they could see the hills of Judea. Once there, it would not be that far until they would climb up to Jerusalem and join the thousands of pilgrims for the Passover celebration.

Thomas wondered if he would see the Rabbi Yeshua and His followers there among the large crowds. He was hoping at least to run into Miriam and Tiny, or maybe Daniel and his family. It would be a little over a day before they got there. The closer they came to Judea, the more people they met on their way, mostly on foot to the Holy City. Thomas was glad they had the cart, even if it was slow going. The little donkey, which he had named Igora, plodded faithfully along without any visible signs of complaint. He felt sorry for the little animal and made sure she was fed and watered at regular times.

"You have not told me much about your family, Thomas," Lucius said into the silence.

"I told you about my wife Melissa. She is very beautiful and I miss her."

"You have no children?"

"No, she didn't want to give up her work when we were first married. After that, I don't know why the subject never came up," he said with a touch of sadness in his voice.

"What is a man without children, Thomas?" Lucius said.

"You don't have any either, do you?" He sounded slightly offended.

"I am not married, my friend. I have been too busy traveling the world and in my wanderings I have never found a woman I wanted to settle down with. To the consternation of my parents, I must say." He shook the reins slightly and reached for the wineskin. "I don't know what it is, ever since I have become interested in the Jewish religion, I feel there is a hole in my life, something I am supposed to do, yet I don't know what it is. I have started searching for a purpose, but how do you look for something when you don't know what it is you're looking for?"

"I have never looked for a purpose, because I always knew I would be a surgeon," Thomas said. "Now I'm not so sure that is enough anymore. Like you, I have no idea what it might be."

"We are two lost souls looking for the secret of life," Lucius said with a smile. "Both of us were so sure of our superior education and talents. What happened?"

"I have no idea, Lucius, I still am convinced, this existence I live right now, is nothing but a strange dream from which I will wake up anytime now. Nothing else makes sense."

"There you go again, carrying on about your dream." Lucius sighed in exasperation.

They drove on in silence the rest of the way until it was time to break for the evening meal and stopped at the side of a grove of olive trees. The olives would not be ripe for many months, until the fall. It was the last of the harvest in the year. A little further back they had found some early grape clusters, which looked barely ripe enough to eat. The fruit was a welcome addition to their supplies.

"Have you ever believed in the afterlife, Lucius?" Thomas asked, savoring the slightly tart grapes after a good meal. He had learned from eating pomegranates to spit the many seeds a good distance with great efficiency.

"I have examined the Hellenistic and Roman gods and studied the Judean religion, but I can't say that any of these beliefs have given me an insight into the purpose of mankind or the possibility of an afterlife, Thomas. None of them seem to change people's behavior towards one another. People act the same, whether they believe in anything or not. The Greek and Roman gods behave worse than human beings with their anger, jealousy and petty power struggles among themselves. The Jews are so bound up with regulations and restrictions of daily living, they are barely able to move without their leaders breathing down their necks with judgment and condemnation. What I dislike most about them, is the attitude they have of having been chosen above all the other people in the world. Why would their God pick out a small group of people, cantankerous and stiff necked to the extreme, and put them above all the rest of humanity? I will grant you, they are one of the most intelligent among the nations, but are hindered by the many restrictions that have been put on them by their leaders."

"What do you think about their God?" Thomas asked.

"From what I have learned about Him, He is remarkable among the fables of the gods of the world. First of all, there is only one. Second, He sounds benevolent and capable of forgiveness and love and really seems to care about His people. Do I believe He really exists? I don't know, although it would be nice. What bothers me about Him most is that He only wants the Jews, which means I don't qualify as one of His children." He looked at Thomas with a sudden, sad little smile. "But you could be."

"I don't believe in Him," Thomas answered without hesitation. "I never have and neither have my parents. The only thing we ever believed to have any lasting value, is science and the pursuit of truth that can be proven without the necessity of faith."

"I don't know about that, Thomas. The more I have studied and understand about life, the more questions remain unanswered. By necessity, that is where faith must come in."

"I only believe what I can detect with the five senses. The rest, science will figure out in time," Thomas said with certainty.

"How do you explain the beginning of life in the womb, Thomas? When did the world come into being and who created it? Even you cannot go back to that time with all your science and bring me proof. I have studied the human body in great detail and yet I cannot understand what makes the heart beat and the blood flow in such precision and harmony. At what point does it start to beat and who tells it to do so? And even if there is chemistry as you tell me, which causes the body to function the way it does, who created *it*?" He leaned back against the trunk of the tree with a deep sigh. "No, Thomas, even you cannot explain all these things with your science." He sighed again. "In every one of us there is a void which seeks those answers and yearns to find the One who created us. Different religions try to fill that void, but I am looking for Him who gives me the reason for being and the understanding that He has destined me to be more than I can ever be on my own. And so I will continue to search until I find Him." Lucius leaned forward with his eyes closed as if in prayer.

The two sat in silence for a long time, each steeped in his own thoughts, until it was once more time to continue on to Jerusalem, with only one more stop for the night at the next village.

After the incident on the road, Lucius changed their travel plans somewhat the next morning. Instead of going straight south, they would travel through the villages of Bethany on the south slope of the Mount of Olives, somewhat off the Roman Road and then on to Bethphage on the western slope of the same mountain, just across the Kidron Valley from Jerusalem.

Chapter 8

It was on the morning of the fourth day since they left Capernaum, they entered through the gate of the Holy City. Coming down from the Mount of Olives, they had passed through numerous campsites filled with the faithful from all across the known world. Lucius told Thomas, since the city would swell over six times its normal size during Passover, they must get there ahead of the main crowd to find lodging. Judging from the endless stream of pilgrims pouring into the city, he doubted there would be any room left anywhere.

"Never fear, we will find a place. I have a friend who promised he will help us find lodging in the upper section of the city. It is where the more well-to-do live." Lucius sounded confident.

"Of course it is, Lucius, you don't know any others," Thomas said with a chuckle.

The cart rumbled over the stone covered streets at the usual slow pace. Along the way they passed rows upon rows of wealthy homes. These were not made of the usual rough exterior, but gleamed in the bright sun with their clean, whitewashed, finely hewn, square stones. The street was crowded with people in colorful Jewish garments, some in simple browns of the poor, but many in finer cloth of muted reds and greens with tasseled prayer shawls in multiple colors. He even spotted a few men with long locks hanging on each side of their face. He was surprised how many Romans and Greeks he saw among the crowd, easily visible in their bright colored togas draped over their white garments. He was sure there were many languages spoken in the crowd, but as usual, all he could hear was English.

Suddenly, all movements stopped as a small contingent of Roman soldiers came marching toward them from the opposite direction. Thomas admired their beautiful red garments underneath the matching red armor. The silver helmets gleamed in the sun with their elongated, brush-like, red tops. Even their shields were red with yellow insignias, which made them resemble shining knights. They reminded him of a movie he had seen.

The crowd moved out of the way in total silence and he definitely sensed their resentment as they stood aside to let the soldiers pass.

"How dare they intrude on us during Passover," he heard an old man grumble, standing next to their cart.

"They are here to keep order," Lucius whispered to Thomas. "This crowd can get quite fervent and sometimes even violent. Many riots have been started, driven by the religious fervor during this time. Make sure you don't get involved in any conversation. There is no way I can get you out of a Roman jail if you are arrested."

"Don't worry, I'll be good," Thomas whispered back. "I think we can go now, they're gone," he said and pointed to the Roman soldiers behind them down the road.

After they drove on for a short distance, they came to a large intersection. Thomas took in a deep breath as he beheld the imposing front of the Temple before him. It was stunning! No wonder, for the Jews there was no other building equal to this Temple with its splendor and magnificence as the spiritual focal point of their God and His people. The massive structure seemed to stretch endlessly as it towered above the city before it. The gleaming limestone of the walls reflected the sun in a way it made the building glow as if in a heavenly light. Thomas marveled at some of the stones, weighing several tons or more. He could not imagine how the builders had managed to lay them with such perfect precision without modern technology.

"Where did they get the building blocks for this temple, Lucius?" He asked in a hushed tone.

"The mountains around here are composed of limestone from what I understand," Lucius answered. He was interrupted by a voice coming from the steps leading up to the main building.

"What is he saying, Lucius?" Thomas asked, because it was too far away for him to make out the words.

"He is reciting the *Shema,* the main commandment of their faith," Lucius said. "This is how it goes,
"Hear, O Israel! The Lord is our God, the Lord alone! Therefore, you shall love the Lord your God with all your heart, and with all your soul, and with all your strength."

"It is from their book called Deuteronomy, Chapter 6," Lucius went on. "I have memorized it, because it contains the main emphasis of their belief. The truly fervent believers carry a copy of this prayer in a pouch tied to their belt. However, I can only guess, because all prayers must be spoken in Hebrew. That is a language I do not know, but maybe you do. It is mostly used for prayer." He looked at Thomas expectantly. "If you do, you will have to translate a lot while we are here, because the coming days will be filled with prayers spoken in it."

"I do remember the *Shema* from going to the synagogue when I was a child. My grandmother taught me to say it in Hebrew," Thomas said with awe in his voice. "I definitely never thought to hear it at Herod's temple in the city of Jerusalem." He felt a stirring in his heart as he looked at the magnificent sight of the Temple. It affected him more deeply than he ever thought it would and for the first time in his life, he felt like a Jew.

"We better get going, Thomas," Lucius interrupted his thoughts. "We must get to my friend's house so he can show us our lodgings for the next four days."

"Do you know where he lives?" Thomas asked.

"I certainly do, because I have been here once before. It was not during Passover nor was it as crowded. Cassius is a Greek and lives in the upper part of the city, like I told you before. It is not far from here." He flicked the reins and Igora reluctantly pulled the cart forward. "Actually, his father is a friend of my father's and he visited our home many times when I was a child. His son Cassius moved here several years ago as part of the business. Like my father, he imports cloth, spices and perfumes and makes use of the busy trade routes to and from Egypt. Cassius was constantly held up to me as an example of stepping into his father's footsteps. I used to hate the boy when I was younger because of it." Thomas chuckled. "He is a very nice person and we are friends now."

It was not long until they stopped in front of a large, white house, one of many lining the spotlessly clean street on both sides. A slave came up to the cart and took the reins of the donkey after bowing to Lucius and Thomas.

"The master is waiting for you." He pointed to the door. At that moment another slave came and showed them into the house. It was arranged like a Roman villa with the walls of the atrium adorned with pictures of lush gardens with flowers, birds and fruit trees. The bright sunlight flooded through an opening in the roof and gave the room a light, airy appearance.

"Welcome to my home, Lucius," a booming voice shouted from the rear. It belonged to a tall, handsome man in his forties. His hair was curled like the typical Greek of that day and his toga hung gracefully over one of his powerful shoulders. His big smile showed a row of perfect white teeth. "You are a sight for sore eyes, my friend," he said as he hugged Lucius with a big bear hug.

"It is good to see you as well, Cassius," Lucius said. "I want you to meet my friend Thomas. He is a Jew from a far-way land called America and is a talented fellow physician."

"Welcome, Thomas. You must be a special person to be called a friend and talented by Lucius. He doesn't bestow those honors on too many people." He snapped his fingers toward the slave standing in back of him. "Get the things from the cart and bring them in, Flavius."

"Yes master," the young man said and ran outside.

"I thought you had found lodgings for us, Cassius," Lucius said, "there should be no need to unload our belongings."

"Nonsense, you are staying with us. I am eager to talk to a fellow Greek. My wife will be delighted to feed you delicious food from home since she has taught the cook to fix many Greek dishes." His laugh boomed throughout the house. "Thomas, come, I will introduce you to her. Be careful, she will ask you many questions since you are from a far-away land. I must warn you, she is filled with curiosity, unlike most of the shy, serious Jewish women around here. She is also quite educated and well versed in Latin and Hebrew, aside from Greek of course. Although lately, she has become interested in some Galilean carpenter, who she says goes around performing miracles. It must be some out of the way Jewish sect and sounds quite absurd if you ask me. I am sure she will tell you all about Him, whether you want to hear it or not." He laughed good-naturedly.

"Thomas speaks many languages as well, Cassius," Lucius managed to say as the man took a rare breath. "He is an unusual Jew in so many ways, as you will see."

"I am looking forward to get to know you, Thomas," Cassius said as he turned and led them further into the interior of the house.

The afternoon had turned into evening and by the light of several oil lamps, they sat on ornate, comfortable couches, upholstered in the finest cloth of blues and purple in what Thomas would call a living room. Slaves stood by, ready to make sure all their wishes were instantly seen to. Thomas sipped wine from a silver goblet as he leaned back, listening to the conversation about their home town Antioch. His mind wondered to his own home in Philadelphia. *It seems so far away, even strange,* he thought. *What in the world am I doing here? I wonder how Melissa is doing? She did forget my birthday the last time I was home. Does she feel guilty now that I have disappeared? The people at the hospital have probably forgotten I ever existed. I wish I could tell Nana where I am. She would be so pleased to have me here and find out I am a Jew after all.*

"I understand you are from a land called America, Thomas?"

He looked up, startled. The voice belonged to Claudia, the lady of the house. She was in her late thirties, a striking, petite, slender woman with shiny, long black hair hanging to her shoulders. Her large, blue eyes sparkled with intelligence as she looked at him with a tiny smile. She wore a wide belt of gold around the small waist of her elegant, yet simple white dress. Large ear rings, matching the belt, hung from her ears, nearly touching her shoulders. "You seemed to be far away, Thomas. Were your thoughts of your distant land maybe, your wife and children? I would love to hear all about them, yet you have been strangely quiet."

"I am listening and learning, gracious Lady Claudia. This land and its people are so very different from where I come from."

"But I thought you were a Jew, Thomas, are you not?"

"Yes, although I do not believe in their God or their customs." Thomas hastened to add.

"I thought all Jews believed in this one God. That is what makes them Jews." Claudia leaned forward with interest. "What is it you *do* believe, Thomas?"

"I put my faith in science and knowledge and the things I can explain and choose to disregard the religious fables, whether Jewish, Greek or Roman," Thomas said and then added after a slight pause, "I don't mean to offend in any way when I tell you that in my opinion religion hinders the full development of a man's mind by putting unnecessary restrictions on his thoughts and actions. To me it is nothing but a crutch for those who do not comprehend, that we, as human beings, are the highest form of intelligence and perfectly capable to run our lives without the help or interference of a deity."

"That is remarkable. I thought every culture has some form of religion, even the simplest tribes of the world. One may not believe in these gods, but they are as necessary as the pillars of a temple." She took a fig and bit off a tiny piece of it, then held out her goblet without a word for the slave to fill it. "You are unusual indeed, Thomas. You must tell me about your country. Where is it and how did you get here?"

"It is indeed far away, across a large body of water to the west. It was settled by people from the north many years ago, barbarians as you call them. They went there in ships to escape religious persecution and have done well since then, although, their basic philosophy is taken in part from the Greeks. For example, I swore an oath to Hippocrates when I finished my medical training."

"How very interesting, Thomas. But tell me, how can these Barbarians, as uncivilized and crude as they are, have managed to travel across the waters and establish such a wonderful country?"

"That is a question I cannot answer you. Maybe they are not as uncivilized as the Romans have you believe," he added with a smile.

"Since you say the people fled religious persecution, what religion did they practice?" Her eyes were set on him with sudden intensity.

"I know this sounds strange, but they mostly believe in this Carpenter from Galilee your husband mentioned you are interested in."

"You know about the Rabbi Yeshua?" Her face showed total confusion. "How can they possibly know about Him?"

"I don't know. All I know, millions believe in Him all over the world where I come from." He looked at her and shrugged his shoulders in a helpless gesture of confusion. "My wife Melissa believes in Him as well. Maybe you can tell me how *you* found out about Him?" he asked.

"I have a friend in Capernaum who told me about Yeshua when she came to see us not too long ago. Her name is Joanna and her husband is Chuza, King Herod's steward. She has been following this man for quite a while now. According to her, this Rabbi goes throughout Galilee preaching and healing people. She began believing in Him when a centurion found his most valuable servant dying of an unknown sickness. The centurion heard of Yeshua and sent some elders of the Jews to Him, asking Him to come and heal his servant. When they came to Yeshua, they pleaded earnestly with Him and said, 'This man deserves to have you do this, because he loves our nation and has built our synagogue.' So Yeshua went with them. He was not far from the house when the centurion sent friends to say to him, 'Lord, don't trouble yourself, for I do not deserve to have you come under my roof.' That is why I did not even consider myself worthy to come to You. But say the word, and my servant will be healed.'
When Yeshua heard this, He was amazed at him, and turning to the crowd following Him, He said, 'I tell you, I have not found such great faith even in Israel.' Then the men who had been sent returned to the house and found the servant well." (Luke 7:2-9)

"Joanna and her husband are not great friends of King Herod's, but they have to live there because of her husband's job," Claudia continued. "She believes the centurion is a good man, a friend of the Jews and refuses to mistreat them in disobedience to Rome. Joanna also told me she has witnessed several other miracles and is convinced this Rabbi is the Meshiah the Jews are waiting for." Claudia leaned forward and looked at Thomas with intensity. "Does your wife believe He is?"

"Yes she does, Lady Claudia, she certainly does and so do all those other millions I told you about. Please don't ask me to explain to you how that can be, I can't. I just know it is so."

"If He is the Meshiah and the Son of God as He claims to be, I just have to believe this is possible," she said. "I heard He is on the way to Jerusalem as we speak and I am going to find him when He gets here," she added with great determination.

"Please, let us know when you find Him," Lucius interjected, "I want to know more about Him as well. Not that I believe He is the Meshiah, but just out of curiosity," he added.

"There she goes again, my fiercely determined wife with her crazy ideas." Cassius sighed with a crooked little smile, looking at his wife with something close to adoration. "I know she will get in trouble, she always does."

"I have invited a Pharisee named Nicodemus to dine with us tomorrow," Claudia said. "He is a wonderful man who is much more open-minded about associating with Gentiles, although he comes when it is dark so he won't be seen."

"What exactly is a Pharisee?" Lucius asked. "I know I should know, but the many different titles the religious leaders have here, it escapes me at the moment."

"They are a sect of the Jews who have devoted their lives to following the *Torah*, the books of the Law of Moses. They firmly believe in following the letter of the law in all its minute detail in order to please God. They are the ones you see walking around with their prayer shawls and more often than not, criticizing others for not being as holy as they are." Claudia was trying hard to find the words. "Nicodemus is not like that. He is a godly man who seeks the truth within the law, rather than just the law. I have had many discussions with him about the coming Meshiah. He has listened to the Rabbi Yeshua and it has sparked his curiosity, because the words this carpenter from Nazareth speaks, are not like any teacher he has ever heard."

"There is a book like the *Torah* called the Bible in my country," Thomas said. "All those who believe in this Rabbi read it diligently. I never have and so I have no idea what it contains. The only thing I do remember is, He was born in Bethlehem and was from the line of King David. I talked with Miriam, his mother and she told me that He was born in a cave since there was no room in the inn. She also shares that angels and shepherds came to worship Him after He was born. That was about thirty years ago during the time of King Herod."

"We have to ask Nicodemus when he comes tomorrow if that goes in line with prophecy about the Meshiah," Claudia said. "That will make for interesting conversation."

"I think we better allow our guests to go to sleep, they've had a long journey," Cassius said as he rose from his cushion. "We will have plenty of time tomorrow to talk. Flavius will show you to your bed chamber." The young slave appeared out of the shadows and waved for Thomas to follow him.

He awoke early the next morning. He had slept soundly and was ready to see the sights of Jerusalem. Tomorrow was the first day of Passover and the beginning of the first of two days of big celebrations with good food and drink all day. As Claudia told him, holiday candles will be lit this night and elaborate meals are served both tomorrow and the day after. They are followed by four days called *chol hamoed*, which are semi-festive days, when most work is allowed. To round out the

Passover celebrations are two more days after that of commemoration of the dividing of the Red Sea. *Nothing like a holiday that lasts six days,* Thomas thought as he reached for his clothes. Flavius stood by ready to help him, but he waved him away, slightly embarrassed at the thought of having someone put his clothes on for him.

As he followed the slave through the house to the dining area, he noticed for the first time the beautiful mosaic floors in certain sections. They were definitely influenced by Roman culture and looked like Persian rugs to him with their rich, colorful, intricate designs. Absent in the house were any pictures or statues of gods, since it would have meant an unforgivable offense to the Jews within the city limits of Jerusalem.

Several slaves stood ready to serve him. A drink of date juice was offered by one as soon as he sat down, while another brought a selection of wheat bread, dried fish, goat cheese and figs. A beautifully designed ceramic bowl, filled with slices of pomegranate was carried in by yet another. Thomas looked at the slaves and wondered if he should greet them, but then thought better of it, since they did not dare look at him, but served him in silence. He did not want to offend his hosts by being too friendly, remembering how it had annoyed Lucius before.

"I see you are up early, Thomas," Claudia said in a cheerful voice as she entered the room. "Please excuse my husband, but he will not arise until later. To me the morning is the most beautiful time of day with the cool air making everything fresh and new. This is the time I do my reading and thinking." She sat down on a couch opposite from Thomas. "I hope you rested well. If there is anything you need, simply let one of the slaves know and they will get it for you. I can't wait to accompany you today, together with Lucius, of course. My husband will not go with us. He hates that sort of thing. Maybe we will run into the Rabbi. The best place to look for Him will be at the Temple." A slave handed her a silver goblet filled with date juice. "For later I have the cook prepare juice from the lotus jujube, a deliciously refreshing drink, although he might be too busy fixing a sumptuous meal for the visit of Nicodemus tonight. It should be an interesting evening of discussing current developments about the Rabbi Yeshua and what is going on with the Passover festivities. I am sure he knows more about that than we do." Thomas was delighted with her animated chatter and simply nodded as he continued helping himself to the delicious food in front of him.

The streets were extremely crowded as they made their way to the Temple area. Vendors were offering *Chametz* items to the non-Jews. As Claudia explained, these are any kind of foods from the day before containing yeast. This includes any leavened grain product or drink made with it like alcoholic beverages and foods which weren't guarded from leavening or fermentation.

"A lot of lambs have given their lives for this festival," she continued as they walked along. "Each family has to purchase a perfect one, not more than a year-old, no later than four days before Passover," she told Lucius and Thomas as they walked on. "I was there one year as the great slaughter of these animals was carried out at the Temple. Starting in the afternoon and continuing until dusk, fathers or other family leaders take their chosen lamb to have it slaughtered under the supervision of the priests. They catch the blood in a basin and then toss it at the base of the altar. After that the father skins the lamb and removes the fat and kidneys to be burned at the altar as a sacrifice. Then the father wraps the carcass in the skin and carries it home where it will be roasted for the main meal during the Passover." She shivered. "It is quite a gruesome procedure, but they all have to do it, according to their Law." She stopped to greet a friend and chatted for a moment before rejoining Lucius and Thomas, and then continued with her story.

"My husband and I were invited to this meal one year. I remember the strange items that were served like bitter herbs, unleavened bread, a fruit-and-nut-paste and a raw vegetable dipped in a tart dressing. We reclined around a table on floor cushions at a specified time in late afternoon for the actual meal. I enjoyed what they called the *Kiddush*, a ceremonial blessing over the wine served with the dinner." She looked at Lucius and Thomas with a smile. "I am sure Nicodemus can tell us the deeper meaning of all this tonight. Come, we will arrive at the Temple in a moment."

The crowd had increased in such a way, they could barely make it through the mass of humanity without losing sight of each other.

"I see the Rabbi," Lucius cried suddenly and pointed to the imposing steps leading up to the Temple. Thomas could make out a throng of people crowding around Yeshua. It took them quite a while of pushing and shoving until they managed to stand close enough so they could hear what was being said.

"Are you the one who was to come, or should we expect someone else?" (Luke 7:20) a man in the crowd asked.

Yeshua replied, "Go back and report to John what you hear and see. The blind receive sight, the lame walk, those who have leprosy are cured, the deaf hear, the dead are raised, and the good news is preached to the poor. Blessed is the man who does not fall away on account of Me." (Luke 7:22-23)

Thomas listened intently. He had to agree with the man, because he had seen Him perform some of the very miracles He was talking about.

Yet he felt confused and immediately reasoned this had to be a dream. It made no sense otherwise, although he was getting tired of this self-imposed argument.

"I have to talk to Yeshua," he said to no one in particular. "I just have to." With that he pressed forward until he stood before Him. The Rabbi turned and looked at Thomas with that knowing smile he had seen on His face before at Cephas' house and held out His hands to him.

"Who are You?" Thomas asked. "How do You do the things You do? I am a doctor from the future and I know *You* know that. Please tell me, I have to understand."

Yeshua leaned closer to Thomas and spoke in a quiet voice, looking at him with an expression that seemed to sear into his soul, "Blessed are your eyes because they see, and your ears because they hear. For I tell you the truth, many prophets and righteous men wanted to see what you see but did not see it, and to hear what you hear but did not hear it." (Luke 10:23-24)

Thomas stood for what seemed an eternity with his eyes closed. He was unable to comprehend the peace mixed with confusion that flooded his heart. *I still don't understand any of this,* he thought, almost in tears. *Yeshua, why did You not explain it to me better?* When he opened his eyes the Rabbi had walked away toward the court of the Gentiles in the Temple with a large crowd following Him closely. Lucius and Claudia had stayed behind with Thomas.

"What did He say?" Claudia asked, her voice shaking with excitement. "He talked to you, Thomas. The Rabbi talked to you!"

"I am not sure I understand what He said, "Thomas answered, barely able to speak. "I don't understand anything."

"Come then, Thomas, we will follow Him into the court of the Gentiles," Claudia said and took his hand. "That is where all the vendors and the money changers are. Maybe there you can buy an offering since you are a Jew. They have doves and lambs and even cattle in there you can purchase."

Thomas and Lucius followed her up the large steps on the left side of the Temple, leading over and across an arch into the inside where Gentiles and vendors were allowed to go. A great commotion was in progress when they walked inside. It was pandemonium with Yeshua right in the middle of it! They stood in utter amazement as they watched the spectacle.

In the temple courts He (Yeshua) found men selling cattle, sheep and doves, and others sitting at tables exchanging money. So He made a whip out of cords, and drove all from the temple area, both sheep and cattle; He scattered the coins of the money changers and overturned their tables.

(John 2:14-15)

Thomas was astonished as he watched this gentle man lose his temper at the sight of the commerce being conducted in this holy place. It somehow made him feel better seeing that Yeshua was a real man with feelings of anger and frustration, just like everyone else. His thoughts were interrupted by the Rabbi yelling at the last few merchants left selling doves.

"Get these out of here! How dare you turn My Father's house into a market!" (John 2:16)

Thomas noticed the men with Him stood to the side, whispering among themselves, but they were too far away for him to hear what they said. He also noticed they hadn't joined in the fray.

"That was quite a surprise," Lucius said. "I didn't think the Rabbi had it in Him," he added with admiration in his voice. "This should cause a great stir among the religious leaders. After all, I would think they make a lot of money renting spaces to the merchants."

"I am totally astounded at His display of temper," Claudia said with disappointment in her voice. "I thought He was a holy man, but this didn't look holy to me. Besides, what does He mean this temple is His Father's house? A little prideful, wouldn't you say?"

"If this is the Meshiah like you suspect, Lady Claudia, then the Temple *is* His Father's house, wouldn't you say?" Lucius looked at her with a mischievous twinkle in his eyes.

"Oh dear, I hadn't considered that," she answered sheepishly.

Chapter 9

They had returned late in the afternoon to give Claudia a chance to oversee the last minute preparation for the dinner she had planned in honor of Nicodemus that night.

In spite of the colorful sights at every corner and the countless vendors praising their wares, Thomas' mind was still filled with the words Yeshua had spoken to him. It felt as if they were etched into his heart. What was it about the man that stirred his soul like no other human being ever had? He knew without a doubt he would have to see Him again to find out.

His slave appeared in the door and bowed to him. "The mistress wishes you to come, the guest of honor will be arriving soon, Master."

"Thank you." Thomas looked at the slave as if seeing him for the first time. He was in his mid-twenties, tall, slender with a handsome, narrow face and blue eyes. His thick, blond hair was cut short and spoke of northern European heritage. He moved with a touch of elegance and grace, leading Thomas to believe he came from an upper class family before Rome captured him and sold him into slavery.

"Where are you from, Flavius?"

"I was born in the far north, a country called Germania, until slave traders brought me to Antioch, where my master bought me when I was but a small boy."

"I am sorry, Flavius."

"Do not feel sorry for me, Master. This family is good to me and being a slave is all I have ever known."

"Have you never wanted to be free?" Thomas asked.

"No, where would I go and what would I do? As long as I serve this master and his family faithfully, I live a good life," he said and looked at Thomas without even a hint of sadness. "This is my home."

Thomas entered the atrium at the same time Nicodemus arrived.

"My dear Nicodemus, how gracious of you to honor our home with your presence," Cassius said as he bowed slightly before a man in a blue, long robe draped over a long-sleeved, white linen undergarment. He pushed his headdress off as soon as he was inside. Thomas guessed he was around fifty with the customary dark beard and hair to match, although it was showing a lot of gray on the sides. His brown eyes sparkled with delight as he reached for Cassius' hands.

"Shalom, Cassius, I am the one who should be honored to be invited.

May the God of Abraham, Isaac and Jacob richly bless you and your entire house."

"Nicodemus, we have awaited you anxiously," Claudia said and stepped forward and bowed to him with a smile. "We are delighted to serve you our best and hope that you might teach us about Passover and your religion." She turned to Lucius and Thomas. "May I introduce you to our two guests who have arrived to celebrate Passover with us, and, like me, have a lot of questions for you."

Nicodemus bowed his head slightly in their direction. "Shalom to you both, my friends, I look forward to get to know you better over the course of this evening." His smile made his face break out into a multitude of friendly wrinkles, which gave him a benign look.

"I will be glad to answer any questions you might have, but the wisdom of age has taught me how little I actually know of the things of our God and His mysterious ways."

"Come, all of you and let's sit down and have some refreshments," Claudia said as she turned and led the group into the dining area.

Thomas could tell Claudia waited politely all through the meal, playing the gracious hostess and listening to the men discussing the "Roman question" as people called it.

"Rome is here to stay," Cassius said with great emphasis. "They are the greatest power in the world and there is no one strong enough to beat them, definitely not this little, insignificant land called Israel." He bowed to Nicodemus. "Forgive me, I did not mean to call your nation insignificant, but against such Roman might, any nation pales in comparison."

"Unfortunately you are right, Cassius," Nicodemus answered. "I am by no means offended." He wiped his mouth carefully with a linen cloth and leaned back into the thick couch cushion made of expensive, imported, blue fabric. "It will take divine intervention of Yahweh to defeat our enemies. Think of the Pharaoh of Egypt. At that time, he was the greatest power in the world, and yet our God managed to destroy him and set our people free with no trouble at all. That is precisely what we are celebrating in these coming days of Passover."

"There is a lot of talk about the Meshiah coming, Nicodemus. What does the Sanhedrin have to say about that?" Claudia asked. "You are the learned leaders of your people, what is your opinion of Him?"

"My dear Lady Claudia, the Sanhedrin is like a hornet's nest of opinions, disagreements and strife. Especially since this Rabbi Yeshua has come on the scene. You see, this 71-member council, the highest political, religious and judicial body of leaders in Israel, is made up of two factions, the Pharisees, of which I am one, and the Sadducees. We meet daily in the Chamber of the Hewn Stone. It is adjacent to the court of the Priests in the Temple."

"What is the difference between the two?" Lucius asked.

"We Pharisees consider ourselves the interpreters of the Torah and believe everything is preordained, but insist people have a free will to choose. We also believe there is an afterlife and put great importance on ritual purity and humanitarian endeavors to earn entrance. The Sadducees on the other hand insist that everything in life is pre-ordained and cannot be changed, unless mentioned in the Torah specifically. But both of the factions adhere strictly to the law of Moses. What also sets us apart is, the Pharisees believe in the coming of the Meshiah and they do not. There is another sect which agrees with us on that. They are called the Essenes. From what I understand, this Rabbi Yeshua's family seems to be part of that sect. The infamous John the Baptizer is His cousin and is an Essene. Many of the members of this sect choose to live a life of poverty or chose to spend much time in the desert, devoted to prayer."

"From what I have heard, the Rabbi from Nazareth is not a friend of the Pharisees or the Sadducees. As a matter of fact, I am given to understand He has severely chastised both of you in his preaching, Nicodemus," Claudia said. "How do you feel about that?"

"This man is an enigma to me, Lady Claudia. Just when I thought Him to be a worker of miracles and a man of God, He throws a violent temper tantrum in the Temple this morning. The Sanhedrin is upset as you can imagine. We make a lot of money for the Temple treasury by allowing vendors to sell their merchandise. After all, it is sold for sacrifices to the Lord God. I don't understand why that would upset this man so."

"Why did you think He was a man of God?" Thomas asked.

Nicodemus sat for a moment, deep in thought. Then he looked up at Thomas with a deep sigh.

"I am a man of deep faith and believe our God does great miracles. But I have never seen any man do the kind of things this Rabbi Yeshua does. And not just one, but so many according to reports from all over Galilee, here in Jerusalem and even in Samaria. As a member of the Sanhedrin, I felt it was my duty to find out if He was from God or not, so I went to see Him the other day."

"You did?" The group instantly leaned closer. "Please tell us what happened," Claudia said, barely able to keep her composure.

"It was a conversation I will never forget. It is seared into my heart and soul and I think about it all the time. As a matter of fact, that is why I asked to come here. I don't feel I can share with my fellow members of the Sanhedrin, but I can openly talk about it with gentiles like you.

"What happened, Nicodemus, tell us." Claudia was almost shouting.

"Well, this is what I said to Him, "Rabbi, we know you are a teacher who has come from God. For no one could perform the miraculous signs you are doing if God were not with him."

In reply Yeshua declared, "I tell you the truth, no one can see the kingdom of God unless he is born again."

"How can a man be born when he is old? I said. "Surely he cannot enter a second time into his mother's womb to be born!"

Yeshua answered, "I tell you the truth, no one can enter the kingdom of God unless he is born of water and the Spirit. Flesh gives birth to flesh, but the Spirit gives birth to spirit. You should not be surprised at my saying, you must be born again." (John 3:2-7)

"You can imagine how confused I was," Nicodemus said to his listeners with a frown. "But I didn't give up and asked Him again, "How can this be?"

"You are Israel's teacher," Yeshua said, "and do you not understand these things? I tell you the truth, we speak of what we know, and we testify to what we have seen, but still you people do not accept our testimony." (John 3:9-11)

"And then He said something that really embarrassed me to no end so that I can hardly bring myself to share it." Nicodemus' voice rose slightly as he went on.

"I have spoken to you of earthly things and you do not believe; how then will you believe if I speak of heavenly things? No one has ever gone into heaven except the one who came from heaven, - the Son of Man. Just as Moses lifted up the snake in the desert, so the Son of Man must be lifted up, that everyone who believes in him may have eternal life." (John 3:12-15)

"I was stunned when He told me unless I believe in Him I will not have eternal life. I was upset, confused and totally shaken by His words. There was some anger, too at His audacity to say such a thing. But He wasn't finished yet. Here are the words that will never leave my mind and he spoke them in the most loving, kind and wonderfully quiet voice."

"For God so loved the world that he gave his one and only Son, that whoever believes in him shall not perish but have eternal life. For God did not send his Son into the world to condemn the world, but to save the world through him. Whoever believes in him is not condemned, but whoever does not believe in him stands condemned already because he does not believe in the name of God's one and only Son." (John 3:16)

There was total silence as Nicodemus leaned back and closed his eyes as if exhausted.

That is the very scripture Melissa's grandmother used on me every time I saw her! Thomas was stunned. *This is also what some of these crazy preachers on TV keep telling the masses and they believe it. I remember that day in the doctor's lounge. Pat Harrison, Chief of Gynecology was imitating one of them, shouting 'You must be borned again!' How they had laughed about the southerners and their fundamentalism. How superior he had felt at the time, but refrained from any comment since he was Jewish. Besides, religion, no matter what kind, was not just useless, but had caused nothing but trouble throughout history. So what was he doing here, discussing whether a simple carpenter from Nazareth was the Jewish Messiah? This is crazy!*

"What does it mean, Nicodemus?" Claudia asked into the silence. "Is He the Meshiah?"

"I don't know."

"Wouldn't there be something about Him in the Torah that you can look up and see if maybe some prophesies or such things point to Him?" Claudia asked. Thomas could tell she felt sorry for the man. Here he was the great teacher in the Sanhedrin and this Rabbi Yeshua had thrown him into total confusion.

"I have spent the last few days studying the Torah, searching for answers," Nicodemus said in utter frustration, "because there is no way I can bring this up at the daily meetings. The others are very angry with the man and think he is preaching heresy. They are even talking about having him arrested." He looked at the group. "You can see my dilemma."

"I was upset this morning witnessing His temper in the Temple," Claudia said, "especially about the part where He told them this was His Father's house. But like Lucius pointed out to me, if He is the Meshiah and the one and only Son of God as He says, the Temple *is* His Father's house."

"In my search of the scripture I came across where it tells in the book of Micah that the Meshiah will be born in Bethlehem," Nicodemus said. "This man is from Nazareth."

"No, He is not," Thomas said, "I know for a fact He was born in Bethlehem. I talked to His mother not too many days ago. What is so strange, she tells that at His birth in a cave near that town, shepherds came and told her an angel sent them to come and worship the child. The only reason she and her husband went there was that they had to go to Bethlehem to be counted since they were of the line of David. How can a child born in a small, dirty cave become the Meshiah? Surely God could think of something better than that."

"I wouldn't be so sure about that, Thomas. This is what it says in the book of Isaiah,

"For to us a child is born, to us a son is given, and the government will be on his shoulders. And he will be called Wonderful Counselor, Mighty God, Everlasting Father, Prince of Peace. Of the increase of his government and peace there will be no end." (Isaiah 9:6-7)

"No one has ever understood that scripture. How can a human child be born and be called Mighty God? Scholars have scratched their heads for generations about the meaning of those words." Nicodemus pulled on his beard in a thoughtful gesture and then went on, "The Meshiah is going to be a king out of the line of David," he said, "because it is what is written in Isaiah,

"He will reign on David's throne and over his kingdom, establishing and upholding it with justice and righteousness from that time on and forever. The zeal of the Lord Almighty will accomplish this." (Isaiah 7:7)

"How can anyone establish a kingdom that will last forever?" Thomas asked. "No kingdom in the history of mankind has ever lasted forever. Believe me, I know."

"I agree with you, but the Holy Scriptures cannot be wrong, because our God does not lie." Nicodemus sounded adamant. "His Word is true and what He says stands forever."

"There is something I am wondering about," Lucius said. "If this Yeshua is the Meshiah, why does He not preach in Jerusalem? From what I hear He stays mostly in Galilee. That doesn't make much sense to me. Here in the city is where the religious leaders and the biggest crowds gather. He would definitely be more successful if He held His big meetings right here instead of in the countryside of Galilee.

"That is a question I have asked myself as well, Lucius. However, when I went to the book of Isaiah, these well-known verses came to mind,

"...in the past he humbled the land of Zebulun and the land of Nephtali, but in the future he will honor Galilee of the Gentiles, by the way of the sea, along the Jordan – The people walking in darkness have seen a great light; on those living in the land of the shadow of death a light has dawned."

"There are quite a few signs that already seem to fit," Lucius said. "I think you need to search for more to be sure, Nicodemus. Who knows, you might find He really is the Meshiah if He fulfills them all. And He would have to in order for you to prove that He is who He says, the Son of God."

"I will be too busy with Passover coming up, but I assure you, I will not rest until I find out if He is the One we are waiting for." Nicodemus sounded determined as he got up from his seat. "I must be going, dear

Claudia. It has been a wonderful, stimulating evening as usual. Cassius, I hope you will allow me to come back sometime when I know more."

"We are counting on it, Nicodemus. You are welcome in our home anytime," Claudia answered before her husband could say anything.

Chapter 10

The next morning Thomas rose early, in part because he could not still his mind. The conversation from last night would not leave his thoughts. *I have to wake up from this dream. This is really getting to me! I am a modern scientist, a talented surgeon and that alone makes me enlightened enough not to believe this stuff. No matter what these people say, it is the 21st Century and this is not real.* He took a deep breath. *I will not allow myself to get drawn into this religious fervor, because I am in control of my mind!*

He was alone in the room. Flavius had not yet arrived to serve him. He liked the young man because of his quiet, efficient ways and ready smile. What a shame he had to spend his entire life as a slave.

"Good morning, Master, what can I do for you?" Flavius said with a pleasant smile. "The sun is barely above the horizon and it looks like it will be a beautiful day."

"Flavius, do you believe in this Meshiah?"

"I have not had a chance to see Him, Master, but He sounds like a good man to me. One of the kitchen slaves, Marcellus, has met him on his way to the market place. He saw Him perform a miracle at the Temple and is convinced He is the Meshiah. But Marcellus is just a kitchen slave, Master, he does not know much." Flavius sounded apologetic for talking so freely. "Please forgive me for being so forward. I am also just a slave."

"No, no, Flavius, I asked you, remember? Where I come from we don't believe in slavery. I think you are an intelligent man and have a right to your opinion."

"I do not have any rights, Master and therefore I am not allowed to have opinions either." Flavius stood with his eyes glued to the floor in a subservient position.

"I want you to look at me, Flavius," Thomas said. "Look at me, when you are with me, we can talk as equals. I would love for you to feel free to say whatever is on your mind, you hear?" Thomas had stepped up to the slave, put his hand under his chin and forced him to look up.

Flavius withdrew from him with sudden fear in his eyes.

"I cannot do that. My master would flog me if he knew I dared to speak to you in that way. I am only allowed to answer if you ask me a question, nothing more, Master. That is the way it has to be. I am only a slave and know my place in this household. Please forgive me for disagreeing with you, I did not mean to offend you in any way." He was trembling.

"Flavius, you did not offend me. I definitely don't want to get you into trouble." Thomas stepped up to the door. "I'm ready to go and break my fast, come, you can help me if no one is up yet."

"The mistress is already eating, Master. She will be glad to have you join her."

Two hours later Lucius and Thomas were ready to make their way into the city. It was the first day of Passover and no Jew was allowed to work on this holy of holiest days, except for preparing the festive meals all through the day.

"Let's go to the Temple, that's where the crowds will be today. I am not allowed into the inner courts, but they will let you in, Thomas. I am glad you are wearing your head covering, because you are going to need it." Lucius sounded excited.

When they stood before the Temple, Thomas looked to the left and saw Antonia, the fortress built adjacent to it. He observed a number of Roman soldiers coming and going. Their bright red tunics under their silver armor made them stand out conspicuously, even from this distance.

"Something is up," Lucius said. "I wouldn't be surprised if there is a riot brewing of some sorts. The sect of the Zealots usually manages to stir up the crowd during this time and it looks like the Romans want to be ready for them."

"The Jews really hate these Romans, don't they?" Thomas said. "Especially Pontius Pilate, from what Nathanial told me. He seems to be the favorite object of their scorn."

"He keeps a tight rein on them, that's for sure. Not because he hates the Jews that much, but he has to keep the Emperor Tiberius happy by keeping the peace. Palestine is notorious for rioting against the Romans. Pontius Pilate was probably sent here for some kind of punishment, because no Roman officer of high rank wants to be stuck in this god-forsaken corner of the world. So these procurators come with a bad attitude right from the start, but the better they manage to control the people, the better chance they have to be recalled to Rome and be assigned to a more popular place in the Empire."

The two stood in the midst of a huge crowd pressing in to get access to the Temple. Thomas was anxious to see more of the interior. He allowed himself to be carried by the mass of people closer to the large steps. Suddenly, a hand grabbed his shoulder in a rough manner.

"Look who we have here, brothers, the stranger who dared to beat us with a rod."

Thomas knew that voice. It belonged to Barabbas. He turned and saw a group of about ten men surrounding the man. He realized there was no way he could take on that many and so he simply stood there and faced them with a look of defiance.

"Let's get out of here, Thomas," Lucius whispered frantically. "He will kill you for sure. I will try to get help." Out of the corner of his eyes Thomas watched him disappear into the crowd, which had immediately made a space when they saw Barabbas accost Thomas.

"You are the one who tried to rob us, all I did was defend myself," Thomas said with as much bravado as he could muster. "I would suggest you be on your way."

"We are going to finish what we started then, Barbarian. How dare you try to enter the Temple on a holy day like today, isn't that right, boys? Let's show him this time who's in charge."

The men with him drew closer toward Thomas. He had no choice but to try to fend them off, even in the face of being outnumbered. He assumed his defense stance as Barabbas raised his fists to hit him. It was all a blur after that as a scuffle ensued between the men and Thomas with the crowd watching and cheering for Barabbas.

"Stop this right now in the name of the Emperor!" a voice shouted above the din. "Make way in the name of Emperor Tiberius!"

Thomas breathed a sigh of relief. Lucius actually did get help.

"Ah, look who we have here," one of the soldiers said as he grabbed Barabbas by the shoulder and spun him around. "Our favorite trouble maker stirring up the crowds as usual, isn't that right, Centurion Antonius?"

"So it is soldier. Take him in and that whole worthless crowd with him, including the man he was fighting with. Let's put them all away before there is any more unrest." With that Thomas was taken between two soldiers and led off toward the Antonia fortress.

"Centurion, please do not take my friend. He was merely defending himself against these ruffians. He is innocent!" Lucius shouted as he followed the man.

"I don't have time to sort all this out. Just answer me one question, is he a Roman citizen?" the Centurion asked Lucius.

"No, he is not."

"Then he comes with us. You might want to find some influential friends who can vouch for him. Otherwise he will stay locked up until a judge can hear his case and right now, that can take a while. Get out of my way, Greek or I will haul you in as well."

Lucius watched helplessly as Thomas was led away and disappeared behind the gate of the fortress.

It was the next morning. Thomas woke up inside the dark, damp prison cell with every one of his bones hurting from lying on the hard stone floor without any kind of straw mat for comfort. He had been thrown unceremoniously in with four of the other men from Barabbas' group. Thank goodness, Barabbas was not one of them. There were no windows or any kind of benches to sit on. All he could make out were the bare, roughly hewn stone walls in the low light of an oil lamp, just outside the iron bars that served as a door. There was not much room for him to move with five people crammed into the small cell with a putrid smell assaulting his nose to the point he wanted to throw up. Visions of his beautiful, tiled bathroom came to his mind as he looked at the single clay container apparently put there in place of a toilet. *This is getting worse. Before I was shoveling manure, now I'm in it,* he thought.

"You better stay on your side, Barbarian or we will beat you senseless," one of the men said with a growl. "I sure don't like sitting in here because of you. Who knows when they will let us out."

"It was Barabbas who started all this as you might want to remember," Thomas said. "I was minding my own business. Besides, I beat the snot out of him the last time I met him, I can do the same with you." He was sick of these morons and sick of the place and the stink. "I have no patience with the likes of you, just leave me alone." His voice sounded menacing enough, it made the man withdraw from him to the other side.

It was two days later when two soldiers opened the iron gate of the prison cell. "Come with us, Jew," they said and pointed at Thomas.

He jumped up and made his way past the others without saying a word. He couldn't wait to get out of the cell and followed the soldier ahead of him up the steps with another one behind. He was sure Lucius had found a way to get him out as he was led into the large courtyard. The bright sunlight blinded his eyes for a moment, until he saw a horse-drawn cart with bars on all sides waiting by the door.

"Get in there," the soldier said and pushed him roughly toward it. "You are taking a ride. Pontius Pilate will let Herod decide what to do with you. He is busy with more important things right now."

"Will you inform my friend Lucius where you are taking me?" Thomas asked.

"What do I care who your friend is. I'm sure after a while he will make inquiries with the magistrate and he will let him know where you are being taken."

"Why are you doing this, I am innocent. They attacked me!" Thomas was shouting by now.

"Be silent, Jew before I beat you. I am in a foul mood today because of all the trouble you Jews cause us every day." With that he shoved Thomas onto the cart and closed the latch behind him. *Once again, no benches or straw to soften the ride,* Thomas thought with disgust.

The rough ride put Thomas into a state of depression. Since the cart was drawn by a horse instead of a donkey, wherever they were going, it would be faster. From what he could tell, they were heading east for a while around the Dead Sea and then straight west. He was fed almost nothing and was given very little water on the way. The two Roman soldiers up front never paid any attention to their prisoner, but talked freely as if Thomas didn't exist.

"Pontius Pilate is disgusted with Herod Antipas as usual," the older one said. "The man is scum in the procurator's eyes. He married his own brother's former wife Herodias and this holy man, they call John the Baptizer, has criticized him for it. Now Herodias wants him dead, but Herod is afraid to do it, because the people really like this guy and could revolt if he has him killed."

"I tell you one thing, these Jews are the most cantankerous people I've ever met," the other answered. "They will riot at the drop of a hat, especially when it has something to do with their religion. From what I hear, this John the Baptizer says he is preparing the way for the Meshiah and hundreds went to see him by the River Jordan."

"What did he do when they got there?" the first one asked.

"From what I could tell, all he did was dunk them under water and mumble something about repentance. The way they fight constantly, they probably have a lot to be sorry for." He chuckled. "I am not interested in religion, not even our own. All our gods are worthless. They have never answered any of my prayers. It's all a bunch of fancy talk and making money off of us poor folks. Our temples should be rich the way we have to buy offerings for everything, just to stay on the priests' good side."

"From what I hear, the Emperor Tiberius is not too keen on Pontius Pilate," the older one said. "One big mistake and our high and mighty procurator is history and he knows it. That's why he doesn't tolerate any problems with the Jews. Tiberius is sick and tired of the continuous trouble with these people. I think that is why he sent Pontius Pilate to Judea, aside from being mad at him. He knows the man is tough and has no trouble keeping them under control better than anyone else."

"I'm glad I'm just a simple soldier and all I have to do is take orders. Can you imagine, everything you do could make the Emperor mad and you could lose your head just like that." He snapped his fingers. "They say Tiberius is getting older and crankier by the day."

"I wish I could go back home," the older one sighed. "I am tired of this godforsaken place. I really feel the people's hate everywhere I go. It would be good to march into Rome and hear the crowds cheer for us for a change. Besides, I miss my family. I haven't seen the wife and kids for two years."

"That is tough. At least I'm not married, but I agree with you. I miss Pompeii, that's where I was born. It is so beautiful there with Mt. Vesuvius in the backyard. It is bigger than anything around here and rumbles and smokes like an angry god sometimes. My father is the overseer for a wealthy landowner. He makes a good living and my parents have a nice little house on the outskirts of town. I joined the Emperor's service to see the world, but I must say I'm ready to go home."

Thomas enjoyed their talk. He tried to remember when Mt. Vesuvius erupted and wondered, if the young man will die when it does in about thirty years. *Maybe I should warn him,* he thought, but dismissed it. Why should he care?

When they arrived at their destination an hour later, all Thomas could see was a huge hilltop fort, located on the northern side of a large body of water. He overheard the soldiers calling it the fortress of Machaerus. He had no idea where or what it was. All he could see was that it was big, built on the side of a steep hill and facing what he thought must be the Dead Sea, because of its size and the relatively short distance they had traveled. It had only been a day's journey from Jerusalem. Whatever it was, he realized it was not anywhere near Galilee and looked more like a prison than anything else. His heart sank. How would Lucius ever find him? And then a terrible thought occurred to him. *Why would he be looking for him? After all, he was only someone he had met a short time ago!*

The horse had a tough time pulling the cart up the steep road to the prison entrance. A guard asked for identification and then let them pass. There were many low lying buildings, separated by high walls arranged in a terrace-like way, hugging the steep hill. The fort had a large, square tower on top. *This is a place one could get lost in forever,* Thomas thought as a wave of fear went through him. *No one will ever miss me, because no one cares enough to look for me.*

"Get out, Jew." The younger of the two soldiers pulled him out of the cart impatiently. "This is your new home, enjoy it." After handing Thomas over to a guard from the prison, he joined his fellow soldier on the cart and the two drove out of the main gate without looking back.

"Welcome to Herod's favorite place for people who tick him off," the guard said with a smirk.

Chapter 11

A week had gone by and Thomas sat in the dark prison cell, his head between his knees. For the first time in his life he was without hope. He had lost some weight as hunger and thirst had become his constant companions. Once a day, someone brought a watery soup to the cell entrance with two or three soggy pieces of bread floating in it. A man named Zebedee was his cell mate, a kind, gentle soul, his body as thin as a skeleton. Thomas had made sure he fed him his portion first of whatever they brought. The man's face was completely hidden underneath a grey beard that had not been cut for years and hung down to his waist. His hair was almost as long. The filthy clothes were more like rags, barely covering his emaciated body. He looked like a shadow, until he spoke. There was a spark in his voice, a strength that belied his weak body.

"I will serve the Lord God all the days of my life, even in this hellish place. He has promised me that I would see the Deliverer before I die. It has been fifteen years since Herod took my young daughter and violated her as he rode through my village of Nain. When I attacked him to save my beautiful Anna, his guards bound me and brought me here. I have no idea what has become of my Anna or my family. I have never heard from any of them. Yahweh will set me free to see the Meshiah and allow me to be with my family once more, whether here or in the afterlife."

Thomas felt ashamed of himself in the face of this man's faith and perseverance next to his own hopelessness after only one week in this place. Zebedee had actually encouraged him and helped him cope since he arrived. He woke up this morning with a feeling of dread and discouragement.

"Zebedee, something bad is going to happen today. I can feel it," he told the old man.

"If you could just trust in Jehovah like I do, you would not give in to such feelings, Thomas. It is the enemy who comes and sows the seeds of sadness into your heart. Give your life to the Lord God Jehovah and the deceiver cannot do that to you."

"But I don't believe in your God," Thomas said. "I wish I could, really, I do." His voice had such a yearning in it, the old man reached over and touched his shoulder.

"God has something very special planned for you, Thomas. I know it. It is the same knowing that I have about seeing the Meshiah before I die."

"How can you say that, Zebedee. Your Meshiah is not going to come and visit you here in this prison, is He?"

"I don't know. All I do know is that I will see Him." Zebedee had a bright smile on his face. That is when Thomas noticed for the first time he didn't have a tooth in his mouth.

It was late in the afternoon when the guard came and led them out into the courtyard.

"This doesn't happen very often, Thomas," Zebedee said. "The Lord has favored us today to allow us to feel the sunshine on our faces. Blessed be the God of Abraham, Isaac and Jacob."

Thomas squinted as they emerged from the dark cell into the bright courtyard. He pretty well had to carry Zebedee, because he was too weak to walk by himself. After his eyes adjusted to the light, he saw a rough looking man standing in the opposite corner. He looked a little like Zebedee with his long, unkempt beard and hair, but without the malnourished state.

"That is John, Thomas. He is a man of God and a messenger of the Most High. They call him John the Baptizer. He told me that he was sent to make straight the path of the Meshiah by calling the people to repentance."

Thomas was surprised. He had heard of the man from Lucius. So this was the guy who had dared to tell Herod Antipas off about marrying his own brother's former wife and got arrested for it.

"John, this is my fellow prisoner Thomas," Zebedee said as John walked over to them. "He has been very kind to me. I have tried to tell him about the Meshiah, but he says he doesn't believe in the Lord God."

John looked at Thomas with piercing, brown eyes.

"You have seen the Meshiah, Thomas, I am sure of it. You have been sent by the God of Abraham, Isaac and Jacob to behold His Son and believe, for He will use you greatly in the far distant future. Do not resist Him, but repent for He has chosen you to serve Him in a different age."

"These are strange words John," Zebedee said.

"They are not to you, are they, Thomas?" John looked at Thomas with a smile. "Yeshua will redeem you in ways you cannot comprehend now. Follow Him and you will be set free."

"Are you saying I will get out of here?" Thomas asked.

"I don't know about that, all I know is that the truth will set you free."

"That means they will figure out I am innocent and let me go, right?" Thomas sounded hopeful.

"Back into your cell," the guard shouted suddenly. "I have already let you stay longer than is allowed."

"I wonder what John meant, Thomas. He said you understood. Can you tell me?" Zebedee sounded curious and excited. "I know when John hears from the Lord, he is always right."

"You wouldn't believe me if I told you, Zebedee." Thomas sat down way back in the corner of the cell with a deep sigh. "I wish I understood any of this, but I don't, no matter what John says."

Two more weeks passed and Thomas had heard nothing from the outside world. He had gotten to love the old man Zebedee and wished he could do more for him. Strangely, it was he who kept Thomas from sinking into despair with his positive attitude and constant talk about the Meshiah.

Thomas had thought about the words spoken to him by John the Baptizer. The way it looked, and if this was real, he would become like one of those crazy TV preachers he used to make fun of. He chuckled. *That'll be the day! He would become the biggest joke to all his friends and especially to the hospital crowd. No one, not even the Meshiah was worth that.*

He had not seen John since that first time. He thought him a little strange anyway with all his religious talk and it made him nervous to hear him talk about his future the way he did. The man was slightly nuts in his opinion.

A shadow appeared in the doorway.

"Is there anyone here by the name of Thomas?" the guard asked.

"I am Thomas."

"Get up and come with me. There is someone here for you."

Thomas turned to Zebedee. "If this means I am being set free, I will not forget about you, old friend. You hold on to that thought about seeing the Meshiah, you hear me, Zebedee?"

"I will, Thomas. I will." The old man was crying.

The guard led Thomas out of the courtyard into a large building. As he entered, he saw Lucius, Cassius and a woman in expensive clothes standing together.

"Thank God you are alive, Thomas!" Lucius cried and ran toward him. "We have been so worried we might never find you." He hugged him with enthusiasm.

Cassius walked up to him with outstretched arms. Thank the gods you are well, my friend. Claudia told me if I show up without you being let go she will divorce me," he said with a laugh. "She has been tirelessly trying to find out what they had done with you. I think they helped her because they couldn't stand her bothering them anymore."

His booming laugh filled the room and Thomas felt good about that.

"Allow me to introduce you to the Lady Joanna, the wife of Chuza, Herod's steward," Lucius said. "She is the one who pulled the right strings with Herod to get you out of here."

"Thank you, my Lady," Thomas said and bowed to her with a grateful smile. "You have no idea what it means to me to be free."

"I am glad I could be of help. My friend Lucius told me so much about you and how much he values you as a friend and a talented physician, I couldn't help but talk to my husband. He in turn approached Herod one day when he found him in a good mood." She smiled at him. "And here you are."

Thomas looked at her, when a sudden thought struck him.

"Lady Joanna, there is an old man back there who has been here for fifteen years. He was put here by the father of the king, because he tried to defend his daughter from being defiled by Herod as he traveled through their village. Is there any way you can help to get him free as well? I am sure no one remembers he is even here."

Joanna turned and waved to one of the guard.

"Another prisoner was to be released together with this man." She turned to Thomas. "What was the name?"

"It is Zebedee, my Lady, his name is Zebedee and he is from Nain. He cannot walk by himself, please allow me to get him," Thomas said.

"Guard, have two men help Zebedee to this room. Do not make me wait too long," she said in an authoritative tone.

"Yes, gracious Lady, right away," the guard said and rushed off immediately.

It took quite a while until four men came carrying a stretcher with Zebedee on it.

"Praise be to God, He has not forgotten His servant and has saved me to behold the Meshiah before I die." Zebedee was crying and laughing and praying at the same time as he tried to get up from the stretcher.

"Stay on there, my friend," Joanna said. "The guards can carry you to my carriage and we will take you to Nain. It is on the way to Capernaum. From what I understand, the Rabbi Yeshua will be in the village in a few days. Maybe you can see Him then."

As they walked out, Thomas saw the elegant carriage standing by the big front gate, drawn by two beautiful black horses. A slave held the head of the animals when they climbed aboard. Zebedee was helped in first and insisted to sit with the slave, who handled the animals up front. Thomas joined him, since he was sure he smelled pretty bad, since he had not had a bath in many days.

Cassius had his own four-wheel cart and left the group to head back to Jerusalem. He was instructed to give Claudia greetings from Thomas with a promise she would see them again next year for the Passover.

After a few miles, before they crossed the Jordan River, Thomas asked if he and Zebedee could bathe before the long journey to Capernaum. Not surprisingly, no one objected.

At a stopover in a town called Scythopolis, they bought new clothes for Zebedee and Thomas and had their hair and beards trimmed at a barber shop. All were amazed how much better Zebedee looked and agreed they would have never recognized him from the man who was carried on a stretcher out of the prison. Zebedee had a perpetual smile on his face as he continued to praise God for his release and insisted, once he was back in Nain, he would see the Meshiah. It was beginning to drive Thomas a little crazy.

The reunion with Zebedee's family was touching. His wife had passed away two years ago, but his son was there with his wife and three children. His daughter was the mother of four by now and came to see her father the same day. A sumptuous meal was prepared for the occasion and they all listened with rapt attention as Zebedee told of his time in prison and meeting John the Baptizer. When he shared what the Lord had promised him about seeing the Meshiah, they smiled benignly, but said nothing.

It was late afternoon by the time they continued on to Capernaum.

Thomas walked into Lucius' house with a feeling of joy and relief. He felt he was coming home. It had been over four weeks since he left to go to Jerusalem. So much had happened and he couldn't wait to start seeing patients again and get back to a normal life.

That evening, he shared with Lucius about the things John the Baptizer had told him.

"I am afraid I don't understand what the meaning is about the far away future, Thomas," Lucius said. "And you are sure he said you would understand?" He looked at Thomas with curiosity. "Do you?"

"Yes, I do, Lucius. It is time I shared with you why I am always saying my life here doesn't make any sense. Let me tell you what happened, about Philadelphia and my life in America in the future in the year 2016. I have no idea why this is happening or how, but I know that it is. Yeshua knows what I am saying is true. I told Him in Jerusalem I was from the future and He *knew,* Lucius. Just like the Baptizer knew. There was one other time. An old man named Jonah told me about taking the message into the distant future at the wedding at Cana. I wish I could explain it better, but I can't. I am a man of science and not given to emotional day-dreams. I deal with reality and not imagination. What I am hearing from you, Lucius and from others, these are things I could not possibly know on my own. And that is what makes it almost impossible for it to be just a regular dream, because one cannot dream facts that one does not know when awake. Yet everything I have seen and experienced in the last few months, I had no idea existed. I have never been to Israel, have never studied archeology and I do not speak Greek, Aramaic or Latin, yet you hear me talk in these languages. All I hear is English, the language I speak in America. If I could put into words how I live in the future, you would not believe it." He looked at Lucius in utter frustration.

"Tell me about your country and how you live. Is it really so different from here?" Lucius sounded skeptical.

"It is, Lucius. It is. We have carts that move without a donkey at a speed faster than a bird can fly. It would only take maybe three or four hours to get from here to Jerusalem on streets paved perfectly even. There are big, shiny carts that fly through the air at even greater speeds than that. It would only take a day to fly half way around the world way up higher than the highest mountains. We have running hot and cold water inside the house which we can turn on and off at will. I do not need oil lamps but simply turn a small handle and lights come on that do not go out unless I wish it. I could go on and on. It is too difficult to describe. And even if I could, I doubt you would believe me." Thomas leaned back into the couch and sighed deeply. "I am here two thousand years in the past and I have no idea how I got here or how to get back. Neither do I know why I was transported to this place and time."

"That is the most incredible story I have ever heard, Thomas and I don't know whether to believe you or not. But one thing I do know, you are not a man given to lies. This may all be in your head and you believe it is true, or maybe it is true. There is no way to tell until you find out why you are here. Could it be that all this has to do with the Rabbi from Nazareth?"

"Are you saying He is the Meshiah and He wants me to see everything He did so I will believe in Him?" Now Thomas sounded skeptical.

"It is the only thing that makes sense. If He is the Meshiah, then He is God. And if He is God, all things are possible, Thomas."

"There is one thing wrong with your theory, Lucius. I absolutely do not believe in God, any god. And therefore I do not believe in the Meshiah either." Thomas felt a deep anger rising up in him and didn't know why.

Two weeks went by and Thomas actually enjoyed the routine of his daily life as a country doctor to the poor. He was on his way to a patient one morning when a carriage stopped next to him. It was Joanna.

"Greetings, Thomas. I hope you have fully recovered from your ordeal in prison."

"Greetings to you, Lady Joanna, I must say I have never been so glad to come home from a trip before. I will always be in your debt for your kindness." He smiled at her and turned to go.

"Wait, Thomas. The Rabbi Yeshua is going to Nain tomorrow. Would you like to come along and see how Zebedee is doing?"

"That is a little too far to walk for my poor feet, Lady Joanna. Besides, I have quite a few patients to see since I have been gone for so many days." Thomas had decided he would not try to seek out the Rabbi any longer. It was just better that way.

"Would you and Lucius come if you could use my carriage? I have a strong feeling you need to be there, Thomas." She looked at him with a bright smile. "As a favor to me?"

"I will tell Lucius and let him decide, Lady Joanna. How can I get in touch with you? *My life for a cell phone.*

"I will simply pick you and Lucius up in the morning. The Rabbi is already on His way there and will arrive tomorrow around mid-day. That way we will all get there at the same time. I asked Him if He wanted to go with us, but He said he would rather walk together with His disciples." She tapped on the carriage door and the driver flicked the reins. She was gone before Thomas could change his mind.

The next day was rather cloudy when Joanna picked them up. Thomas had been eager to ride to Nain and see how Zebedee was getting along. He had grown fond of the wonderful old man during their time in prison together.

"I hope it won't rain," Joanna said as they drove along the hard, uneven road. Even in this nice carriage, it was still a rough ride and they were tossed several times rather violently. It took three hours until the outskirts of the small village of Nain came into view. They had not seen the Rabbi along the way, but there were large crowds heading in the direction of the village.

"He is really getting popular these days," Joanna said. "The crowds are getting bigger by the day and there are times when He just goes off into the mountains by Himself to pray. It must be hard to be pressed in by crowds day after day and be begged to heal the many sick they bring with them."

It was just then they saw four men carrying a stretcher with a child on it.

"I wonder what is wrong with the little girl," Joanna said as the carriage drove by. "I feel so bad riding in this thing while these poor people walk. That is why I rarely take it when I accompany the Rabbi."

The small village of Nain was surrounded by a stone wall for protection. As they got closer, they saw Jeshua and a large crowd walking along. Joanna stopped the carriage and they got out and joined Him and His men.

As He approached the town gate, a dead person was being carried out – the only son of his mother, and she was a widow. And a large crowd from the town was with her. When the Lord saw her, his heart went out to her and he said, "Don't cry." Then he went up and touched the coffin and those carrying it stood still. He said, "Young man, I say to you, get up!" The dead man sat up and began to talk, and Yeshua gave him back to his mother. *(Luke 7:12-15)*

The crowd was astonished and Thomas could hear them shouting and praising God. That is when he saw Zebedee. The old man had gained some weight and looked well. He watched him push through the crowd and fall on his knees before Yeshua. "I can now die in peace, because I have seen the Meshiah as the Lord promised I would." Zebedee held on to Yeshua's robes and cried out in a loud voice, "This is the One we have been waiting for. He will set our people free and save us from our sins. Thank you, Lord, You are faithful in all you do and reach out to the poor and needy with compassion. You have saved me from prison and set my soul free to worship You for all eternity."

Yeshua reached down and raised Zebedee up and smiled at him; and then His gaze fell on Thomas. *He knows,* Thomas thought, *He knows everything.* Thomas stood and stared at the man, wanting to run up to Him and ask Him to explain, but he found he couldn't move. *I want to believe, but I can't, because this is not real.* He felt tears filling his eyes and brushed them away, angry and frustrated. *Why do you want to mess with someone who doesn't believe in You or hasn't asked to know You? I was fine without You; why won't You leave me alone?* He was screaming on the inside, surprised no one could hear him. Yeshua was still looking at him and Thomas could hear Him speak clearly in his mind,

"Blessed are the eyes that see what you see. For I tell you that many prophets and kings wanted to see what you see but did not see it, and to hear what you hear but did not hear it." (Luke 10:23-24)

Thomas looked away in frustration. *If this is the Meshiah, why can I not believe in Him? If you are God, why can't You just talk to me? I am a scientist, not a dreamer. Why do You reach out to me in a way I cannot understand?* Thomas stood transfixed as he watched the crowd worshipping this Yeshua. He felt alone, hopeless and angry. *I hate this. I don't want to be religious, I just want to be a surgeon in my hospital in Philadelphia and heal people for real, not just in this alternate reality?*

He turned around and walked off to the side of the road where the carriage stood. He pressed his face against the soft neck of the horse and began to cry.

When he finally raised his head and stepped away from the animal, a great anger, shame and bitterness filled his heart. He had been made a fool of by this man. He was and always would be a man of the 21st century, educated and gifted, wealthy and successful. Not this sniveling religious fanatic, trying to hang on to a simple carpenter from a tiny village in nowhere.

Chapter 12

After several hours the crowd had dispersed. Joanna, Lucius and Thomas were invited to join the festivities that had turned from a funeral to a resurrection party with much singing, rejoicing and good food. It was the first time Thomas had a chance to get a closer look at the men with Yeshua. To him they seemed simple, uneducated fishermen, with even a tax collector among them and others with low paying jobs he didn't know about. They kept mostly to themselves and stayed close to Yeshua.

"I hear you are a physician, Thomas." The man had walked up from behind silently so that it startled Thomas when he heard his voice. "Shalom, my name is Judas, son of Simon Iscariot. I'm one of the men with the Rabbi."

"I can see that, how very nice for you." Thomas wasn't the least bit interested in talking to the stranger or get into a religious discussion with him. He was done with that. He looked at Judas and was not impressed. Everything about the man spelled slick, oily and dishonest. His eyes had a shiftlessness to them which made Thomas want to hold on to his wallet, had he still carried one. Strings of dark, curly hair hung over the man's forehead as if he was trying to hide his eyes. A leather bag hung over his shoulder and he was most careful to hang on to it at all times.

"Since you are a physician, I am sure you get paid handsomely for healing people, Thomas," he said in a higher than normal voice, which immediately grated on Thomas' nerves.

"What is it to you, Judas? I don't ask you how much the Rabbi pays you to work for Him."

Judas looked at Thomas with surprise, oblivious to his dislike of him. "You sound like an angry man. Maybe you don't get paid at all like me?"

"Again I ask you, what is it you do, Judas?"

"I am in charge of the money."

"How much *does* the Rabbi get paid when He heals somebody?" Thomas said just to be nasty.

"Funny you should ask that." Judas stepped closer to Thomas, looked around first and then whispered close to his ear, "He doesn't charge anything, but lives on what people give Him. Can you imagine how rich we would all be by now, if He only heals those who can pay? I have tried to tell Him that, but the man won't listen to me. After all, I am the expert on money matters." He sounded proud of himself.

"Did you study finance?" Thomas was making fun of him.

"Sort of, I stole for a living before the Rabbi asked me to follow Him." Judas chuckled. "I guess He didn't know that or He wouldn't have put me in charge of the purse."

"Does that mean you still dip your fingers into the till every now and then?" Thomas was having fun with this.

"How did you know?" He looked at Thomas with sudden concern.

"I thought your Rabbi knows everything," Thomas said with a touch of sarcasm.

"He knows a lot, but I am smarter than He is when it comes to money."

"Judas, you don't sound to me like you believe in this Rabbi being the Meshiah, do you?"

"If He was, He wouldn't have put me in charge of the purse, would He now?" He looked at Thomas with a sly grin. "I know He heals people and many think He is special, but even I know the Meshiah will be born in a palace and fight the Romans and throw them out. But hey, if He is the Son of God, I'm along for the ride while it lasts and make a little bit of money at the same time."

"You seem to have it all figured out, Judas. Good luck to you."

"Wait, Thomas, you never told me what *you* believe about the Rabbi."

"I don't believe anything. I am a physician, a learned man of science and totally not interested in this nonsense." Thomas felt good saying it.

"Why are you here then?"

"A noble lady invited me to join her and a few friends to see the Rabbi," Thomas answered. "I'm just along for the ride, like you say." Thomas turned and walked away without giving the man another chance to continue the conversation.

I'm done with this guy. He is a slimy character and another reason for me to be sure Yeshua is not the Meshiah or He wouldn't allow this thief to handle His money. Thomas started to feel better. He was in control again.

"How exciting to watch the Rabbi raise the young man from the dead," Joanna said as she walked up to Thomas. "No one in Israel has ever seen anything like this since Yahweh parted the Red Sea. I am honored I can be a part of His followers." She smiled up at him and touched his arm slightly. "Aren't you glad you came?"

"I am, Lady Joanna, thank you for inviting me." Thomas decided he would be polite and not mention his decision to stay away from further contact with Yeshua. After all, he owed this lady his freedom.

"I want you to meet Cephas, one of the men with the Rabbi. Come, I will introduce you, Thomas." She pulled him over to a rough looking man with unruly hair on both head and face. His compact body was covered in a long-sleeved robe, held together by a rope. He gestured excitedly as he talked with Lucius and spoke with a strong, deep voice.

"Lucius, you are a Greek, how can you know our ways or our religion? We are the chosen people and our God has always taken care of us. The Rabbi Yeshua will be the One to put the Romans in their place, you'll see. With His power to heal people and drive out demons, He will have no trouble driving out the Romans who dare suppress the Jews."

"Cephas, I want you to meet my good friend Thomas. He is an Israelite, yet comes from a far-away land," Lucius said as Thomas walked up to them.

"Shalom, Thomas, it is very nice to meet you," Cephas said, "They also call me Peter. What do you think of the Rabbi raising a man from the dead? We are His closest helpers and without us He probably could not do the things He does."

Thomas had to smile at the puffed up attitude of the man. He knew Cephas had no idea how Yeshua did what He did. "I am glad the Rabbi has you to rely on, Cephas," Thomas said with a cynical little smile. "And what is it exactly that you do?"

"Hrmph." He cleared his throat. "I assist Him in many ways too hard for you to understand, I'm sure," Cephas said, slightly embarrassed and at a loss for a better answer. Thomas could tell, he had a habit of speaking before he thought.

"I am sure He values your input in religious matters as well, since you are one of His assistants." Thomas was enjoying this, fully realizing this simple fisherman had no clue what was going on. *That's another reason to doubt Yeshua. The man has no idea how to pick experts to help Him run the show,* Thomas thought.

"Here is another one of our group I want you to meet," Joanna said before Cephas could answer. "Thomas, I want you to meet Andrew, the brother of Cephas."

Thomas could see the family resemblance. "Shalom, Andrew, it is good to meet you." He could see Andrew was younger than Cephas, with an open, friendly face, unlike his more serious older brother. He had a habit of combing his thick, brown hair with his hands when he was excited.

"What a day. The Rabbi is amazing, wouldn't you say, Thomas?" His face was animated as he spoke. The brown robe hung on him loosely since he was quite skinny. Unlike his brother, he seemed humble and childlike in his admiration of Yeshua. "I stand amazed each time He heals someone. There is no doubt in my mind He is the Meshiah,"

Andrew said with total conviction.

"And here is Thomas, called Didymus, another one of us," Andrew said as he turned to a tall, skinny young man. "He is the one who asks the Rabbi many questions about everything. "Meet Thomas, Thomas," Andrew said, laughing.

Thomas liked the kid. He was young, yet had a studious look about him. His tiny brown eyes sparkled as he looked at Thomas with great curiosity.

"I like to know about things before I believe anything," he said. "They laugh at me, but I think one should not just have blind faith, but have it be rooted in knowledge."

"You are a man after my own heart," Thomas said. "It must be our name or something that we think alike in this area. For instance, have you asked the Rabbi how He does all these miracles?"

"I have many times."

"What has He told you, Didymus?"

He answers me the same way each time with these words,

"By myself I can do nothing." (John 5:30) "For the very work that the Father has given me to finish, and which I am doing, testifies that the Father has sent me." (John 5:36)

"Why does the man speak in riddles?" Thomas said more to himself than to Didymus. "I have talked to Him as well, but each time He speaks to me, I have no idea what He is talking about."

"I can certainly understand that; it happens to the rest of us constantly. The Rabbi gets frustrated with us at times when we don't understand what the deeper meaning of His words are. But then He tells us, the Holy Spirit will teach us things later on when He is no longer with us."

"Where is He planning to go?" Thomas asked.

"I have no idea; He hasn't told us yet."

"Well, Didymus, you keep on asking Him all those questions, maybe someday He will give you an answer you can understand." Thomas bowed slightly and walked over to where Lucius was talking to a very unusual looking man.

"Thomas, this is Matthew, another of Yeshua's men," Lucius said.

The little man bowed low to Thomas and smiled.

"Some also call me Levi." He was short, rotund and totally bald. His full, curly beard covered most of his face and his tiny eyes almost disappeared in the folds of his fat, rosy cheeks. He reminded Thomas of a miniature Santa Claus. "How delighted I am to meet you, Thomas. I heard from Lucius that you are a fine physician." He chuckled in anticipation of his next statement. "However, with the Lord in our midst, we no longer need your services, I should say."

"I hear you were a tax collector, Matthew. I am surprised, given the reputation of most men in your profession, the Rabbi chose you to be one of His apostles. Taxes and religion don't exactly go well together, do they?" Thomas looked at him with a slight grin.

"Let me share with you how I was chosen by the Master. I was sitting at my booth and Yeshua simply walked up to me and said, "Follow Me." (Luke 5:27) I was in shock and knew He had made a mistake. But then, to thank Him, I gave a great banquet for my fellow tax collectors and friends to introduce them to the Master. But the Pharisees and the teachers of the law who belonged to their sect, complained to His disciples, "Why do You eat and drink with tax collectors and sinners?"

Yeshua answered them, "It is not the healthy who need a doctor, but the sick. I have not come to call the righteous, but sinners to repentance." (Luke 5:29-32)

"You see, Thomas, the Lord Yeshua measures with a different measuring stick. His ways are not our ways and yet He is the most wonderful person I have ever met. Since I have been with Him, I have returned the monies I took that were above what I was allowed to take. Not only that, I have asked many to forgive me for my former ways of cheating on them. I am a different man from the one I used to be." He chuckled with an infectious smile. "Even my wife and children tell me I have become a better person than I was before."

"Does that mean you have given up your tax collection business?" Lucius asked.

"I still have a hired servant who runs it for me," he said. "He has strict instructions not to charge more than what is required by Rome, though."

"It was good to meet you, Matthew," Thomas said and walked on, amazed by the sincerity of the man. Standing to the side, he looked at the apostles gathered around Yeshua. They seemed a close-knit group, bound together by their zeal to follow Him. The Master, as they called Him, sat at a table with a glass of wine mixture in His hand, talking animatedly. Thomas couldn't make out what was said, but they were laughing and seemingly having a good time. He stood and watched them for a long time until Yeshua's eyes caught his. He smiled at Thomas with a nod of reassurance, rose from his seat and walked over to where Thomas stood.

"There is a way that seems right to a man, but in the end it leads to death." (Proverbs 14:12) "What good will it be for a man if he gains the whole world, yet forfeits his soul? Or what can a man give in exchange for his soul?" (Matthew 16:26)

Thomas was unable to speak. This time he knew what Jeshua meant. The Rabbi was aware of his anger and bitterness, his frustration and determination to avoid Him in the future. Yet there was no judgment, no rejection or accusation in Yeshua's voice, just love. And it was this love that hit Thomas with such tangible force, he began to shake. Yeshua put His hand on his shoulder in an encouraging gesture, smiling at him with His knowing smile.

"Why do I have a feeling You will never let me go," Thomas said with resignation in his voice and walked away.

Chapter 13

Several months had passed. By now Thomas was well known as the physician of the poor. Instead of working as a skilled surgeon, he had settled for being a general practitioner, something he always knew was totally beneath him. In his opinion, ordinary medical students without superior talent settled for that, not someone like him with a gifted mind and hands to match. There were a few situations where he was able to put his surgical skills to good use, but most of the time, because of lack of anesthesia and the right tools, he was forced to rely on the simple, natural remedies of the time. He felt extremely frustrated, knowing many died, when it would have been so easy to treat them in the hospital back in Philadelphia.

The poor in Capernaum came to rely on him in a way he had not experienced before. He would never get used to being paid in fish, grain, grapes and figs. Lucius on the other hand, seemed to have no trouble fleecing the rich as he raked in the money with his upper crust clientele. In contrast, Thomas with all his modern knowledge, he had to settle for being second best. And that was something he had never experienced in his professional life. There was one good thing in all this, Lucius was gracious and accepted his "fees" as payment for staying with him.

Thomas still thought about the Rabbi from time to time and wondered why He did not heal anyone in His own hometown. There were many stories being told of His miracles in the countless villages in Galilee, but hardly any in Nazareth. As a matter of fact, Thomas heard one of his patients tell, Yeshua had been thrown out of the synagogue there and had to leave town because they wanted to throw him over the cliff. (Luke 4:28-30) It made him wonder if those most familiar with Him had rejected His claim of being the Meshiah, because they knew He was only a simple carpenter's son.

Thomas was glad he didn't have to deal with that religious nonsense anymore and had made it abundantly clear to Lucius he was no longer interested in talking about the man.

"What happened, Thomas, did He upset you?"

"Not really, this whole religious fervor upsets me. And let's face it, it is *all* people want to talk about these days. I am tired of it and wish to stay a man of science. I want to help the sick get better through my knowledge instead of using faith as a crutch for any and everything they cannot explain. The thing is, Lucius, unlike them, I have so much more knowledge of how nature and science works than everyone else around here. What they call a gift from Yahweh, I call the product of either lucky circumstances or the natural way things work. For example, a good harvest is not a gift from God, but the result of the right soil, combined with the right amount of rain at the right time. It's that simple."

Lucius respected Thomas' decision and stopped bringing up the subject of Yeshua. However, they had many opportunities learning from each other about how to treat the sick. Thomas was amazed to learn of the countless natural remedies that actually worked sometimes, without having to deal with dangerous side effects of modern treatments and their chemicals. *Maybe I'll go into homeopathy when I get back home.* He smiled. To a surgeon that was even worse than being a general practitioner.

Getting back home, what a novel idea, he thought. There were days he actually didn't even think about home or his former life. Thomas' thoughts were interrupted by a young woman entering the front door of the office.

"Master, my daughter is very sick with a fever. Can you come and help her?" She was crying. "She is our only child and has been ill for two days. I don't have any money with which to pay you."

"I will come with you and take a look at her," he said with a reassuring smile. "What is your name?"

"I am Sarah, the wife of Caleb, the apprentice to the blacksmith. My little girl's name is Ruth."

He grabbed his medical bag and followed her to the poorest section of town through narrow streets with steep steps in places along the way.

"Tell me about your daughter. How old is she?" he asked the woman on the way there.

"She was born three seasons ago last spring and has been healthy since then. I take good care of her."

"I am sure you do, Sarah. Children at that age get fevers quite often. Most of the time it is nothing to worry about and will subside in a few days," he said.

He had to duck his head when he entered the more than modest two-room hut. The little girl was lying on a straw mattress in the corner, her face flushed from the high temperature. He palpitated her stomach. Thank goodness, it was soft and pliable. She was coughing and her nose was stopped up. It was only a cold. He put his ear to her chest and checked for any lung problems, but couldn't hear any sounds of pneumonia.

He turned to the mother.

"Boil some rosemary twigs in water and rub her little body with it. Then brew some white willow tea, it will help bring down the fever. Make sure she drinks a lot of water. Not a wine mixture, just water. Boil it first and allow it to cool and then make her take as much of it as she will drink. You may add some pomegranate juice if you have any."

"Yes, Master. I will do that. I am so grateful for your help." She put a handful of figs into his hand before he left. He looked at them and rolled his eyes as he walked back to the office. *Another big fee for a big medical miracle.* He felt like a country doctor in the Middle Ages and wondered if his surgical skills were completely atrophied by now. It was hard to visualize his operating theatre in these surroundings. Gleaming steel instruments, bleeping monitors and technical equipment everywhere, while admiring medical students sat behind a glass wall on the balcony above, watching him perform medical breakthroughs. Instead here he was, walking on dirty, narrow streets, being asked to cure the common cold. His mother used to say a cold got better after a week with a doctor and seven days without one. He sighed. How long could this ridiculous, demeaning nightmare go on?

Lucius met him at the door when he got back, waving his arms and shouting praises to every god in Greece and Rome he could think of.

"You are not going to believe what happened, Thomas. We have been invited to a big dinner at the palace of King Herod Antipas in Sepphoris in three days."

"How did you manage that, Lucius? Bribe one of your rich clients?"

"Of course not, but I did help one of them with a slight medical problem. A distant relative of Herod had a boil on his leg. I lanced it and sterilized it with wine and bandaged it like you showed me and it got better in a few days. He is very grateful. Naturally, I asked him if it was alright to bring along my business partner and he said it was."

"Are you sure it's alright with the King? What I mean, does Herod know we are coming?" Thomas asked. "I would hate to get thrown into prison again for showing up uninvited."

"Of course it is. Herod will never know we are there. We will probably sit in the very back of the great hall, too far away to be seen or heard by him, but just the thought of being in the presence of a king is exciting." He looked at Thomas, confused that he was not as impressed as he was. "Don't you think so, Thomas? I have never even been near royalty before," he added, totally in awe at the thought.

"From what I remember from my history lessons, Herod was not the finest specimen of humanity," Thomas said. "I also remember talking to John the Baptizer when I was in prison. He is the one who told Herod he was wrong to marry Herodias, his brother's former wife. Herod sent him to prison for it."

"I didn't know about that, Thomas. You better not say anything when we get there. I don't think even Chuza can get you out of prison a second time talking like that."

It was three days later and they were on the way to Nazareth. From there it was only a short distance to Sepphoris, the palace Herod Antipas had resurrected to its former glory.

"You may not know the story of Herod and his wife Herodias, Thomas. She is the granddaughter of Herod the Great and his wife Mariamne. Our present illustrious king Herod Antipas was actually married to the daughter of King Aretas IV of Nabatea. However, Antipas traveled to Rome and there met and fell in love with his half-brother's wife, Herodias. They agreed to marry after Herod divorced his wife, Aretas' daughter. She heard of the plan and fled to the prison you were in, Machaerus, from where her father's forces whisked her away back to her country. You can imagine this has not gone over well with Aretas. I am sure he and Herod will come to blows in the not so distant future."

"I have heard Joanna tell me about this palace," Thomas said. "She says it is fabulous beyond anything you can imagine. She told me it makes her sick every time she sees the splendor and then thinks about the poor and needy everywhere else."

"Her husband Chuza will be busy tonight, I imagine," Lucius said. "She has asked us to stay at their house after the banquet. I am looking forward to talking to her about the Rabbi." Lucius was careful not to say anymore on the subject for now.

The sun was sinking low in the sky when they approached the palace of Sepphoris. It was built on top of an isolated hill in the plain of Galilee. Herod called it Zippori, "my little bird", for its view. The Romans renamed it Sepphoris. Even from the distance, it looked massive. Thomas was surprised it was located only about four miles from Nazareth.

It took them quite some time to make it up the hill to the main gate. The little donkey was exhausted by the time they were allowed to enter the huge courtyard. A slave took the reins and assured them he would feed and water the animal, while another asked them to follow him into the inside of the huge building.

Everywhere Thomas looked, there were breathtakingly colorful, intricate mosaic images of flowers, battle scenes and gods and goddesses in lush gardens on the walls and floors as they advanced further into the inner rooms of the palace. Hundreds of oil lamps had already been lit along the long hallways leading to the great banquet hall. They could hear the hum of countless voices, mixed in with music, the closer they got.

Thomas stood transfixed when he saw the large number of people in the biggest banquet hall he had ever seen. The tables, set in the finest silver and gold with countless candelabras lit by wax candles, were laden with an abundance of the most exotic selection of an endless variety of delicacies. It was a glittering picture of opulence such as he had never dreamed could exist. Countless slaves were busy carrying pitchers of wine and other beverages hoisted on their shoulders, ready to refill anyone's glass whenever a guest indicated he was ready for more.

"If you please, Master," a slave said and pointed to two chairs toward the back of the hall. "These are your seats."

"You are right, Lucius, Herod will never know we are here. We'll have a hard time seeing him with the head table so far away," Thomas whispered as they sat down.

"That is not a head table, Thomas. Those are two thrones you are seeing, one for Herod and the other for his wife Herodias."

"I seem to remember she has a daughter named Salome," Thomas said. I remember that because I saw a play at the theater once. She is the one that asks for John the Baptist's head on a platter."

"What? That is crazy, where do you get such an idea, Thomas?" Lucius sounded frantic. "I would advise you not to talk such ridiculous nonsense here or you will end up in Machaerus for sure," he whispered in Thomas' ear.

"I am telling you it's going to happen, you will see," Thomas whispered back, "maybe even tonight."

He looked around and saw Joanna sitting on the opposite side of the table. She nodded to them with a big smile and waved. Before they could return her greeting, loud trumpets sounded and the huge, ornate doors of the great hall opened wide. The crowd hushed instantly and everyone rose from their seats. Herod and Herodias entered, holding hands as they looked at each other as if deeply in love and then waved at the guests with their other hand. Both were dressed magnificently in garments the colors of purple and gold, studded with diamonds. They each wore crowns made of gold, decorated with huge precious stones. The people bowed deeply until the couple had made it to the two thrones in the front.

Herod and Herodias stood smiling at the crowd and then waved for everyone to sit down. Thomas was mesmerized by the stunning woman at Herod's side. He got a good look at both of them when they passed by. No wonder Herod had fallen in love with her. She was actually taller than he. Her face had the classic signs of beauty with large eyes, perfect bone structure and an aquiline nose that gave her a stunningly beautiful profile. He noticed a cold, haughty look in her dark, sensuous eyes that even her broad smile could not hide.

Herod on the other hand was overweight in a flabby sort of way, which results from too much rich food and no exercise. His tailor had performed a miracle hiding the mountains of rolls underneath the folds of his garment. A heavy gold chain hung from his thick, fleshy neck, set off by the solid purple toga draped gracefully across one shoulder.

Before he sat down, he raised his hand and shouted, "Hail Caesar!"

"Hail Caesar," the crowd echoed dutifully in return.

"Hail King Herod," someone shouted with much greater enthusiasm.

"Hail King Herod," the crowd repeated.

Herod and Herodias waved and sat down. The crowd followed and the place was soon filled with the chatter and clatter of the banquet. It was hard for Thomas to know which of the delicacies to try first and decided he would follow Joanna's example as he watched her take a selection of fruit first. After that she reached for small pieces of the exotic meats which Thomas had no idea what they were. In the end, he made up his mind to try a little of everything and then go back for more of what he liked most.

An hour went by and the guests were getting to the point of being filled and started to concentrate on having their wine goblets filled regularly by a slave standing behind each chair. The low chatter of the crowd at the beginning of the meal was soon replaced by loud, boisterous laughter, evidence of the effects of the drink.

No one paid much attention to a group of beautiful young girls, who appeared seemingly out of nowhere and began dancing in a sensuous way in front of the king. Herod gave them only a fleeting glance and continued to consume large amounts of food from what Thomas could make out. After the dancers had finished, a richly dressed slave came in, leading a sleek cheetah on a diamond studded leash in front of the two thrones. The animal sat down next to Herodias in a regal pose as she fed it with meats from the table. The crowd looked on in awe for a few moments and then returned to their chatter. Throughout the evening, a good number of musicians and dancers performed in stunning, elaborate costumes, while still more food and drink was brought in by numerous slaves. They were followed by jugglers, a magician and other entertainers in what seemed a never-ending procession of performers.

I wouldn't want to be a cook tonight, Thomas thought, as he patted his full stomach, finishing up his dessert of dried pears boiled in wine and covered with a honey glaze. It was delicious.

Suddenly the sound of trumpets interrupted the revelry of the guests. A single young girl appeared in a gown made of ultra-sheer material that didn't leave much to the imagination. Her forehead was covered by a gold head band, studded with rubies and diamonds. Thomas realized she couldn't be more than thirteen or fourteen and knew it had to be Salome, the daughter of Herodias.

"Now watch what happens, Lucius. When she is done, she will ask for the head of John the Baptizer, just like I told you before," he whispered.

The girl moved slowly at first and then, directly in front of Herod Antipas, her lithe body began gyrating faster and faster in fluid, sensual motions for what seemed a long time. Herod followed her every movements with his beady little eyes. Thomas was sure he was drooling.

Finally, the girl sank to the floor in a graceful heap, looking up at Herod with an inviting smile and whispered, "Happy Birthday, your Majesty."

"By all the gods, it is Salome!" Herod shouted into the silence. He leaned over to Herodias with a smile and held out his pudgy hand for hers and kissed it. His large, golden crown was held by a shock of curly, black hair as he bent over and beads of sweat poured down the sides of his puffy, red face. His thick lips, in a perpetual state of pouting, were drawn apart in a sensuous smile.

"You have outdone yourself, my daughter," he finally said as he let go of Herodias' hand and turned back to Salome. With a wave of his jeweled hand he raised her up and motioned for the young girl to step closer.

"Whatever it is you want, I will give it to you, up to half my kingdom. Just say the word and it is yours."

Thomas looked at Lucius. "Now watch it, she will ask for John's head."

Lucius sat mesmerized, whether from seeing Thomas' prediction being fulfilled or from the gruesome request about to be spoken.

The girl whispered something to her mother. Herodias answered her back in a low voice. Salome looked at her mother, stunned for a moment, then nodded her head in agreement and turned towards Herod.

"I want the head of John the Baptizer on a platter, my king."

There was a sudden silence in the great hall, except for the slaves filling the glasses and clearing away the many dishes. Lucius took in a deep breath and looked at Thomas with an expression of surprise and wonder. None of the other guests dared speak for fear of saying anything wrong as they stared stoically toward the macabre scene up front.

Herod Antipas looked at Herodias with a helpless gesture of frustration and regret, as if ready to deny the request.

"You promised my daughter to give her whatever she asks for," Herodias said in a silky, smooth voice as she looked at her husband first and then at the guests. "A king cannot break his oath, my lord."

Herod stared at his wife in disbelief and even fear, then at the girl and finally at his guests.

"I have sworn an oath and I shall keep it." He waved to his guards, and in a loud voice ordered that John the Baptizer was to be beheaded in prison and his head brought to him at once." (Matthew 14:6-10)

Even from the back of the hall, Thomas could tell Herod Antipas was upset. He noticed the atmosphere of the evening had become somber as the crowd was trying hard to deal with what had just happened, yet fearful of acting or saying anything that might further upset the King. Only Herodias was laughing as she reached over and stroked Herod's arm in a sensuous and possessive manner.

"Thank you, my lord. You have made me a happy woman tonight."

Thomas looked over at Joanna and saw she could barely hold back her tears. He heard Lucius whisper to her after she asked to be excused, "We will follow you in a few minutes. Wait for us in the courtyard and we will leave together."

They arrived an hour later at the spacious villa of Chuza and Joanna. It was situated between Sipphores and Nazareth, on a large estate given to them by Herod Antipas. Even in the dark, Thomas could tell it was a luxurious place, hidden behind a large iron gate amidst a cluster of trees. In spite of the late hour, several slaves saw to their needs when they arrived.

Joanna ordered the servants to bring refreshments and the inevitable wine mixture as soon as they settled into the plush couches made of the finest fabric, with large pillows everywhere.

"I am so glad to be out of that evil place," Joanna said after she made sure everyone was settled in comfortably. "I hate to go there, but especially for occasions like this. Herod and Herodias are two godless people who are raising a daughter in the same immoral ways. However, what happened tonight is the worst I have ever seen. The Rabbi will be very sad to hear about it when I see Him in the coming days. He has spoken about John, who is actually His cousin. He told us, John was born to fulfill the role of Elijah, having been sent to prepare the way for the Meshiah, like the scripture foretold." Joann had recovered from her shock and seemed revitalized by talking about Jeshua. "He was baptized by John and from what I hear tell, as Yeshua was praying, heaven was opened and the Holy Spirit descended on Him in bodily form like a dove. And a voice came from heaven: "You are my Son, whom I love; with you I am well pleased." (Luke 3:21-22)

Lucius sat and listened in rapt attention, while Thomas frowned at the unlikely tale.

"I have talked to John while I was in prison, Lady Joanna. He definitely did not look like a prophet to me or someone risen from the dead." Thomas shook his head in disbelief.

"You don't believe any of this, do you, Thomas?" Joanna asked gently.

"No, I don't. It all sounds too fantastic for my scientific mind," he said with a polite smile. "I have made up my mind to rely on my knowledge and talents instead of a poor carpenter from Nazareth." He looked at Joanna with an apologetic little smile. "I do not mean to offend you, dear lady, but I have never been religious and I intend to stay that way."

"What happened that made you turn away from Yeshua, Thomas?" she asked with surprise. "I thought you believed in Him like we do."

"I thought I did for a short time, but then nothing makes sense what He says to me or some of His actions. I know He is a good man, but that is all He is."

"What about the miracles?" she asked.

"I don't know, I can't explain them, but then I can't explain anything about my being here or the life I lead right now." His frustration was evident.

"Thomas says he comes from the future," Lucius said. "He foretold what happened tonight with Salome before it ever happened. His story is just as fantastic as that of the Rabbi."

"If you come from the future and you believe something as incredible as that, why can't you believe the Rabbi is the Meshiah?" Joanna asked, trying to work through what she had just heard. "Does Yeshua know about your strange story?"

"I believe He does and yet He refuses to explain it to me. That is why I am so angry with Him. It is as if He is making fun of me and I feel humiliated and angry with Him for using this strange way to communicate with me. I am a man of science, not a dreamer. If He is the Meshiah and knows all things, why can't He talk to me in a way I can understand? Instead, He constantly speaks in riddles and parables." Thomas took another sip of the wine mixture to calm his nerves. "Each time I talk to Him or about Him I get upset and I am tired of it."

"That is why Thomas has decided he does not want anything to do with Yeshua or even talk about Him anymore," Lucius said to Joanna.

"That is a shame, Thomas. You are missing out on the greatest event in human history, namely God Himself visiting us in flesh and blood."

"Why do you think God feels He has to do that?" Thomas said, barely trying to hide his sarcasm.

"I don't understand that part yet, but I will. For now, I think it is time for us to get some rest. It is late. If you don't mind, I will have Marcellus show you to your rooms." She rose from her seat and summoned the slave standing by the door with a wave of her hand.

Chapter 14

There was a subtle change in Thomas during the many days that followed. He felt good again, in control of his life. At the same time, he was no longer satisfied to be known as the doctor for the poor. After seeing the opulence of Herod's palace, he decided it was time he earned some real money, the way a talented physician had the right to expect.

They were sitting on comfortable couches after a delicious dinner. Lucius had just returned from visiting one of his rich clients in Tiberias.

"It is amazing what these people will pay just to have me come and essentially do nothing but make them feel better by giving them herbal tea and sympathy. I wish I had some of the instruments and medicines you say they have in your time," he said to Thomas.

"We could both make a real fortune," Thomas answered as he took a piece of lamb, spread some mint jelly over it and put it in his mouth. "That brings me to a point I wanted to discuss with you for a long time, Lucius. I have proven myself and have worked diligently treating every poor creature in this flea-bitten town for the past year. Don't you think it is time you made it possible for me to share in your good fortunes by passing some of those rich clients on to me?"

"I was wondering how long it would take you to ask me, Thomas. You definitely deserve a share of the income, since you do the same amount of work I do." Lucius took a sip of wine mixture and leaned back into the plush cushion. "What do you say, I spend more time with the Rabbi Yeshua and you take over some of my clients? I have enough money to last me a lifetime. It is time I remember that I came here to study Judaism. And who better to learn from than the Rabbi Yeshua?"

"You still see Him? I thought you had given up on Him like I have, since I haven't heard you mention Him in a long time," Thomas said.

"I have not said anything, because I know you do not want to talk about Him. There have been many more miracles all over the area since the last time you saw Him. He is truly amazing and I have come to believe that He could possibly be the Meshiah." Lucius was careful how much to say so as not to upset his friend.

"So you wouldn't mind if I took some of your patients?" Thomas was elated.

"Absolutely not, let's start tomorrow. I have an appointment with an important official at the palace. He is complaining of an upset stomach and is in much pain. Why don't you go and see him? You can use the cart and the donkey. Whatever you negotiate for a fee, belongs to you."

Thomas was excited. Finally, he was getting somewhere. *Forget the poor and make enough money to buy my own house and servants,* he thought and then smiled. *Let Lucius waste his time on religion, while I get rich.*

He felt re-energized as he let Igora find her way toward Sepphoris. It had become a challenge to figure out how to make do without the help of technology and modern remedies. He had learned to dispense herbs and ointments and combine them with helpful treatments out of the storehouse of his vast scientific knowledge. His reputation as a good doctor was great among the poor. As soon as he could do the same with the rich, he was home free toward a better, more independent life. It was not that he didn't enjoy staying at Lucius' house, but a grown man had to make his own way.

He thought about stopping at Miriam's house as he passed through Nazareth, but thought better of it. No reason to get stirred up about Yeshua. Life was getting good and he didn't need the distraction. He saw quite a few people walking along the way. It was not until he noticed a woman with a small child and a heavy bag on her shoulders that he stopped and asked if she wanted a ride. She looked at him with real fear in her eyes and shook her head, afraid to say anything. That's when he remembered a woman could not be seen alone with a man, who was not a relative. He shrugged his shoulders. He had tried. Was it his fault these people were so backward?

It was mid-morning by the time he arrived at the palace. The guard let him in without a problem when he told him he was the doctor coming to see the honorable Josephus. A slave took care of the cart and donkey and another showed Thomas inside the palace. This time, he was not nearly as awed as he passed the many beautiful rooms and decorations. He was shown into a sitting area adjacent to a small courtyard with a large fig tree and a water basin lined with colorful tiles. There were exotic birds in cages filling the air with their chirping.

"Shalom, I am Magdalene, the wife of Josephus." She was an older woman with gray hair held up with several silver combs. Her long, flowing gown was gathered at the waist by a silver belt.

"Shalom, gracious lady Magdalene," Thomas said and bowed. "I am Thomas, the physician. I have come to see if I can help your husband."

"I am glad, Thomas, because Josephus is in great pain. Come, I will lead you to him." She walked to an open door a few feet away and waved for Thomas to enter.

"Josephus, my dear, the doctor has finally come. His name is

Thomas."

It took Thomas a minute to get used to the dark interior. A man in his middle-fifties was lying on a bed, a painful expression on his face. He looked pale and perspiration stood in great drops on his forehead. "Shalom, Thomas, I hope you can help me, because this pain is terrible."

"Tell me where it hurts, Sir." Thomas stood at the side of the bed.

"Right here," Josephus said and pointed to his abdomen. "I have been relieving myself quite violently since yesterday and now I am ready to throw up. I also have a terrible headache." His voice sounded thin and pitiful.

Thomas removed the bedcover and touched his stomach. It was extended and painful to the touch. It sounded like the man had diverticulitis, judging without blood tests.

"Josephus, you have an inflammation of your intestines. Have you been eating a lot of figs?" Thomas asked.

"I love figs and eat them with every meal. Are you saying they were spoiled?"

"Not at all, what I *am* saying is, the little seeds in the figs have gotten stuck in the folds of your bowels. After some days they rot and spoil and cause an infection. That is what gives you diarrhea. I will give you a tea to calm down the infection in your bowels and then I must ask you never to eat figs again."

"That is most unfortunate," Josephus said. "Are you sure about this? I have eaten figs all my life and they have never bothered me before." There was doubt in his voice.

"As our body ages on the outside, so do all our organs inside as well, Sir. We must therefore treat them much more gently and watch what we eat. If you stay away from all fruit with seeds, nuts and any other foods like coarse barley bread that still has partial kernels in it, these incidents will not happen again. Make sure they grind the grain real fine before they make your bread with it."

"When will I feel better?"

"With the tea I am giving you and by withholding food for a day, you should feel better and be well in a day or two."

"Thank you so much for treating my husband and helping him to stay well, Thomas," Magdalene said as he stepped out of the room. "I will see to it that all is done the way you say. I will instruct the cook to only feed him food without seeds in them, just as you suggested."

"I will stop by in two days and see how your husband is doing, noble lady."

"That is fine, I will see to it you will be handsomely rewarded for your trouble," she said with a smile. "I told Herodias you were coming and she wants to see you at once as soon as you are done here. Come, I will lead you to her." She waved to a female slave and said, "You stay with the master until I return."

"Is Herodias sick?" Thomas asked, surprised at the summons.

"I don't know, but I am sure if she is, she does not want anyone to know," Magdalene whispered. "She does not take me into her confidence." She leaned closer to Thomas and said in a low voice," You are a handsome man, please beware and be careful when you are alone with her."

Thomas looked at her shocked, but said nothing. *This could get interesting – and very dangerous,* he thought.

The closer they got to the royal chambers, the more opulent the surroundings became. He was a little nervous, especially after what Magdalene had said. He remembered Herodias from the birthday banquet and knew well her effect on men. She reminded him of a sleek panther stalking his prey. He would have to be careful, no sense in losing his head over her, literally speaking. He chuckled on the inside.

"You are not Lucius are you, handsome?" Herodias asked as soon as he walked in. She was sitting on a gold embroidered couch facing a green, lush courtyard with a large pool shaded by palm trees on two sides. She took a cluster of grapes and in a lascivious gesture, pulled one off with her lips and looked at Thomas with large, brown eyes filled with desire. Both upper arms had dozens of narrow gold and silver bracelets that gleamed as the sunlight reflected on them. Her dress was made of the finest linen in a bright, green color, clinging tightly to her well curved body. A single strand of a gold necklace enhanced her ample cleavage perfectly. "Magdalene, who is this handsome creature?" she asked with a sensuous smile.

"Your Majesty, this is Thomas the physician. I called him to look after my husband as you might remember," Magdalene said as she sank into a low curtsy.

"Ah yes, although he looks more like a god, don't you think?"

"If you say so, your Majesty. He has diagnosed Josephus' ailment right away. His skills as a physician are to be admired."

Thomas heard a slight tremble of fear in her voice.

"Your Majesty, it is a great honor to be summoned by you. How may I be of service?" Thomas asked to get Herodias' attention away from Magdalene.

"You may leave us, Magdalene," Herodias said as she waved her hand in a dismissive gesture and turned to Thomas. "Have a seat, Thomas." She pointed to an ornate chair close to where she sat. "Can I get you some refreshments? It is a long journey from Capernaum."

"Thank you, your Majesty. I will take some wine mixture if it is not too much trouble."

Herodias nodded to one of the slaves and Thomas was handed a silver goblet immediately.

Herodias stretched like a cat as she studied Thomas from head to toe. "You are a fine specimen of a man, Thomas. I am sure you have a wife and children?"

"I do have a wife, but no children," he answered. "Is there anything I can help you with, medically speaking, your Majesty?"

"You could give me a thorough examination to make sure everything is alright," she said with a sly smile.

"I am sure your royal physicians can do that much better than I. After all, I am only a country doctor," he answered, trying not to look at her.

She looked at him with disappointment.

"Oh well, it was a nice try. I do get bored in this lonely place, far away from anywhere. It is time we moved back to Tiberias." She leaned towards Thomas. "If you moved there, you could become one of the royal physicians, would you like that?"

"It would be a great honor to be chosen for such a task, but at this time I am rather busy attending many clients in Galilee. Thank you for thinking so highly of me, your Majesty." Thomas hoped she was not going to order him to move to Tiberias and held his breath.

"What a shame. That's all, you can go now," she said and waved him out with a dismissive gesture. "A slave will show you the way out." Her voice suddenly had an icy ring to it.

Thomas got up, relieved the audience was over, he bowed low before he followed a male slave out the door. He breathed a sigh of relief when he got back on his cart and on the road back to Capernaum. *Royalty around here is not all that it's cut out to be,* he thought, *I'll take an audience with the Queen of England any time.*

Chapter 15

When Thomas returned to the palace two days later, there were several officials with their wives who wanted his medical advice. Apparently, Magdalene had shared how much better Josephus felt since he had followed his treatment. Thomas spent the day prescribing remedies and giving medical advice. That is when he found out the rumor was running wild, he was the secret physician to Herodias. His adamant denial only served to confirm it in the minds of those who spread it. The good thing was, he had made more money in that one day than he had in a whole year serving the poor. Looking back later, this day would prove to be the pivotal point on his way to becoming the preferred physician to the rich, not only in Capernaum, but also in Tiberias, Herod's new capitol to the west on the Sea of Galilee.

It was almost evening by the time he got back to Capernaum and found that Lucius had gone to a meeting. He leaned back into the big cushions of the couch after a good meal and closed his eyes. It had been a good day. He loved the idea he could practice medicine and actually make money at the same time. If this kept up, he could soon buy a horse and transportation better suited to his status. It felt good to be the best again. He shuddered at the thought he had almost bought into this religious fervor and made a fool of himself. He wondered about Lucius. Had he become a follower of Yeshua? What would that do to their business arrangement and friendship? Maybe it was time to think of finding a place of his own?

A messenger arrived a week later from King Herod. Thomas was summoned for a medical consult with the King. Lucius looked at Thomas with a strange look of apprehension and worry.

"This could be your undoing, Thomas," he said. "This man is not only evil, but very dangerous. Can you imagine what happens, if you cannot cure him and he actually gets worse from your treatment? He not only could be angry with you, but cut off your head. The man is a maniac and has killed plenty of people for less, including members of his own family."

"You forget my superior medical training," Thomas said. "I will know what is wrong with him and take precautions to make it very clear whether I can help him or not. I am in a perfect place to become more successful than I was even in my former life in Philadelphia."

"Success isn't everything, Thomas. I am learning from Yeshua that it is more important to gain treasures in heaven than riches here on earth."

"You collect treasures for eternity and I work on getting rich down here. We'll see who is happier in the end," Thomas answered in a condescending tone.

"You are changing, Thomas," Lucius said with great sadness. "You sound as arrogant as when you first came."

"That is not arrogance you hear, my friend, but self-confidence. That is the way I used to be. I liked it then and I like it now. What's more, I am in control of my life and career, because I am good at what I do."

"I hope you will receive everything you think you deserve, Thomas. However, I pray the price you have to pay is not too steep in the end. Riches can disappear in a moment, but values of goodness, mercy and faith in a loving God bring you treasures that can never be taken from you, no matter what happens."

"You are really getting too serious, Lucius. It must be because you have been with Yeshua too long and sound like all the other sad people that follow Him." He looked at his friend with a sudden thought. "Could it be you are a little jealous of my sudden success or that I am smarter than you?"

Lucius looked at him with true sorrow in his eyes. "You are on a dangerous road to destruction, Thomas. I pray that the Lord God have mercy on your soul." He reached out and touched Thomas' arm with a gentle gesture of affection. "I will always be there for you if you should ever need me, remember that."

"Well, I have to be on my way. The king sent a carriage for me. The slaves are waiting outside." Thomas grabbed his bag and walked out the door without looking back. Lucius sank into a chair with a heavy sigh as he listened to the clatter of the horses fading into the distance.

King Herod was resting in a large bed in his opulent chambers. A number of members of the court stood around him in solemn, subdued groups, while several slaves offered wine in silver goblets. When Thomas was shown in, he bowed low before the king.

"Shalom, your Majesty. I am Thomas, the physician you commanded to attend you." *It sounded good. He had practiced on the way how to talk to a king.*

"Finally. It took you long enough. I don't like to be kept waiting," Herod snapped, apparently in a foul mood. "None of my physicians have been able to help me. I hope you can do better, Thomas," he said in a weak voice. "I am feeling worse every day and think I am dying."

"Oh no, your Majesty, you will live for many more years," the group of people in the room said almost in unison. Thomas could hear more fear than sincerity as they spoke. Herodias stood at the side of the bed, holding Herod's hand.

"I told you this man is good at his trade, my lord, allow him to attend you without all these people in the room." She waved her hand dismissively toward the courtiers and they left immediately.

"Come closer, Thomas," Herod said with a weak wave of his pudgy hand.

"What is troubling you, Sir?" Thomas asked with a slight bow.

"I am being poisoned, I am sure of it. For all I know, it is my lovely wife."

Herodias smiled at him with a look of concern in her dark eyes.

"I assure you, my husband, I am your most loyal subject and would never think of doing such a horrible thing."

"Yes, yes, of course you wouldn't, you sly cat. After all, where would you be without me?"

"That is so true, my lord."

"Can you tell me what your symptoms are, Sir?" Thomas asked before this weird conversation could get any worse.

"He is weak, parts of his body are swollen and he has open sores on his gums. He has already lost several of his teeth. Needless to say, this has made him very irritable at times," Herodias answered instead. "Which of course is understandable under the circumstances," she hastened to add when Herod looked at her, anger rising in his eyes.

"Watch your tongue, woman or I will have it cut out for saying such a thing about your king."

"My lord, could you tell me what you like to eat?" Thomas interrupted him before she could answer.

"What do you mean, what do I eat?" He was still annoyed.

"What foods do you consume every day? Please tell me, it is very important, Sir."

"I eat only meat. That is all I like. Meat and wine and other spirits to wash it down," he finally said.

"Do you eat any fruits or vegetables at all each day?" Thomas asked.

"I absolutely despise vegetables and don't care much for fruit. That is food for the common people. I keep my strength up with solid things like meat."

The richest man in this part of the world has scurvy! Thomas thought and almost smiled. Instead, he looked solemn and pretended to be deep in thought before he opened his medicine bag and rummaged around in it for a while. Finally, he found a bottle of water mixed with honey. He kept it in there to give to those who could not be helped, but still wanted some medicine to make them feel better. *This was too easy, but he had to be careful not to make it look so.*

"I will have to examine you, Majesty to find out what it is that has you vexed. This might be extremely serious, but I have no doubt I can cure it. Please allow me to look into your mouth and check out your stomach. Most diseases lie hidden beneath the surface and can be detected only by pressing on the body. For now, I will give you a spoon full of this medicine. It will help with some of the symptoms for a little while." He filled a wooden spoon with the honey water and guided it into Herod's mouth. "Please, open your garments so that I may look and feel your stomach," he said as he stepped closer to Herod.

It took two slaves ten minutes to remove the layers of his clothes until the countless rolls of fat were exposed. Thomas pressed and probed his stomach and found no symptoms of any kind indicating any other illness he could diagnose without modern x-rays or a CT scan.

"This is indeed serious, your Majesty," he said. "I am glad you called me or you would indeed have been in danger of dying." *I am not lying; without some form of vitamin C, this man would indeed die.* "I will have to consult with your head steward and have him fix my secret remedy for you as soon as possible."

"My head steward, what does he have to do with medicine? Are you a quack, Thomas?" Herod was screaming at him.

"I am sorry, but it is the only way for you to get better. As a matter of fact, I can promise you will feel well after a week, if you take this drink I will have him prepare for you daily. It contains very special ingredients which will make you well, my lord." Thomas stood and looked at Herod, waiting for him to summon Chuza.

"Get me my steward right away," Herod said to a slave by the door.

"I will consult with him outside in the outer chamber, if that is alright with you. You will need your rest after the medicine I have just given you." Herod leaned back in his pillow and closed his eyes.

"Do you want me to stay with you, my love?" Herodias asked as she leaned over and kissed his forehead.

"That would be nice, my pet," the king murmured and held her hand.

Chuza, Joanna's husband, came rushing up to him after a few minutes, totally out of breath.

"Why am I being summoned to the King? What have I done wrong?" That is when he saw Thomas. "What are you doing here, Thomas? Is there a problem with the King?" His face was pale with fear.

"Please, do not worry, Chuza. You have done nothing to incur the wrath of the king. I am the one who needs to talk to you and I must ask you to listen to me carefully." Thomas put his hand on Chuza's shoulder to calm him down. "Do you have lemons in your kitchen?"

"Of course we have lemons."

'You also have pomegranates, right?"

"Yes, of course, what is this all about?" Chuza was getting upset. "These are ridiculous questions, Thomas. What is going on?"

"Just listen, Chuza and do what I tell you if you want both of us to stay alive." Thomas spoke in his most professional, authoritative tone and Chuza calmed down. "Every morning and every evening you squeeze the juice of two lemons into a goblet and then fill it up with a small spoon full of honey and the rest with the juice of pomegranates. Bring this to the king yourself and see to it that he drinks all of it. Do not allow anyone else in your kitchen to see what is in it. Just tell the slaves it is a secret medicine for the king and no one is allowed to know what it is, under pain of death. If you don't make him drink this twice a day every day for the next two weeks, he will die and you will get the blame, do you understand me?" Thomas sounded urgent.

Chuza nodded his head in agreement.

"Once Herod is returned to health, he still has to drink this drink twice a week for the rest of his life or his illness will come back," Thomas went on. "I will make sure he understands that."

"Thomas, this sounds ridiculously simple. Are you sure it will work?" Chuza sounded worried. "You realize you and I could lose our lives if it doesn't."

"It will work, Chuza, don't worry. He has this disease because he refuses to eat fruits or vegetables and consumes only meat and alcohol. There is enough of the life-giving ingredient in lemon and pomegranate juice to make up for it. You may consider trying out some delicious desserts with fruit in it at least twice a week or as often as he will eat it. Just don't tell him how simple this is and let him believe it is a secret medicine. Pretend you don't know what it is and that I will give you a supply to last until the next time I come."

"I understand, Thomas. You are indeed a great physician, but also a great businessman." He smiled at Thomas with a knowing smile and left for the kitchen to prepare the first drink.

After two weeks Herod's health was back. The entire court marveled at how Thomas the physician had brought the king back from the brink of death. Which, given the strict medial facts, was not so far-fetched. Herod would have died from scurvy in the not too distant future without the added vitamin C in the mystery drink. Needless to say, Thomas' fame spread like wild-fire throughout Galilee and he was in high demand with the royal court and the wealthy of the area, especially in Tiberias. A lot of Romans and Greeks lived there and Thomas was a daily visitor in attendance to the upper crust of the new city.

"I am actually in competition with the Rabbi," he told Lucius one day as they sat and talked at the end of the day. "But I make a lot more money than He does." He chuckled.

Lucius looked at him with concern, but said nothing. Thomas had shown him the two sleek horses he had bought and the carriage to go with them, as well as a slave to take care of the animals and to serve as driver.

"I remember when you first came you did not like slavery. Now you own one," he said to Thomas with mild surprise in his voice when he saw Marcellus, the young slave boy. What happened to your convictions, Thomas?"

"I am just trying to fit in, Lucius. No sense in bucking the system, like they say in my country."

Two days later, he had another summons to see Herod.

"I hope he took his medicine," Lucius said.

"No, it doesn't work that fast. He would have to go for quite a long while to develop vitamin C deficiency again. I have no idea what it might be," he said as he got into his new carriage and they sped off to Sepphoris, with Marcellus holding the reins.

"I have not thanked you properly for what you did for me, Thomas," Herod said when Thomas was shown into the audience room. There were countless officials and some of Herod's relatives standing around the throne. "We have decided to honor you with a villa located between Capernaum and Tiberias, my new capitol. It belonged to a relative of mine who has displeased me and I banished him and his family to Gaul. I give it to you and make you my personal physician at the same time." The crowd applauded and crowded around Thomas with smiles and handshakes.

"Before I accept your most generous offer, my lord, I must tell you that I am greatly honored by your marvelous gift. However, I would like to be able to still see other patients as well. Since you are in such perfect health right now, there wouldn't be enough for me to do." Thomas held his breath and wondered if he had blown it with the refusal of exclusivity as Herod's doctor.

"Ah, the man wants to get richer by treating the rich," Herod laughed. "Why not, I owe you my life, Thomas, your wish is granted. Just make sure you are always available whenever I summon you."

"I am always at your service, my lord, you can be sure of that." Thomas breathed a sigh of relief and bowed deeply before Herod.

Chapter 16

When Thomas returned from Sepphoris before the sun set, he found Lucius at dinner with Chuza and Joanna.

"How nice to see you again, Thomas," Joanna said with a warm smile. "It has been a long time. I hear you are a very busy man these days."

"What a pleasant surprise to see you," he said and hugged her in a warm embrace. "And you, Chuza, I didn't know you would be here."

"I have told them about your adventures at the palace, Thomas, how you have impressed the royal court with your medical talents. Herod is heard telling people you saved his life every chance he gets. Your fame must be spreading far and wide." Chuza looked at him with admiration.

"You don't know the latest," Thomas said and looked at the three. "Herod gave me a villa as a gift in appreciation for curing his illness. It lies between Capernaum and Tiberias. That way I can see clients in both directions." He smiled at Lucius. "It looks like I will be moving out, my old friend. I shall miss you and our talks and delicious dinners after work. I shall never forget how you took me in when I was homeless and in need of a job."

"I shall miss you as well, Thomas," Lucius said with a sad smile. "I remember the day you came into my office, telling me I need your help to run my medical practice. I thought you were arrogant and prideful at the time." He smiled. "That seems a long time ago and we have both changed since then."

"My life has definitely changed and it is still changing," Thomas answered. "What am I going to do in a big house all by myself?" He suddenly realized that he would be quite alone in a world that was not his own. This sounded like a dream. Or was it?

"I bring you greetings from Yeshua, Thomas," Joanna said. "He has missed seeing you. I have no idea how He manages to remember anybody He has seen only a few times when He deals with large crowds every day."

"Does He have a message for me, Joanna?" Thomas asked against his better judgment.

"As a matter of fact, He did tell me to share this with you." She frowned as she tried to remember. "Ah, here it is.

"For there is nothing that will not be disclosed, and nothing concealed that will not be known or brought out into the open. Therefore, consider carefully how you listen. Whoever has will be given more; whoever does not have, even what he thinks he has will be taken from him." Luke 6:17-

18

"Does that mean anything to you, Thomas?" Joanna asked.

"No, as usual it doesn't. The man speaks only in riddles and only once did I understand what He said." Thomas was getting upset. "You see, every time I talk about Him I get aggravated. Why can't He speak in a plain language I can understand?"

"I don't know, Thomas. If it doesn't mean anything to you now, it will in the future," Joanna said. "He acted very loving when He told me He missed you. I think He knows you are looking for answers to your life."

"I have my answer," he retorted with angry defiance. "I am successful, rich and getting richer by the day. And now I have a villa and all the comforts of home. What more do I need?"

"What about your soul, Thomas?" Joanna asked gently. "Is it right with your soul?"

"I have a wife who doesn't love me or need me. I live two thousand years in the past and nothing makes any sense. What could be more right with my soul?" He leaned over and looked at the three of them. "The only thing that is real for me right now is my riches and my comfortable life. The other is, I am doing what I love to do more than anything else, practice medicine. There is nothing else of value I need." He leaned back with a deep sigh. "I will be moving out tomorrow, Lucius. An official from the palace is coming to take me to my new villa." He smiled at the group. "We will have a banquet and I plan to invite all the new friends I've made since I've come here. Just give me time to move in and get settled."

There was a strained silence. Joanna looked at Thomas with a look of profound sadness. "Thomas, you have become a dear friend to all of us in such a short time. We will miss your enthusiasm for medicine and helping the poor the way you did. I ask the Lord God to reward you for your kindness toward them and grant you insight into the things that really matter - faith. Yeshua says He came into the world that we might be saved from our sins by believing in Him."

"You want me to believe that a simple carpenter can take away my sins?" He leaned forward with anger in his voice, "I have led a good life, saved countless people's lives by healing them with my medical knowledge and surgical talents. I have never stolen anything, killed anyone or committed any other criminal acts. What would Yeshua need to save me from, Joanna?" Thomas reached for his glass of wine on the table and took a long sip to calm his nerves. "And if what He says is true and God did send His Son to die for us, and this Yeshua is His Son, give me one good reason why that would be necessary. All God has to do is forgive mankind and have done with it. Instead, He sends this Yeshua and condemns Him to death. What kind of a ridiculously cruel thing is that? Can you or your Yeshua explain that to me, Joanna?"

"Why would God condemn Yeshua to death, Thomas? He is very much alive and in no danger. He is the Son of God; no one can kill Him." Joanna was getting upset now.

"I have news for all of you, He will be arrested, tried and they will hang Him on a cross in Jerusalem in about two years at Passover. I know, I am from the future and millions all over the world will still believe He is the Meshiah."

There was a stunned silence.

"This cannot be true, Thomas. It simply cannot. I know Yeshua is the Son of God, the Meshiah who was promised to my people so many years ago by the prophets. And while I cannot explain this to you right now, I know some day I will." She sounded adamant and looked at Thomas with a strange fire in her eyes. "I don't care what you say, it cannot be true. Our Meshiah will set us free and set up a government that will last for all eternity. And nothing and nobody will ever tell me otherwise, not even you, Thomas." She sounded angry. "You come here and tell us you are from the future. That is what is ridiculous. No one can do that. There must be something wrong with your mind or you wouldn't say such a thing."

"I am sorry, Joanna, I shouldn't have upset you like this. You are right, there is something wrong with my mind. Please pay no attention to what I said." He realized he had said too much in his anger.

"We are all sincerely fond of you, Thomas," Lucius said in a gentle tone, "and we know you do not lie. But at the same time what you say is so unbelievable that it could not possibly be true. Even if you believe what you are saying, we don't, yet we still care about you and will remain your friends. As a physician, you understand the mind can play tricks at times and that is what is happening to you. What you need is some rest in your new villa and you will see everything will be alright."

"I understand, Lucius. Please forgive me. I will not mention this ever again." He looked at the three with a pleading smile and realized he was now truly alone in this time and place.

As much as everyone tried to continue with a normal conversation, Chuza and Joanna soon decided it was time to retire.

The next day, a man named Jonas came under orders from Herod to take Thomas to his new villa. It was situated about half an hour away from Capernaum to the west, on a road along the Sea of Galilee toward the city of Tiberias. Thomas had instructed Marcellus to load his belongings on the carriage and follow them to his new home.

"The King has instructed me to hand over the proper papers of ownership of this estate to you as soon as we arrive," Jonas said. "I am one of the scribes of his court and handle the transfers of property for His Majesty.

"How big is the estate, Jonas?" Thomas was almost afraid to ask.

"I do not know the exact size, Sir since I have never been there. According to the papers ,you now own a large amount of land, a vineyard and many fields of grain and several orchards of figs and olive trees. Approximately one hundred slaves are also a part of the holdings. Some of them work in the house, but most are laborers in the fields. You have an overseer, a freedman named Issus. He is a Greek and has been a paid servant for many years. As I understand, he would be the one to give you better details of the condition and size of the estate."

"I see." Thomas was speechless. He, the one who was against slavery, now owned one hundred of them. *I guess it is all part of the deal.*

It was getting close to mid-day when the two carriages turned into a winding, long driveway, lined with huge sycamore trees, leading to an ornate gate. Two slaves opened it as they approached and bowed low. A large, impressive sandstone villa, built in Roman style, stood in the midst of a cluster of trees as they drove through. A group of about thirty people stood at the front door. A middle-aged man rushed up to the carriage and helped Thomas and Jonas down.

"I am Issus, the overseer, Master. I welcome you to your new home. We are all ready to serve you and await your orders," he said with a low bow. "These are your house slaves, worthless and lazy most of them, but with a firm hand, they will serve you well," he said with a wave of his hand toward a group of about thirty slaves. They in turn bowed low and kept their eyes downcast, afraid to be caught looking at their new owner.

"Thank you, Issus," Thomas said, "this is Jonas, a scribe at Herod's court. He is here to turn this place over to me. Please show us inside and have refreshments served so that we can finalize the legalities properly."

"Of course, Master, please follow me," Issus said and with a hard stare ordered the slaves back to work.

Thomas was impressed with his new home. The influence of Roman culture was everywhere with mosaics of gods and goddesses as well as scenes of lush gardens with exotic plant life on the walls and floors everywhere. The atrium was a large entrance hall with an opening in the roof to allow the sun to fill the room with bright light throughout the day. It illuminated the beautiful wall paintings with their intense, vivid colors in a way Thomas had not seen in pictures in museums of his time. Right underneath the opening was a pool to catch the rainwater with a large stone statue of some god at one end. Even the ceiling was laid out with colorful mosaic tiles in intricate designs. Leading off the atrium were several doors which apparently led to other rooms.

"This is the triclinium," Issus said and pointed to a room with three couches arranged around a low table. *That must be the dining room,* Thomas thought. Once again, the walls had mosaic tile designs that looked like tapestry. Three slave girls were setting the table with finely painted earthenware, filled with an assortment of grapes, figs, dates and the inevitable pomegranates. Several types of cheeses and meats were laid out on wooden platters. In front of two colorful plates stood two elegantly designed silver goblets filled with the wine mixture.

"I hope this will be satisfactory, Master," Issus said as Thomas and Jonas sat down. Issus made no move to join them and stood a little to the side by the door. Thomas assumed an overseer did not eat with the master at the same table.

"I will call you when we are done with the formalities, Issus. I will have you show me the rest of the house," he said.

"Very well, Master," Issus said and left.

After they had finished the meal, Jonas pushed the dishes aside and spread out his papers for Thomas to inspect and sign.

"This is a land grant from King Herod Antipas to you, Thomas. It is for life and can be passed on to your heirs in perpetuity," he said. "If you die without heirs, all this will return to the royal treasure. It includes the land, the house, the slaves and the profit from your land. Of course you will be expected to pay the yearly tax as required by the King. It is due once a year after the harvest in the fall and will be collected by a tax collector from either Capernaum or Tiberias. I am not sure which one." He smiled a rare smile. "I am also sure they will find you when the time comes. I hope you realize, that you are required to pay taxes not just to Herod, but to Rome as well. And if you are a Jew, you must pay the Temple tax. There is a lot less left over than you might think at the end of the year," he added with a sigh.

"That does not seem to change wherever you go," Thomas said.

It was not long after the formalities were over, Jonas rose. "It has been a delight to be of service, Sir, but I must get on my way. It is a long journey back to Sepphoris. I hope whatever gods you serve will look with favor on you and this house for as long as you live." He bowed and followed a slave back to his carriage.

Thomas sat back down on the couch, still stunned by what he now called his own. He found it hard to believe all this was his. At that moment a beautiful young woman walked into the room.

"My name is Lydia, Master. I am the one who sees that all your needs are met in the house. Please let me know how I may serve you."

He was stunned by her graceful, lithe figure, her long, black hair and flawless olive-toned skin. Her large brown eyes dominated her heart-shaped face, set off by full, red lips.

"What is it you do, Lydia?" was all he could manage to say.

"I serve your meals, keep your bedroom clean and see to it that you have everything you need. I am also responsible for the slaves who are assigned to you personally to make sure they behave and obey you at all times."

"Thank you, Lydia, I am sure you do a fine job at whatever you do. I will let you know if I need anything." He was embarrassed, because he caught himself staring at her.

"May I serve you in any way, Master?" It sounded like the voice of a child and came from the entrance off of the atrium. She was a beautiful little girl, no more than ten. "My name is Helena and I am one of your house slaves."

"Hello, Helena," Thomas said with a gentle smile. "And what is it you do in this house?"

"I am here to see that you have everything you need, Master."

"And what if I don't need anything, Helena?" he asked with a twinkle in his eyes.

"Then I just stand here until you do." She lowered her eyes, but not before a tiny smile crossed her face.

"Where are you from, Helena?"

"I was born in Rome into the household of one of the great senators." Thomas could hear she was proud of that fact.

"How old are you?"

"I do not know that, Master, because I do not know numbers.

"How did you come here to Galilee?"

"The last master bought me when I was old enough to be taken from my mother. He was a relative of King Herod and lived in this place. I don't know where he is now, but I heard the King got mad at him." Her hand flew to her mouth in fear as soon as the words were out. "Forgive me, Master."

Thomas laughed. "You are a bright girl, Helena. I like you and we are going to get along just fine. Let's just hope the King doesn't get mad at me, hey?"

"Oh no, Master, no one could ever get mad at you as nice as you are." Thomas was touched by her childlike sincerity.

A feeling of uneasiness came over him. This young girl was beautiful and intelligent and yet she was a slave. His slave! He cringed. This would take some getting used to.

"Helena, do you think you could show me around the house? I am sure you know all the rooms," Thomas said and got up. "You can even show me where you live."

"I don't think you want to go there, Master. It isn't near as nice there as your rooms." Her little face looked eager and bright with large blue eyes and long, blond hair. She was of slender build and looked at him with apprehension. "I will show you your study and the living room and the courtyard out back. That is my favorite." Her face was animated as she spoke.

She led him back to the atrium and from there to what looked like a living room with several couches and a low table. He was surprised how little furniture there was. Another door led to a bedroom with a wooden bed with a thin padding on it. It also had a couch. The room was of a good size and seemed to be the master bedroom. His bedroom! He turned to look for Helena. She stood in the door, trembling in fear he might ask her to come in.

"Helena, is this my bedroom?"

"Yes, Master," she whispered.

"I promise you, I will never ask you to come in here." He smiled at her and walked out of the room and heard her sigh with relief.

She took him to four more bedrooms leading off of the atrium. All were small and had only a bed in each. The area between the atrium and the courtyard looked like a study for the master of the house. It was more like a passageway to the second part of the house and allowed the owner to oversee the entire area on both sides.

"Do you want to see the courtyard, Master?" Helena asked.

"I want to see the kitchen first, Helena."

She turned toward a hallway and headed to a door way down at the end. He was appalled when he saw a dark room, lit by a tiny window with smoke penetrating the air from a fire in the cooking area. The walls were black with soot and the smell of spoiled fruit hung in the air.

"This is Esther, the cook, Master," Helena said and pointed to a young woman standing over a table, cutting meat. She jumped back in surprise, almost dropping the big knife.

"Forgive me, Master, I did not know you were coming, I would have cleaned up better." She bowed low and he could tell she was scared.

He smiled at her and then looked at another woman standing by the far end of the kitchen.

"That is Octavia, Master," Helena said. "She is in charge of all the house slaves."

"I am happy to serve you, Master." She was a woman in her late forties, with premature gray hair held back by a dirty scarf, and eyes that spoke of a hard, joyless life. She struck Thomas as a harsh task master.

"Have Issus bring some workmen and make two more windows in here so the smoke from the fire has a place to escape outside. After that, have them wash the walls and paint them white. I want it done right away."

"Yes, Master," Octavia said with a surprisingly strong voice. "If you don't mind me saying so, I don't think this will be necessary, because Esther is a worthless slave who doesn't deserve anything else."

Her tone irritated Thomas. He realized she was barely hiding her displeasure.

"I am sorry this does not meet with your approval, but I insist." He looked at her with a harsh glare. "I will not tolerate your insolence Octavia. Do I make myself very clear?"

"Yes, Master."

He noticed her disapproval before she walked out. He turned back to Esther. "In a few days I will want to talk to you about fixing some dishes I am used to from my home."

"I am here to serve you, Master," she said, wiping her greasy hands on a piece of cloth on the table. "Let me know how and I will try," she said before he left the kitchen. Helena led him back toward the main house. Before they went in, she motioned for him to turn to the left. As he walked through the door he stepped into the bright sunshine into a peaceful, lush green enclosure with several large trees and ornately carved benches under each. He looked at the long, low buildings on the opposite side of the courtyard.

"Over there is where I live," Helena said and pointed to them.

"At least you have a nice garden to sit in and enjoy this peaceful oasis," he said with a smile.

"We are not allowed to enter this garden, Master. It is for you only."

"How do you get to your place then, Helena?"

"There is a side door on the other side of the buildings which is for slaves only."

"I don't think I want to sit here all by myself every day, Helena. Maybe you can keep me company." He looked at her with an inviting smile and noticed a hint of fear in her eyes.

"I am here to serve you and if you want to talk to me while you rest, then that is what we will do." She tried to sound confident. "You are not like the other master. He never wanted to talk to any of us."

"Did he have a family?" Thomas asked.

"Oh yes, he had a wife and children."

"Did they treat you well?"

Her face clouded over and she seemed to withdraw within herself and whispered, "Yes, Master."

He stood before her and lifted her chin up to look at him.

"Helena, I will never mistreat you. You will be safe with me," he said and smiled at her.

"I am glad you came, Master. I will tell the others of your kindness." Her eyes filled with tears of relief and he could only guess at her cruel past filled with abuse.

Chapter 17

He woke up early the next morning. The sunlight made a square on his bed covers coming through the window high up on the wall. He rested on the surprisingly comfortable mattress for a long time. It was hard to believe this estate was his with a hundred people to go with it.

"What can I do for you, Master?" The voice belonged to a man in his fifties. He stood by the door, waiting.

"What is your name?"

"I am Abraham, Master. I was the personal attendant to the former owner of this house. I have come to ask if you wish me to continue to serve you or would you rather have someone else?"

"You will do fine, Abraham. I like a glass of lemon juice with honey first thing in the morning. Be so kind as to have that ready when I get to the table."

"Will you not need my help to get dressed, Master? I laid out the garments for you to wear last night. I hope they are to your liking." Abraham looked much older than he actually was. His thick, curly hair was completely grey and his face was lined with deep wrinkles. He looked Jewish to Thomas with his prominent nose and brown eyes.

"Are you from Galilee, Abraham?"

"I am, Master. I was born in Nain many seasons ago and have served in this house since I was a young man." Abraham stood, waiting to help Thomas with his clothes.

"How did you get to be a slave?"

"I had a wife and a child and owned a small parcel of land. Herod the Great was our king and he increased our taxes so much in order to build his palaces, I fell behind and had to borrow to make up the difference. When I could not pay the money back, my land and house were seized and I was sold into slavery to the owner of this house. He was a Roman and I was in his service for many years. When he died, the family could not pay for the upkeep and the King took it for unpaid taxes. He gave it to his relative, who also lived here with his family for a few seasons. When they left, the house was without an owner until you came."

"Does your family still live around here, Abraham?"

"No, Master. My wife took our little son and fled to Judea before I was sold. She made it to Jerusalem to her relative's house and served in their household. I got to see them once many seasons ago when the master went there for Passover. My son is grown now and has a family of his own. He, his wife and their four children, took his mother to live with him when she got too old to work."

When Thomas finished getting dressed, he left for the dining room.

Abraham followed right behind him and served his breakfast with great efficiency and care.

"Might there be anything else I can do for you today, Master?" he asked when Thomas was finished. "I hope you don't think I am being forward, but you don't have too many garments for a man in your important position. If you would allow me, I will order a tailor to come and measure you for new clothes befitting your station." Abraham stood, unsure of himself if he was in trouble for suggesting such a thing.

"Abraham, that sounds like a wonderful idea. I have no idea what I need and will leave it up to you to order whatever you think is appropriate. However, let's not get too fancy, shall we? I don't want to look foolish and show off my new wealth in a way that would look offensive."

"Leave it to me, Master, I will make it so you will be the best dressed master in Galilee, but still look like it is nothing for you to wear such expensive finery."

"Abraham, when was the last time you had a new garment?" Thomas asked.

"Never. The slaves don't get new clothes, Master. We wear whatever is thrown away by the master and his family."

"This is what I want you to do, Abraham. When the tailor comes, have him bring with him everyone in his workshop and plenty of cloth to choose from. I want him to measure every slave in this household for a new garment," Thomas said. "It is time the servants in this place are well dressed, well fed and in good health. Also inform Issus of this order and tell him I wish to speak with him this morning. After that is done, I want to examine every household slave to see if they are healthy. I am a physician and will not allow anyone to be sick if I can help it." *This is a good way to get to know everyone in this house. Also, if I have to have slaves, I might as well treat them right. I realize I'm doing this to relieve my guilt, but maybe this will make up for being a big slave owner.*

Abraham stood and looked at Thomas with a look of such joy and gratitude, it embarrassed him.

"Master, are you sure you want to do this for us? Such a generous thing has never been heard of in all the years I have been a slave here. May the God of Abraham, Isaac and Jacob bless you, my lord and give you back a hundredfold in return for your kindness. I will send a messenger to the tailor and let him know of your order right away. There will be rejoicing in this house for sure." Abraham's face was beaming.

"Good morning, Master." It was Helena.

"Well good morning, Angel. I was wondering where you have been," he said with a smile. "I need to see your bright face every day as soon as

I come to break my fast. That way all will be well for the rest of the day."

"Master, that is an easy task and I will never fail to be here as you ask." She bowed low before him. "I hope you slept well. May the gods favor you today."

"Helena, I don't believe in gods, so let's not mention them in this house. If there should by chance be a God, one is enough for me."

"You believe like the Jews then?"

"I am a Jew, Helena, but I don't believe in their God or their customs. I come from a far-away land where no one worships gods. We believe everything has a reason and a purpose; and life runs well without worrying about deities that don't exist."

"I have never heard anyone talk like that in all my life. How very strange, Master. But if that is what you say, then that is what we will do." Her look of childlike trust tugged at his heart and he wished he had a daughter just like this sweet young girl.

"Master, Issus is here to see you," Abraham announced. "May I show him in?"

"Please do." Thomas had laid awake for a long time last night, thinking what it might take to run a place like this. He didn't have a clue and would have to rely on Issus. He had seen some ledgers in the study and knew they would contain some facts and figures he needed to familiarize himself with the financial status of this estate.

"Good morning, Master. I hope you are refreshed and doing well." Issus stood by the door, waiting for Thomas to wave him in.

"Let's go to the study and go over the books, Issus," Thomas said. "This would be a good morning for you to tell me about the overall status of this estate."

"Very well, Sir," Issus said and followed him out.

It took all morning to go over the books. To his surprise, Thomas found out this was the time of the wheat harvest and the grapes would be ready in a week or so. The barley had already been brought in and Issus was waiting to take it to Capernaum and Tiberias to sell it. Since he had known there would be a new owner, he had waited till now to receive his orders from Thomas of what to do with it.

"You do what you have done for many years, Issus. I rely on your judgment and business sense. If you do well, there will be a nice bonus for you.

"Thank you, Master, I will not let you down." It was the first time Thomas saw the man smile. From glancing at the books, he realized if he never treated another patient, he would still be a rich man with the income from the land. *Good for you, Herod, you old sod. I hope all your ailments are that rewarding for me.*

The medical exam of the slaves produced a few things he saw needed to be done for some of the older ones. Overall, he was surprised how healthy everyone was. He did notice there was not one overweight person among them and most were a little too skinny. He would improve their food and see to it no one ever went hungry.

"Octavia, I want you to make sure every house slave takes a bath at least twice a week." He looked at her sullen, tired eyes.

"Yes, Master, although they don't get that dirty working inside the house," she said in a grumpy tone. "It will spoil them if they get to bathe more than once a month and then I can't get any work out of them."

"You let me decide what I think is right, Octavia," Thomas said in a sharp tone. "In addition, the cook and the kitchen staff must wash their hands before they prepare a meal. This is very important. It will keep disease away, do you understand? It is caused by tiny things you can't see that make us ill if we don't wash them away before we eat the food. If they get into our stomach, they can cause sickness and even death."

"No one has died in this house for a long time, without all this fuss." Octavia clearly did not want the additional work and had been around long enough to voice her opinion.

"If I find out that you don't follow my orders in this, I will find someone else to do your job, is that clear?" He looked at her with a hard stare. "Octavia, I will treat you well as long as you do as you are told, even if you don't understand or agree with my orders."

"Yes, Master, I am sorry." Her eyes betrayed her disapproval before she could lower them in submission.

He spent the next few days getting to know the way the household worked. Once that was done, he was ready to travel and treat the sick again. Playing the rich, lazy landowner was not his style.

Every day, messengers had come to call on him to visit the sick, but until now, he had told them he would not be available. Yet today, when one of the most prominent Pharisees in Capernaum asked him to join him at his house for dinner, he knew it was time to come out of hiding and go back to work. He presumed someone in the house was sick and needed his medical attention. He had never met Ezra, a powerful leader of the local synagogue, but had been told he was a vehement opponent of Yeshua. *At least he won't preach to me about the Meshiah,* Thomas thought.

"Abraham, I will need you to draw a bath after the mid-day meal and lay out my good clothes. I am invited to dine at the home of Ezra, a prominent Pharisee tonight."

"Master, that is wonderful. Maybe he can tell you something about the Rabbi Yeshua everyone is talking about." Abraham sounded excited. "I hear He is a great preacher and healer. Some even say He is the Meshiah."

"I have met the man, Abraham and I am not impressed, so let's not talk about Him anymore." Thomas sounded angry.

"Forgive me, Master, I am just an ignorant slave. I shall not mention Him again."

"See that you don't."

The mention of Yeshua had instantly put Thomas in a foul mood. He had not thought about Him in a long time and was glad of it. His life was good and he didn't need his good fortune spoiled by the Carpenter and His talk of the kingdom of God.

It was the first time the master had been short with Abraham and the old slave wondered what went wrong when he had met the Rabbi from Nazareth. But it was better not to bring the subject up again. He would have to tell Lydia about it so she might be careful not to mention anything about the Yeshua when she served the master at table. He had started talking to her as of late and asked her a lot of personal questions. Abraham knew the master saw that she was a beautiful young woman with her long, black hair and smoldering dark eyes. The new garments would look very becoming on her and Abraham wondered if she would end up being his mistress. After all, the man was alone and without female companionship. It would be only too natural for him to want her for his bed. Besides, she was his slave and he could do with her what he wanted.

Abraham knew Lydia was a follower of Yeshua, because she had met Him several times when she was sent to Capernaum with Issus to buy delicacies for the master's table. Octavia had put her in charge of going to the market place, since she was very good at getting the best food for the best price. As a matter of fact, she had witnessed Yeshua perform a miracle just the other day when he healed ten men of leprosy. Even Issus, who had taken the grain to market, had been there and confirmed what she told the rest of the slaves. Everyone had been excited, even the ones who did not know anything about the Meshiah, since they believed in pagan gods.

Marcellus, the young slave boy, who Thomas had bought when he still lived with Lucius, drove him to the Pharisee's house. Markus, a man of about twenty-five was with him to make sure they would return safely should it be dark on the way home. The two sat up front while Thomas sat in the enclosed carriage by himself. He was delighted to have been invited to dinner, because he missed the company of his friends Lucius and Joanna and her husband. He had thought about visiting Lucius, but had decided against it, because of his newly found zeal for Yeshua. Neither could he forget how they had looked at him when they thought his mind was not right when he told them Yeshua would die on the cross.

Anger rose in Thomas. What was it that caused him to feel humiliated every time he got near the Carpenter or talked to someone about Him? No matter how hard he tried, he knew this alternate reality had to do with Him, but he couldn't figure out what. The man got killed two thousand years ago, for heaven's sakes; what was so upsetting about that? And why would the thought of Yeshua bother him to such an extent?

They had reached the large house of Ezra and Marcellus helped Thomas down from the carriage.

"Wait in the courtyard for me. I might not be long."

"Yes, Master," Marcellus said.

A slave stood ready to lead Thomas into the house. To his surprise, there were many guests and he wondered why he had been invited if not to tend to a sick person.

"My dear Thomas, I have looked forward to meeting you. Imagine, a Jew who has managed to gain the favor of Herod Antipas. That is indeed rare." Ezra was a tall man, dressed in a royal blue *tallit* with elaborate, artistic embroidery on the four cornered garment and with the all-important tassels at the bottom. It was the customary clothing worn by a prominent religious leader and showed the wearer was a devout adherer of the Mosaic Law. Ezra's face had a hardness to it that took away from his handsome features. His eyes were a remarkable blue as he looked at Thomas with calculating coldness.

"I am very happy to meet you, Ezra," Thomas said and bowed. "I had no idea this was a large gathering for dinner. I assumed you summoned me to tend to a sick person."

"You are right on both counts, Thomas. This is a large dinner and we have a sick person. There is only one thing, I have invited the Rabbi Yeshua to attend to see if He will heal someone on the Shabbat. There are many Pharisees and experts of the Law here tonight, who want to see if He will break the commandment and disobey Yahweh by working on this day of rest."

Thomas was furious to be involved in this religious nonsense, but he knew he had no choice but to stay and watch silently. He spotted Yeshua sitting on a couch in the large living area. All eyes were on Him as he spoke in a low voice. Thomas couldn't hear what He was saying. He moved closer when Ezra left him to greet another guest. Yeshua looked at him with a strange, serious look and nodded. Thomas noticed He was not smiling this time, but neither did he have the feeling the Rabbi was upset with him.

That's when Thomas saw a man sitting in front of Yeshua. Thomas could tell with one look he had severe edema, probably from congestive heart failure. His breathing was labored from the fluid inside, restricting his lungs. The man didn't say a word to the Rabbi, but just looked at him with fear, as if pleading for his life, while desperately trying to catch his next breath. There was total silence in the room as everyone watched intently what the Carpenter was going to do.

Yeshua asked the Pharisees and experts in the law, "Is it lawful to heal on the Shabbat or not?" But they remained silent. So taking hold of the man, he healed him and sent him away.

Then he asked them, "If one of you has a son or an ox that falls into a well on the Shabbat day, will you not immediately pull him out?" And they had nothing to say. (Luke 14:2-6)

After what seemed a long, uncomfortable silence, Thomas was astounded that no one commented when the man walked out, completely healed. Instead, there was an angry murmur coming from the religious leaders. Yeshua sat quietly with his hands folded in his lap and looked at the people in the room with a smile.

Finally, Ezra asked his guests to sit at the table in the other room. Immediately there was a great rush as everyone tried to find the best seat, pushing and shoving. Finally, a servant showed Thomas to a seat way in the back. It just so happened, Yeshua was sitting across from him. Before long, the slaves brought out the food, but before they started to eat, Jeshua got up and told them a parable about grabbing the seat of honor when invited to a banquet. The further He got into the story, the more embarrassed everyone became. He concluded by saying, "For everyone who exalts himself will be humbled, and he who humbles himself will be exalted." (Luke 14:11) When He sat down, He looked straight at Thomas, and this time He smiled.

"Yeshua, I did not try to find the best seat, but waited until a slave showed me where to sit," Thomas said, feeling like an idiot.

"He who is not with me is against me, and he who does not gather with me, scatters." (Luke 11:23)

Thomas could barely hold his frustration and anger at the remark. *Yeshua knows I have rejected Him.* His mind was a jumble of emotions as he looked at Him and it somehow made him even angrier. Once again, he felt totally humiliated by this quiet spoken man, who had said nothing outwardly upsetting to him. Yeshua continued to teach about other things during the rest of the evening, but Thomas was too upset to listen and was glad when it was finally time to leave.

On the way home, Thomas sat inside the carriage, the usual turmoil and emotions filling his soul after meeting Yeshua. In spite of not thinking about Him for so long, he felt as confused as ever and wished he could talk to someone. But there was no one. He was essentially alone in that big house, filled with thirty people who were afraid of him, no matter how nice he treated them. *No wonder, he owned them!* He couldn't even handle his own life, least of all direct and control a hundred people.

He had already noticed how easy it was now to get angry and lose self-control and dismiss their feelings as unimportant. He wondered how it would affect him after a time, when everyone has to agree and do exactly what he says, without the possibility of expressing any other thoughts than what they thought he wanted to hear. He was surprised he had no idea what they really thought or how they lived. Did they get married, have children, a happy life and live like normal people? It suddenly came to him, he had no idea, because he had never asked them.

Embarrassed, he pushed the thoughts out of his mind and wondered instead what happened at that dinner tonight. As usual, he felt totally confused when he wondered about Yeshua healing a person with congestive heart failure. Other than a heart transplant, no one could cure that in Philadelphia either. Yet the man simply tells this desperately sick person to go home and he is healed! The idea that this might just be a dream occurred to him, until he dismissed it like he had done so many times before. If this was happening in Philadelphia in the year 2016, everybody would believe Yeshua was the Son of God. It couldn't be, because no one can do those things unless they are God and there is no God. And if this is real, why would God send His Son to die? That doesn't make any sense either, even in 2016.

He vaguely recalled Melissa's grandmother telling him about the resurrection of Yeshua. Well, if that is true, then he will definitely be around to see it. Maybe then he will understand. This reality in which he lived, had told him many things he never knew. Maybe it will explain that, too. If his calculations were right, it will be two years from now until Yeshua will be arrested and crucified. Let's see what his life will be like till then. The way things look now, it could not go better. He was a rich man and getting richer by the day. His fame as a physician was only superseded by Yeshua and that was ok. There is one thing different, all the right people like him and hate the Rabbi. We'll see who comes out ahead in the end.

Chapter 18

He woke up in a foul mood. His mind was still in turmoil and he did not want to face the people out there who were a part of his property. The very thought made him cringe and he wanted to yell at someone.

"I am glad you returned safely, Master," Abraham said as he walked in. "It was very late."

"I don't think you should concern yourself how late I get back, Abraham. I am not a child and don't need anyone to check up on me." He looked at the old man with a frown. "Just leave me alone, I don't want to talk to anyone today."

"Yes, Master." Abraham looked shocked and left without another word.

Well, that went great. Now he felt even worse. It wasn't his fault they were here and they were his slaves. *Why can't I just get home or wake up or something!*

Finally, he got up and dressed.

Helena stood in the door of the dining room, unsure whether to come in. Abraham had told her to stay away from the master since he was in a terrible state. "I think something awful happened to him last night and he is dreadfully upset and might yell at you."

"Good morning, Master. If I smile, will you feel better?" she asked with a thin little voice.

Thomas looked up from his food and saw her, small and scared, nervously twirling a strand of hair with one finger.

"Come, Angel and smile. It *will* make me feel much better." He held out his arms and she flew to him, sobbing.

"I don't want you to be mad at me, Master. It is my job to make you happy every morning and if you are mad, then I have failed you." She buried her head in his garment, still crying.

"Now, now, there is no need for that, child. I could never be mad at you, because you are my sunshine." He held a piece of bread with cheese up to her. "Come here, sit and eat with me, just the two of us." He turned to Lydia and said, "Bring a cup and a plate for Helena. She is going to eat with me this morning so I won't be sad anymore."

"I can't do that, you are my master and I am not allowed to eat with you at the same table," the girl said, looking at him with fear in her eyes.

"Who says?"

It took a second and then a broad smile lit up her face. "Nobody, because you say I can."

"Sit right here then and we'll pretend you are my daughter and I am your father. Then we can have breakfast together every morning, isn't that right, Lydia?"

"Yes, Master it is," Lydia said as she put the plate and a cup of juice in front of Helena.

"Would you like that, Angel?"

"You mean I could be your daughter and eat at the table with you every day?" She looked at him with astonishment. "I can't even imagine such a thing, Master."

"I can. And since I am the master, let's do it, what do you say? I always wanted to have a daughter just like you, and now I have one. Imagine that." He reached over and stroked her hair gently.

"Are we just pretending for one day or for tomorrow as well?" She sounded unsure of herself.

"We don't have to pretend at all. I just declare that from today on you are my daughter and you may sit at my table and eat with me every day."

She looked at him and then stared down at her plate. "You are just making fun of me, aren't you, Master, because you are angry today. It isn't real, is it?"

"Look at me, Helena," Thomas said gently. "I am not making fun of you, I promise. Do you remember the day I came and told you I would never hurt you?"

"Yes Master, I remember and you never have."

"So why would I start now? I have no family, no one to love and no one who loves me," he said with great sadness in his voice. "You are the only one I feel I can truly love with all my heart."

"It sure would be nice to have a father, Master. Someone like you who is good and kind and never hurts me."

"Just like I promised you that day and I have kept my promise, so I want to tell you today that I give you the freedom to live in this house as if you were my child."

"What does that mean, Master?" She asked, her large eyes nearly filling her little face.

"For one it means you do not call me master anymore."

Her hand flew to her mouth. "What would I call you then?"

"How about Thomas?"

"Oh no, I couldn't do that, I will get flogged by Octavia the first time she hears me."

"What would you like to call me, Angel?" For some reason he couldn't wait to hear her answer.

"I don't know, Master, no one has ever loved me."

"You can take your time." He turned to Lydia. "Get me Octavia right now, I wish to speak with her."

"Yes, Master."

Helena looked frightened when the woman walked in. Octavia was horrified when she saw Helena sitting at the table with Thomas.

"How dare you sit there, get up at once," she screamed at the girl. "I will have her flogged immediately Master, so that this never happens again." She made a move to pull the girl away from the table.

"Hold it Octavia, I have given Helena permission to sit here with me any time she wants to without punishment of any kind."

"You have no idea how to handle slaves, Master. They must be kept in line and taught to know their place. Let me handle this and you won't have any trouble with her in the future." She stepped closer to Helena, ready to grab her by the arm and pull her away.

"Octavia!" Thomas shouted in a loud voice. All the anger from last night and this morning was released in that one shout. "You will never touch this child, do you hear me? She is like a daughter to me and will be treated as such by everyone in this house. One more outburst like you showed today and I will sell you to the next slave trader, do you understand me?" He was shaking with such anger as he had never known. "You are the one who does not know her place and I will not tolerate your insolence and rebellion toward me any longer. I will run this house the way I see fit and treat the people here with the dignity they deserve. If you don't like it, then it's time you leave."

"I am sorry, Master, I had no idea. Please, I don't want to be sold. I have been here for so many years, this is my home. Please, Master, please don't sell me. I will change, I promise." Octavia was screaming as she knelt before Thomas, tears streaming down her face. "I am sorry. Please don't sell me."

Thomas was horrified at seeing her on the floor before him. He had become the very thing he never wanted to be, a slave master threatening his slave with being sold just because he was angry.

He took a deep breath. "Octavia, get up at once. Of course I will not sell you, I was angry. Please forgive me." He reached down and pulled her up. "It is alright, we are all a little on edge today." He looked at the woman with a stern look. "You must understand that I am different from most masters you have ever known. I do not enjoy owning slaves, because I think slavery is wrong. But since I have them, I have to make the best of it." He looked at Octavia, his calm had returned.

"I still need your help to run this house and I do not wish to interfere in how you do that on a day to day basis. But when I ask you to do certain things, I expect to be obeyed. And in my treatment of Helena, you will do what I say. She is no longer my slave, but my daughter. In time I will make it legal. You will treat her with kindness and respect and most of all, she is no longer under your supervision. Do I make myself very clear? I love her like she was my own and I want her to be treated as such. Make sure you inform the other slaves of her new status. She will have one of the bedrooms in this house for her own. She can choose which one and you will see to it that it is furnished nicely and with everything she wants. You will also let her choose a young slave girl for a companion and a servant for her with a room next to hers."

Helena sat at the table and listened in awe and wonder, while Octavia vacillated between relief of not being sold and astonishment about the new status of Helena.

"Yes, Master, I will do as you say." She straightened up her garment and wiped the tears off her face. "This has never happened before; please forgive me for not understanding. I will change my ways and try to understand yours. You are so very different." Her face had a sudden soft touch to it Thomas had never seen. "I have never had a kind master like you in all my life," she said with wonder in her voice.

"There is one more thing, Octavia, I never, and I mean never, want you to flog another slave in this house. You can punish bad behavior by other means, but I will not allow physical abuse. That includes withholding food or water."

"Yes, Master, I understand."

He looked at Helena. "Is there a girl your age that you would like to have stay with you in the house?"

"Oh yes, Master. Her name is Sarai and we are best friends. She works in the kitchen."

"Do you know this Sarai, Octavia?"

"Yes, Master, she is the same age as Helena and has been with us all her life. She was born to one of the slaves named Miriam. The old master sold her to a caravan slave trader some seasons ago."

"Who is her father?"

"I don't know, Miriam never said."

"Was it the master, Octavia?"

"I think so. The mistress got mad at Miriam and demanded he get rid of her." She sounded scared. "I am not trying to be critical, Master, but you asked me," she hastened to add.

"One more thing, is there a slave who can read and write in this house?"

"Yes, Master. His name is Olyssus and he is a Greek. From what he tells, he used to be the teacher of the son of a Roman centurion and was brought here to introduce him to the Greek and Latin language, until the boy grew up. He was then sold to the Roman master of this house a long time ago. Olyssus now helps Issus with keeping the books."

"Have him come talk to me, Octavia," Thomas said. "You can go now."

He turned to Helena with a big smile. "I have a thought about what name you can call me. In my country, when you love your father very much you call him Daddy. I would love it if you would call me by that name."

"Daddy?" She said the word with awe in her voice and then repeated it several times. "Daddy, Daddy. That sounds good to me, ma...Daddy." She jumped up and flung her skinny little arms around Thomas' neck and whispered, "Thank you, Daddy."

"Why don't you choose which one of the bedrooms you would like for your own? Choose one for you and one for Sarai and then let Octavia know to prepare them for you the way you like it. I have work to do now. Make sure you come and eat with me at mid-day."

"Yes, Daddy," she said and savored the name as if it was a delicacy in her mouth.

Thomas spent the afternoon talking to Olyssus about becoming Helena's teacher. The man was not near as old as Thomas had thought from what Octavia had told him. In his fifties, with gray hair and intelligent blue eyes in a studious face, Thomas was not sure he could still see to read since there were no glasses available. His hands were long and slender and free of calluses or other signs of hard labor.

"I want her to learn to read, write, math and speak Greek and Latin, Olyssus. And include the girl named Sarai as well in your lessons. At the same time instruct Helena to act like a young lady of means, so she will know how to conduct herself in society. Make sure she understands she is no longer a slave."

"Yes, Master, I will be happy to be a teacher again and will do my best." He bowed low and Thomas could tell he was excited. "How may I address the young lady now that she is the daughter of the house?" he asked.

"Miss Helena will be fine, Olyssus," Thomas said. "It will help her get used to her new status. "When you return, have Sarai come to see me," he added.

"Yes, Master."

A few minutes later, a little dark-haired girl came into the study, trembling with fear and glued to the doorway.

"Come in, Sarai, I won't hurt you," Thomas said with a smile. She was even smaller than Helena, her Idumean heritage quite evident. *That actually makes this little girl a distant relative of Herod Antipas,* he thought. Her brown eyes and somewhat dark skin were a definite give-away that the former master of the house was the father.

"Has Helena told you that you are to live in this house and be her servant, Sarai?" Thomas asked.

"Yes, Master, but I didn't believe her." She was still trembling. "I am sorry I didn't and now I am in trouble."

"Come here, Sarai." He waved her closer. "You are not in trouble and this is the best thing that has ever happened to you. You will be her servant and friend at the same time and will live in a room of your own right next to Helena's. You will even get to wear pretty clothes and learn to act like a lady, won't that be wonderful?"

"Oh." She stared at him in awe. "I cannot imagine something like that could ever happen to me in my whole life." Her little face, half covered by her thick, curly hair, had lit up as if a light had gone on inside. "This is really true, Master?"

"Yes, Sarai, it is. Now go and find Helena and the two of you select your rooms and bring your things over here from the slave quarters. Have one of the servants help you if you need it." He stopped her before she left. "You may walk through the courtyard from now on, Sarai. It is much closer."

"Thank you, Master," she said and ran from the room, her shabby little garment flying in tow.

As the days passed, Thomas felt like he had a family with Helena and Sarai sharing his meals and his life. For the first time he truly wished Melissa could be here with him. He was sure they could be happy together now. To cover up his longing for her, he dove full time into his medical practice and was on the road most every day to see the sick in Tiberias, Capernaum and the surrounding villages of Galilee. Although he did not do much surgery, he still enjoyed practicing medicine. As time went on, he became richer and more in demand with the many well-to-do clients, since his superior knowledge of medicine gave him an advantage over other doctors. To his astonishment, he had found out, that most healers were religious men, woefully ignorant and superstitious in the treatment of their patients. Given that fact, he definitely felt superior to all of them.

The deeper insight he got how the rich lived, the more cynical he became about their lives and decadent behavior with its dire consequences. He found syphilis and STD rampant, yet could do nothing to cure any of them without the aid of antibiotics. All he could do was warn them about having sexual relations indiscriminately. Gout and liver cirrhosis from the large amount of daily alcoholic consumption, as well as strokes and heart attacks were quite common due to the rich diet of delicacies clogging their arteries. In vain he tried to tell them to cut back and eat more fruits and vegetables, since these were considered foods for the common people. It astounded him how few vegetables were grown in Israel.

By talking to the many wealthy Romans, Greeks and rich merchants from the known world, he began to see what a totally separate life the rich lived from the poor. He was horrified at how the Galilean peasants suffered from the high taxes Herod Antipas demanded for his many building projects. Add to that the Romans with their tax to Caesar, plus the religious Temple tax, and none of the lower class could ever hope to achieve anything other than bare survival. Hunger, malnutrition and constant debt payments made their life miserable and steeped in abject poverty. This made for the perfect breeding ground of unrest, riots and hatred towards the rich, the king, the Romans; and even furthered feuds between Galileans and Samaritans. Many young sons and daughters were sold into slavery or indentured service as families struggled to survive on even the most minimal level.

Thomas was sure many slaves in his service started out that way. Since he couldn't help all of them, he decided to ignore their plight and concentrate on his own happiness instead. He learned, in order to overcome his guilt, he stopped letting the plight of his people get to him after a while by allowing Issus and Octavia to run the estate and forbidding them to mention anything of a personal nature to him. In so many words, in the midst of untold misery, back-breaking work and untreated sickness and disease, especially with his field slaves, he lived a life of comfort and opulence, without allowing their hardships to touch him in a personal way. Deep down, however, in the waking hours of the morning, he was overcome at times by the thought that he had become exactly like the slave owners in the South he had judged so harshly. But just like them, his were only fleeting thoughts, outweighed by reasoning in favor of necessity, economic considerations and personal comfort. In a relatively short time he had become a rich landowner and prominent physician to the wealthy in this remarkable, mysterious new reality.

Chapter 19

One morning, a messenger came with news Lucius and Joanna were on their way for a visit. Thomas didn't know whether to rejoice or be annoyed. It had been many months since he had even thought about them or Yeshua. Instantly, he felt tension rising inside and vowed he would not allow any conversation touching on religion. On the other hand, there was so much he wanted to share with them about his life and Helena. She had become his daughter by legal adoption not too long ago and was given the name Helena of Philadelphia.

He had no idea how long his friends planned to stay and had Octavia prepare the house for all eventualities. Thomas was nervous about the visit. He loved both Lucius and Joanna, but when they dismissed his story about coming from the future and declared his mind unfit, he felt cut off from them on so many levels. He would never forget the feeling of loneliness which came with the realization, he could never confide in anyone about this again, and that included these two, his closest friends.

It was mid-morning when his guests arrived in Joanna's carriage. Thomas sent Marcellus out to show them into the house and met them at the door.

"How wonderful to see you," he said and hugged them both. "Welcome into my home. It has been too long."

"You look well Thomas," Lucius said as he looked around the atrium, impressed. "I must say you really made out well for someone whom I hired to clean instruments almost two years ago."

"It is good to finally see you again, Thomas," Joanna said. "I have missed you so much. Chuza says he sees you at Herod's parties sometimes or when you look after the health of the king and his court. I always ask him to share with me how you are doing, but he never seems to know anything. You must tell us about your good fortune and your new life." She sounded genuinely glad to see him. Lucius on the other hand seemed more reserved than Thomas remembered him.

"Come in and allow me to serve you some refreshments. It is quite a journey out here." He pointed to the cushions around the dining table and asked them to sit and then turned to Lydia. "Have Helena come in and join us, I want her to meet my friends."

"Yes, Master," she said and left.

"This is my newly adopted daughter Helena of Philadelphia," he said as the girl entered the room. "Helena, these are my dearest friends Lucius and Lady Joanna."

The girl looked at them with a shy smile. "I am glad to meet you."

She bowed to them. *Abraham has taught her well.*

"You are a very beautiful child," Joanna exclaimed. "Look at her, Lucius, she is gorgeous." She turned to Thomas, "You have done a good thing to adopt this girl. I know she will bring you a lot of joy, "she said as she reached out to Helena. "Come here, child, let me look at you." She took her hand and held it. "Your father is a good man; may the Lord God bless him richly for his kindness toward you."

"We are not allowed to talk about God, dear lady. Daddy says there is no God." Helena looked at Joanna without reproach. "But Lydia says there is a God and His name is Yeshua."

"And who is Lydia, Helena?" Joanna asked.

"She is a slave in this house and serves the food at mealtime."

There followed an uncomfortable silence.

"Tell us how you are doing, Thomas? I am so sorry I have not heard from you in such a long time." Lucius tried to bring the conversation around to a more acceptable subject.

"I have been extremely busy moving into this house and learning how to be a landowner," Thomas answered. "You know how I feel about slavery; and here I end up with almost a hundred of them." He looked at Helena with a warm smile. "This little girl marched right into my heart on the first day, when she decided it was her job to make me happy. She has wrapped me around her little finger since then. I always wanted a little girl and here she is." He hugged Helena with great affection. "She is the sunshine of my life, aren't you, Angel?"

"Yes Daddy."

"What does she call you, Thomas? I don't think I have ever heard that word," Joanna said.

"It is an affectionate term for a good father in my country," he said.

"It sounds lovely, Helena."

"Thank you, my Lady," she said. "Daddy says it is only for fathers who are kind and wonderful and never hurt me." She turned to Thomas. "May I be excused, Daddy? Sarai and I are playing a game and I would like to get back and finish it."

"That is fine, run along."

"It sounds to me like she really loves you, Thomas. I am glad. Everyone needs to be loved by someone", Lucius said as he followed her with his eyes. "It makes me almost sorry I don't have children."

There was an uncomfortable lull in the conversation. Thomas felt Yeshua was standing in the room between them like a shadow and felt stress building up inside.

"I am still traveling with Yeshua, Thomas," Joanna finally said. "I told Him I was going to visit you and He sends His love."

"Thank you Joanna, I am sure He has better things to do than bother with me." There was a hint of sarcasm in his voice. "I have not heard or seen Him for a long time and the people I associate with these days have dismissed Him as a fraud and I tend to agree with them."

"He may be many things, Thomas, but He is no fraud," Lucius said. "How can you say that when the blind see, the lame walk and those with demons are set free? I am a physician and know illness when I see it. I have seen Him heal so many people, there is no way He can fake them all. Even if you don't want to believe He is the Meshiah, why can't you at least agree that He is a very unusual man?"

"I do not deny His miracle power, Lucius. I just don't believe He is the Son of God or that the only way I can get to heaven is if I believe in Him." He looked at Lucius and Joanna with his jaw set. "If you wish to stay in my home I must ask you to honor my request not to talk about Yeshua. I am sorry I have to say this, but let's face it, this carpenter's son has destroyed my friendship with you, Lucius. I am sick of hearing about Him or talking about Him and would prefer not to ever think about Him again. If we can do that, then you are welcome to stay in my home for as long as you like. I miss both of you and don't really have any other friends but you." He had spoken with quiet authority and both Lucius and Joanna realized he meant it.

"Yeshua is my life, Thomas," Joanna said. "I have nothing else I would rather do than follow Him wherever that leads me. My heart would be empty if I can't talk about Him and share with others about His message of hope and the coming of the kingdom of God." Her voice shook with emotion. "As to your assertion that He has destroyed our friendship, it is you who is essentially doing that with your closed mind and refusal to tolerate our belief. Lucius and I have come to reach out to you and see if we can agree to disagree and still discuss subjects where we are on opposite sides." She looked at him with such love, Thomas had a hard time standing his ground.

"I agree with you, Joanna, but I still wish we could talk about other subjects during your stay."

"And I wish you could explain to us why it is so difficult for you to talk about or believe in a man who has done nothing but good by healing and teaching people about God's love," Lucius said. "How is it that *you* can heal people and expect to be respected for it, but it upsets you when Yeshua does it? And why would you hate someone who reaches out to the poor and tells them God loves them so much that He sent His only Son to set them free?" Lucius sat back and took another sip of wine mixture.

"I wish I could explain my real situation to you both," Thomas said, "but since you think I am demented when I try to tell you the truth, there is not much I can say on the subject." Thomas was calm as he spoke. "I am not a man given to emotionalism or fantasies. I am a scientist." He looked at Lucius. "And I have proven that to you, have I not?"

"Yes, you have, Thomas," Lucius answered. "Your medical knowledge is far beyond anything I have ever heard of or even imagined."

"Then where do you think it comes from?" Thomas asked. "I had to learn it from someone or somewhere in a place so advanced, it makes it impossible it could be from this time." He leaned forward and looked at the two with a hard stare. "I am from the future, from the year 2016 and I have no idea how I got here or what I am doing in this time. That is why I feel I am living a dream and none of this is real. And if it isn't real, then why would I believe anything your Yeshua says or does, Joanna?"

"I know why you are here, Thomas," she answered without hesitation. "You were sent here to accept the Yeshua as your Meshiah."

He stared at her for a long time as her words hung in the air like a tangible presence and finally said in a low voice, "Why would He bother, I am an atheist without any desire to believe in any god of any kind."

"Could it be, there is someone in your life who has been praying for you?" Joanna looked at him with a gentle smile.

"My wife Melissa believes in Yeshua, but she hates me. I have done some awful things to her and I am convinced she would never do that, because she wants to divorce me." He stared down at his hands. "As you can see, I am not a very good man, so why would your Yeshua want me? I am sure He picks good people like you who follow Him and do what He says."

"Let me tell you what He told us not too long ago," Joanna said.

"I did not come to call the righteous, but sinners to repentance." (Luke 5:32)

"Well, at least I qualify in that area," Thomas said with a chuckle.

"We find ourselves in a peculiar situation," Lucius said as he looked around. "All of us believe in a fantastic story we insist is true. One, God has sent His Son to earth, and the other Thomas came to visit us from two thousand years in the future. Both stories have enough truth in them we can't deny them outright, but not enough proof to substantiate them as proven, scientific facts. This is indeed a dilemma, but it should not prevent us from accepting each other's beliefs without getting upset. There is a saying in Greece when you can't change or explain something "It is what it is.""

"You are not going to believe this, Lucius, that is a buzzword in my country as well at the moment."

The atmosphere had suddenly changed. A feeling of friendship and warmth filled the room and they realized their relationship had been restored.

"What do you say we go and sit in the courtyard and enjoy the beautiful scenery?" Thomas said. "I will have Lydia serve us the mid-day meal out there under the large sycamore trees."

"That sounds wonderful, Thomas," Joanna said and got up. "I can't wait to see your beautiful home anyway. I still can't believe Herod gave it to you."

"The old fox is so happy I cured him, he would have given me his kingdom if I had asked for it."

"How is he doing, Thomas?" she asked.

"As long as he takes his fruit drink twice a day, the illness he had will not return."

"So there is no secret medicine in it like everyone says?" Lucius asked.

"No, of course not, it is a simple case of vitamin C deficiency, one of those chemicals I told you about. It is found in sufficient amounts in lemons and other fruits and vegetables we normally eat. But because the man eats only meat and drinks large amounts of alcohol, it results in a life threatening illness, easily fixed by making him drink two fruit drinks a day." Thomas waved his hand in a circular motion. "And look what those two drinks have given me." He laughed. "Herod actually thinks fruits and vegetables are for poor people, while meat is for the rich. Guess who has the last laugh with this prideful reasoning? The man will probably die from his liver being destroyed by the alcohol and when that happens, only Yeshua can help him."

'Your medical knowledge is truly amazing, Thomas," Lucius said with admiration in his voice. "I miss our daily talks when you taught me some of what you know."

Over the next two days, they freely shared their unlikely stories with each other, one about the kingdom of God and the other about the distant future. It was on the second day Joanna asked a question that had been on her mind ever since Thomas had mentioned the subject many months ago.

"Thomas, you said that Yeshua will be convicted and die on the cross in Jerusalem. I have never forgotten it and wonder if you can explain it further." She shifted in her seat. "The reason I bring this up, because the Rabbi has made several mentions that He came to die for our sins. No one wants to believe Him, but since you told us, explain what you meant by your remark."

"I am not too familiar with the belief of the Christians, as they are called in my time. They have two festivals that are celebrated world-wide. One is His birth with the story of Yeshua being born in Bethlehem in a stable, which has already happened, as you know. The other is called Easter and it deals with the death of Yeshua on the cross at the hand of the religious leaders and the Romans. Pontius Pilate is the one who will give the go-ahead to have Him crucified. Other than that, I don't know much. My wife's grandmother tried to tell me that I have to accept Yeshua into my life and get saved, as she put it. She spoke of His crucifixion for our sins and all that." He looked at Joanna as he went on. "Here is where it gets interesting. She also said He would be resurrected from the dead, which I found highly unlikely at the time and still do, by the way."

Joanna and Lucius hung onto his every word and sat in silence for a long time after he was finished.

"I remember Jeshua saying things I didn't understand at the time, Thomas. Hearing this, however, it is beginning to make sense," Joanna said into the silence. "This is what the Master told us last week,

"The reason my Father loves me is that I lay down my life – only to take it up again. No one takes it from me, but I lay it down of my own accord. I have authority to lay it down and authority to take it up again. This command I received from my Father." (John 10:17-18)

"Do you also understand why He has to die?" Lucius asked.

"No, I don't. But I have an idea. I can ask my husband if we could go to the next Passover and visit with Cassius and Claudia. Once there, we would be able to ask Nicodemus to give us an idea what the Torah has to say on that subject," Joanna said. "It would be extremely interesting to find out what the prophets have written so long ago. We can all go together, wouldn't that be wonderful?"

"It sure would, especially since Thomas has a fancy carriage and speedy horses instead of my little cart and Igor," Lucius laughed. "You will admit, old friend, it was quite a trip. I will never forget how you beat up those three guys on the road."

"Yeah, and look what it got me in the end, a month in prison," Thomas said with a broad smile.

"The meal is served, Master," Lydia said. "I have arranged seating and a table under the tree over there." She pointed to the opposite side. "Miss Helena asks permission to take her meal in her room, since she is engaged in a game with Sarai, Master."

"That is fine, Lydia. We are ready."

It was a feast consisting of an abundance of fruit, cheese and lamb with wheat bread dipped in mint sauce.

"That is one good looking woman, Thomas," Lucius said between bites after Lydia had gone into the house. I am surprised you had not noticed."

"I am married," Thomas said with regret in his voice. "Trust me, I have noticed many times. I have had one affair already and lost the love and respect of my wife, I don't want to do it again."

"Theoretically speaking, your wife has been dead for two thousand years, old boy." Lucius chuckled. "What is there to stop you?"

"Nothing if this life is real, everything if it isn't," Thomas answered.

"Gentlemen, this is no conversation with a lady present," Joanna interrupted. "But I must say, she is very beautiful and I couldn't blame you if you were tempted. I have seen her at some of the meetings with Yeshua. I am sure she is a follower."

"Helena says Lydia told her she was," Thomas said. "Since I have forbidden anyone to speak of Him in this house, she has not said a word about Him to me."

"I think you should ask her, Thomas," Lydia said. "She might tell you things I don't remember or haven't heard Him say."

"I try not to talk to her too much for fear of getting involved with her in any more than the barest necessities," Thomas said. "Like my old servant Abraham says, she is my slave and I can do with her what I want. My problem is, I have everything I have always wanted, and yet somehow there is still something missing I have no idea what it is. Strangely, I do not miss my wife Melissa all that much. How can I be lonely with all this?" He made a sweeping gesture around the courtyard.

"There is nothing easy about life, even in beautiful surroundings like these, Thomas. That is why the Master told us, "Do not store up for yourselves treasures on earth, where moth and rust destroy, and where thieves break in and steal. But store up for yourselves treasures in heaven, where moth and rust do not destroy, and where thieves do break in and steal. For where your treasure is, there your heart will be also." (Matthew 6:19-21)

"And another time He said, "But seek first his kingdom and his righteousness, and all these things will be given to you as well." (Matthew 6:33)

"This man has an astounding wisdom that is beyond anything I have ever heard in my travels," Lucius said. "And He uses such simple words, even a child can understand most of the time," he added.

"Then I must be an idiot, Lucius, because I never have a clue what He is saying when He talks to me." Thomas said with a touch of the old anger in his voice.

The two days went by fast and Thomas was sad to see his friends leave and felt relieved their relationship had been restored. He would make sure to visit with them more often from now on. His heart was a little heavy when he watched their carriage disappear in the distance, until he saw Helena run up to him, her blond hair flying in the wind. "I won Daddy, I won!"
"That is great, Angel."

Chapter 20

Lydia was standing in the door the next day when he walked in.

"Make sure the girls get something to eat, Lydia," Thomas said as he walked by her.

"Yes, Master."

Darn it, she is beautiful, he thought as he went to the courtyard and sat down under the big tree, thinking how well the visit went. It was a great feeling to have his friends back.

"Master, I need to speak with you." It was Lydia.

"What is it?" He tried to sound distant.

"I would like to go into Capernaum tomorrow." She stood with her head down, waiting for his answer.

"Why?"

"I am not allowed to mention the person I wish to see, Master."

"Is it the Rabbi Yeshua?" he asked.

"Yes it is, Master."

"Why do you need to see Him, Lydia?"

"There is an old woman named Esther in the slave quarters. She is bent over and cannot straighten up. She is getting worse every day. Octavia says she must be sold or turned out of the house, since she can no longer work." Lydia was clearly uncomfortable. "I know it is forbidden to talk about the Rabbi, but I thought if I take her to Him, He will heal her." She did not dare look up as she stood waiting for his answer.

"Bring her to me, Lydia, I will take a look at her," Thomas said.

"Yes, Master."

"Wait a minute before you go. Why did I not see her when I examined everyone?"

"Esther begged not to see you for fear you might sell her."

A few minutes later, a petit woman, bent over from the waist, was led into the courtyard by Lydia.

"This is Esther, Master," Lydia said.

Thomas saw immediately that the poor woman suffered from some kind of curvature of the spine. He could not tell exactly what, but guessed it could be caused by either severe arthritis or scoliosis.

"Are you in a lot of pain, Esther?" he asked.

"Yes, Master. It hurts all the time now," she said, looking up at him with the most pitiful expression. "Octavia says, since I can't work anymore, I have to be sold." She pointed at herself with a helpless gesture. "Who is going to buy me, I am worthless and only good enough to be put down and have done with it."

"Esther, I am not going to sell you and we are not going to allow you to die," Thomas said with a smile. "I know what your illness is, but there is nothing I can do for you." *It looks like Ankylosing spondylitis.* "This is when the bones in your back are fused together. I am sure you have had this for a long time and it is very painful, isn't it?"

"Yes, Master, it is." She stood before him, with her body bent over in such an angle, she couldn't even look at him. He figured she had walked around, staring at the floor, for the last ten to fifteen years.

"I have to go to Capernaum tomorrow. I will take you and Lydia with me and let her ask the Rabbi Yeshua to heal you." He looked at Lydia with a smile. "I have a feeling you know Him well, don't you, Lydia?"

"Yes, Master, I do. I am sorry, I know I have disobeyed you, please forgive me."

"Please don't be sorry, let's see if Yeshua will do what I can't. I will leave in the mid-morning hour. Make sure you are both ready to accompany me. Tell Marcellus to make room for you and Esther inside the carriage. It is more comfortable for Esther that way."

It was a clear, sunny day when they got on the way. It had taken Marcellus and Lydia a good bit of time to get Esther into the carriage. She cried out in pain as Marcellus finally lifted her onto the seat, because she was unable to climb in. Thomas sat up front with Marcellus so the two women could have enough room inside. He had never sat up there and actually enjoyed the view. When Marcellus flicked the reins for the horses to speed up, Thomas stopped him.

"We have to go slow, because the pain would be too much for Esther if it gets bumpy," he told him. "Try to avoid any holes and uneven spots in the road, Marcellus."

"It will take a long time to reach Capernaum that way, Master," the young man said with a frown. "You will be late for your appointment."

"I will be fine, Marcellus. You see, if the patient I am supposed to treat is really sick, he won't mind waiting, as long as I make him feel better once I get there, isn't that right?"

"Yes, Master. Where are we going when we get to Capernaum?"

"I think Lydia said the Rabbi was preaching in the synagogue since it is the Shabbat," Thomas said. "You can drop the two women off there and then drive me on to the house of the honorable Gaius Maximus on the other side of town."

"Yes, Master."

There was a large crowd in front of the synagogue when they

arrived. When Lydia and Marcellus helped Esther out of the carriage, a Pharisee walked up to them, gesticulating wildly with his hands.

"You can't bring her in today, it is the Shabbat and it is unlawful even for the Rabbi to heal on this day of rest. Take her and bring her back tomorrow." He was shouting to make sure everyone heard him.

"She is going in, Sir and there is nothing you can do to stop her." Thomas had gotten down from the carriage and stood in front of the man. "Can't you tell she is in a lot of pain? I would suggest you let the Rabbi decide whether He wants to heal her or not."

"And who are you that you would dare speak to me in that way? Don't you know I am a leader in this synagogue and have not only the authority, but the duty to see that the Law of Moses is obeyed in all things?" He stared at Thomas defiantly.

"And I am Thomas of Philadelphia, the personal physician of King Herod and I dare you to stop me from accompanying this woman into the synagogue." He raised himself up to his full height as he spoke with an equally loud voice.

The Pharisee, hearing who Thomas was, looked around for support from the crowd, but found none. The people had parted to let Esther and Lydia pass into the women's section of the synagogue. Thomas followed, choosing a seat up front to make sure the Pharisee would not throw Esther out if he left. Also, he had decided he wanted to watch closely what Yeshua would do.

It was not long until a murmur filled the synagogue. The Rabbi had arrived. He sat down in the front and waited for the service to begin with the *Shema.* After that, several men took turns to expound on verses from the Torah, but Thomas knew everyone was waiting for Yeshua to go up front and teach. It was quite a while until He finally took His place at the lectern. He looked at Thomas with His usual smile as he nodded to him. In spite of himself, Thomas felt his heart beating faster when he saw those eyes directed at him with an intensity that was unsettling.

Yeshua did not say anything, but looked up to the women's section, until he spotted Esther. When He saw her, he called her forward and said to her," Woman, you are set free from your infirmity." Then He put His hands on her, and immediately she straightened up and praised God." (Luke 13:12-13)

Thomas smiled, wondering what the Pharisee had to say about this, when he saw the man step up to the front. Indignant because Jesus had healed on the Shabbat, the synagogue ruler said to the people, "There are six days for work. So come and be healed on those days, not on the Shabbat." (Luke 13:14)

He fastened his look on Thomas and then on Yeshua with a

disapproving stare as the crowd grew silent.

Yeshua answered him, "You hypocrites! Doesn't each of you on the Shabbat untie his ox or donkey from the stall and lead it out to give it water? Then should not this woman, a daughter of Abraham, whom Satan has kept bound for eighteen years, be set free on the Shabbat day from what bound her?" When he said this, all his opponents were humiliated, but the people were delighted with all the wonderful things he was doing." (Luke 13:15-17)

Thomas smiled. Finally he understood something Yeshua said. The comments of the crowd about the hypocrisy of the leaders on the way out were priceless. *Nothing much had changed in two thousand years. Religion was still the same legalism it had always been.* He loved how the Rabbi got right to the crux of it, in a way that left no question of what He was saying. *Why is it that most Christians choose to be like the Pharisees instead of Yeshua?* he wondered.

"Master, I am healed." Esther ran up to him, with her hands raised and jumping like a young girl when he arrived outside the synagogue. "The Yeshua healed me, look!" She stood before him, her spine completely straight and normal, the way it should be.

"I can see that, Esther. I am so very happy for you. See, I didn't have to sell you and you didn't have to die, isn't that great?" He looked at her with great affection and smiled mischievously. "I wonder what Octavia has to say about that."

"Master, thank you for taking Esther and staying for the service. They would have never allowed us in if it hadn't been for you," Lydia said. "You are so very kind."

Before Thomas could answer, Yeshua walked up to them. He turned to Thomas and said,

"Ask and it will be given to you, seek and you will find, knock and the door will be opened to you. For everyone who asks receives; he who seeks finds, and to him who knocks, the door will be opened." (Matthew 7:7)

"Thank you, Master, for healing my slave. I don't understand anything about You, but I do know that You are a good man," Thomas said. "If You could just speak to me in real life, I could believe in You," Thomas said without anger in his voice.

Yeshua looked at him with that knowing look. "I tell you the truth, whoever hears my word and believes him who sent me, he has eternal life and will not be condemned, he has crossed over from death to life." (John 5:24)

Thomas stood motionless and stared after Yeshua, watching Him walk away from the enthusiastic crowd. His confusion had returned, but there was no anger.

Since it was the Shabbat, Thomas had to take the women with him to his clients house. They would have to wait in the carriage with Marcellus until he was done, since all businesses were closed.

Gaius Maximus was a rich Roman merchant, dealing in cloths and jewelry and a friend of Herod's.

"I have called you, because my wife is ill. Herod tells me you saved his life and performs miracles like that Jewish carpenter," he said as Thomas walked in. Gaius was a younger man with typical Roman features. His hair was styled in fashionable waves. A prominent, curved nose gave his features a masculine look, softened somewhat by his lively blue eyes. He wore a dark, blue toga made of the finest materials and had gold rings on every finger. There was no doubt, he was a wealthy man.

"I am a man of science, not religion, Gaius and use my medical knowledge to perform healings without the use of faith," Thomas answered. "It would be much easier if I could do what Yeshua does, but unfortunately I can't. May I inquire what is wrong with your wife?"

"She is bringing up her food every morning and feels quite ill and weak for an hour or two," he said. "I am extremely worried. We have not been married for too long and I truly am fond of her. Her father is a senator in Rome and he would not look kindly on his daughter getting sick after I take her to this god-forsaken place to live."

"May I see your wife in private, Sir, in order to examine her?" Thomas asked.

"Of course, I will have her personal slave woman be there to assist you." Gaius said, not wanting Thomas to be alone with his young wife.

"That will be fine, Sir, just have her show me the way."

"The physician is here to see you, my lady," the woman said as they entered a room adjoining the large atrium.

"Have him come in, Felicity," a high, feminine voice answered coming from the large bed.

Thomas looked at her. She was a lovely young woman with stunning, large blue eyes and long, brown, wavy hair. Her skin was flawless, which brought out the classic bone structure even more. She held her hand out to Thomas in a weak gesture.

"I am Thomas, your physician," he said as he took it. "I am here to see what is wrong, if anything, my lady." He smiled.

"There has to be something wrong or I would not feel so horrible and bring up my food each morning and sometimes even during the day. That has never happened to me before."

"Do you mind if I touch your stomach, my lady?" Thomas asked.

"If you must, although my husband will not like that. He is a jealous man who loves me very much." She tried to smile.

"That is alright, my lady, Felicity is here to see to it I do not do anything that will upset you or your husband." He waved to the slave to remove the gown from the women's abdomen and palpated her stomach as gently as he could. She was definitely pregnant. "How long have you been married, my lady?" he asked.

"Just one moon cycle."

And when did you have your last monthly cycle?"

"About three months ago."

Oophs. "You may put her clothes back on, Felicity," he said. "And then leave us."

After the slave left he turned to the young woman.

"You are with child and it has been quite a bit longer than one moon cycle, my lady. I hope that will not present a problem with your husband." He tried to put this as gently as possible.

She looked at him with a terrified expression. "The gods help me, I am doomed." Tears filled her eyes as she looked at Thomas. "What am I going to do?"

Thomas realized he didn't even know her name. "Do I take it your husband is not the father of this child?"

"No, he is not. I was in love with a slave in my father's house. He was a wonderful man and we gave in to our passion only a few times until I was sent here to marry Gaius Maximus."

"What is your name, my lady?'

"I am Petronia."

"Well, Petronia, I cannot change the course of nature. Your husband will figure out this child is not his when you deliver," Thomas said with compassion. "Do you have any idea what he might do to you?"

"He could kill me if he wants, but he will probably send me back to my father or worse, have me cast away." She began to sob. "I have no idea what to do." Suddenly she looked at Thomas, her face showing a glimmer of hope. "Can you remove the child from my womb? You are a doctor, aren't you?"

"I do know how to do that, Petronia, but it is dangerous. Infection can set in easily and you can die."

"I would rather be dead than bear the shame that awaits me when my husband and my family find out."

"It would have to be done very soon, before the baby grows anymore." Thomas was torn. While he had no qualms about the abortion, the risk of infection was enormous, plus his reputation would be ruined if she died under his care. On the other hand, this woman's life was in danger from the punishment her husband might inflict on her if he found out."

"Will you help me, Thomas?" She was pleading now. "I am desperate."

"I will help you, but you have to take your slave woman into your confidence. I cannot do this alone. Also, you will have to have it done somewhere other than here in this house, because your husband and the rest of the servants would surely find out. Can you arrange that?"

"I will think of something. When will you be able to do it?"

"As soon as you let me know where you will be, I will make the medical arrangements."

"I will send a messenger to let you know as soon as I can get away." She sounded better and her tears had stopped flowing.

"I will tell your husband it is a case of indigestion and that it will improve with the medicine I will give you. It is just water with honey, but you don't have to tell him that." He reached into his bag and gave her the small container with the liquid.

On the way home he insisted to sit with Marcellus again. He was too distracted to deal with the two happy women in the carriage. He had never done an abortion himself, but had observed many as an intern. It was not that he was against it and didn't care if other doctors performed them. It was just that personally, he couldn't deal with the idea of taking a baby's life. He realized it was legal, but knew, scientifically speaking, every human being started out as a fetus. In medical school his professor had stated unequivocally, as soon as there is cell division, there is life and he had sworn an oath to preserve life and do no harm to his patients. He cringed. And then it came to him, maybe this was just a dream, so why should he care?

The entire household was in uproar when Esther walked in, rejoicing and praising God. Lydia described in detail what had happened and everyone was in awe at the healing power of Yeshua and Thomas' kindness. Helena asked permission to give a big dinner for all the house slaves and Thomas agreed. For days there were preparations under way and even Octavia was found smiling more often than not. Esther was reinstated in her old job of running the slave quarters and she went about it with a vengeance, demanding that all rooms be cleaned and the straw bedding renewed for starters.

Thomas stayed to himself, pondering and preparing for the surgery he would perform. It would take some doing to find the right instruments and much stronger alcohol than just wine for Apolonia. When the messenger came after four days, he was ready.

When it was over, he tried hard not to think about it. Everything went well and Apolonia returned home to her husband. Since he didn't hear anything further, he assumed she was doing well. He promised himself he would not do it again. It was simply too risky and too uncomfortable.

The dinner was held in the courtyard with music, dancing and good food and wine. Thomas had agreed to be present and it was some time before the slaves felt free enough to eat and drink with the master and his daughter serving them. When the music started, Thomas asked Lydia to dance with him. There were shouts and laughter to cheer them on and he felt light-hearted for the first time in months. His desire for her only increased as he held her close. Lydia remained shy and distant, no matter how he tried to loosen her tongue by encouraging her to drink. She stuck to her one glass for the evening and that was it.

"Do you not like to drink, Lydia?" he asked as they danced. His hand was on her back as he smiled at her.

"I like it fine, Master, but I don't like to feel out of control of my senses."

"I am sure you know how beautiful you are, Lydia. Is there anyone in your life that makes your heart beat faster?" He smiled at her.

"No Master, I have not found a man that interests me as of yet. I can't say that I am looking either." She spoke in a whisper.

"Do I interest you, Lydia?" He asked and held his breath.

"You are my master and I am your slave. I have no right to be interested in you, yet you can do with me as you wish." She looked at him with sadness in her eyes. "We live in different worlds and the only thing I can ever be to you is your mistress, but I don't want to be that to any man. Yeshua says that the Lord God loves us all the same and that there is no difference between men and women, slave and free. I would rather be without a man and remain a slave than your mistress and become a whore." Thomas was taken aback by the vehemence in her voice.

"I promise you I will never make you do anything you do not want to do, Lydia. But know that I am very attracted to you and would like to spend some time in your company," Thomas said.

"I am here to serve you, Master. All you have to do is ask," she said in a monotone voice.

"I don't want you as my slave, but as a friend, Lydia," he said, feeling a little foolish, because she had him in the palm of her hands.

"I don't know that it is possible to be your friend and your slave at the same time," she said, "but I will try to obey you in all things in whatever you ask me to do, just as I always have."

"I don't think you understand, Lydia. I don't want obedience from you, but a relationship, where we can talk and discuss things that are on our heart."

"I don't think I can do that, because you will always be my master and therefore it is impossible for you to ever be my friend."

The music had stopped and he had no choice but to let her go. His heart was heavy as he left the ongoing festivities and went into the house, overwhelmed with a sudden feeling of utter loneliness.

Chapter 21

Weeks went by and when Lucius sent a messenger to say it was soon time to make the journey to Jerusalem for Passover, Thomas was ready to go. He sent a note letting his friend know they would take Marcellus along to see to the horses and Abraham as his personal servant.

"Abraham, in a month it is time to go to Jerusalem and I am going to let you come along so you can be with your family," Thomas told the old man.

"Oh Master, that is wonderful, thank you."

"I have been thinking, you are getting on in years, I would like to give you your freedom so you can stay with your wife and son, would you like that?"

Abraham stared at Thomas and then sank to his knees. "Oh Master, this is too great a joy, my heart cannot contain it. May the God of Abraham, Isaac and Jacob bless you not just in this life, but in the life to come. I do not deserve such a blessing." His skinny body shook violently as he cried.

"You deserve it, Abraham, for your faithfulness to me and just because you yearn to be free to be with your family."

The news of Abraham being freed spread through the household within minutes, since one of the slaves had overheard their conversation. There were some who were glad for the old man, but others took it hard, because they also wanted to be free.

Thomas found his favorite spot on the bench under the sycamore tree in the courtyard. He hated to see Abraham leave, but going to Jerusalem was the perfect chance for him to be reunited with his family after so many years.

His thoughts went to Lydia. He had tried hard to ignore her, but each time he saw her, he wanted her more. She did not seem to notice and was the same she had always been, reserved, yet friendly and efficient in her service to him. Her presence in the room made him feel guilty, angry and short tempered, no matter how hard he tried to tell himself it was ridiculous to be under the spell of a woman to this extent. He started to look for faults and criticized her almost every day for little things. Yet the more he did, the more guilt he felt and that in turn put him in a foul mood. It was a vicious cycle which he did not know how to stop.

He blamed Yeshua for having influenced her to believe in her new morality, because he was sure she had been the former master's mistress at one time or another. Darn it, she was his slave and he could do with her what he wanted. He felt a helpless anger rise up within him that hadn't been there for a while. Melissa didn't care about him after all this time. She had probably found someone else by now. Why couldn't he take what was his? What was it about the girl that made him worry about what she thought or believed?

"Bring me some wine," he growled when a slave came to ask if he needed anything.

"Yes, Master."

He sat for a long time under the tree, drinking one goblet after another until he felt almost sick. And still, the feelings of helpless rage would not go away. A dark cloud of crushing loneliness descended over him that made him want to scream and lash out at somebody or something.

"It is getting dark, Master. Maybe it is better if you come inside." It was Lydia.

"Help me get to my bed," he said, slurring the words. "And then get out of my sight, I never want to see you again," he said as he got up on unsteady legs.

Lydia turned and waved two men to help her and together they managed to get to him into his bed, where he fell asleep within seconds.

The next morning he woke up with a giant hangover. He groaned when Abraham came in to help him get up.

"Get out! I don't ever want to wake up again." He moaned and held his head. It had been in medical school since the last time he got so drunk he did not remember anything about last night.

"You have an appointment in Tiberias this afternoon, Master," Abraham said. "Do you want me to send a messenger to tell your client you are sick?"

"That sounds like a good idea, Abraham, because I really am sick."

"Maybe you wish to sleep some more, Master. It might make you feel better. I can come back later."

It was two hours later Thomas walked into the dining room on unsteady legs. His head was pounding and he slumped into his seat.

"Where is Lydia? Why hasn't she brought my breakfast?" he growled at Abraham.

"You commanded her to be gone for good, Master and to get out of your sight forever."

"You have got to be kidding! I was drunk, Abraham, really drunk." He looked at the old man with bloodshot eyes. "Tell her I want to see her immediately and never listen to me when I am drunk."

"She will be happy to hear that, Master. She has been in her quarters crying her eyes out all night," Abraham said.

"Good morning, Daddy. You look awful, are you not well?" Helena came in with a big smile. "I missed you at breakfast earlier, but Abraham said you wanted to sleep some more." She sounded bubbly and bounced on the couch, which made his head hurt.

"Angel, I have a terrible headache, please be nice and quiet and don't shake the couch."

"What is wrong, I don't want you to be sick, Daddy." She was suddenly close to tears.

"It is nothing serious, my little sunshine, I must have had some bad wine last night, that's all. Go back to your lessons and I will see you for the mid-day meal."

"I hope you will be better by then," she said and left the room.

"Can I be of service, Master?" It was Lydia.

"Where have you been? The one morning I sleep in you stay in your room being lazy."

"Yes Master," she said and a tiny smile crossed her face as she looked at him. "It shall never happen again."

"Have you ever been really drunk, Lydia?" Thomas asked as he took a sip of fruit juice.

"No I have not." She looked at him, still smiling, "I can't say that it does much for people the next day, does it?"

He groaned and put his head in his hands.

Over the next few days his drinking bouts in the evening became a habit as his desire for Lydia grew. It was the only way he could dull the thoughts of being trapped in a life that wasn't real and riches he didn't earn within a reality that seemed like a dream with no way to escape. Thoughts of Melissa swept through his mind, mixed in with the picture of Lydia's loveliness. Added to that, he was outdone by a simple carpenter who healed people he wouldn't have been able to help, even in the 21st Century. His reliance on science, technology and modern medicine was useless and therefore, he was useless. The only surgery he had performed lately was killing an unborn child, something he said he was never going to do. These thoughts ran through his mind like a loop day after day and he was helpless to stop them until he was drunk enough to fall asleep.

He wondered when this nightmare would end while he sat under his favorite tree again one evening.

"I brought you something to eat, Master. It will keep you from feeling bad." It was Lydia.

"You mean it will keep me from getting drunk?"

She didn't answer as she put the food in front of him on a small table.

"Answer me, Lydia." He was angry to be confronted by his weakness.

"I am sorry, Master. I am only trying to help."

"You are trying to help? You are the one that put me in this position of being a drunk, because you won't go away." His voice had an angry edge to it.

"I am sorry," she whispered.

"Sorry for what? Rejecting me because your Yeshua suddenly wants you to be pure and holy when you were a whore before? I am your master and can do with you what I want, yet you have the audacity to turn me down. I know you were the mistress to the last owner of this place, so why do you reject me?" He took another deep gulp of the wine. "Answer me!" he shouted.

"I belong to you, Master. I told you that you are free to do with me as you wish and I will obey." She stood in front of him with her head down.

"So you give me permission do you? How dare you? Don't you realize you are nothing but a miserable slave and I am your owner?" He stared at her, trembling with anger and frustration as she remained silent.

"I will prove to you that you do not own me, woman," he shouted and rose from his seat. "Go to my room. Now! I will show you that Yeshua does not have any control over you or me."

When they reached his bedroom, she stood motionless as he staggered inside. "What are you waiting for, take your clothes off and do what you know how to do best."

"Please Master, do not do this, I beg you. Do not defile me in this way," she cried as she looked at him with pleading eyes.

"Women have thrown themselves at me and you call this being defiled?" With a sudden rage of anger, he struck her face with his hand and then pushed her onto the bed. "I will show you what it feels like to be defiled."

When it was over, Lydia left the room, sobbing quietly.

A sense of gloom hung over the house the next morning. Everyone was aware of what had happened. Lydia stayed in her quarters, refusing to eat. She took some juice from Abraham, but would not speak. When he entered Thomas' room, the master laid on the bed, staring at the ceiling without acknowledging him.

"Would you like some food, Master?"

"Get out. I don't want to see anyone," he said without looking at the servant.

"Yes Master."

When the old man left the room, Thomas buried his head in his arms as sobs shook his body. The great Chief of Thoracic surgery had raped an innocent woman! According to the laws of his time, he belonged in prison. That much for being a man of superior intellect and stature next to these uneducated people of ancient times! Modern man had not changed in two thousand years. *He* had not changed and had treated a woman he said he loved worse than the woman he was married to. One he raped, the other he had cheated on – again. What a miserable piece of scum he was. The real scary part in all this was, he wanted a drink and it was only morning.

That's when he suddenly remembered the words of Yeshua, "For there is nothing that will not be disclosed, and nothing concealed that will not be known or brought out into the open." (Luke 6:17)

When he finally walked into the dining room, Helena was sitting at the table by herself. She did not look up as he sat down.

"You did to Lydia what the other master did to me, Daddy." Tears were running down her cheeks.

Oh God! He reached for the juice without a word as they sat in silence. When he tried to touch her hand, she withdrew it and fear filled her eyes. "Are you going to do it to me as well?"

He looked at Helena with a look of such sadness that she reached out her hand to his.

"I am so very sorry, Angel. I never want to hurt you, never. You are the only sane thing in my life right now. I promise I will never hurt Lydia again."

"Why did you hurt her, Daddy?"

"I was angry and drunk."

"The other master was like you. He would get drunk and then hurt me. I wish you wouldn't drink anymore, Daddy. Maybe then you won't hurt Lydia anymore either."

Thomas looked at Helena and held out his arms to her. "Come, let me hug you and tell you that I love you and will never break my promise to you."

"Did you promise Lydia you wouldn't hurt her like that?"

"I did."

"If you broke your promise to her, maybe you will break it with me, too."

"Let me explain something to you, Helena. When you grow up and fall in love with a boy, it is a different kind of love than a father has for his child. It is a grown-up love that can hurt as much as it can give joy. My love for you is not like that. It will always be the same and never hurt or leave you." He leaned over to her and kissed the top of her blond hair. "Does that make any sense to you?"

"I think so. Are you going to say you are sorry to Lydia, Daddy?"

"Yes, but I don't know if she will ever forgive me."

"I know she will, because the Rabbi Yeshua says we have to forgive even those who are our enemies. And Lydia tries very hard to do what the Rabbi says," Helena said with assurance. "I didn't know if I could love you anymore when I heard what you did, but if you are sorry then I have to do what Yeshua says as well, Daddy."

Thomas sat and held the little girl as if he never wanted to let her go; and it was as if all the dread and shame gave way to a sense of relief. *Maybe Yeshua's ways are not so far-fetched after all.*

"It is almost time for you to leave for your appointment, Master," Abraham said. "The carriage is ready and waiting for you." The old man stood with his head bowed low for the first time in a long while.

It was four hours before Thomas returned from his visit to the house of a wealthy Roman in Tiberias. He was getting tired of treating these spoiled, wealthy people, who suffered from nothing more than the consequences of overindulgence of food and licentious living. The trouble was, without modern medicine, there wasn't much more he could do than tell them to go on a diet and live a clean life. *He was a fine one to talk!*

He got out of the carriage, tired and disgusted. The dread to meet Lydia made him cringe.

"Have my bath prepared before the evening meal, Abraham," he said. It would feel good to get rid of the sand and sweat from the trip.

"Right away, Master." Abraham said with a distant tone in his voice.

"When I am done here I want you to get me Lydia. I need to talk to her."

"She has not come out of her room, Master. I don't know if she will obey you."

Thomas looked at Abraham with a sad expression, "I know you judge me for what I did. I want you to know that I agree with everything you are thinking. I have behaved abominably and I am sorry. I have let all of you down and I doubt anyone in this house will ever respect me again."

"We truly thought you were different, Master," Abraham said and did not dare look at Thomas.

"I did too, my old friend. I did too. Just ask Lydia if she will see me. If she doesn't, I will not force her."

Thomas sat at the table by himself. Helena had gone to stay with a friend in the next village accompanied by a slave woman and Sarai. He was grateful no one bothered him as he ate.

"You wanted to see me, Master." Lydia stood with her head down.

"Please, sit down at the table," he said and pointed to a seat opposite to where he sat.

"I am a slave, I am not allowed to sit at the master's table," she said in a monotone voice.

"Since I am the master and I tell you to do it, don't you think it's alright? Please, Lydia, sit with me."

She sat on the very edge of the cushion, her head still down.

"Please look at me, Lydia. I have never been so sorry about anything in all my life. I don't expect you to forgive me, but I am going to ask you anyway. I am not just sorry, but horrified that I could behave in such a way toward anyone, but especially you. You are a beautiful, sweet and wonderful girl any man would be proud to love. Instead, I abused you like a slave and a cheap whore last night. To me you are none of those things, but a woman I desire and can't have, because I am married. I know there is nothing I can do to undo what I did, but I can give you your freedom. And that is what I am going to do. It will take a few days to make it legal, but from this day on you are free to go where you wish."

She looked at him and tears began to roll down her cheeks.

"I do forgive you, Master. Not just because the Rabbi says I should or you are setting me free, but because I want to. I know you are a kind and gentle man, but I can feel you are very unhappy about something. I wish I could help you, but I don't think that is possible since both of us are bound by circumstances we cannot change. I thank you for my freedom. I will return to my home in Samaria and see if my parents will allow me to live with them."

"How did you become a slave, Lydia?" he asked.

"My story is like Abraham's. My father sold me when I was a little girl, because he could not pay the taxes so many years ago."

"Will he take you back?"

"I don't know. My family may reject me since I am no longer a virgin and no man will want to marry me now."

"What will you do?"

"I do not know, Master."

"I have a friend named Lucius in Capernaum. Maybe you could run his household as a freedwoman. I am sure he would pay you enough money so you can live a good life in his house. You will want to know that he is a follower of Yeshua and a physician like me. If I ask him would you be interested?"

"Yes, thank you, Master, that sounds wonderful." She looked at Thomas with a look of love and regret as she wiped the tears off her face. "You are a man capable of great kindness and great cruelty at the same time. I pray that the Lord will help you choose which one you want to be in the end. I wish you would go and listen to Yeshua and learn how to live a righteous life and believe in Him; and so save your soul at the same time."

When she rose from her seat he got up as well. They stood for a moment and looked at each other, when, suddenly, he leaned forward, took her face in his hands and kissed her gently on the lips. "I could have loved you, Lydia, if I was free," he said with great tenderness.

"I could have loved you, too, Thomas," she whispered and left the room without looking back.

Chapter 22

"This is what I have longed for, Master, to see my wife and son again," Abraham said with great emotion as they entered through the gate of Jerusalem. "It has been many seasons; I wonder if they will recognize me."

The trip had been uneventful due to the comfort of Thomas' horse-drawn carriage and overnight stays in upper class accommodations on the way. It was a time of sharing and discussion about the Meshiah between Joanna, Lucius and Thomas. He still insisted all this was religious nonsense, while the others tried to convince him that Yeshua had come to deliver Israel from the Romans.

"I am telling you He won't," he said. "I have no idea why He came, but it wasn't for that. In my time a lot more people all over the world believe He is the Meshiah than now, but the Romans have nothing to do with it. They fade into history and give way to a religion called Christianity, which is based on the Christ or better, Yeshua."

"Can't you remember more about their belief, Thomas?" Joanna said. "Surely, you must have some idea why He came if not to establish His kingdom in Israel."

"It isn't that I don't remember. I don't know, since I did not believe in religion of any kind. I wish I had paid more attention to my wife's grandmother. She tried to tell me, but it was all nonsense to me at the time, and still is."

"Do you at least remember what she said to you?" Joanna asked.

"Some of it. It had to do with accepting Yeshua into your heart and giving Him your life, because He died for our sin. She called it being saved."

"How could He possibly die for our sins?" Lucius asked.

"I remember Yeshua saying something about that," Joanna said. "Let me think, how did He word it?" "For God did not send his Son into the world to condemn the world, but to save the world through him. (John 3:17)

"But save the world from what, if not from the Romans?" she wondered.

"What about your wife, didn't she tell you anything?" Lucius asked.

"We agreed when we got married that we wouldn't talk about religion, and we didn't. I know she believed in Yeshua, but she never mentioned anything about Him to me."

"How can you be married to someone and never talk about something as important as religion?" Joanna wondered.

"My marriage was not the greatest," Thomas said sheepishly.

"That brings me to a point about marriage," Lucius said. "That slave girl Lydia you recommended to run my house? She is great. I have no idea why you would let someone so beautiful and talented go."

"She didn't tell you?"

"No, she didn't and even when I asked her, she withdrew mysteriously and wouldn't answer." Lucius said. "What happened, Thomas?"

"If she won't tell you, then I don't think I will either. Let's just let it rest, it is better that way."

"Master, we are here! This is my son's house," Abraham shouted suddenly. They had stopped in front of a small, but clean dwelling in one of the more modest neighborhoods in Jerusalem. A young man in his early thirties came toward the carriage and stopped when he saw Abraham.

"Father, is that you?"

"Jesse, my son!" Abraham cried and jumped down from the carriage and ran toward him. They embraced with shouts of joy and tears.

"Is this your master?" Jesse asked when he finally let go of Abraham and turned toward Thomas, who had gotten down from the carriage.

"Shalom, Jesse, I am Thomas and I am no longer his master. He is a freedman and has come to stay with you."

"Oh, may the God of Abraham, Isaac and Jacob be praised!" An older woman had stepped out of the door and ran toward Abraham. "My husband has come home." She buried her head in his chest as sobs racked her body. They stood so for a long time until Jesse said to Thomas, "Would you care to come in and join us in a meal? It would be an honor for this house to serve the master that set my father free from bondage."

"Thank you Jesse, but we must get on. My friends and I are expected at the house of Cassius and Diana. We will be there over Passover. Maybe we can visit later, but for now I want you and your father to enjoy being together. He has been a wonderful servant to me and he deserves his freedom."

"Thank you again, Master, may the Lord God richly bless you for your kindness."

Before Thomas returned to the carriage, Abraham turned to him and said, "You were the kindest of all the masters I have had and I thank you. The Lord would have you know that just when you think all is well with your life, a great calamity will befall you. But remember, it is to show you that earthly riches are but for a moment, while the kingdom of God will last forever. He will never leave you nor forsake you, Thomas, even in your darkest hour. Remember these words, because they will give you comfort in the difficult days ahead." Abraham was shaking and his son had to steady him. "You will see the Meshiah in all His Glory, but not until you turn to Him, totally broken." Abraham looked at Thomas with great sadness. "How I wish you could be spared what is to come, but it is because it comes, that you will gain your life." Slowly Abraham turned and walked into the house.

Thomas stood and stared at the old servant, stunned by his words. He had never heard him talk this way and wondered what it all meant.

The evening everyone had been waiting for finally arrived. Nicodemus walked in with a big smile and greeted everyone with an even bigger hug.

"You sure don't act like the rest of those Pharisees, Nicodemus," Diana said. "As usual, we are waiting to hear about Yeshua and what you have found out in the Torah about Him."

"Will you let the man come in first and have a good meal before you inundate him with your silly questions, woman?" Cassius said.

"I will try, dear, but it isn't easy. Just because you are not interested in this, the rest of us are." She looked at her husband with an affectionate smile and asked the guests to be seated at the table.

"Thomas, I hear you have quite a reputation as a healer at the court of Herod Antipas?" Nicodemus said.

"I was fortunate to be called to treat a disease that required very little on my part, but had dramatic results in that it saved his life. I take no credit for it, since it is common knowledge where I come from," Thomas said with an embarrassed smile.

"And where do you come from?" Nicodemus looked at him with curiosity. "You speak Greek quite fluently, like an educated man."

"I am from a place called America and a city named Philadelphia," he said.

"That means brotherly love, but I am sure you already know that," Nicodemus said.

"I do know that, I just wish everyone who lives there did love his brother. Unfortunately, that is not the case as with most human beings." Thomas said. "I myself included."

"This is true for everyone, for it says in the Torah, "How then can we be saved? All of us have become like one who is unclean, and all our righteous acts are like filthy rags; we all shrivel up like a leaf, and like the wind our sins sweep us away." (Isaiah 64:6)

"What you are saying Nicodemus, even the Pharisees, no matter how hard they try to obey everything in the Torah, can ever be righteous enough before God," Joanna said with astonishment. "I thought if you strictly adhere to the Law of Moses, it would be enough to earn favor with God and so gain eternal life?"

"Believe me, I have struggled with this all my life. Since I belong to the sect of the Pharisees and try so hard to be perfect, I know I am only a sinful man who fails every day, in spite of my efforts."

"Then no one can ever be righteous." Joanna said into the sudden stillness. "Could that be why Yeshua says He is the One who came for our sins? I heard him say that the other day to those of us who are close to Him,

"I am the gate; whoever enters through me will be saved." (John 10:9)

"From what I can gather, He claims to be the Meshiah who came to save us from our sins," Nicodemus said. "In order to understand what He means by that, I went to the Torah and studied all the passages that refer to the coming Meshiah. I was astounded to find that there is nothing there about military battles or defeating the Romans, but they all refer to a spiritual battle. You remember when we spoke last, I found the scripture about the Meshiah being born in Bethlehem and a child growing up and being called Mighty Counselor and Prince of Peace and son of God. There is no way the scripture could possibly refer to a human being, since no human can ever become a god or be perfect."

"So how can Jeshua be a god since He is a human being?" Thomas asked.

"I am glad you asked that," Joanna said. "Not that long ago, Yeshua and His apostles went to Nazareth and I went with them. While there, I had a long talk with His mother. Miriam is a devout, humble and kind woman who would never lie to anyone. I asked her about Yeshua and about what happened when He was born. She verified that angels and shepherds came to worship Him, but then she said something that was even stranger." Everyone leaned forward with great anticipation. "This is what she told me. Before she was married to Joseph, an angel appeared to her and told her she would bear a son and was told to call Him Yeshua, which means 'Salvation'. When she told the angel that she had not been with a man, he told her the Holy Spirit would overshadow her and she would be with child. At first she did not know what to say other than the Lord's will be done. But then, after two months went by, she found herself pregnant and she still wasn't married nor had she been with a man. This child, the One we now know as Yeshua, was not conceived through normal means, but through God Himself."

"That is what the Torah says," Nicodemus cried, "Therefore the Lord Himself will give you a sign: The virgin will be with child and give birth to a son and will call him Immanuel." (Isaiah 7:14) "And the name

Immanuel means 'God is with us'," Nicodemus continued. "That is what was missing. I could not find how this could be, since so far all the other prophesies I found fit the Rabbi."

"What about the part of throwing out the Romans and establishing a kingdom that will last forever?" Joanna asked.

"Like Thomas said last year, no human kingdom will last forever. That means the scripture is talking about a spiritual kingdom. It has to, because nothing else makes any sense."

"Yeshua is always talking about 'Repent, the kingdom of God is near'. That is beginning to make a lot of sense, given what we have just heard," Joanna said. "Not too many days ago, He was telling us after being asked by the Pharisees when the kingdom of God would come,

"The kingdom of God does not come with your careful observation, nor will people say, 'Here it is,' or There it is,' because the kingdom of God is within you." (Luke 17:20-21)

"And then toward the end He said something very strange that sounds like what Thomas has told us,

"But first he must suffer many things and be rejected by this generation." (John 17:25)

"That is what is going to happen, Nicodemus," Thomas said. "Where I come from, millions of people believe that Yeshua was the Meshiah, not because He threw out the Romans, but because He was killed on the cross and rose again after three days. They believe He died for their sins and established a kingdom called the Church. Two thousand years later, it is still going strong."

Nicodemus looked at Thomas with astonishment, and then a sudden realization came to him.

"This is incredible. It fits the scripture in Isaiah perfectly. Let me read it to you from the Torah," he said and reached for a book he had placed carefully on the table when he first sat down. "No one has ever been able to understand what it means and who the prophet is alluding to. Until now." He flipped a few pages, sat back on the couch and began to read.

"Who has believed our message and to whom has the arm of the Lord been revealed? He grew up before him like a tender shoot, and like a root out of dry ground. He had no beauty or majesty to attract us to him, nothing in his appearance that we should desire him. He was despised and rejected by men, a man of sorrows, and familiar with suffering. Like one from whom men hide their faces he was despised and we esteemed him not.

Surely he took up our infirmities and carried our sorrows, yet we considered him stricken by God, smitten by him, and afflicted. But he was pierced for our transgressions, he was crushed for our iniquities, the punishment that brought us peace was upon him, and by his wounds we are healed." (Isaiah 53:1-5)

"Let me pick out some verses in the chapter and you will see why I think Yeshua is talking about giving His life," Nicodemus went on. "This is what it says, "For he was cut off from the land of the living; for the transgression of my people he was stricken. He was assigned a grave with the wicked, and with the rich in his death, though he had done no violence, nor was any deceit in his mouth.

Yet it was the Lord's will to crush him and cause him to suffer, and though the Lord makes his life a guilt offering, he will see his offspring and prolong his days, and the will of the Lord will prosper in his hand. After the suffering of his soul, he will see the light of life and he will be satisfied, by his knowledge my righteous servant will justify many, and he will bear their iniquities."

"…because he poured out his life unto death, and was numbered with the transgressors. For he bore the sin of many, and made intercession for the transgressors." (Isaiah 53:8-12)

"What this is saying, if Yeshua gets put on the cross and suffers death like I know He will, He is the Meshiah according to that prophesy," Thomas said. "Because that is what my wife's grandmother tried to tell me. She called it salvation."

"I have no idea what you are talking about, Thomas, but what you are saying is correct," Nicodemus said with awe. "It is the first time this scripture has made sense to me." He scratched his beard. "I just came from a meeting with the Sanhedrin this morning. There was great upheaval about Yeshua and His message. They are furious with His criticism of them and the big crowds following Him. The worst is, they cannot explain the miracles, signs and wonders He is performing everywhere. How can they fight those?" He looked at the others with a sudden concern. "There is more and more talk to have Him arrested and charged with heresy and blasphemy. And the punishment for both is death."

"You don't think our own people are going to kill their Meshiah?" Joanna said with horror in her voice. "I could understand if it was the Romans," she added.

"It will be both," Thomas said.

There was a sudden silence after that as everyone stared at him.

"Are you telling us that we have waited for all these hundreds of years for the Meshiah and then, when He comes, we will kill Him?" Nicodemus asked almost in a whisper.

"I think so. My knowledge of what happens is sketchy at best, but that is what the followers of Jeshua believe in the future," Thomas said.

"Actually, it is the religious leaders who have a lot to do with it. And Pontius Pilate. I don't know how it all happens, but that much I do know."

For the first time Thomas felt he knew more than everybody else. He was not near as impressed with the scriptures Nicodemus had read as the rest of them. Sure, it was amazing how they seemed to fit, but then, a lot of it made no sense, just like everything else Yeshua did or said. It must be a religious thing to talk in riddles. Give me science and facts. There is never any doubt about what is being said. He was getting tired of this discussion.

"Are you a prophet, Thomas?" Nicodemus asked.

"No, I am definitely not a prophet. I don't even think I believe most of what has been discussed here this evening."

"Then why should we believe what you said about what is going to happen to Yeshua?"

"You probably shouldn't, since I don't think any of this is real anyway." He looked confused.

"Don't pay any attention to him, Nicodemus. Thomas goes off on his dream journey every once in a while. We have learned to ignore it," Lucius said.

Suddenly, there was a loud knock at the door. Cassius waved for the slave to wait until he got there to open the gate to the courtyard.

"In the name of the Emperor, open this gate!" a loud voice shouted.

"Oh my lord, I have no idea what could be wrong for Roman soldiers to come knocking on our door," Diana said with fear.

Before Cassius could say anything, four Roman soldiers walked into the courtyard.

"We are here for Thomas, the royal physician of Herod Antipas," one of them said. "Is he here?"

"What do you want with him?" Cassius asked, trying to sound calm.

"That is none of your business, Greek. Just show us where he is."

Before Cassius could answer, Thomas stepped outside and faced the soldier. "I am Thomas, the physician. What can I do for you?"

"You are to come with us to the house of Pontius Pilate, Sir."

"Why?"

"That is not for us to know. All we know is that we were ordered to bring you to the procurator's home right away."

"Here we go again," Lucius muttered under his breath. "Every time this man walks into Jerusalem, he gets into trouble."

"I will be alright, Lucius, don't worry. I will be back as soon as possible," Thomas said with a forced smile.

"Let's go, physician. We do not wish to keep the procurator waiting."

Thomas was helped into an official looking carriage when they got to the street. *At least I'm not arrested,* he thought as he sank into the soft seat. It took quite a while, even with the two sleek, black horses racing down the road, until they came to a large estate on the edge of Jerusalem. The huge gate swung open as they approached and without slowing down, the carriage made its way to the front of a spacious Roman villa.

Several slaves were ready to assist him and showed him into the house without delay. He realized by now, someone was desperately in need of medical attention, when a tall, imposing man walked up to him and said in an authoritative voice, "I am Pontius Pilate. Please, come with me. My daughter is in great distress and needs your help." The man looked distraught as he rushed Thomas down into the inner sanctum, passing by a maze of rooms.

Suddenly, Thomas heard an earsplitting scream, like a woman in labor.

"She has been in labor for the last twenty hours and the physician thinks there is something wrong. I would strongly suggest you do your best to help her. I don't trust these Jewish quacks."

Thomas entered a room with four women standing around a large bed, crying and wailing. The young mother was screaming as another contraction racked her body, while a doctor stood by wringing his hands.

"Get all these people out," Thomas commanded. "You too, Procurator, leave only the doctor and two slaves. I need hot water and clean linen as well as more light. Light many more oil lamps so I can see what I'm doing. Hurry!" he yelled at the slaves. "And bring me a large container with lots of undiluted wine in it."

He walked up to the mother and lifted her legs to see how far she was dilated.

"Wait, you may not touch my daughter in that area, physician," Pontius Pilate yelled.

"Then you find yourself another doctor, because that is the only way I can help her. Besides, I told you to get out. Do it!"

Pontius Pilate was so stunned to be spoken to like that, he did as he was told and left the room.

When Thomas examined the mother, he realized the baby was not lined up in the birth canal. This would not only be difficult, but extremely painful as he had to turn it around to face the birth canal while still in the womb.

"What is your name, great lady?" he asked her.

"I am Petronia, please help me," she said and then started to scream again as another contraction started.

"Try to take deep breaths, Petronia. I know it is difficult. Just do it, it will help with the pain." He leaned over her and took her face in his. "I will have to reach inside you and turn the baby around and that is going to hurt terribly. Whatever you do, try not to push." He turned to the doctor. "Hold her hand and don't let it go but try to restrain her to keep her from moving." He waved to a slave. "You go on the other side and take her hand and do the same. Do not let her move! Get another slave in here to help with the oil lamps," he yelled to no one in particular. "I need more light."

He put his hands into the wine and soaked them for a few minutes all the way up to his elbows, hoping the alcohol would help disinfect them sufficiently to avoid infection.

"There is nothing to be done, physician," the doctor said with a smirk. "I have already tried all the remedies and they have not helped."

Thomas ignored the man and reached inside the mother with one hand. He felt the baby's backside against the opening of the birth canal. With his hand he pushed the body further in and then turned it until he could grab the feet and pull them into the opening. Petronia screamed and would have jumped up if the three people hadn't held her down.

"It won't be long, Petronia, you can push now as hard as you can. The baby is coming feet first, but that's alright."

It took another fifteen minutes until the first little foot appeared and then the other. He grabbed them both and pulled, while encouraging Petronia to keep pushing, until suddenly, the baby slipped out and landed on the linen sheets. It was slightly blue, but after a minute of gently massaging his body, it pinked up nicely. Thomas gave it over to the slave for cleaning amidst lusty cries of protest.

"It is a boy, Petronia. You are the mother of a strong, healthy boy." Thomas said with a smile.

"Oh, thank you, I am so happy and tired at the same time," she said as her head fell back on the pillow.

Thomas washed his hands in the wine and dried them off with a fresh linen cloth. Two slaves were busy cleaning up the afterbirth and replaced the soiled linens with fresh ones.

"Petronia, keep the area down there as clean as you possibly can. Wash it with undiluted wine when you relieve yourself each time. Make sure you start walking around by tomorrow. Your physician here will tell you to stay in bed for several weeks. Do not listen to him. It is better to walk right away to keep the blood from clotting and will make you feel stronger much sooner."

"I will. Thank you so much, Thomas," she said and took his hand. "I know you saved my life and that of my baby."

"You can let the family come in now," he said to the slave.

He stepped aside when the baby's father and Pontius Pilate, together with his wife, came rushing in.

"You have not disappointed me, physician," Pilate said after kissing his daughter and having admired his grandson. "Herod, that sly old fox, knows how to get the best of everything, including a good physician."

"Thank you, Sir. Your daughter will be alright. Please allow her to get up and walk around as soon as she wants. The sooner, the better, no matter what your physician says. There is nothing more I can do here, so I would like to get back to my dinner, if that is alright with you, Sir."

"I must say, I haven't been yelled at by anyone like you since I talked to the Emperor the last time I had an audience with him," Pontius Pilate said with a smile, which softened his strong features and made him look even more handsome. "Here is your pay. I can never reward you enough, Thomas. You have no doubt saved my daughter's life and that of my first grandson. If there is ever any favor I can do for you, let me know." With that he put a large bag filled with coins in Thomas' hand.

"You are most welcome, Sir. It is always rewarding to bring a new life into the world." With that Thomas bowed and followed the slave back to the carriage.

Chapter 23

When Thomas returned to Galilee a week later, his fame had already spread before him. Every rich family wanted their child delivered by the preferred medical expert to Pontius Pilate. Especially the Roman citizens in Galilee clamored to have him as their personal doctor. For many weeks after the trip to Jerusalem, he spent more time on the road than at home.

His wealth increased a hundred-fold and yet, he was not happy. He missed both Abraham and Lydia. The house seemed empty without them and Helena agreed. She had been very fond of Lydia and had taken her on as a surrogate mother. Thomas didn't know what he would have done now without Helena. She still saw it as her mission to make him smile every morning as they had breakfast together. She had changed from the shy little slave to a self-confident girl, assured of her father's love. Olyssus had taught her and her slave girl Sarai a lot of things a lady of society should know. She took it all in like a sponge. Thomas was proud of her and took her along to many dinners he was invited to and introduced her as his daughter. No one ever questioned it.

He was sitting in his carriage one day as Marcellus drove him to Tiberias. It was a long ride and his thoughts went to Abraham and the words he had spoken to him. Should he believe what the old man said or just dismiss it as emotionalism, he wondered. What if it was true? That's when he decided to make sure Helena would always be taken care of. He would have a scribe come to his house and draw up a will. If nothing else, it would make him feel better. In it he made Helena the legal owner of the estate and all his property, including the slaves if anything should happen to him. Should he die while she was still under age, Lucius would assume guardianship.

It was done two weeks later without Helena's knowledge. She had become one of the wealthiest heiresses in Galilee.

It was on a bright, sunny morning. He was in his carriage on the way to Sepphoris, when he met Yeshua and his twelve apostles walking down the narrow road. A large crowd followed them. When He passed the group, Thomas told Marcellus to slow down.

"Would you like a ride, Rabbi, I am going through Nazareth on my way to Sepphoris," he asked as he leaned out of the carriage.

To his surprise, Yeshua nodded His head and joined Thomas inside and sat down across from him without a word. Thomas studied the carpenter carefully and realized He looked like any other man. As a matter of fact, he looked quite ordinary. If this was the Son of God, why couldn't God have made Him look handsome at least? He wasn't tall either, but of normal height, like most of His people. His hair was a little wavy and of a warm, brown color. There was one feature that was different from all the people Thomas had ever met. Yeshua's eyes had a look of serenity, yet power, of kindness, yet strength and most of all, they were filled with love. It was this love that touched Thomas' heart deeply every time he looked at Him. He sensed a certain feeling of peace in his heart instead of anger like before.

"Yeshua, I know you know all about me," Thomas finally said into the silence. "You know I come from the future and am stuck here in the distant past. I know You know all my arguments whether to believe in You or God. If my life here was real, I would believe in You, but it isn't. I can't believe in what feels like a dream. You are not real, so why shouldn't I believe in my many possessions and the comfortable life I live now. I am a famous physician and attend kings and even Pontius Pilate. I have arrived at the pinnacle of my profession in a short time. What more could I ask for?"

"But woe to you who are rich, for you have already received your comfort. Woe to you who are well fed now, for you will go hungry. Woe to you who laugh now, for you will mourn and weep. Woe to you when all men speak well of you, for that is how their fathers treated the false prophets." (Luke 6:24-26)

"You sound like Abraham," Thomas said. "He also told me terrible things are going to happen to me. Why? What did I do wrong?"

"The knowledge of the secrets of the kingdom of God has been given to you..." (Luke 8:9)

"There You go again, what good does it do me if I don't understand? Why won't You speak plainly to me? I have tried to ignore You, hate You and deny You, Rabbi, but it is no good. I somehow cannot get away from You. Why won't You just leave me alone and never bother with me again?" Thomas asked in utter frustration.

"For the Son of Man came to seek and to save what was lost." (Luke 19:10)

"You are right there, I am lost. Lost in this past. Lost to my wife, to Lydia and to a job I loved. I have gained riches far beyond anything I ever dreamed of and yet You tell me I am to blame for being rich. What is wrong with being rich? Why can't I be a good person and still be rich?"

"If you want to be perfect, go sell your possessions and give to the poor, and you will have treasures in heaven. Then come, follow me."

(Matthew 19:21)

"I can't do that, because I don't want to give up all that I have earned."

"How hard it is for the rich to enter the kingdom of God! Indeed, it is easier for a camel to go through the eye of a needle than for a rich man to enter the kingdom of God." (Luke 18:24-25)

"Are you saying I will not make it?"

"What is impossible with men is possible with God." (Luke 18:27)

"At least tell me something, are You going to die on the cross like they say in the future where I come from?"

"…and everything that is written by the prophets about the Son of Man will be fulfilled. He will be handed over to the Gentiles. They will mock him, insult him, spit on him, flog him, and kill him. On the third day he will rise again." (Luke 18:31-33)

"So that part is true then. Why do you have to die?"

"I am the gate, whoever enters through me, will be saved." (John 10:9)

"What do I need to be saved from?" Thomas asked.

Yeshua replied, "I tell you the truth, everyone who sins is a slave to sin. Now a slave has no permanent place in the family, but a son belongs to it forever. So if the Son sets you free, you will be free indeed." (John 6:34-36)

"I am not a slave, but a free man. Why would I need You to set me free?"

"For judgment I have come into this world, so that the blind will see and those who see will become blind." (John 9:39) "If you were blind, you would not be guilty of sin; but now that you claim you can see, your guilt remains." (John 9:41)

The only noise was the carriage rolling across the hard surface of the road as they sat in silence for the rest of the way.

Many weeks passed and his life had settled into a pleasant routine. He poured all his love into Helena and watched her develop into a young woman of society. She had learned to speak Latin and Greek quite well by now. He had hired a slave named Jacob to teach her the tenets of the Jewish faith. His own feelings of loneliness and longing for something more remained and he had started to accept frequent invitations to attend the many festivities at the homes of the rich in the area. He became a regular at Herod's banquets and enjoyed the opulence and excitement of the court. It was there he found entertainment with the many beautiful slave girls available to him through Herod's generosity. Since there was no love or commitment involved, he reasoned it was alright. Besides, none of it was real, and who cared. Since he couldn't have Lydia, why not enjoy life.

He was sitting under his favorite tree in the courtyard after two days at the palace of Sepphoris.

"Lucius the physician and Lydia are here to see you, Master."

Thomas jumped up when he saw Lucius and Lydia walk into the courtyard. His heart took a second beat when he saw her stand behind his friend with a slight smile on her face. She was as beautiful as ever, even more so. There was a glow about her that had not been there before.

"Greetings, my friend," Lucius said as he hugged Thomas. "It has been a while since we have seen each other. I hope you are doing well."

"Greetings to you, Lucius. I am well indeed." He turned to Lydia with a smile. "And how are you, Lydia? I hope this man treats you well. You look as lovely as ever." He bowed before her.

"Shalom, Thomas, it is good to see you," she said in a quiet voice. "I am very well, thank you."

"Markus, bring some wine and refreshments," he ordered. "Let's celebrate with good friends."

"Thomas, Lydia and I came to tell you something," Lucius said after they had finished with the amenities. He squirmed in his seat. "I hope you will not be offended in any way."

"Why would I be offended, my friend. I cannot think of two people I love more in this world other than my daughter Helena," he said. "What is it you want to tell me?"

"Lydia and I have decided to get married. I hope that does not present a problem for you."

Thomas looked at the two people before him in stunned silence. His eyes settled on Lydia. She looked down at her hands. They were shaking slightly. He was desperately trying to think of something appropriate to say, but nothing would come. Lydia. Seeing her he knew he was still in love with her and would always be. A sense of terrible loss and loneliness washed over him. All the riches he had amassed, all the fame he basked in, yet the one thing he really wanted was slipping away forever.

"Thomas? Did you hear what I said?" Lucius said. "We are in love and want to get married next month."

Thomas looked at his friend as if waking up from a dream. "I heard you and I am very happy for both of you." It was all he could do to sound casual. "I will give you a wedding feast here at my house. It will be the biggest celebration in memory and will last for seven days. And we won't run out of wine."

"I don't think we can accept that, Thomas," Lydia said before Lucius could answer. "We want a quiet, private ceremony with the Rabbi officiating and just a few friends."

"I understand," Thomas said and tried not to look at her. "I really do understand, Lydia."

"I don't think you do, Thomas. Lucius knows what happened between us and we both still consider you our best friend. Since we follow the Rabbi, we have learned to forgive and still love those who have done us harm. Yeshua has taught me to love my enemies and do good to those who have spitefully used me. I am not just talking about you, Thomas, but about the other master who owned me before you came. It gives me peace in a sense I have never known and allows me to love you with a love that is different from what I thought I had for you." She looked at him with such genuine affection, he couldn't help but smile.

"I am glad you are happy, Lydia, truly I am. When I get back to my wife I will try to love her the way you love if I ever figure out how." He took another sip of wine and hoped it would calm him to the point he could think straight.

"Without the Rabbi you never will," she said as she took Lucius' hand. "Lucius and I have found what it means to be happy by trusting in the Meshiah and His ways."

"I can see that." He sat back and closed his eyes. "Maybe someday I will find something I can be happy about." His voice sounded forlorn.

"Won't you accept Yeshua and find out?" she asked. "He will show you how."

"I don't think I can. I talked to Him not too long ago. He is a good man, but I still don't understand anything He says." He looked down at his goblet. "This is all I have now, this and my little girl until I go back to where I came from." He shrugged his shoulders. "I feel it is time for me to wake up, but I don't know how to do that either."

He was glad when they left and sat under the tree and got drunk.

Chapter 24

After they left, he started drinking again on a regular basis. It was only in the evening, so it would not interfere with his practice. Being a doctor was all that held him together. He tried to hide his alcohol problem from Helena and didn't start drinking until she had gone to bed for the night. He knew his life was unraveling, the richer he got and the more his reputation as a physician spread. Yet there were days he imagined himself more successful than the Rabbi Yeshua. His 21st century knowledge of medicine definitely had its rewards and he didn't need faith to heal people.

Lydia and Lucius had gotten married. He did not attend the wedding, because he had started drinking that morning and was in no shape to go anywhere by noon. It was better that way, all things considered. After they had come to tell him of the marriage, he had avoided them altogether and found people in high society more to his liking. There was no talk of the Rabbi there and definitely no restraint about morals. People in those circles treated ethics and principals more or less as small inconveniences. Tiberias and Sepphoris were places with a Roman culture, built on loose Roman values in the midst of Galilee. Thomas started to feel comfortable there and blended in perfectly. He even insisted that Helena was introduced into society circles to learn how the right people lived. He was sure she would be a part of that when she got a little older.

He made many friends in high places and felt comfortable with them, since he was richer and smarter than most of them. His favorite place was the bath house in Tiberias, a place of opulence and leisure for the upper class, with hundreds of slaves catering to their every need. It was here the gossip of Herod's bizarre escapades, the political problems of Pontius Pilate with the Jews in Jerusalem and the latest news from the Emperor in Rome were discussed. Thomas wished he could remember more of the history of that time, but even if he did, he knew better than to mention he was from the future. There were times he even forgot about it as he got more and more involved in the life of a rich landowner and famous physician. Life was good and he did not allow himself to be unhappy anymore. Only on rare occasions did he experience loneliness, but had learned to drown it in alcohol to the point he would not remember it the next morning.

It was on one of those bad days, as he drove up to the house, he looked forward to an evening under his favorite tree and drown his bad mood in wine. He was coming home from a long trip to see a client and in no mood to talk to anyone. As soon as he walked into the house he found the slaves in turmoil. Helena had disappeared!

"What do you mean she has disappeared? Who was in charge of watching her?" His angry voice carried all over the house. Octavia stood before him, trembling.

"I have no idea where she could be, Master. She was here for breakfast and since then no one has been able to find her. We have looked everywhere."

"Olyssus, did you not say anything when she didn't show up for class?"

"Yes I did, Master. That's when we found out she was gone. I was waiting for her as usual and when she did not come, I went into the house looking for her." The old man was shaking in fear.

"I will kill the slave who has not done his job." Thomas was beside himself. "Octavia, where is Sarai?" he yelled.

"She is gone, too, Master."

"There will be hell to pay for everyone if you do not find her unharmed." He slumped into a seat in the office. His mind was reeling. He had no idea what could have happened to her and realized, he had not paid much attention to his daughter in the last few weeks.

"Master, the cart is gone and so is the donkey," a young slave said, totally out of breath from running. "Marcellus is gone as well."

He was stunned. His slave had escaped with his daughter! Where on earth could they have gone and why? He stared in front of him, guilt starting to fill his mind. He had been consumed with his work and pleasures and had neglected the only human being that meant anything to him. *Oh God!* Was there no end to his failures in this wretched life?

Suddenly, his eyes fell on a piece of papyrus in front of him. He took it and unfolded it carefully.

My dear Daddy,

I have gone to Lydia's house, because you are too busy to be my Daddy anymore. I still love you, because Yeshua wants me to, but I don't feel that you love me anymore. Also, I still want to believe in Yeshua instead of all those other gods your new friends like. I am sorry if I have disappointed you and wish I had done better. Love, Helena.

Thomas sat and stared at the note. His little girl thought he didn't love her anymore. She was all he had left, all that really mattered anymore, yet he had ignored her.

"Bring me Marcellus as soon as he returns." His voice sounded menacing.

"Yes, Master, he just drove up and is taking care of the donkey."

Thomas watched Marcellus walk in, tired and weary from the journey.

"Come here, slave," he yelled. "How dare you take my daughter out of this house without my permission. Who do you think you are?"

"She ordered me to do it, Master, I had to obey her," Marcellus answered, shaking in fear. "I am sorry, Master."

"Octavia," Thomas shouted. "Take this worthless slave and have him beaten with twenty lashes. I will teach you to disobey me, boy! You are lucky I won't kill you," he said in a low voice and slapped his face. "Get him out of my sight and do as you're told, Octavia."

"Yes, Master," she said and took Marcellus' arm and led him away to the slave quarters.

Early the next morning he was on the road to Capernaum to Lucius' house. A young slave named Andrew drove the carriage. *He would never trust a slave again. They were all the same, disobedient and irresponsible.* He had made up his mind, he would not allow Helena to be involved with Lydia or Lucius or anyone who believed in Yeshua. It was the Rabbi's fault she ran away, because she wanted to be with people who believed in Him. He would introduce her to Roman culture and society, so she could find a suitable husband and live a life worthy of her status. He was in control of this life, not Yeshua!

Helena ran up to him when he arrived.

"Daddy, I am sorry for running off like that. I just couldn't stand for you to be gone all the time." She hugged his neck and kissed his cheek. "I am so glad to see you."

He pushed her away and walked into the house. Lucius and Lydia stood to greet him.

"Shalom, Thomas, how good to see you," Lydia said and bowed to him.

"Greetings, old man, I am glad you finally made it here to visit us. We would love for you to take the mid-day meal with us," Lucius said.

"I am afraid this is not a friendly visit, Lucius. I am here to pick up Helena. I am extremely upset she ran away. It worried me to death. I have punished Marcellus for bringing her here without my permission." He turned to Helena. "Get your things and come with me, we are going back right away."

"But Daddy, I like it here with Lydia and Lucius. Why can't we stay a while?"

"Don't argue with me, you are in enough trouble. Do as you are told and get your things." There was no doubt he meant it, judging by the tone of his voice.

Helena stomped in the back of the house to get her belongings and ran to the carriage, crying. "I told you he doesn't love me anymore. Come on Sarai, let's go."

"Thomas, are you sure you can't stay?" Lucius asked.

"I am sure. From now on I want her to stay away from this house until I say otherwise. Thank you for taking care of her." He turned and went back to the carriage. Sarai was sitting with Andrew at the front.

"You are angry with me, Daddy."

"Yes I am. You had no right to tell Marcellus to take you this far away without me knowing where you are going. I have had to punish him for your bad behavior."

"What did you do to him?" She sounded alarmed. "I like Marcellus, he is my friend."

"That doesn't matter. The point is you are no longer a slave and you need to stop associating with slaves."

"But he is not a slave to me, he is my friend, just like Sarai." She looked at Thomas with astonishment. "How come you want me to be mean to the slaves when I know they love me? I used to be one of them."

"That is right, you used to be, now you are not. You are the daughter of the richest man in Galilee and it is time you act like it. From now on you will learn Roman ways and behave like a lady of the upper class and not like a common slave." Thomas still sounded angry.

"You have changed, Father," Helena said and looked straight ahead with tears in her eyes.

"Why are you calling me Father?"

"Because you are no longer the Daddy I used to know. You are drinking again and your rich friends hate Yeshua and believe in many gods. I hate them and will never be one of them, no matter what you say. I love Lydia and Lucius, they are kind and follow the ways of Yeshua. They treat their slaves with respect and do not punish them when they have done nothing wrong." She was crying now.

"You will do as I say. From now on, we will no longer associate with them because all they talk about is Yeshua and His crazy ideas of the kingdom of God. And that is final."

"And I will never be a Roman," she said with determination, "and that is also final."

It was late in the evening and he was sitting under the tree with a goblet of wine in his hand. His mind was filled with anger. He hated the thought about being involved with slaves. In the end Helena was still a slave and would always be one. He was sad that she rejected his offer to give her a life of luxury, while all she wanted was to follow Yeshua. How come an eleven-year-old could believe in Him and he couldn't? Not only that, she turned to the people who did and away from him and his new friends. No matter what he did, no matter where he went, Yeshua was always there somehow. The realization made him even more angry.

"Master, please forgive me for disturbing you," Octavia said with her head bowed low. "Marcellus is really hurt from the beating. There is blood all over and he is crying because his back is bleeding badly. Can you come and take a look at his wounds?"

"I don't care, he deserves what he got. Maybe next time he will know better." Thomas took another sip of wine. "Go away, I don't want to bother with a slave right now."

It was five days later when Octavia came and reported to Thomas that Marcellus was delirious. When Thomas went to the slave quarters, he found the boy with a high fever and a massive infection. By the time he tried to treat his wounds, sepsis had set in and it was too late. Marcellus opened his eyes and looked at Thomas. With great effort he whispered, "I am sorry, please forgive me, Master. I forgive you, just like Yeshua says to do." And with that he died.

Thomas sat in the straw that was his bed and wept. This boy had died for no other reason than being Helena's friend. He walked out of the slave quarters across the courtyard and sat down under the tree and stared straight ahead without seeing. He had killed a human being by refusing to treat the wounds inflicted on his orders. What kind of a physician was he? What kind of a man had he become? He would get life in prison for this crime back in Philadelphia. Was there no end to the evil in his heart?

"I tell you the truth, everyone who sins is a slave to sin." (John 6:34)

Thomas heard the words in his mind as clearly as if Yeshua was sitting right next to him. He understood. He had become a man bound to sin in every area of his life. *I am no better than my slaves. They are chained to me without any chance of being free, just as I am chained to my wretched failures with no way out.* He sat and stared and felt nothing, except he wanted a drink.

The next morning Helena was already at breakfast when he entered. She didn't look at him.

"I want to go live with Lydia and Lucius, Father," she said without emotion. "I don't know you anymore. You have become just like your Roman friends, heartless and evil toward the slaves. I am a slave and I will always be one. God loves me anyway, Yeshua says. He tells us there is no difference with Him what we are, just so we love others." She wiped the silent tears off her face. "I don't care about being rich. I don't want or need your money, all I wanted was for you to love me. But in your eyes I am and always will be just a lowly, common servant. Please, allow me to go and live in Capernaum, I beg you."

Thomas couldn't answer. He sat, as if his heart was made of stone, without feelings or emotions.

"You will stay here, don't ask me again," he finally managed to say into the silence. His tone was harsh.

Helena got up from the table and left without a word, sobbing silently.

It was a house filled with silent mourning. Marcellus had been greatly loved by everyone with his cheerful, friendly demeanor. Helena was heartbroken. She refused to sit at the table with Thomas and took her meals in the kitchen with the slaves. The two had stopped speaking to each other altogether. No one in the house dared to be around the master for fear of doing something wrong. They performed their chores meticulously, driven by dread and terror of doing something to displease him.

Thomas was glad when he was called away to visit an important patient. The journey would take two or three days. Maybe when he returned things would be better. He was on his way to Bethsaida with Andrew driving. It is situated on the very eastern tip of the Sea of Galilee. A messenger had come to ask if he could see a prominent Roman official who apparently had fallen ill of an unknown disease. He had learned to diagnose without the modern convenience of technology and found, it was not all that impossible to come up with a correct diagnosis. What was much more difficult was the remedy. Even with his fame, he had lost many patients because there was no treatment available to combat even the simplest illnesses without surgery or antibiotics.

They had been on the road for quite a while on the way to Capernaum. It was a beautiful drive along the lake on the right as it glistened in the bright sunshine. His mind calmed down somewhat as his eyes looked out over to the mountain range on the other side of the large body of water. He could actually make out some fishing boats way in the distance.

As they turned around the bend, a large crowd sat on a hillside to the left. They were clustered in groups, listening to a man standing on a small rise. The carriage was almost past it, when it came to a sudden stop with a jolt. Andrew jumped down to check what was wrong. One of the wheels had come loose and was ready to fall off.

"We have to stop until I can tighten it, Master," Andrew said with fear in his voice. "It is not my fault, I checked everything before we left." The man was shaking as he looked for signs of anger in Thomas' face.

"Well, fix it." Thomas said in a harsh tone. "And be quick about it."

"Yes, Master."

Thomas looked toward the crowd and frowned. He had no doubt it was Yeshua they were listening to. He also had no choice but to sit down on the grass and hear what He said until his carriage was fixed. The voice of the Rabbi, usually soft and low, carried His words with amazing clarity.

"Watch out! Be on your guard against all kinds of greed; a man's life does not consist in the abundance of his possession." And he told them this parable: The ground of a certain rich man produced a good crop. He thought to himself, 'What shall I do? I have no place to store my crops.'

Then he said," This is what I'll do. I will tear down my barns and build bigger ones, and there I will store all the grain and my goods. And I'll say to myself, 'You have plenty of good things laid up for many years. Take life easy; eat, drink and be merry.'

But God said to him, 'You fool! This very night your life will be demanded from you. Then who will get what you have prepared for yourself?'

"This is how it will be with anyone who stores up things for himself but is not rich toward God." (Luke 12:15-21)

Thomas stared at the Rabbi in disbelief. *He knows! He knows what I've done.* He cringed and could not stop looking at Yeshua. Even from the distance he could feel His eyes on him with a love that tore into his heart like a sword. *He still loves me, even now. No one else does, not even Helena. How can that be? I am evil, mean and filled with hatred for myself. I am an adulterer, a rapist and a murderer on top of a greedy bastard! How can anyone love me?* Thomas put his head on his knees to hide the tears. *I am the most evil man I have ever known. I have amassed riches and possessions and yet at the same time have driven away all the people around me I truly care for. How could I not know this is the man I really am without the façade of human civilization? Yeshua knew it all the time and He still loves me.*

"Master, the carriage is fixed, we can go on now," Andrew said.

Thomas looked at his slave with eyes so filled with sorrow, Andrew held out his hand in spite of his fear to help him up. "You will be alright, Master."

"No, Andrew, I will never be alright again."

Chapter 25

Weeks had gone by and Thomas and Helena never spoke. She stayed with Sarai and the other slaves and refused to be in the same room with him. Olyssus still gave her lessons every day and she became proficient in Greek and Latin. Unbeknownst to Thomas, there was a large group of slaves who met in the slave quarters to discuss the latest teachings of the Rabbi. Helena was very much a part of it. They met in the evening and on days when Thomas was on the road. Issus was the leader and he brought back news each time he returned from Capernaum to buy and sell grain and other crops. Many times he shared with the group how he witnessed Yeshua heal many and it caused great excitement, since these miracles confirmed He was the Meshiah. Over time, the meetings caused in many slaves a desire to forgive the master for the death of Marcellus, because it was what Yeshua preached and expected of His followers. Helena had a particularly hard time to forgive her father or reach out to him as his daughter. She had lost her trust in his goodness and love and didn't know how to get it back. He turned out to be no different than her former master in many ways with his cruelty, anger and drinking.

Thomas made sure he was gone as much as he could in order not to have to face the people in his house, but especially Helena. A wave of regret washed over him every time he saw her and it made him angry and then he would drink. It was a vicious cycle he could not escape.

"You have no choice but to forgive your father, Helena," Sarai said after one of the clandestine meetings. "How can you follow Yeshua and not do what He says to do? I know the master still loves you."

"I know he does, Sarai, but how can I trust him again? He gets so angry when he drinks and then does mean things. I am scared of him. He killed Marcellus when he didn't do anything wrong."

"I don't think he meant to kill him, he just didn't treat him, that's all." Sarai looked at Helena with a look of concern. "How can you ever think you can stay mad at him and live in this house as a follower of Yeshua?"

"It feels terrible, Sarai," Helena said. "It is like living in a dark tomb."

"Only you can make it light again by forgiving him and try to love him again." She looked at Helena and took her hand. "Come, I will go with you. Together, it will be easier."

"Daddy, can I talk to you?" Her voice was thin and she looked like the little girl he remembered. Thomas was sitting at the table, eating his mid-day meal. He looked at Helena with a look of surprise.

"Of course you can talk to me. Come and sit right here." He looked at Sarai, "you, too."

"Thank you, Master."

What is it you want to say to me, Angel?"

"You haven't called me that in a long time, Daddy."

"Just like you haven't called me Daddy in forever." He smiled at her with a sad little smile. "I still love you, you know that?"

"Yes I do and I still love you, too."

"We have to talk about what happened with Marcellus, don't we?"

"Yes, we do. Did you mean to kill him, Daddy?"

"Of course I didn't, you know that."

"No, I don't know that anymore. You are different now and I am scared of you." She was crying.

"My Angel, I am so sorry I have failed you in every way a man can fail his daughter. I have failed everybody, especially Marcellus and for that I am deeply sorry. Believe me, I would give anything to undo what I did." He reached out to her and she flew into his arms, burying her head in his chest.

"Please forgive me, Helena," he whispered into her ear.

"I do, I forgive you like Yeshua says to do and that will make it like it never happened, Daddy. Just promise me you won't drink again."

"I promise."

It was three weeks later. He sat under his favorite tree. This time without a drink. He had kept his promise to Helena and their relationship had mended better than he could have ever hoped. Life was good again and maybe there was hope he could restore his friendship with Lucius and Lydia. His thoughts went to the first time he met Lucius and the camaraderie and friendship they had enjoyed. And to Lydia and his feelings for her until he messed things up.

Talking about feelings, he hadn't been feeling well for a while and experienced a certain muscle weakness in his hands he couldn't explain. He looked down and felt a slight numbness and a few skin bumps on both hands. He touched the bumps and rubbed his hands over them to relieve the numbness, but couldn't. That's when he saw the rash on the side of his right thumb. With growing alarm, he touched the inside of his nose and realized he had noticed a sore for quite a while and remembered the several nosebleeds during the last few weeks. He felt for his earlobes and realized they were enlarged.

A feeling of sudden dread came over him. These were the typical signs of early lepromatous or multibacillary leprosy! Instantly the words of Abraham came to his mind.

"The Lord would have you know that just when you think all is well with your life, a great calamity will befall you. But remember, it is to show you that earthly riches are but for a moment, while the kingdom of God will last forever. He will never leave you nor forsake you, Thomas, even in your darkest hour. Remember these words, because they will give you comfort in the difficult days ahead. You will see the Meshiah in all His Glory, but not until you turn to Him totally broken."

This is the calamity Abraham spoke of. He was a leper! Thomas sat stunned and his mind reeled as he desperately tried to deny what he knew to be medical evidence. He thought hard to remember what he had learned about the disease. As best he could recall, leprosy was caused by a bacteria related to the tuberculosis bacterium. It is spread by body fluids as well as droplets from the upper respiratory tract. The symptoms start in the skin and the peripheral nervous system and then spread to other parts like hands, feet, face and earlobes. After that comes the disfigurement of the skin and bones, twisting of limbs and curling of the fingers to form the better known claw hand. Facial changes include thickening of the outer ear and collapsing of the nose. Tumor-like growths may form on the skin and even on the optic nerve and cause blindness. Most of the deformities are caused by nerve damage and result in loss of pain sensation.

He must have contracted the disease when he treated the poor when he first worked for Lucius. *That's the thanks I get for being kind.*

If he was in Philadelphia there would be no problem to treat this, but here, while not a death sentence, here it meant banishment to a leper colony for the rest of his life. It seemed ironic, instead of a life sentence in prison for his crimes, Yeshua sentenced him to a life of misery as an outcast of society in Galilee.

Without treatment he had some time to set his life in order and then disappear into the living hell of leprosy. If he was careful, there was very little chance he could infect anyone unless he sneezed or coughed on them. He didn't think his facial features had changed yet. If not, no one need know about this until it was time to leave behind all that he knew. If there was ever a good time to wake up from this nightmare, this was it!

He would have to tell Lucius. He was Helena's guardian. He would also have to change his will and leave the estate and all that it entailed to her *now* instead of when he died. It would be years before that happened, but he would not be here to run things. This way Helena was the owner and Lucius her guardian. He would ask Lydia if she would be there for her until she grew up and leave her a large amount of money to be independently wealthy.

All he was, all that he owned and everything he had been so proud of would be gone, including the memory of his accomplishments as a royal physician. In this day, people tended to cast out those who contracted the disease and treat them as if they had never existed. He would be forgotten in two worlds and vanish without a trace in both.

He sat under the tree, filled with fear and without hope. After gaining status, riches and success, he had lost it all in one instant, just like Yeshua knew all along he would.

The weeks passed and his symptoms got a little worse each day. Yet so far, there were no outward, visible signs for anyone to suspect anything was wrong. He had spread the news that he was getting ready to retire and turned down most requests to see patients any longer, until one day he stopped altogether. He still had not told Lucius or Lydia, but had turned over his estate to Helena two days ago without her knowledge. It was now time to go visit his friends to inform them of their new responsibility as the girl's guardian.

He took a deep breath as the carriage turned into their courtyard.

"Thomas, how wonderful to see you. We were wondering if the news of your retirement is true," Lucius said as he met Thomas at the carriage.

"It is, Lucius. I am now a man with nothing to do but lie around and enjoy life," he said with a forced smile and stepped back to avoid Lucius' hug.

"That is something I find hard to believe, old friend. Come inside, Lydia will be glad to see you. She is pregnant, you know." Lucius was surprised to see his friend withdraw from him.

"I am happy for both of you." Thomas followed him inside.

Lydia looked radiant and greeted Thomas with great affection, but he stopped her from hugging him. "We were getting worried about you hearing all this talk of your retirement. What is going on, Thomas?"

"I have come for a special purpose and need to talk to both of you. Please hear me out, this is very important."

"Allow me to serve some refreshments before we get started. You are probably thirsty and hungry from your journey," Lydia said and ordered a slave to bring food and drink.

After finishing the meal, Thomas leaned back.

"I think it would be better if you dismissed the slaves and make sure we are alone. What I have come to tell you needs to stay between us."

"You sound very mysterious, old friend, but I will do as you ask," Lucius said and dismissed the servants with a wave.

Thomas looked at his two friends with a sad smile.

"I have come with a sad story that will upset you both very much. Let me start at the beginning. When I came here over two years ago, I was alone and Lucius, you took me in and allowed me to work for you. Since then I have spent my life amassing an enormous amount of riches and status so that I will never lack anything. Throughout this entire time, Yeshua has tried to reach me with His message, but I have never listened to Him or understood what He tried to tell me. Instead, I turned to Roman society and their gods to find entertainment and fulfillment. In the process I almost lost you, my daughter and every moral value I ever believed in in exchange for riches and fame." Lucius and Lydia were listening to him in rapt attention as he went on.

You may recall, when we dropped off Abraham at his son's house in Jerusalem, the old man gave me a word I will never forget.

"The Lord would have you know that just when you think all is well with your life, a great calamity will befall you. But remember, it is to show you that earthly riches are but for a moment, while the kingdom of God will last forever. He will never leave you nor forsake you, Thomas, even in your darkest hour. Remember these words, because they will give you comfort in the difficult days ahead. You will see the Meshiah in all His Glory, but not until you turn to Him totally broken."

"Not too long ago, when I was on my way to Bethsaida, I heard Yeshua preach to a crowd. It was right after the horrible incident with Marcellus and his death. The Rabbi looked straight at me and said these words, which I have said in my heart many times,

"This is what I'll do. I will tear down my barns and build bigger ones, and there I will store all the grain and my goods. And I'll say to myself, 'You have plenty of good things laid up for many years. Take life easy; eat, drink and be merry.'

But God said to him, 'You fool! This very night your life will be demanded from you. Then who will get what you have prepared for yourself?'

"This is how it will be with anyone who stores up things for himself but is not rich toward God." (Luke 12:15-21)

"These were warnings I did not heed and instead continued to trust in myself, my riches and my status of being the great royal physician and preferred doctor to Pontius Pilate."

"But you are all those things, Thomas," Lucius said.

"Yes, I am, my friend, but what I failed to see is what you and Lydia have seen long ago. These things do not make me happy or help me find the key to the kingdom of God Yeshua is talking about. My eleven-year-old daughter knows how to believe, yet I still don't."

"What are you talking about, Thomas?" Lydia asked with concern in her voice.

"I have leprosy."

"Oh my God," Lucius said in a whisper and stared at Thomas with horror.

"There is no doubt, I know the symptoms. In my time in the future this would be no problem, but I fully realize what this means for me right now. I have made preparations to leave and that is why I am here. I have turned all my worldly possessions over to Helena. She is as of this moment the legal owner of my estate. I have also given a large sum of money to you, Lydia, which will make you independently wealthy for the rest of your life with the request that you be her mother. You, Lucius I have designated as her guardian until she is of age and have put you in charge of running the estate. You may take as much money in compensation as you wish for your trouble so that neither one of you will ever have to worry about having enough money to live comfortably." He leaned forward. "Please do not worry, this disease is not contagious unless you come in contact with a person's bodily fluids. That is why I would not allow you to hug me. Until there are outward signs, I will remain in my home. When the time comes, and I will leave that up to you, Lucius, I will go to 'The Tombs' and disappear forever into the leper colony."

He leaned back and closed his eyes as tears streamed down his face. "I have lost everything just like Yeshua knew I would and tried to tell me so many times. Yet I didn't listen. I have failed as a man, a human being and as a father and I stand before you and ask you to forgive me, for I have failed both of you as well. Especially you, Lydia. For the things I have done I would be thrown in prison for the rest of my life in my world. This will amount to the same and I can only hope I will prove myself somehow in the terrible place I am going."

"Come with us and let Yeshua heal you," Lydia said with hope in her voice. "He knows you and will make you well if you believe in Him."

"That's the point, I still don't believe and He knows it, even if my life has now turned into a horrible nightmare."

He rose from his seat. "A scribe will come and have you sign some papers to make all this legal. I thank you for your love and support during the last two years and hope you will have a good, long life together." He started to leave.

"Just a minute. This is not over," Lucius said with a sudden firmness in his voice. "When you go to The Tombs, we will take care of you and see that you have food and all the comforts possible. We will not leave you destitute, Thomas, not ever."

"How long do you think it will be until you have to go there, Thomas?" Lydia asked.

"I don't know, maybe a few weeks at most, until I can no longer hide the signs of the disease."

"Have you told Helena?"

"No, and I don't want to. I will ask you to tell her and everyone else that I died. I will leave the details to you," he said.

"Oh dear Lord," she said and started to cry. "This is so horrible, I can't believe it."

"Maybe it's only a dream, Lydia and none of this is real. Maybe I will wake up and I am back in Philadelphia in my comfortable home and once again be the big Chief of Thoracic Surgery. Wouldn't that be nice," he said wistfully.

.

Chapter 26

"Daddy, you don't snuggle with me anymore," Helena said one evening as they sat under the tree. You used to hold me and tell me stories."

"You are too old for that, Angel. When you get to be twelve you have to learn to act like a young lady and not like a baby." Thomas cringed. How he would love to hold her close, but he was afraid she would see his advancing signs of leprosy. He did notice his nose was enlarged and his hands had lost most of their feelings. He was beginning to drop things. It was almost time. He had sent Andrew to get Lucius to come and make the final decision. It had been two months since he told them.

Thomas had not left the house at all since then and spent most of his time in the courtyard. It had become his refuge. The slaves noticed a new kindness and a gentle spirit they had never known him to have before. Gone were his outbursts of anger as he talked with them and instead, he asked about their private lives. They did not know what to make of it, but accepted the new master with relief and joy.

"Greetings, Thomas. I have come as you asked." It was Lucius. "Let me look at you." He stood in front of Thomas and studied his face and hands. "You have changed, old friend. Your nose and ears have changed shape. Your beard helps hide the evidence somewhat, but your fingers have gotten larger and I don't know that you can hide those much longer." He was close to tears. "I have asked Yeshua to come and heal you, but He did not answer me. At least He knows where you will be, maybe He will come there and touch you. Remember, He healed ten lepers last year, why couldn't He do the same for you?"

"I hear He is really busy these days with huge crowds everywhere. It is getting closer to the time when He will go to Jerusalem and be killed. In a way He is doing the same thing I am, going from being famous to losing everything." Thomas looked at Lucius and got up from his seat. "I am ready. Will you drive me there? I don't want Andrew to know where I am going," he said. "I have packed a few things and I am taking my medical bag. Who knows, maybe I can still practice medicine in there. Other than that, I don't really know what to take going into a leper colony, do you?" He smiled a sad little smile. "Let me talk to Helena one more time over the mid-day meal and then after that we will leave."

They were on their way. Thomas looked back one last time before the estate was out of view.

"How will you tell Helena?" he asked Lucius.

"I don't know. Lydia and I think it would be better if we told her the truth. She is old enough to understand and could actually visit you sometimes. That brings me to a point. With your knowledge of the disease, how exactly is it passed on?"

"Mostly through nasal discharge coming into direct contact with another person. It is actually not that easily transferred. Medically speaking, no one would have to go to a leper colony if the proper precautions were taken. It is caused by bacteria; a minute organism we cannot see with our normal eyes. If you have leprosy and you sneeze into someone's face, the bacteria gets into their mouth and from there into the lungs and then spreads throughout the body. After that it can take many years for it to start multiplying. Or, like with me, show up sooner."

"So if you stayed in your house and never got physically close to anyone, there would be no danger for anyone else to get it?" Lucius asked.

"That is right."

"Could you not do that instead of going to The Tombs?"

"I think the authorities would take action if they found out and would force me to leave," Thomas said, "because they would be too afraid of being infected. Some of the slaves would surely tell."

"What you are saying, if we brought Helena to the outskirts of The Tombs, she could visit with you without being in danger. To me that would be better than telling her you are dead."

"Let's see how things work out first. Just tell her I went on a long trip and have been delayed until we see how everything looks," Thomas said. "I don't want to hurt her any more than I already have."

"You have not ever really told me how you are handling all this, Thomas. Your entire life is crumbling and there is nothing you can do." Lucius looked at his friend, close to tears.

"I am being punished for what I have done. I truly thought I was a good person when I started on this journey," he answered. "Instead I found out that, given the right circumstances, we are all capable of such evil, it is hard to believe. The things I was so sure I would never do, I have done and the things I thought I would always do, I have cast aside, like decency, morality, kindness and compassion for others. I never saw my pride, never understood how arrogant I was, how puffed up with knowledge and education. What is knowledge when your soul is corrupt, what are riches, when you are poor inside toward others. Yeshua knew the real me all the time, yet He still reached out and tried to tell me. I wish His love was real and not just a religious thing. It is my greatest desire to do better when I wake up from this nightmare. I have promised myself I am going to try to be a better person when I get back to my world."

"Yeshua says that on our own we can never be better than what we are inside, Thomas. We all try to be good, but it is just not possible on a daily basis," Lucius said.

"I know I have been through enough to do better. I have learned a lot in the last two years and I can do it if anybody can." Thomas sounded sure.

"Let me tell you what Yeshua told us,

"The good man brings good things out of the good stored up in his heart, and the evil man brings evil things out of the evil stored up in his heart." (Luke 6:43-45)

"Didn't you just tell me you had no idea there was such evil in your heart, Thomas? Trust me, it is still there and will rear its ugly head again if the circumstances are right," Lucius said. "That is what Yeshua is trying to tell us," he added. "Listen to what He also said, "For out of the overflow of his heart his mouth speaks." (Luke 6:45) "The way you think, Thomas, you are still proud and think you can do it all without Him."

"I don't think you understand me at all, Lucius. I am intelligent enough to know that when I know something is wrong, I will simply avoid doing it in the future. What I'm saying is, I have learned from my mistakes. I am sure I would never do the things I've done again." Thomas was adamant.

Lucius looked at his friend with great sadness and knew Yeshua was not through with him yet. *What will it take?* he wondered.

"There are provisions in the back of the cart," he said. "They should last you for two weeks. Someone, either myself or Lydia or one of our slaves who serves Yeshua, will bring you whatever you need every two weeks. We will find a meeting place and figure out how to do this on a regular basis." He looked at Thomas with a reassuring smile. "We will not leave you or forget about you, do you understand?"

"Thank you Lucius. I will know more when I get there and have settled in. For all I know it won't be all that bad."

"It will be very bad, Thomas. I have heard terrible things about the place. I pray the Lord will be with you and protect you."

They drove on in silence for quite a while until they came to a large rock formation. A big sign stood at the entrance. 'The Tombs. Stay out!'

"This is it, Lucius, I will have to go it alone from here."

"No, you don't. I will drive you further in. You can't carry all that stuff by yourself. Besides, who is going to stop us?" Lucius said with grim determination.

A narrow path led uphill and stopped abruptly at the top of a steep ravine. A make-shift large, wooden basket, held by a strong rope dangled down all the way to the bottom. When Thomas looked over the edge of the rift, he saw it was empty and proceeded to pull it up by the rope until it reached the top.

"This is how they get food and supplies down there," he said as he started putting some of his belongings in it.

"Thomas, you need to go down those steps over there and wait until I let the basket down," Lucius said. "Otherwise someone will come and steal your stuff."

Thomas hesitated for a moment, looking at Lucius. "This is it, old friend," he said with an awkward smile and then carefully took a few steps down and disappeared into the steep ravine.

"Let me know when you're there," Lucius shouted after him.

It was a long way down on narrow, rough, stone steps. Thomas felt slightly dizzy and was glad when he reached the ground. He pulled on the rope and Lucius lowered the first basket down, filled with clothes and his medical bag, followed by many more until all his belongings were piled up around him.

"You must be a rich man," a voice said behind him. "That is a lot of stuff. Care to share?"

Thomas turned around and was taken aback by a large man with horribly deformed limbs. His face was unrecognizable because of a sunken nose and big bumps across his forehead. It reminded him of the movie 'The Beauty and the Beast'. The rest of his body was covered in a loose-fitting, dirty garment.

"I just got here and no, I don't care to share," Thomas said. "I give you something if you show me where I can find a place to call my own. I'm new."

"There is a place a little down the hill in a low cave. You are too tall to fit in it. Then there is another place right over there, but that is for people who have money and can pay rent to Brutus. He charges five denari for a month."

"Thomas, are you alright down there?" He had forgotten about Lucius.

"I'm fine, Lucius, you can go, I will see you in two weeks in this spot," Thomas yelled and turned to the man. "If you help me carry my stuff to where this Brutus is, I will give you a denari," he said.

"I can't use my hands, my fingers are gone."

"So how were you going to steal my stuff if you can't use your hands?"

"I have friends in high places," the man laughed good-naturedly and pointed to another figure behind him. "This is Crassus and I am Markus. We take care of each other. He doesn't see and has hands and I have eyes, but don't have fingers. It works." He smiled a horribly twisted smile.

"Come on, Crassus, you can help me carry my stuff to see Brutus," Thomas said. "I will reward both of you if you don't try to run off with it. I have money and if you help me we can do business together."

"That sounds good to me. Markus, what do you think?" the blind man asked his companion.

"Let's go," Thomas said and piled some of the stuff on Crassus' outstretched arms. "Here, Markus, you can carry some of it in your arms as well. I will guide Crassus if you will lead the way."

The sun was low on the horizon and Thomas knew he would have to find a place before dark. Countless dark figures, hidden underneath dirty, stained garments, stood at the entrance of the many caves and watched them closely as they made their way toward a large entrance in the rock.

"This is Brutus' place," Markus said and pointed to a big man watching them as they approached.

"I can see you are a wealthy man, stranger. I guess you want a place to stash all that stuff?"

"My name is Thomas and you must be Brutus."

"I am. How much can you afford to spend on a place?" he asked with a sneer. His face was crude with bushy eyebrows and yellow stained teeth, half of them missing. He leaned on a long wooden pole for balance, since one of his feet was deformed to the point of a clump of flesh. His hands were huge with some fingers down to stumps. Thomas stepped back because of the foul odor of the disease emanating from his body.

"I hear you have a place I can rent. I can pay if it is acceptable," Thomas said.

"Ah, we do have a rich man here." He stepped forward and held out his hand. "For you that will be twenty denari for the month."

"I will give you ten and we will call it a deal," Thomas said.

"It's a deal, friend. My slave here, Ruth is her name, will show you where your fancy accommodations are. "Come here, Ruth!" he yelled into the cave. "Show this rich man to the cave that was occupied by Markus Venetius." He turned to Thomas with a sneer. "The man died the other day. No big loss, he was getting too bad off to get around anyway. A guy needs to learn when it's time to bow out, I always say." Brutus spit on the ground, barely missing Thomas' feet."

"I hope you do when your time comes, Brutus," Thomas said in a sarcastic tone as he turned and followed the woman, waving for Markus to bring Crassus along.

It was early the next morning. Thomas woke up, sore all over from sleeping on the bare rock. He had to discard the straw that was left from the former occupant, since it smelled horribly. He stepped out of the small cave. The sunlight was bright on this side of the ravine. That was good, since it would be in the shade by noon. He looked around. So this is what his home would be for the rest of his life. A feeling of dread rose up and made him cringe. *If his colleagues in Philadelphia could see him now.* He hadn't thought about them in a long time. He wondered how Helena was and if she missed him. Should he allow her to come visit him? It would be too gruesome for her as his disease progressed.

"Shalom, you are new here, aren't you?" At one time she must have been a beautiful woman, tall, slender and walking with a sway as she approached him. "I am Magdala, the prostitute. I was a famous woman at one time until this dreaded scourge got the better of me. But I can still plie my trade if there is a need." She leaned forward with a seductive smile that looked bizarre, given her deformed facial features. "You are a handsome, rich man. I can tell." She looked at him closely. "I think I have seen you before." Her voice took on a smooth tone. "I was a famous dancer in my time." She suddenly clapped her hands. "That's how I know your face, you are Thomas, Herod's personal physician." She laughed a shrill laugh. "Oh my, how the mighty have fallen."

He cringed.

"What's to keep us now from doing what comes natural," she said with a short little laugh.

"I am not interested Magdala. Go away." He was embarrassed and went back into his cave.

"You can't hide from me for long, physician, none of them can," she shouted after him.

As the day wore on, he had arranged his things in the cave in a way it looked somewhat livable. He even found some straw to make a place for a bed, even if it was flea infested. It was actually quite cool deeper inside the cave and he put the bag with the fruit and cheese back as far as he could. His provisions may not last for two weeks, but some would hold up if he was careful until Lucius brought more. He hid the money pouch in a crevice he found up in the ceiling. That was good, he would need money to buy some things. Surely, the town of Capernaum provided some basic necessities for these poor wretches, like fresh straw and some food items. Even if they charged for them, he had enough to buy whatever he needed.

He sat in the entrance of his cave and watched as dozens of dark figures, wrapped in ragged clothes moved like shadows up and down the sandy path in front of his dwelling. Every one of them was showing signs of the disease. Some hobbled on stumps without toes, others hid their sores and bumps all over their bodies with lose-fitting rags. Most of them had hands with fingers missing or disfigured faces covered with hood-like wrappings made from worn-out cloth. An eerie silence hung over the camp. Not far down, a big fire pit was apparently used for a public cooking area. A dozen people stood waiting for their food to finish cooking. He spotted several stray dogs waiting for scraps to fall on the ground.

Suddenly, he spotted a movement inside his cave. When he looked closer, he saw a rat scamper lazily along the wall without taking any notice of him. He took the wooden rod he had brought and chased it out by trying to hit it. That made him wonder how he could keep his food supply from being eaten by rats and other animals like dogs and cats. He looked around the cave and then took the cheese and dried meat and wrapped them in a heavy piece of cloth and tied a rope around it. There was a sharp, pointed piece of rock sticking out way up on the edge of the ceiling. He took the other end of the rope, tied it around the rock and hung the bundle with the food way up high so no four-legged animal could get to it. His hands felt weak after handling the rope and he had to rest. There was no pain, but the numbness in his feet and hands drove him crazy. His fingers had no feeling in them whatsoever.

He went back outside and sat in the shade of the entrance. This was his life now. The crushing reality of this hellish existence began to fill him with an overpowering dread. This was all there was, all there would ever be, a life among walking shadows in varying degree of decay. It was like a horror movie, except he was part of the cast.

"You are new around here." The voice sounded muffled through the cloth held in front of the face.

"Yes, I am."

"My name is Philip, what's yours?" The man sounded young, but Thomas couldn't tell.

"I am Thomas."

"I heard from Magdala that you are a doctor, is that right?"

"It is."

"We need a doctor in this place, there are many who are sick and dying around here."

"No kidding," Thomas answered in a sarcastic tone. "Who would have thought."

"My brother is sick with a fever. Can you help him?" He pointed down the path. "We live down there. You want to come and look at him?"

"There is nothing I can do for anybody. I don't have medicine of any kind and I can't heal him without it. My name is not Yeshua." He was angry.

"But you could look at him anyway. Maybe you can tell what's wrong with him." He sounded like he wasn't going to go away.

"Please leave me alone, there is nothing I can do. I am sorry about your brother. I hope he feels better," Thomas said and went into the cave. He sat down and put his head on his knees as sobs shook his body. The enormity of his situation and the hopelessness of his surroundings overtook him with a force that made him feel physically ill. When he lifted his head he stared into the dark end of the cave and wanted to scream. PLEASE, SOMEBODY WAKE ME UP!

And here he had worried about being a good man in this place. He couldn't even be a man, but was reduced to a life worse than that of an animal. How do these people manage to survive in this hellhole? What was there to live or wake up for every morning? He had to laugh as his look fell on his medicine bag. It would be a blessing to get sick and die in this place. And here he thought he would arrive and be the great physician among these people. Yes, by all means, let's call 911 and have the ambulance come and take them to his hospital and he would perform surgery in a sterile surgical suite....

He started to laugh, a hysterical laugh that wouldn't stop until it changed into screaming.

"Why did you let this happen to me? You knew it would all the time. Why didn't you heal me? I hate you, Yeshua, I hate you, I hate you! Let me die!" He whimpered like an animal in pain. "I am Thomas Peterson, MD, Chief of Thoracic Surgery at Mercy Hospital in Philadelphia in the year 2016. This is a terrible nightmare. Please, somebody wake me up!"

No one came to check on him, no one cared, because they had all been there. Finally, the screaming stopped and turned into uncontrolled sobbing. He collapsed on the straw mattress and curled up into a fetal position and finally fell asleep from exhaustion.

Chapter 27

When he woke up the next morning, it was a gray and dreary day. Heavy clouds covered the sky and the air smelled of rain. He hated the thought of waking up and tried to go back to sleep, but the urge to relieve himself was too insistent. The container in the back of the cave reminded him of the prison cell in Macheraus. When he finally sat up, he saw the rat sniffing for crumbs from the meal he had last night. He stared at it and was amazed it was not the least bit afraid of him, but scuttled over and nuzzled at his hand. He realized it was the former owner's pet! He laughed to himself. The only creature to love him now was a rat!

"I see you found Apolonia," a voice said from the entrance. "She was Markus' friend. I am Leah."

"Go away, I don't want to talk to anyone." His tone was distant.

"They all say that when they first get here," she said. "But after a while you have to talk to someone or you go mad." She sat down in the entrance way. "I have been here for a long time and I have seen it all. Magdala told me you are a physician. It won't do you any good in this place, will it? We are all sick and so are you. What will help you is to realize you have to do anything you can to stay alive or you are not going to make it."

"Why should I want to stay alive, Leah?" he asked, his voice filled with sarcasm. "This is not living; this is hell on earth."

"Yes, it is, but it is the only life we have." She pushed back her head covering and Thomas saw her face, horribly marred and distorted. From the way she acted and talked, he figured she was middle-aged, about fifty, but he couldn't be sure. "You might as well take a good look; it is only going to get worse." She pointed to her face and body. "I count myself fortunate, at least I am not blind and I can still use my limbs."

"You call that fortunate?" He spat out the words.

"Yes, around here it is. What is your name?"

"Thomas."

"Well, Thomas, you will get used to this since you don't have a choice." She sat down in the entrance with great effort and leaned against the rock. "I see you have a lot of things in here. They will not last, because word has gotten around that you are a wealthy man. The first time you leave this place it will all be gone. I have already heard the gang talk about you."

"What gang?"

"Oh, that would be Brutus and his cohorts. He has about ten low life criminal types who take everything from everyone and sell it to the rest of us."

"What can you do to stop them?"

"Nothing, unless you have someone to watch your stuff when you have to leave," she answered.

"And you want to be the one to do it?" Thomas smirked at her.

"It's better than lose it, isn't it?"

He looked at her. "What are you asking in return?"

"I need protection. You look like a good man. If I move in with you, they will leave me alone. Otherwise I am only a woman for the taking for these creeps."

"Are you saying you want to stay in here with me on a permanent basis and live with me?"

"Yes. I would cook for you and keep this place clean." She leaned over and looked around outside. "I am the first one to ask, there will be others. But I am the one with the least problems. The others are much worse off and can't work hard like I can."

Thomas looked her over carefully. She was ugly as sin with lesions covering her face, but her brown eyes looked friendly. The rest of her body was probably ravaged by the disease as well.

"Well, Leah, let me think about it. Come back later and we will talk."

"You are making a mistake, Thomas. They are waiting out there for you and will beat you up to get your stuff if you remain in here alone," she said. "At least let me take your food and hide it for you."

"You really think I'm stupid, don't you? If I give it to you I will never see you again."

"Suit yourself. It will be gone whether you hand it over to me or not. Except with me, it will be safe, by yourself it will be gone and then you have to buy it back from them."

"I will take my chances. I know how to defend myself." He knew he could still rely on his self-defense abilities.

"I will leave you then and come back later. I hope you will be alright by then." She got up with great difficulties and hobbled away.

No sooner had she gone, when the entrance was filled with the figure of a huge man. It was Brutus with his men behind him.

"Hand over your stuff, rich man, I am here to collect," he growled menacingly. "Hand it over or we will teach you what it means to be uncooperative."

"Go away, Brutus. I am not just going to give you my stuff because you ask for it. It is mine and you have no right to it," Thomas answered as he pushed the man away from the entrance into the rain outside.

Brutus stumbled backward and hit the muddy ground with a look of surprise on his face. His men stepped back in fear when they realized Thomas was holding a rod, ready to use it.

"Make no mistake, you come near me I will kill you with this," Thomas said as he shook the staff at them. "I know how to defend myself against a bunch of crippled morons like you." He looked down at Brutus with contempt.

It took the big man an enormous effort to get back up with one useless foot, until his men helped him. When he was finally standing before Thomas, his face was a contorted mask of hatred.

"You will be sorry for this, Physician. No one treats Brutus this way," he growled with clenched teeth. "I will kill you if that is the last thing I do."

"Help yourself and find out you're going to end up in the same position you did a minute ago. Now get away from me and don't let me see your ugly face again," Thomas said with contempt.

He stood with the rod in his hand and watched them leave in the pouring rain. He realized he had made a mortal enemy on the second day of his stay. He would have to be careful.

"You did good, Thomas. I'm impressed." It was Leah. "But they will be back when you least expect it. Probably at night when you are asleep. And you do have to go to sleep sometime, Thomas."

"Go away, I don't want you, nothing personal. I cannot handle living with someone right now. I have enough to do to get used to this hellhole."

"I will be waiting and watching, Thomas. There will come a day when you will need me. Before it was free, now it will cost you." She looked at him with hurt and rejection in her eyes and walked away into the rain.

He sat down at the entrance and looked at the surroundings for the first time since he got here yesterday. Little Apolonia came running and cuddled in the folds of this robe. He stroked her glossy, dark hair and she went to sleep.

The Tombs was a deep gorge with one side rising up to the plateau where the road was they came on. The other was made up of a long stretch of a rock formation with a number of caves formed by rainwater as it washed away the soft lime rock over time. A narrow dirt path ran in front of the caves which made him think of a street with row houses in a poor neighborhood in the big cities. Missing were the little yards in the front. Here there were only piles of sand which turned into thick mud in the rain.

There had to be a water source somewhere. He would have to find it since his supply of wine would be gone soon. The 'street', if you could call it, was empty. Apparently everyone stayed inside during bad weather. He watched the rain run down in a rivulet across from him on the other side of the entrance. Water! He hurried inside and found a mid-size clay pot he had brought and positioned it so the water could run into it. That would last him for two days if not more. He would have to go back and remember the camping trips he had gone on when he belonged to the boy scouts. It was a long time ago, but what else did he have to do?

He wondered where he could wash himself. Maybe there was a stream nearby. There had to be something like it or the people here couldn't survive. He would ask someone when the rain stopped. But it didn't stop for two more days. By then the road was so muddy, it was impossible to walk without sinking into a thick layer of sludge. Most of the people were unable to get around since their feet were crippled. Only those who still had normal legs were slowly leaving their caves.

Brutus and his cohorts had not returned. He was beginning to relax. Maybe they had learned their lesson and would leave him alone. He did notice that no one spoke to him. As a matter of fact, when he ventured out to the cooking area, everybody totally ignored him. More than that, he realized they were afraid of him. Or better, afraid of Brutus, if they associated with him. Apparently the man had a strangle hold on this community and ruled it with an iron fist.

He didn't mind being left alone. He was still in a state of shock finding himself in this abyss of hopelessness. His mind was a blank and the only thing that kept him sane was Apolonia. She turned out to be a most affectionate little animal and clung to him with unconditional love. He felt a ridiculous tenderness as he fed her bits of cheese and small pieces of bread, which was pretty stale by now. Because of the rain, it had mold on the corner. He made himself eat it since it would provide some antibiotic effect in this filthy environment.

Another week went by and he had not heard or seen any sign of Brutus or his men. He was on his way to the small brook that ran on the edge of the gorge, fed by a spring coming out of the side of the rock. The people stepped away as he approached. Without hesitation he took his clothes off and waded into the water. It felt cold, but wonderful. He would finally feel clean and didn't care if anyone was watching. He had brought another set of clothes and put them on and washed the filthy ones he had worn for a week. He felt invigorated when he made it back to his cave. The moment he walked inside he realized that everything he owned was gone! Apolonia ran to him through the empty space with a delighted squeal. He carefully laid out his wet clothes on the rocks outside to dry in the sun as a cold anger rose within him. The bastards!

"I told you this would happen, but you wouldn't listen, would you? Now it is too late. You have nothing." Leah stood behind him. "You are just like every other man I have ever known. They think they can handle everything by themselves and the gods forbid they would take advice from a woman." He turned around and looked at her. She wore a smirk on her face as she went on, "Unless you have some money stashed away, you are out of luck and will starve to death for all anyone cares around here, including me."

"Get away from me, woman. I don't need you!" he yelled at her, "and stop coming around and heckling me." He took a threatening step toward her and she walked away laughing a vicious little laugh. "You'll come around, physician, just wait and see."

He went inside and reached for his money pouch hidden in the ceiling. Thank the gods, they hadn't found it." It would be a week before Lucius came back with fresh supplies. He could buy some stuff until then and make due. He stuffed the money back in the hiding place when he heard voices outside.

"You got tired of your old furniture, did you physician?" It was Brutus and his men. Maybe you want new stuff. I just got a new load of goods, you want to buy some?" He was laughing. "Come by my place and look around, I will give you a good price."

Thomas looked at the man with an ice cold stare. "I will make you feel sorry, Brutus. For now, I will buy my things back if you deliver them to me here. I will even pay your price. Like you say, I am a rich man and money doesn't mean anything to me." He stepped closer and looked him square in the eyes. "If you ever do this again I will kill you with my bare hands." His voice was so filled with hate, Brutus stepped back with fear in his eyes.

"Fellows, get the stuff and put it back in his place while I conduct business with him." He turned to Thomas and held out his hand. "That will be twenty denari, physician."

"When I have my stuff back you will get your money, not before. Now get away from me until they bring my things and don't show your ugly face before then."

When Brutus came to collect the money, Thomas looked at him with a calculating stare.

"I want to make a deal with you. I am a rich man. If you play your cards right, you can make more money off of me than you would stealing my stuff. I will pay you twenty denarii on top of the ten for the rent if you promise to leave me and my things alone and tell everyone else to do the same. Think of it, it will be a steady income without the danger of me bashing your head in the next time you come near me or my things. What do you say?"

"That sounds like a deal, Physician. How do I know you are going to pay me regularly?"

"If I don't follow through, all bets are off and we can go back to fighting each other," Thomas answered.

Thomas walked back into his cave. Twenty denari meant nothing to him. Lucius would bring him money any time he needed it, according to their arrangement. He would have paid more just to get his things back and be left in peace.

An hour later, he was busy arranging his possessions in the cave and before long, everything looked the way it had been. He even bought some more bread while he was at it. Apparently Brutus ran a thriving little grocery store. Thomas didn't know whether the food he sold was stolen or whether he had an outside supplier. Thomas didn't care as long as he could buy enough food for himself on a regular basis to fill in until Lucius could bring more. Things didn't look near as bleak as they had when he first got here. He knew he could make it, given the circumstances, no matter what Leah said. After all, he was intelligent, resourceful and rich. Money could get him anything, even in this place.

The days went by in a never ending, boring succession. Each morning he made a scratch into the wall so he wouldn't miss when Lucius came to see him. According to his markings, tomorrow was the day. He didn't recall that they set a time, so he was forced to spend hours waiting by the basket. After a while he decided he would climb up the steps to see his old friend and find out about Helena and Lydia. It took forever to make it up since his muscles were weakening. But finally, he reached the top and sat on the ground, looking down the road for the cart. It was two hours later he saw the unmistakable big ears of Igor.

There were two people sitting on the cart, but he couldn't make out who it was at first. Finally, as they came closer he realized it was Lucius and Helena! She jumped off while they were still quite a distance away and ran toward him, her beautiful blond hair trailing behind her.

"Daddy, I'm here!" she shouted, her arms waving.

"Don't come any closer, Angel," he said and held his hands out with a gesture to stop her.

"I don't care, I want to hug you." She was crying and laughing at the same time.

"No, Helena, you must stop right there or I have no choice but to go down into the gorge.

She finally stopped three feet in front of him and looked at him with horror. "Daddy, what happened to your face?"

"I know I don't look too good, but this is still me, your Daddy who loves you more than anyone in the world. It's only on the outside I have changed. I'm still the same on the inside." He waved for her to sit with him on the ground. "Greetings, Lucius, how good to see you. Come, let's sit and talk. It has been a long time since I have seen both of you. Tell me how things are in the real world. How is Lydia?"

"She is going to have a baby, Daddy, did you know that?" If it is a boy they are going to name him Thomas." She was bubbly and happy and soon forgot about his looks.

"I know. You will have to help Lydia take care of it, won't you?" he asked.

"I can't wait to have a little brother or sister. It will be so much fun. Lucius got me a doll so I can practice how to hold it and all that."

"How are you, Thomas?" Lucius said after a while. "You have survived your first two weeks. "How is it down there?"

"You don't want to know, my friend. It is not a place anyone would ever want to live, but I have managed to make it somehow and settled into some sort of routine," he said. "Believe it or not, they have a vendor down there who sells items like food and other necessities. I will need some more money. Did you bring any, Lucius?"

"Of course I did, I have it right here. Let me know if it is enough. If not, I will come back tomorrow with the horses and bring you more. We all want you to have every comfort possible. I also brought plenty of food. When you are ready, we will load it into the basket for you."

"Thank you, old friend. It makes life more tolerable down there knowing you are there to help me."

"When are you coming home, Daddy?" Helena asked. "I miss you and think you have stayed here long enough."

"I will never come home, Helena. I have leprosy and all who do, have to stay in this place."

"What about when you get well?" she asked with disappointment in her voice.

"I will never get well, only worse," he said and looked at her with great sadness.

"Yes, you will. I will ask Yeshua to make you well and then you can come back home." She was close to tears. Promise me, Daddy, if I take you, you will come with me to where He preaches and then I can ask Him to heal you like He does with all the other sick people."

"I don't think He will, Helena. Please don't ask me to do this. I won't because I am very angry with Him. He knows where I am and did not do anything to stop this disease when I saw Him a few weeks ago. What makes you think He will heal me if I went now?"

"He can't heal you if you're angry with Him, Daddy. You have to give Him your heart and tell Him you're sorry. I know, because I have been with Him many times when I go with Lucius and Lydia."

"You take her with you to follow Him, Lucius?" Thomas sounded angry. "I don't want you to do that. I won't stand for it. She is my daughter and you will do as I say."

"No, Thomas, she is under our legal care and we decide, not you. There is no way we will leave her alone with the slaves and go off with Yeshua on His trips."

"How does He feel about having children bothering Him?" Thomas asked.

"Let me tell you what happened one day when His disciples asked who was the greatest in the kingdom of heaven. This is what He answered them as He asked a little boy to stand with Him,

"And he said, "I tell you the truth, unless you change and become like little children, you will never enter the kingdom of heaven. Therefore, whoever humbles himself like this child is the greatest in the kingdom of heaven." (Matthew 18:2-4)

"He loves me, Daddy," Helena said before Lucius could go on. "He has told me many times. And when He talks to me He always asks about you. That means He loves you, too." She looked at Thomas with her big, blue eyes. "I think we should go see Him together when you are ready and ask Him to heal you." She smiled at Thomas. "I know He will heal you even if you don't think so. He says if I have faith as little as a tiny mustard seed I can move big mountains of trouble. And you look like you are in big trouble, aren't you, Daddy?" Before he could stop her she touched his hand and said," I have enough faith for both of us, because I love you."

Chapter 28

Thomas returned to his cave with an ample supply of figs, dates, grapes and things like cheese, meat and a wineskin filled with the best wine. Little Apolonia liked grapes and squirted juice all over the floor as she bit into one.

After his visit with Helena and Lucius, he realized how much he missed them and his home. He would never be able to go back there. A sudden anger flooded his mind. Yeshua knew he had leprosy. Why didn't He heal him? It would have been nothing for Him. Instead He allows him to languish in this rat hole. If he ever thought the Carpenter could be the Meshiah, this killed that notion. No Son of God would act like that, just because he didn't believe in Him.

Thomas decided he would have to learn to cut out all feelings of love and longing in order to survive. He didn't want to be torn up inside every time he thought of the people he loved. This was the here and now and he would have to make the best of it. There was no way he would ever allow himself to be drawn to anyone for fear of losing them. He was alone and would stay alone, no matter what happened.

"You sure have an abundance of food, Thomas," Leah said as she stopped by the entrance.

"Yes, and I didn't need you to get it or have it be safe, did I?"

"You must really be a wealthy man to pay Brutus all that money every month." She looked at Thomas with envy. "Would you give me some food or money?"

"Why, you threatened me the last time we talked that I would have to pay you for your favors. Why should I?"

"I'm sorry, I didn't mean it," she said, trying to sound contrite.

"You absolutely did mean it, Leah. You are one of those who hang around men who have the most to give you. If I was poor, you wouldn't give me the time of day."

"That is true. I would have starved to death if I hadn't, even when I was a child. My mother was a prostitute from Greece and she kicked me out of the house when I was ten. I have taken care of myself ever since."

"And the best you could accomplish was to become a common whore?"

"I was very beautiful once," she said wistfully.

"I was good looking once, too. So what? Nothing in life lasts, not looks, not riches or status. It can all be taken in a moment's notice." He sounded bitter. 'I put no faith in any of that anymore and instead live for the moment. And for this moment I don't want you or need you."

"You are a mean man, Thomas. Have you always been like this?"

"I tried nice. It doesn't pay. I tried being good, nothing came of it either. The only thing that really works is mean and looking out for number one. Having money is all that stands between me and misery in the end. Let's face it, I am miserable, but at least I am somewhat comfortable." He looked at her with disdain. "Get lost, I don't like scum like you."

She walked away, dejected and hunched over and disappeared in one of the caves down the road.

He felt anger at the way he had acted, but he had to learn to avoid being soft. After all, he couldn't feed everybody here, so why waste his feelings or food on an ugly whore?

Over the next few days he ventured out of his cave, because he no longer feared for his stuff being stolen. The people treated him with new respect as he walked up to the cooking place. He was a rich man under the protection of Brutus.

His eyes fell on a slender woman in her early twenties. She appeared shy and withdrawn and stood to the side to wait her turn at the fire. When no one let her approach, Thomas took her piece of meat and put it on the fire.

"Thank you, Sir," she said in a whisper.

"What is your name?"

"I am Esther from the city of Tyre."

"I am Thomas."

"I know. Everyone knows who you are."

"How long have you been here, Esther?" Thomas asked in a gentle voice.

"For two seasons, Sir," she said with profound sadness in her voice.

"Were you a slave?"

"No, my father was a blacksmith and moved his family to Capernaum shortly before I got the sickness. That is why I know who you are. You used to be the physician of the poor in Capernaum until you became famous at Herod's court." She tried not to look at him and hid her face under a large head scarf.

"Come and eat with me when our food is done. My place is just down the road," he said with a smile.

"I am not allowed to visit a man without a chaperone, Sir. My father would not like that."

"Your father is not here, Esther, what difference does it make?" Thomas sounded irritated.

"I am also a follower of Yeshua and he wants me to obey not only my father but Him as well." She shrank back from Thomas in fear. "Please do not force me, Sir, I beg you."

"Then come and just talk to me, I promise not to hurt you," he said and took her meat and his and walked toward his cave. She followed reluctantly, fear showing on her face. She reminded him of Lydia with her gentle brown eyes and thick, long dark hair. She wore a loose robe, but he could tell she had a beautiful figure. There were no signs of leprosy on her face and her skin was flawless.

"Sit down and let's eat some of this good food." He offered her grapes and encouraged her to drink from the wineskin. She soon began to relax as he urged her to drink and eat all she wanted.

"Why don't you take your scarf off so I can look at you, Esther," he said with a smile. "It's alright. We all have unsightly signs of this terrible disease."

Slowly she dropped the scarf and let it fall down to her shoulders. She was stunningly beautiful with a pure innocence that took his breath away. "You are a very pretty girl, Esther."

"I wouldn't know, Sir, I have never looked at myself," she said and smiled at him as she took another grape. "You are being very kind to me, Sir. Thank you, but I think I should be going now."

"Please, don't go. I get very lonely. Won't you stay and keep me company just a little longer? Here, have some more wine." He handed her the wineskin.

"This tastes very good. I have never had wine before, Sir."

"You can call me Thomas, Esther, because we are friends, aren't we?" He smiled at her and in spite of his disfigured features, she responded in kind. "Thank you, Thomas. I would like to be your friend. I think that would be alright with my father and Yeshua."

They sat for another hour and she had no idea she was getting inebriated until she could not keep her eyes open any longer. Gently he led her to the straw mattress in the back of the cave. She tried to push him away and began to cry, but stopped resisting after he pinned her down.

After it was over she rose from the mattress, and after straightening out her garment, left the cave without looking back. He turned his face against the wall and went to sleep.

The next day he forced Esther to move in with him by telling her she was a disgraced woman and had no choice but to live with him if she ever wanted to please her father or Yeshua. She believed him and literally became his slave, cooking, cleaning and taking care of his needs. He became the envy of every man in the camp, because Esther was by far the most beautiful woman there.

She was extremely quiet and subservient and never disobeyed him in any way. He never allowed himself to feel anything for her, but treated her as he had his slaves. She was just another convenience and nothing more. He wouldn't allow it, because deep feelings were a thing of the past.

His heart became more hardened and callous to the suffering of others as time went on. He stopped allowing Helena to come visit and demanded that one of Lucius' slaves bring the supplies. A great darkness of mind came over him as he learned to take advantage over others by buying their soul with his money. He not only bought things, but bought their loyalty with his riches and could get them to do anything he wished. His power became greater than that of Brutus and it was only a matter of time until the two of them would come to blows over who ruled this unlikely kingdom.

He would not allow any kind of thoughts of regret or guilt about anything he did. Nothing mattered in this horrible dungeon, just his personal comforts and the control he had gained over the others in the camp. They had become his slaves and he the master. And this time he didn't even try to treat them with kindness, but with a cruelty and harshness he had never known he was capable of.

It happened on a moonlit night. Thomas was asleep in his cave when he heard the voices outside. They belonged to Brutus and his men. He rose from his straw pallet and took his rod, which he always kept close by and silently crept toward the entrance. He hid in the shadows until the men stopped in front of his cave. Brutus carefully hobbled toward the entrance, a long knife in his hand. Thomas allowed him to walk past him into the cave and then hit him over the head as hard as he could. Brutus dropped like a rock. He groaned as he tried to get up. Before he could rise, Thomas raised his rod again and again with such frenzied fury, he couldn't stop until Brutus' head was a mangled bloody mess on the floor. Thomas stepped over him to where the others stood.

"You want to try me? I'm ready. I will kill all of you if I have to," he shouted and stepped toward them. They fled as fast as they could, seeing their leader was dead.

Thomas stood, his breath coming in shallow gasps. He had just killed a man in cold blood. Well, Brutus had asked for it for a long time. Now there was no one to oppose him. He was the undisputed leader of this miserable place.

"Get back inside!" he shouted at Esther who stood frozen in fear, staring at the bloody corpse.

By now several people had heard the commotion and stood in front of the cave on the other side of the dirt path.

"What are you looking at? The man tried to kill me so I got to him first. I need some men to carry this miserable excuse of a man to the garbage dump. There is money in it if you will help," he added.

Before the sun was up, all evidence that anything had ever happened in the cave had been cleaned up by Esther. Thomas sat in the sunny spot by the entrance enjoying his breakfast of grapes, cheese and bread. Little Apolonia helped with the crumbs.

Afterwards he walked over to the place that used to belong to Brutus. One of the men stood guarding the food and other items for sale.

"This is now mine and you work for me, is that clear?" he spat out. "Do you have any problems with that?"

"No, Master, I don't. I just want to know if I can still work here for my food," he said in a whiny voice.

"You can stay for now until I see what all this is. If you can help me find out what this business is all about, I will consider keeping you on. Just remember, you cheat me, the same thing that happened to Brutus will happen to you."

"Yes, Master. I will do as you say, just don't hurt me."

"Stop whining and get to work," Thomas said in a harsh tone and took his time going through the inventory. He found many items that used to belong to him. Now they were his again. He smiled. He was not only rich, but powerful again.

When he returned to his cave, he found Esther crying.

"Thomas, I think I am pregnant. I am afraid. How can I bring a child into this terrible place?" She looked at him with pleading eyes.

"I will not allow it. There are ways to get rid of the baby. I will get some herbs I know will work and I will help you," he said without emotion.

"But that is my baby, I cannot allow you to kill it, Thomas," she said with surprising force.

"You will do as I say and that's it, woman. I am the master and I decide what is to be done."

She cowered before him and sat in the corner of the back of the cave and wept silently.

The next time the slave came to deliver the supplies, Thomas ordered him to come back that day and bring him a supply of oil made from an herb called Pennyroyal from Lucius' medical supplies. It was delivered that afternoon by Lucius himself.

"What is this for, Thomas?" Lucius asked when he put it into the basket.

"I have to help a woman out, Lucius, don't worry about it."

Thomas, we are all worried about you and haven't seen or spoken to you in months. Are you alright? Helena misses you terribly. Please, come up and talk to me."

"I can no longer climb those steps," Thomas lied. "I am fine. Give my love to everyone. And thank you for the medicine." With that he turned and left Lucius standing way up on the bank.

Two days later he forced Esther to take the mixture in spite of her tears and pleading. The next morning she started bleeding. By that afternoon she was dead.

The day after, Thomas moved into Brutus' cave, since it was the biggest one in the camp. It was as if Esther had never existed.

Thomas ruled the camp with an iron fist and proved to be more cruel than Brutus had ever been. He inspired fear in everyone and encountered no resistance to whatever orders or demands he made. No one dared speak to him or engage in conversation unless spoken to. He sensed a seething hatred in the people, but didn't care. *Let them hate me, what difference does it make?* He didn't like a single one of the crippled miserable misfits who lived there.

Chapter 29

Several weeks went by until he noticed one morning that his vision was a little cloudy. At first he thought there was smoke in the air, but then he realized his eyes could not focus. He knew the leprosy had progressed to his optic nerves and with a sudden jolt he realized he would be blind before long. *Oh God!* He sat in front of his cave and stared down on the street below. People were walking and talking as if nothing had changed. He wanted to scream at them I AM GOING BLIND! But then, many of them were already in that state, so his problem would not cause anyone to lose sleep. He tried to remember how long it would take to render him helpless, but he couldn't. All he knew, there was nothing to be done, he would go blind. With sudden dread he realized he would be at the mercy of those he had so cruelly mistreated. He groaned. *Why are you doing this to me, Yeshua?* He wanted to scream, but no sound came out. The position he had so carefully built up in this place would crumble and he would be worse than nothing – again!

Every day his eyesight got slowly worse. He told no one as fear took over his whole being, since he was certain there was not one person who would help him. No one would lead him by the hand like Markus did for Crassus. He would be on his own.

He was not just losing his eyesight, but his hands and feet had gotten a lot worse as well. He now walked by leaning heavily on his rod and had lost two fingers on the right hand. They simply fell off one day and he hadn't noticed. Not only did his eyes get dim, his body was deteriorating at an alarming rate and he realized with sudden fear, His reign as undisputed ruler of this miserable realm was coming to an end.

Soon the men working for him began to notice he couldn't see very much. They became more and more lax in their jobs and even refused to obey him at times. It was on a sunny morning he woke up in total darkness and realized he was completely blind. When he called for his servant, no one came. He could not feel his way along the walls because he had no feeling in his hands. He staggered to where he thought the exit was and knew he was outside when he felt the breeze on his forehead. He called out for someone to help him, but no one answered.

That's when he heard the voices down in the street.

"Come on, big man, what are you going to do to us now, hey? We have already taken all your stuff and even your food. Come and get us, rich man, where is your money?" He knew it was one of his workers he had beaten a few days ago for stealing a piece of bread.

"I will lead you to the pot if you give me ten denari, rich man," another taunted him. "But I'd rather not. I want to see you mess all over yourself." There was continued laughter and taunting.

Thomas stood rigid, his head held high. He turned to go back into his cave. His body trembled in fear as he slumped down on his mattress. "PLEASE, SOMEBODY GET ME OUT OF HERE!" he shouted, but no one heard him. There was total silence and darkness. The blackest darkness he had ever experienced. He put his head on his knees and sat motionless for hours. When he finally got up to find the waste container, he could not find it and had to relieve himself wherever he stood since he had no idea what part of the cave he was in.

Two days went by and no one came to check on him. He had not had anything to drink or eat in all that time and was ready to give up and lie down and die.

"Come on, Physician, I brought you some food. You don't deserve it, but I feel sorry for you." It was Leah, the prostitute. "I have always had a soft spot for you, even though you are a miserable excuse for a human being," she said as she handed him some bread with cheese on it. "Here take this, it will help."

"Nothing will help," he said as he stuffed the food into his mouth and took a long drink out of the wineskin. "Just let me die."

"Not so fast, first I want all your money and stuff. In return I will take care of you."

"You can have it. It means nothing to me now."

"Good. I want you to tell the people out there that you are giving it to me for taking care of you."

"I will."

"I told you some day you would need me and I would make you pay. Today is that day, Physician."

"Thank you, Leah."

"Don't thank me. I am getting richly rewarded for what I am doing for you. Like you told me, I stick with the guy with the most money and you are still it around here. Before I forget, I also want this cave for my own," she added. He couldn't see the smirk on her face. "You can stay here with me until I get tired of you and then I will throw you out the way you threw me away."

"Please, lead me to the entrance and let me sit in the sun for a little while," Thomas said. I want to feel the warmth of sunshine on my face.

"I will do that, but then I am going to be gone for a while and you better not go inside and soil the place because you can't find the waste container. I am tired of cleaning up after your mess." She sounded harsh and pulled him up with a hard jerk. "Come and don't give me any grief."

It felt good to feel the rays of the sun on his face. He would give anything if he could see its brightness one more time.

As the days went by, he fell into a deep depression. The only time he moved was when Leah made him get up and eat and relieve himself. The rest of the time he lay on the straw mattress in the back of the cave.

"You stay back there Thomas, since you can't see the sun anyway," Leah said. She totally ignored him most of the time and walked the street, telling everyone how rich she was now.

As Thomas lay there for hours, his mind went to the time when this nightmare began. He had a hard time imagining himself as Chief of Thoracic Surgery of a large hospital in the year 2016. How had he come all the way from there to this hellhole, blind, crippled and hated by everyone?

He had been so sure he was a good person, intelligent, educated and successful. Sure, he had cheated on his wife, but he did say he was sorry and tried to mend their relationship. His problems started when his life got involved with Yeshua, the mysterious carpenter who said He was the Meshiah. *What if He really is?* Thomas cringed. This entire journey had its beginning with that question and it was now coming to an end. He wished he could have gotten an answer before he died. But what good would it do if he found out Yeshua was the Meshiah? If the man had tried to show him what a failure he was as a human being, as a husband, father and a physician, He had succeeded. Thomas recoiled as his horrible sins suddenly piled up before him like a horrendous nightmare. They paraded in his mind with such clarity, it took his breath away. He was an adulterer many times over, a repeated rapist, a cruel slave owner, responsible for the death of three people and the killer of two unborn babies. Add to that greed and the desire for fame and recognition, he was no better than King Herod, maybe even worse.

It occurred to him that he had tried three times to gain recognition and power over people through money. The first time as a surgeon in Philadelphia, the second time as the physician for the rich and powerful and the third time here in this miserable hellhole. And it was this desire of wanting absolute power over others that had destroyed him. This was why Yeshua came. To take away his sin of pride, the arrogance that declared he could be good and be a righteous man in his own strength. The words of Melissa's grandmother resounded in his mind.

"Whoever believes in him is not condemned, but whoever does not believe stands condemned already because he has not believed in the name of God's one and only Son. This is the verdict: Light has come into the world, but men loved darkness instead of light because their deeds were evil." (John 3:18-19)

That is what Yeshua tried to tell him, the Light came and he chose darkness and became a part of such evil as he never thought possible. His current blindness was the outward sign of his sinful, dark soul.

It was too late. He would die without ever seeing light again, without ever being able to tell Yeshua He was sorry. He began to sob uncontrollably. Not just because of his current situation, but more so because he had missed the Meshiah who had tried so many times to draw him. It was at that moment he gave up as his mind sank to the very bottom of his existence. *Yeshua, please let me die since I am not worth saving.*

When the slave came the next time to deliver the supplies, there was no one to receive them. When it happened again a day later, Lucius drove the carriage to The Tombs by himself. When no one reacted to his calls, he reluctantly took the steps down to the bottom. He saw a lonely, shadowy figure staring at him as if he was a ghost in his fancy clothes.

"Where can I find Thomas the physician?" he asked. He could not figure out if it was a man or a woman hidden underneath the loose garments and head cover.

"He lives at the end of the road in the last cave," the voice said. "He may be dead by now, who knows."

Lucius hurried as fast as he could until he stood in front of the last entrance.

"Thomas, are you there?" he shouted.

It took a long time for Leah to stick her head out. She was stunned to see a man in expensive clothes standing there shouting for Thomas.

"What do you want?"

"Where is Thomas?"

"He is in here, but he can't come out. He is blind and never gets up from his bed anymore. Every morning I think he is dead, but then I find him still breathing," she said with resignation. "I am tired of taking care of him."

Lucius brushed past her into the inside of the cave. It took his eyes a minute to get used to the darkness.

"Thomas, it is Lucius, where are you?"

"Lucius, is that you?" Thomas' voice was a whisper. "You shouldn't have come. It is too dangerous."

Lucius looked at his friend and began to weep. "What has happened to you, my friend?"

"I am blind Lucius, and too sick to get up anymore. My hands and feet are numb and weak and I have lost most of my fingers and toes. Just leave me here to die, it is better that way."

"I cannot do that, Thomas. We are going to see Yeshua. He will heal you, I know He will." He reached down and pulled Thomas up with both hands. "Come, I will take you to Him."

"I can't make it up the steps."

"You have to, I insist."

It took almost an hour for Thomas to reach the top of the ridge. His body was shaking with weakness and several times he almost lost his balance and crashed to the bottom.

"You will be fine," Lucius said. "I am glad I brought the carriage. No one can see you inside."

"I do not want to go to your home, it is too dangerous," he said in a weak voice. "I am in a bad way."

"I know you are, but I promised Helena if you ever agreed to go see Yeshua, she would be there at your side. We will go pick her up. She can sit with me up front."

Lucius drove the horses as fast as they could run until they came to a halt in front of his house.

"I will go and get Helena. I won't be a minute." He rushed inside and came back with her. Her excitement turned into shock as she looked inside the carriage.

"Yeshua will touch you, Daddy, you will see," she finally said and smiled at him even though he couldn't see it.

"Where are we going, Lucius?" Thomas asked.

"Yeshua is preaching by the lake. He has just come down from the mountains and a lot of people are going there to see Him. As if to confirm his words, there were more and more people making their way toward the lake. It was not long before he saw the apostles and Yeshua standing under a large tree, waiting for everyone to get there.

"We are close enough, Thomas. You can make it to Him if you walk slowly. Helena will lead you, just put your hand on her shoulder," Lucius said as he helped Thomas down from the carriage. Several people stared at them and ran away when they saw Thomas. Some even grumbled and told him to go away, but Lucius glared at them and they walked on in a hurry. Yeshua is standing with his men a few feet in front of you under a large tree," Helena said and stopped.

Thomas stood, trembling as he felt Yeshua approaching and fell to his knees sobbing,

"Master, I am a wretched, sinful man and you have known all along what was in my heart. Yet I would not listen. Please forgive my pride, my arrogance and the horrible crimes I have committed. I am not worthy of anything but death and eternal punishment. But I know you love me, you always have and told me you have come for the lost. I am lost and blind and crippled and deserve to be punished for what I have done. Forgive me, Master. But you said you died for my sins on the cross so that I may live. I give you my life, my body and my mind to do with as you wish. You are my Meshiah and I take you into my heart from this day forward." Thomas kept his face down and added almost as an afterthought,

"Lord, if you are willing you can make me clean."

Yeshua reached out his hand and touched the man.

"I am willing," He said. "Be clean." (Matthew 8:2-3)

Thomas felt a gentle pain spread through his body, followed by soothing warmth filling his entire being. He opened his eyes and saw Yeshua smiling at him with His familiar, knowing smile. Thomas felt such love as he had never experienced. He grabbed the Rabbi's robe and said between sobs,

"Thank you for forgiving me, Lord, thank you for your love and for allowing me to finally see."

He looked at his hands and feet. They were healed and strength was returning to his body. He got up and turned around and swept Helena into his arms. "I am healed, Angel. Yeshua healed me!"

"I told you all along He would, Daddy," she cried. "I told you He loves you."

When Thomas turned back to Yeshua, He looked at him with a special intensity and said,

"Go rather to the lost sheep of Israel. As you go, preach this message: The kingdom of heaven is near. Heal the sick, raise the dead, cleanse those who have leprosy, drive out demons. Freely you have received, freely give. (Matthew 10:5-8)

Thomas bowed low when he felt Yeshua's hand on his head in a gesture of blessing while He spoke,

"Blessed are those who are persecuted because of righteousness, for theirs is the kingdom of heaven.

Blessed are you when people insult you, persecute you and falsely say all kinds of evil against you because of me. Rejoice and be glad, because great is your reward in heaven, for in the same way they persecuted the prophets who were before you." (Matthew 5:3-12)

Thomas stood transfixed as he realized, for the first time he understood everything Yeshua had said.

Chapter 30

The carriage turned into the long driveway up to his house. Lucius held the reins as Helena sat inside snuggling up to Thomas.

"You are coming home, Daddy. I never thought you would come home, not ever," she said with a happy sigh.

"And here I thought you knew all along Yeshua would heal me." He laughed.

"I did, but then I didn't. I don't know. I am just glad He did. Does that make any sense?"

"It does, it does indeed, Angel."

All was quiet when they stopped at the front entrance.

"I wonder where everyone is," Helena said as she jumped down. "Do you need any help, Daddy?"

"When Yeshua healed me He did a perfect job. I feel wonderful and have all my strength back," he said and jumped down with a spring in his feet.

"Master, you are back!" It was Octavia. She stood with a look of surprise and fear as she bowed to him.

Thomas walked up to her with a big smile. "I have returned from the dead and I am alive, Octavia, thanks to Yeshua. He healed me of leprosy."

"You had leprosy? Oh my God. We didn't know."

"Yeshua healed my Daddy, Octavia," Helena cried as she ran past her into the house.

"I am very happy to see you well, Master," Octavia said as she looked at him closely. "I will inform the rest of the household and prepare your rooms."

"Octavia, I want you to get all the slaves together in the courtyard first. I want to talk to them."

"Yes, Master, right away." She hurried inside, her face a mask of doubt and fear.

Thomas went straight to the courtyard and sat down on his favorite bench and waited for everyone to arrive. He looked around with a feeling of such gratitude, his eyes filled with tears. *Thank you, Yeshua, I don't deserve this.*

One by one the slaves appeared and stood at a respectful distance, waiting for him to speak. The news of his leprosy had spread instantly and they did not know whether to believe his claim of having been healed.

He looked at them and smiled.

"I stand before you as one who has returned from the dead. I was banished to The Tombs for all this time and have returned after Yeshua healed me today. While in that hellish place and close to death, I had a chance to review my life and the terrible way I treated all of you. I want to ask your forgiveness just as Yeshua has forgiven me. My life is in His hands now and I will dedicate it to His service. I can never make up for what I did to Marcellus or my cruel behavior toward many of you, but I can try to do better in the future." He looked at them with compassion. "I now understand what it means to be in bondage to someone and be a slave. I was a slave to sin and depravity and had no way out until the Master set me free. I want to do the same for you. I give all of you your freedom as of today."

A stunned silence filled the air. They stared at him, sure he had made a mistake, until someone in the back started to cry. Octavia walked up to him and then slowly fell down on her knees.

"Now I know you speak the truth, Master. You have not only been healed, but you have become a true follower of Yeshua."

"Please do not call me master any longer, Octavia. There is only One and I am not qualified to tie His shoelaces."

Suddenly the group before him broke out in excited chatter amidst hugs and shouts of joy, until one of the older women held up her hand and motioned for silence.

"I have nowhere to go, Master. What am I going to do? I have served this house all my life and will starve if I have to leave." She began to cry.

Thomas held up his hand.

"I will still need servants and so you may stay if you wish. Except from now on you will get paid for your service. Those of you who want to leave may do so, the rest of you are welcome to remain for as long as you need a place to stay." He stood and smiled at them. "I no longer own this estate; my daughter Helena does. I will only be her guardian until she is old enough to run it by herself."

Octavia stepped up and raised her hand for permission to speak.

"I wish to stay in my position, Master, if you'll have me." She turned to the rest of the group. "Raise your hand if you want to leave." Ten hands went up while the rest of them stood, smiling.

"I will stay," a young man said. "Now that I will have some income, I can ask my favorite girl to marry me." He looked at one of the servant girls with a big smile as she blushed.

"It will take a few days for your freedom to be made legal and then I will decide how much each of you will get paid. Until then, I would really like to have my rooms prepared now," he said with a big smile. "It has been a long time since I have had the comforts of home."

"Esther, bring food and drink for the master," Octavia shouted. "Rachel, change the linens on his bed and Ruth you do the dusting. Paul, you take the master's bags and put them away."

"Octavia," Thomas said with a little laugh, "I don't have any bags. I came with nothing but these clothes on my back." He turned to Paul. "What you can do is draw a bath for me and shave this beard off and cut my hair so that I can feel like a human being again. And then bring me fresh clothes and throw these away. I never want to see them again."

News of his return spread fast across the region of Galilee and requests for his service as a physician poured in. But Thomas had decided he would return to what he had been in the beginning, the physician of the poor. He divided his time between his practice and when possible, followed Yeshua to hear Him preach to the crowds as often as he could. He knew the time of His crucifixion was getting closer. It was three months till the next and last Passover.

He still liked his favorite place under the tree in the courtyard, except now it was for praying instead of drinking. Octavia brought him some juice on a platter. "Will there be anything else, Master?" she asked.

"Octavia, I know you and many others are meeting in the slave quarters to discuss Yeshua and His teachings."

"Do you want us to stop?"

"No, of course not, but I would like to come and share what happened to me, if that is alright with everyone," he said. "I think it will help you understand and appreciate Yeshua to an even greater degree. Have Issus come as well, I also know he leads it."

"You never stopped us, Master," Octavia said. "You could have."

"I know, I just didn't care enough at the time, I guess."

"You really have changed, everyone can see it. There is a new softness and love coming from you that has never been there before. Yeshua not only healed your body, but your soul as well."

"You have no idea how true that is, Octavia. That is why I want to share and give Him all the credit for my recovery and change."

"We will be meeting tonight, Master. If you want to come, I will let everyone know. We meet after sundown in the slave quarters."

"How about after dinner right here, wouldn't that be better? Before you go, Octavia, isn't there any way you can call me something other than master? I don't want or deserve the title."

"That may be true for you, but for us that is what you are, our master. We understand how you feel, but this is something we want to keep calling you."

"If you insist, I guess I can't change your mind."

"I will prepare everything for the meeting." She bowed and left with a smile.

Twenty-one people showed up for the gathering and stood around his favorite bench. He walked in and sat down without saying a word. No one dared speak. Finally, he said, "This is your meeting, what do you usually do?"

"We share the words Yeshua has taught us, Master," Issus said. "After that we pray to God and give thanks and praise like the Torah says to do."

"Then we better do that. I will simply sit here and be a part of your meeting until you ask me to speak, Issus," Thomas said.

After a while, everyone felt a little more relaxed with him being there and soon Issus gave the floor to Thomas. He remained seated on his bench and asked everyone to sit down on the grass in front of him. While he did not tell them he came from the future he stayed with the story of coming from a far- away country called America. What he did share was his pride, arrogance and desire to be rich and famous, his descent into immorality and his sin of killing Marcellus with his callous behavior as well as his abusive treatment of Lydia. When he came to the part of living in The Tombs, he left nothing out and several women in the audience began to wipe their eyes. Of course there was great rejoicing as he concluded how he was healed by the Rabbi.

When he was done, there was silence for some moments, until Issus spoke with great emotion.

"Master, we are honored to have you share what Yeshua did for you and know He has truly changed you. Not only are all these men and women free now, but we are brothers and sisters in His kingdom. I served you before because it was my job, now I serve you because I am honored to do so. May the God of Abraham, Isaac and Jacob bless you and this house and all of us in it in the days to come," Issus added.

"I know I have changed, but I am still capable of great evil unless I ask Yeshua to help me," Thomas said. "It is my greatest desire to be a better person in every way. Someday I know I will leave this place, but until then I ask the Lord to help me be the best I can be and serve Him by serving you as a kind and righteous master. Thank you for staying on."

A month had gone by since Thomas had left The Tombs. At first he tried hard not to think about the horror of the place, but as time went on, his heart felt for those he had left behind.

It was early morning one day when he set out to Capernaum to visit the sick. His journey took him past Lucius' house and he stopped and knocked on the door.

"Shalom, Thomas, come in and break your fast with us," Lucius said as he stepped into the house. Lydia will join us shortly."

"I have come to talk to you, Lucius and before you dismiss my idea, hear me out," he said as they sat enjoying juice and fruit. "My thoughts are turning more and more to the people I left behind at The Tombs. I think the Lord is telling me to go and invite them to come and listen to Yeshua. Will you go with me?"

"No, Thomas. My time of childbirth is near, you cannot want Lucius to take a chance of getting leprosy by going into that awful place," Lydia cried out. "I won't allow it." She had walked in and stood in the door.

"I won't ask him to go down into the gorge with me, but he can stay on top and wait for me until I return, Lydia," Thomas reassured her.

"Are you sure it is the Lord telling you to do this, Thomas?" Lucius asked.

"Yes, I'm sure."

"Then I will go with you, my friend. The Lord will protect me, Lydia. Please don't worry." He turned to Thomas. "When do you want to go?"

"I'm on my way right now," Thomas said. "I brought food, kitchen utensils and other items I know they need. When they see me lowering them down in the basket, those who can walk will come. Before I give them the stuff I will have a chance to tell them what happened to me."

It was an eerie feeling as Thomas drove past the sign 'The Tombs, Stay out'. He remembered the last time he came and a shiver of fear ran over him.

"You are scared, aren't you?" Lucius asked.

"Very. This brings back too many horrible memories." He cringed as they drove up to the point where the basket was. "I will go down and wait for you to let the stuff down," he said and slowly got out of the carriage.

It took all the courage and faith he had to walk down the many steep steps. He was shaking by the time he reached the bottom and almost vomited at the horrible, familiar smell assaulting his nostrils. It was not long before several shadowy figures approached him, greedily watching the items he had piled around him.

"You remind me of a rich man we had here a while back the way you bring all your stuff with you. He didn't end up too well. No one knows what happened to him, but we were all glad when he was gone. He was the meanest man we ever had here."

Thomas recognized the voice of Markus. "I know who you are talking about, Markus. You are right, he was mean and greedy and deserved what he got," Thomas said.

"How come you know my name? Your voice sounds familiar, but you don't look like him."

"I am Thomas the physician and I have come to tell you all what happened to me." He looked at the dozen or so people standing around him.

They stared at him in silence until Leah spoke up. "You couldn't be him, he was near death when his friend came and took him away."

"You are right, Leah, I was half dead and now I am alive, because Yeshua healed me."

"I have heard of Him, He is some religious fanatic going around claiming He is the Meshiah," she said with disdain in her voice.

"He is the Meshiah and he has healed hundreds of people, many of them lepers. He came to save us from our sins." Thomas looked around. "You all remember me, mean, greedy, the one who killed Esther and murdered Brutus? The one who made you pay for every piece of bread and charged you rent for your caves until he became blind and you left him to die. Leah, you came and took care of him in exchange for all his possessions." Thomas smiled at Leah. "I came to thank you for not letting me die, but more than that, I came to ask all of you to forgive me for what I did to so many of you. Yeshua did not just heal my body, He healed my soul as well and gave me a new spirit. I have come to ask you if you want to come with me to hear Him and be healed like I was and accept Him as your Meshiah."

"He would never bother with a prostitute like me, Thomas," Leah said with a sneer.

"He bothered with a murderer like me, Leah. Don't you think He will accept you? Come with me and find out, my carriage is waiting up top. What do you have to lose?" He pointed to the ridge above. "I will take you to Him." Thomas looked at the group of people standing in front of him. "You don't have to stay in this stinking hole, come and follow me and let Yeshua set you free." He pointed to the pile of stuff. "This is for all of you if you want it. It is my gift to you to make up for what I did."

Thomas turned and slowly walked back up the steps. No one followed him. As he reached the top, a voice shouted," Wait, Physician, I will go with you. You know me. I always hang on to the man who has the most." It was Leah.

"We will go with you, Thomas." It was Markus with Crassus in tow. "If this Yeshua can heal you, He can heal Crassus and make him see again."

"Come on up, I'll wait for you," Thomas shouted down, "anyone else?" No one else answered.

"You are indeed a rich man, Thomas," Leah said with a look of appreciation on her hideous face as she settled into the carriage. Thomas helped Crassus and Markus inside and then sat up front with Lucius.

"There is a big meeting today, Lucius, let's take them there," Thomas said as he took the reins.

They were met by huge crowds on the way. Thomas guessed them to be in the thousands, on their way to see the Carpenter from Nazareth on a hill by the Sea of Galilee. The crowd was angry when Thomas helped the three lepers out of the carriage and made them sit down on the far side of the hill.

"You have no business bringing them here," a man shouted at him. "We don't want unclean people near us, take them away." Others began to murmur, but Thomas ignored them and looked for Yeshua. When he could not find Him, he started to worry. These people were not going to tolerate his friends for very much longer.

A woman came over with a cane in her hand and shook it with a threatening gesture. "You take these monsters away from here or I will beat them myself. And there isn't a single person here who won't help me."

She was more scared than furious as she stepped toward them, ready to strike, when a hand reached from behind and took the cane away from her. It was Yeshua. She looked at Him and without another word sat down quietly. He turned to Thomas and smiled. Only this time it was a smile filled with joy.

"Master, I brought you some of my friends from The Tombs. I told them what You did for me and how You could heal not just their body, but also their souls." He pointed to Leah, Crassus and Markus.

"I am not worthy for You to bother with me, Lord," Leah said. "I was a prostitute all my life. I only came because Thomas told me You would not mind." She pointed to Crassus and Markus. "These two are much better than I am. They have helped each other for many years. You see, Crassus is blind and has hands, while Markus has eyes but no fingers. Together they get by. So you might want to heal them, even if you don't think I am worthy. It's alright, I am used to it."

Thomas could see Yeshua was touched by her humility. He reached out with a look of compassion, took her head covering off and put His hands on her horribly deformed face. Thomas couldn't see right away what happened, because Leah was turned away from him. When she looked back in his direction, her face was beautiful and smooth! "My

Lord, you are the One they said would come and deliver us. Thank you."
She was crying as she touched her face with a mixture of awe and joy.

While she was still speaking, Yeshua reached out and touched Crassus' eyes. The big man stood in amazement as his vision returned and fell down on his knees before Him. "Thank you, Lord, You are indeed the Meshiah like Thomas says." When Thomas looked at him, he realized all signs of his leprosy were gone.

Markus stretched out his fingerless hands to the Rabbi and touched His robe in a pleading gesture. When he let go of the hem, to his astonishment, he was made whole. He fell on his knees and sobbed. "I am not worthy Lord. Thank you for healing me."

Thomas stood amazed. Before he could say anything, Yeshua walked away into the crowd.

"Thomas, you were right, He is the Meshiah," Leah said between sobs. "I am healed, my God, I am healed!" She turned to Crassus and Markus. Both stood frozen to the ground. "Yeshua made you well, He made us all well." With a sudden burst of emotion, she hugged both men and they cried together with joy, relief and gratitude.

Thomas and Lucius stood and watched them with awe and wonder until Leah, always the practical one said, "What are we going to do now and where are we going to live?"

"You are going to come and live at my house until we can figure out what to do," Thomas said. "I have plenty of room and you can work for your keep as time goes on."

They looked at each other and then at Thomas. "I would have never thought you could be kind like that," Leah said. "This Yeshua has really done a job on you, hasn't He," she added with a chuckle.

"Let's stay and listen to the Rabbi some more," Lucius said. "We can join that group over there." He pointed to where the woman sat who had tried to hit them with a cane.

She looked at the three with shame. "I am sorry I was so angry before. I just didn't want to become unclean like you."

At that moment they heard His voice from the distance.

Yeshua called the crowd to him and said, "Listen and understand. What goes into a man's mouth does not make him unclean, but what comes out of his mouth, that is what makes him unclean."

Then the disciples came to him and asked, "Do you know that the Pharisees were offended when they heard this?"

He replied, "Every plant that my heavenly Father has not planted will be pulled up by the roots. Leave them, they are blind guides. If a blind man leads a blind man, both will fall into a pit." (Matthew 15:10-14)

"We know about that don't we, Markus?" Crassus said with a happy grin.

The Rabbi's voice continued,

"Don't you see that whatever enters the mouth goes into the stomach and then out of the body? But the things that come out of the mouth come from the heart, and these make a man 'unclean'. For out of the heart come evil thoughts, murder, adultery, sexual immorality, theft, false testimony, slander. These are what make a man unclean." (Matthew 15:17-20)

"We know about that, too, don't we?" Thomas said and looked at everyone in the group.

"You can say that again," Leah said with a sad smile. "That has been my life up till now, but not anymore. I want to become a follower of Yeshua after I have not only changed my clothes, but my heart as well."

It was several days later; Thomas was invited to a Pharisee's house in the town of Capernaum. Just before he entered the carriage, Leah approached him.

"I would like to go with you, Thomas."

"It will be after sundown before I return," he said. *She is going back to her old life,* he thought with regret. "I can't stop you. Come on." He waved for her to join him in the carriage. Leah wore a nice dark blue garment and large, gold earrings. She clutched a bag to her body so as not to break something in it. He did not ask what it contained, but could not help but show his disappointment. *Once a prostitute, always a prostitute,* he thought with disdain.

They did not speak much on the way. He guessed Leah felt his disapproval. When he arrived at the Pharisee's house, he left her in the courtyard without a word and went inside. To his surprise he found Yeshua reclining at the table, talking to his host and the many other guests. Yeshua nodded at Thomas with that old familiar, knowing look. Thomas was shocked. What could it possibly be he had done wrong?

It was an hour into the evening, when a woman who had lived a sinful life in that town learned that Yeshua was eating at the Pharisee's house. She brought an alabaster jar of perfume, and as she stood behind him at his feet weeping, she began to wet his feet with her tears. Then she wiped them with her hair, kissed them and poured perfume on them. (Matthew 7:37-39)

The woman was Leah! He had judged and accused her wrongly. That's why Yeshua had looked at him like He did. Thomas missed what was said until he heard Yeshua say, "Therefore, I tell you, her many sins have been forgiven – for she loved much. But he who has been forgiven little loves little." Then Yeshua turned to her, "Your sins are forgiven."

The other guests began to say among themselves, "Who is this who even forgives sins?"

Yeshua said to the woman, "Your faith has saved you; go in peace." (Matthew 7:47-50)

On the way home, Thomas looked at Leah.

"I am sorry I judged you, Leah. I thought…"

"I know what you thought, Thomas, I don't blame you. I saved that bottle of perfume all these years. Now I know why." She smiled at him with a radiant smile. "I am free of my sins, saved from my bondage of evil and I am going to follow my Meshiah wherever He leads me. Tomorrow I will leave your house and go back to Capernaum and find Him, because He has made me whole."

"I will take you and will help you look for Him, Leah," Thomas said.

"I told you I always hang with the man who has the most riches," she said with a sheepish grin. "And Yeshua is richer than any man I've ever known."

Chapter 31

"I am closing my practice, Lucius," Thomas said. "It is two months until Passover. The time has come for the Meshiah to be tried and crucified in Jerusalem and I want to be there."

"Are you certain that is going to happen?" Lucius asked. "Why would anyone want to kill a man who does so many astounding miracles, feed thousands of people with a few loaves of bread and two fish and preaches even for enemies to love each other? It doesn't make any sense."

"Remember the scriptures in the Torah Nicodemus found? He told us this way is the only way they make any sense." Thomas sounded adamant. "Also, before I was healed by Yeshua I thanked Him for dying for my sins on the cross and He did not tell me I was wrong."

"I do remember that, but at that time I didn't think about it as being strange." Lucius looked at Thomas with an expression of regret. "I wish I could go with you, but Lydia is due to deliver any day now. Maybe you could stay until she does and help me bring our child into the world."

"Of course I will, Lucius. This way I have time to let everybody know I will no longer be available as a physician."

It was a week later when a messenger arrived to let Thomas know Lydia was in labor. Thomas and Helena immediately made their way to Capernaum. Helena was excited, since it would be the first time she was allowed to assist Thomas. Thirty minutes into the ride, one of the wheels of their carriage broke and they were stranded for hours until finally, an old farmer gave them a ride. By the time they arrived at Lucius' house, Lydia was in hard labor.

"She does not look good, Thomas," Lucius said when they walked in. "Something is very wrong."

"Let me take a look, Lucius," Thomas said as he rushed into the room where Lydia lay on the bed, pale and weak, with contractions coming every minute. Yet before Thomas had time to wash up, the child was born.

"I want to see my baby," Lydia said in a weak voice. "I don't hear him cry, is something wrong?"

Lucius leaned over her and with tears streaming down his face and said, "Lydia, my love, our son was born dead. There was nothing anyone could have done. I am so sorry."

She looked at Lucius and whispered, "I am sorry, my beloved husband, I tried so hard to be good."

"It was not your fault Lydia," Lucius said.

"The baby has been dead for several days in your womb and an infection has set in," Thomas said. "There is nothing I can do." He held her hand and looked at Lucius with great sadness in his eyes.

"Am I going to die, Thomas?" Lydia asked.

"Yes, Lydia, I am so very sorry." Thomas sounded heartbroken. "All we can do now is put you into the hands of Yeshua." He leaned over her as he continued. "I want you to give your life over to Him right now, can you do that? Tell Him you trust Him and thank Him for dying for you on the cross. Tell Him you believe He is the Meshiah who came to save you. If you can do that just shake your head in agreement and He will accept you as one of His chosen ones."

She slowly nodded her head before she closed her eyes and went to sleep.

Thomas turned to Lucius. "I am so sorry, my friend. I wish I could have done something. In my time I could have, but here all I can do is trust Yeshua to do with her as He decides. If she dies, she and your son will live with Him in eternity. That is why He came, to make it possible for all of us to become children of His kingdom.

"I don't think I want to live without her, Thomas," Lucius said as he sat by the bed, completely heartbroken. "I love her and wanted to get old with her."

"I know, my dear old friend. She is a wonderful, special person and I love her, too," Thomas said.

Two days later Lydia died from a massive infection as Lucius held her in his arms.

"I will never love a woman like that again," Lucius said in a voice filled with sadness. They were on the road to Jerusalem. "I was so sure I had found my purpose in life, to be a husband and father as well as a physician. Now it is as if I no longer have anything to live for."

"We are going to Jerusalem to witness the greatest and most famous trial the world will ever see, Lucius. Even in my time everyone knows about Yeshua being tried, crucified and then resurrected after three days." Thomas sounded excited. "What an honor it is for me to be here to witness it all."

"How can you be glad about the Rabbi being crucified?" Lucius asked. "It still makes no sense to me."

"Because by giving Himself as the perfect sacrifice to the Father, it is the only way He can save mankind from sin and reunite us with God since Adam and Eve messed things up in the beginning. I remember the words Melissa's grandmother told me so many times. Except then, they didn't make any sense, now they do. I so wish I had paid more attention to her so I could understand more of what she was trying to tell me."

"Since you know what's going to happen with Yeshua, do you also know what will become of me? I feel lost and useless right now and wish Yeshua had healed Lydia. Why didn't He?"

"For one, you didn't ask Him, Lucius, did you? You told me before that you are looking for a purpose. I do believe you will have one yet to come. For some reason I have the feeling that since you are in my life, your name will be known in the 21st century."

"I wish any of this made any sense." Lucius sat with his shoulders hunched over and his head down. "I feel my life is over and I wish I could follow Lydia. I am nothing unusual and have no doubt my name is not going to survive into your distant future."

They sat in silence as the carriage rumbled along. It was slow going, because of the two carts filled with supplies as well as several of Thomas' servants traveling behind them. Thomas had sent word ahead to rent a villa in Bethany, a small village two miles outside of Jerusalem on the side of the Mount of Olives. Helena sat with Octavia and Sarai up front on a sack of flower with Esther and Ruth, the two house servants in the back. Since the barley harvest was in full swing, Issus had to stay behind and run the estate and oversee the field workers. Igora's two-year-old colt was running free next to his mother. Helena had insisted on bringing him along since he was her pet. She had named him Star for the white markings on his forehead.

The roads were not yet filled with pilgrims since it was still two weeks to go till Passover. It had taken this long for Lucius to come out of his deep depression after Lydia's death. He was still in a sad state and it was all Thomas could do to get him to come along. It would be another day until they reached Bethany.

"I talked with Joanna the other day," Thomas said. "She will be there a little closer to Passover. Her husband is going this time since Herod has decided to come to Jerusalem this year for the festivities. They will stay in a place of their own, but I am sure we will get to see them while we are there.

"She was very kind and helpful in my time of grief," Lucius said. "I even think she spoke to Yeshua about all this, but said He didn't say much of anything. In her words, it was as if He understood and agreed Lydia had to die. I must say I am more than a little upset with Him about that. He has healed all these other people, why not my Lydia?"

"Since He is the Meshiah, He knows what the future holds for you, Lucius. Maybe He has other plans for your life than just being a husband and physician in Capernaum," Thomas said.

"What else could I possibly be good for? Now I am alone without hope or purpose and if Yeshua is going to get killed like you say, Thomas, then I won't even have Him," Lucius said with bitterness in his voice.

"I have a feeling you will not be alone nor without hope or purpose. Yeshua will use you in the days to come in ways you cannot see right now. Remember how both of us said when I first came, that we are sure there has to be more to our life?" Thomas sounded sure. "I am certain we will understand some day and look back on this time as days of preparation for greater things to come."

Lucius didn't answer.

It was late afternoon when they reached Bethany the next day. Everyone was tired and glad to have arrived at the rented villa. It was a spacious house, situated on the side of a hill, with Jerusalem visible in the distance. Before long, they sat down to a good meal with wine, bread, cheese and lamb fixed by Esther, the cook.

"This is the first time I have been to Jerusalem," Helena said, excited. "I can't wait to see Yeshua and see what miracles He is going to do here."

"The more miracles He does, the more the authorities seem to hate Him," Thomas said between bites. "I'm afraid it will be a time of great joy as well as sorrow, Angel."

"It is all about your talk about the future again isn't it, Daddy?" Helena sounded skeptical. "He is the Meshiah and that means He can't die."

"I agree," Lucius said.

"I have tried to explain it before," Thomas answered with slight annoyance. "Not only does the Torah agree that He must suffer and die, but it also states that He will be resurrected after three days. Joanna confirms that Yeshua has tried to explain it to His followers numerous times, but no one wants to hear it. This is why He came, to offer Himself to the Father as the perfect sacrifice for the sin of mankind. In the future there will be no more sacrifices necessary, no more killing of lambs or doves to approach God. He is the one and only perfect offering for now and forever to make it possible for all of us to come to the Father and so be cleansed from all unrighteousness.

"So what happens next, Daddy?" Helena asked.

"I have no idea, because all I know is what my wife's mother tried to tell me and she did not go into any more detail than what I have told you. We simply have to wait and see. The exciting thing is, we will be there to watch the whole thing."

"Does that mean I can go with you?" Helena asked with great anticipation.

"Of course you can. We all can," Thomas said as he looked around the table with a smile. "Let's get a good rest tonight and then tomorrow we go into Jerusalem together."

Just as always, Thomas was in awe as the Temple came into view. This time he was somewhat more aware of the great significance of the historical as well as the spiritual aspect of this magnificent building. He still couldn't believe he would experience the greatest event in human history right here among the gleaming, white walls of this magnificent edifice. The thought took his breath away and he made Andrew stop the carriage.

"I will never get used to this," he said to Lucius and Helena. "It is simply fabulous."

"Why didn't you ever go and see it in your time?" Lucius asked.

"Because it isn't there anymore, Lucius," he said with great sadness. "This temple will be destroyed in seventy years by the Romans."

"I simply cannot believe that, Thomas," Lucius said. "Why on earth would they do that? I can understand them closing Jerusalem for Passover, but not destroying the temple. That doesn't make any sense."

"Wars and armies rarely make much sense. Not now and not then, nor in the distant future, yet it is and always will be the favorite means of mankind to sort out their differences."

Just as they were ready to drive on, an expensive carriage stopped alongside theirs and a woman's face parted the heavy linen curtain.

"Aren't you Thomas the Physician?"

"Yes my Lady, I am," Thomas said and bowed.

"I am Claudia Procula, the wife of Pontius Pilate. It is urgent that I speak with you," she said.

"Is your daughter unwell or her baby?" Thomas asked.

"No, they are fine. Please follow me to my home, I beg you," she said in an agitated voice.

"Of course, great Lady," Thomas said and motioned for Andrew to follow her carriage.

When they reached the large estate, slaves rushed up to help everyone off the carriage and ushered them into a comfortable room with several couches and tables.

"Please follow me, Thomas," Claudia said. "Make sure to bring refreshments for our guests, Sylvana," she said to a slave nearby as she pointed to Helena and Lucius.

Thomas was mystified what she might want from him since he

could not detect any sign of anyone being ill. She led him to a small courtyard with beautiful plants and a water fountain springing from a basin, covered by rich, colorful tiles and pointed to a group of comfortable couches. "Please have a seat. I will have Petronia bring us some fruit and wine."

Thomas took the silver goblet and leaned back, waiting to find out what this was all about.

"I am sure you have heard about this Rabbi Yeshua," she finally said without wasting any time on amenities as she took a deep sip of her drink. "I have seen Him several times and I have heard Him speak. I am convinced He is a good man." For her age she was still a good looking woman, her slender figure hid by an expensive long, flowing gown. Her black hair, interspersed with grey, was arranged in thick braids around her head, accentuating her classic features. Her dark, brown eyes showed a keen intelligence as she sat across from Thomas with her long, slender legs crossed gracefully.

"I have also met Him, great Lady," Thomas said. "I agree with you and actually believe He is the Meshiah, the long awaited Savior of the Jews."

"I don't know about that, but what I do know is that my husband is in great danger." She leaned forward. "You see, Thomas, I had a dream and in this dream I saw this Rabbi stand before Pontius, beaten, wounded and with a crown of thorns on His head and blood running over his face. My husband stood in front of Him and did not know whether to condemn Him or not, while the crowd was screaming to crucify Him. I ran up to Pontius and begged him to let the man go, but he just ignored me and ordered Him killed." She was shaking by now. "I was so upset about the dream that I had to stay in bed all day weeping. When I spoke to Pontius about it, he just looked at me as if I was a hysterical woman and left for the day." She was crying by now. "I don't know why this dream won't leave me alone, but I am still greatly troubled for the soul of my husband and I don't understand why. Neither do I know of anyone I can talk to since everyone seems to want this man dead, until I saw you."

"Great Lady, I know your dream is real and what you saw will come to pass in just a few days from now. There is nothing you can do to change what is going to happen, but you can warn your husband again. While he will not listen, I want *you* to listen to me. This man Yeshua is the Son of God, sent to die on the cross for our sins. Instead of coming to free the Jews from the Roman bondage, He came to free us all from the bondage of sin. It was ordained that way by God from the beginning of time when sin came into the world. If you will accept this and accept Yeshua into your life and heart, you also will be set free to follow Him.

If you have any more questions, ask a member of the Sanhedrin by the name of Nicodemus. He will explain it to you in greater detail." Thomas took her hand. "Listen to me carefully. Three days after Yeshua is killed, He will rise again. When you hear about it, do not dismiss it as rumor, for it will be the truth. Seek out His followers and maybe you will be one of those who will see Him after He has risen."

"What will happen to my husband for what he is going to do?" she asked with fear in her voice.

"God forgives everyone, even one like Pontius Pilate, if he repents and turns to Him. You can be a great influence on him in the days to come after all this has taken place."

Claudia looked at Thomas with a mixture of fear, confusion and hope.

"I will do what you say, Thomas. Not only have you saved my daughter's life, maybe you have saved mine and my husband's with your words. Thank you for your kindness and wisdom toward us. I know we don't deserve it." She looked down on her hands. "I am fully aware we Romans are not the easiest masters to serve.

Chapter 32

It was two days later. The road from the Mount of Olives, which led through Bethpage and Bethany on toward Jerusalem, was filled with an ever increasing crowd of pilgrims. It was ten days till Passover and Thomas was getting excited as well as anxious about the events ahead.

"Master, I spoke with a woman at the market place today," Octavia said as she served Thomas his breakfast. "There is great wailing and crying in Bethany. A man named Lazarus died four days ago. He and his two sisters Mary and Martha are friends of Yeshua and the sisters had hoped the Rabbi would come back from Perea, where He was preaching and heal their brother. They sent a messenger to Him to ask Him to come, but the messenger returned yesterday, saying the Rabbi told him He would not be able to make it until later. Everyone is upset."

"I can certainly understand that," Lucius said with bitterness in his voice. He had walked in and heard the tail end of the conversation. "He didn't come to heal my Lydia either."

"Why don't we go and see what's going on, Daddy," Helena asked as she joined them at the table. "I would like to go to the market place and see what they have to sell. Maybe I can buy some presents to take back home for some of my friends."

"We can certainly do that, Angel," Thomas said. "It is better than fighting the crowds in Jerusalem. I need a day of rest. Maybe Yeshua will return while we are there. I know He will definitely show up soon," he added, thinking of what was to come soon.

Since the market was just down the road from their house, they decided to walk, since it was still cool. Thomas, Lucius and Helena leisurely strolled through the small row of stalls with vendors praising their merchandise. They couldn't help but pick up on the main topic of conversation in the crowd.

"I always told you this Rabbi is a fraud. No one can do the kind of things people say He does." a stout woman said in a loud voice. "I have no idea why Lazarus and his sisters ever bothered with Him. I warned them just the other day to be careful not to get involved with this strange fanatic."

"Imagine Him saying He is the Meshiah. How ridiculous is that?" an old man said with disdain. He had gnarled hands and sat on a rickety chair behind his display of breads. "I told my wife to stay away from Him, because He will come to no good."

"I agree, the authorities are looking into His claims and I can tell you, they are not too pleased with the crowds following Him and claiming He fed five thousand people." Another sturdy, middle-aged woman picked up two loaves and put them into her basket. "I forbid my son Caleb to follow him just the other day, because there is going to be trouble, you can count on that. This carpenter is just another one of those who claim to be the Meshiah with nothing to back it up," she added in a voice filled with contempt.

"If He had healed Lazarus, maybe that would be different, but from what I hear, He refused to come." The old man laughed. "He probably realized He couldn't raise him from the dead, so He stayed away."

"From what I understand, Mary and Martha are terribly upset and disappointed," a young woman with a child in her arm said. "They were really counting on Him to come back in time to heal him since they are such good friends and all."

"They are probably embarrassed now after all their lofty talk about Him." Another vendor had joined the conversation. He was a short, little man with a sizeable waist, which spoke of too much wine and good food. "I spoke with Martha just the other day and she told me how the Rabbi had healed many people right here in Jerusalem over the last three years. She couldn't stop singing His praises." He rolled his eyes mockingly. "Now what is she going to say about Him?" He laughed. "These religious fanatics, they come and go and the world goes on as it always has and the blasted Romans are here to stay." He turned and went back to his stall, shaking his head so hard his hat nearly fell off.

Thomas and his group stood and listened with great sadness.

"I almost have to agree with them," Lucius said. "He did the same thing to me and let my Lydia die without bothering to come. After all, Joanna told Him about her, but He didn't bother to save her." His eyes were moist as he went on. "He could have healed her, what is it to Him? He healed so many others, why not my Lydia?"

Thomas and Helena looked at each other and didn't know what to say, since they had the same question in their hearts. Helena took Lucius' hand and smiled up at him.

"We love you, Lucius, and so does Yeshua," she said gently.

Suddenly, there was a great commotion in the market place. People came running toward the road, following a woman in the opposite direction of the pilgrims. She was heading towards Bethpage and away from Jerusalem.

"Let's follow them, maybe Yeshua is coming," Lucius said.

"I think this is one of the sisters running to see the Rabbi," Thomas said. "Let's go, we don't want to miss this."

They caught up with the woman just as she reached Yeshua as He was coming down the road towards them. It was Martha, the sister of Lazarus, judging by the conversations they overheard from the crowd. As they got closer they could hear what was said.

"Lord," Martha said to Yeshua, "if you had been here my brother would not have died. But I know that even now God will give you whatever you ask."

Yeshua said to her, "Your brother will rise again."

Martha answered, "I know he will rise again in the resurrection at the last day."

Yeshua said to her, "I am the resurrection and the life. He who believes in me will live, even though he dies, and who ever lives and believes in me will never die. Do you believe this?"

"Yes, Lord," she told him. "I believe that you are the Christ, the Son of God, who was to come into the world." (John 11:21-27)

Thomas was astonished at the woman's faith. Even in the face of her brother's death, she still believed Yeshua was the Meshiah. He knew the Rabbi would do something to reward her for her trust in Him. What could it be? Lazarus had been dead for four days, even He couldn't do anything to change that.

It was then Mary, her sister, ran up to Yeshua.

She fell at his feet and said, "Lord, if you had been here, my brother would not have died."

When Yeshua saw her weeping, and the Jews who had come along with her also weeping, he was deeply moved in spirit and troubled. "Where have you laid him?" he asked.

"Come and see, Lord," they replied.

Yeshua wept.

Then the Jews said, "See how he loved him."

But some of them said, "Could not he who opened the eyes of the blind man have kept this man from dying?" (John 11:32-38)

"I agree with them," Lucius said as he stood with a stony face filled with anger and bitterness.

Thomas put his hands on his friend's shoulder and started to say something, when he heard Yeshua say,

"Take away the stone."

"But, Lord," said Martha, the sister of the dead man, "by this time there is a bad odor, for he has been there four days."

Then Yeshua said, "Did I not tell you that if you believe you would see the glory of God?"

So they took away the stone. Then Yeshua looked up and said, "Father, I thank you that you have heard me. I know that you always hear me, but I said this for the benefit of the people standing here, that they might believe that you sent me."

When he had said this, Yeshua called in a loud voice, "Lazarus, come out!" (John 11:39-43)

Thomas was shocked. There was no way the man would come back. After four days, even someone who wasn't a physician would know that.

"I hope He is not making a fool of Himself," he muttered under his breath.

"You and me both," Lucius mumbled so only Thomas could hear.

The dead man came out, his hands and feet wrapped with strips of linen, and a cloth around his face.
Yeshua said to them, "Take off the grave clothes and let him go." (John 11:44)

Thomas and Lucius looked at each other in total disbelief. The crowd stood stunned, unable to speak.

"I knew Yeshua could do it," Helena said into the silence and took Thomas' hand. "I just knew it."

Suddenly, Lucius slowly moved toward Yeshua. When he reached Him he fell to his knees and sobbed. "I am sorry for having been angry with You about not healing my Lydia. I give my life to You and ask You to use me in whatever way you wish. Forgive me, I am a sinful man and not worthy, but all You have to do is say the word and I am made whole." He continued sobbing until the Master put His hands on his shoulders and raised him up. Then He put one hand on Lucius' head and held it there while He spoke a silent prayer and then turned and walked away to join Lazarus and his sisters.

When Lucius returned to join Thomas and Helena, he had a radiant smile on his face.

"Now I know I have a purpose. I have no idea what it might be, but I don't have to. Yeshua anointed me for a task He has for me to do and I will do it to the best of my ability," he said and hugged Thomas and then Helena. "Come, let us go home and celebrate. I have been made whole."

On the way back to the house, they came upon a group of men who had come to mourn for Lazarus. They could hear what they were saying as they walked behind them.

"This is terrible. What on earth are we going to do if this Rabbi continues with these miracles? We have to let the Sanhedrin know about this," one of them said.

"I don't know," another said. "The man did raise a dead person back to life after four days." He looked at the others. "Four days! There is no way He could have made that up. I smelled the stench for heaven's sake!"

"We know, but think of what the Romans might do to us and our nation if this gets worse and this Rabbi declares Himself King of the Jews. They will shut down the Temple for Passover and then move in the troops. Pontius Pilate will not hesitate one minute if Yeshua threatens him like that." The man was shaking with fear. "I live in Jerusalem and I don't want my family to get hurt when the Romans destroy us all because of this man. Let's go and tell the chief priests. That's all we can do," he added. The others nodded in agreement and continued on to Jerusalem as Thomas and his group turned off the road toward his rented villa.

"Thomas!"

He turned around to where the voice was coming from. A woman was running towards him. It was Leah!

"Wait for me!" She waved her arms and Thomas could see a big smile as she got closer.

"Leah, my goodness, it is you! How are you?" They hugged each other with genuine joy.

"I was hoping I would see you here, Thomas," she said and looked at him when he let her go. "You are looking good. A far cry from that wreck of a human being I saw so many months ago."

"Speak for yourself, you didn't look that great either when I saw you last," he said, laughing.

"Praise God for Yeshua, He saved us both, didn't He?" she asked.

"What are you doing here?" Thomas gave her an inquiring look.

"I am a follower of the Rabbi, Thomas. I told you I would be." She smiled with a radiance Thomas could hardly believe. He remembered her hard, cynical face from The Tombs.

"He must be treating you alright, Leah, you look wonderful."

"He is the Meshiah, Thomas, and I am honored to serve Him. I have gained riches I never dreamed existed and cannot believe I was ever a prostitute. The best thing is, no one treats me with scorn because of it, least of all the Rabbi. There is a whole group of us who follow him wherever He goes and we get to see the many miracles and wonders He performs." She was bubbling with excitement. "I can't wait to see what He is going to do this year at Passover, although He keeps telling us He will be arrested and killed by the chief priests. We have tried to persuade Him not to come here this year, but He won't listen. It is as if He knows what must happen." She had calmed down and looked thoughtful.

"He does know what must happen, Leah. Don't be upset when it does. He will rise again after they kill Him and you will get to see Him then, trust me." Thomas tried his best to put her mind at ease, knowing what was to come.

"That is pretty strange talk, Thomas. But then you were always strange with your predictions of the future and such things. He is the Meshiah, He will never die. Don't you know that?" She looked at Thomas, fear showing in her eyes. "I am a little afraid, you are usually right about what you say is going to happen." She forced a smile as she turned back toward the road. "Maybe this time you are wrong, Thomas."

He followed her with his eyes and felt sorry for the things she would have to go through in the next few days.

"Daddy, are you coming? We are ready for the mid-day meal. Come and join us," Helena shouted from the doorway.

He walked inside and sat down at the table with the others, deep in thought about the things to come.

"Cassius sent a messenger," Lucius said later on that afternoon. "Nicodemus will be at their house tonight and we are invited. It seems he has something he wants to talk to us about. I have a feeling it is about the Sanhedrin and Yeshua. Things are not looking good for the Rabbi."

"I wouldn't imagine they are," Thomas said. "These are hard days coming up for all of us. Maybe Nicodemus has some details we don't know about."

Nicodemus was not his jovial self when he walked in that evening. His face was drawn and his eyes had a profound sadness in them.

"Welcome my friend," Cassius said. "You do not look like you have good news for us."

"Come and sit and refresh yourself," Diana said as she led him to where everyone else was seated already. "We are anxiously awaiting news about the Rabbi."

Nicodemus nodded to Thomas and Lucius as he sat down.

"You were right with everything you told us would happen, Thomas. There was a meeting this morning and it is pretty well decided by Caiaphas that Yeshua will be tried." He sat down with a heavy sigh. "No matter what I said, they wouldn't listen to me; we are going to kill our Meshiah just like the prophets said we would."

No one spoke for a moment until Nicodemus said into the silence, "He has to be the perfect sacrifice so we can have a relationship with the Father. No one else qualifies except His Son. That is why Yeshua will be called the Lamb of God, sacrificed for our sin and so gain for us what was lost through Adam and Eve. It horrifies me that I am going to be part of those who condemn Him," Nicodemus said as his eyes filled with tears. "He hasn't done anything wrong and everybody knows it."

"Can you tell us what went on at the Sanhedrin?" Thomas asked.

"It all has to do with politics. The Chief Priest Caiaphas is convinced Yeshua will cause the people to make Him King of the Jews. That in turn would force the Romans to send their legions and destroy our nation. They will view His claim as insurrection and close the Temple and kill the members of the Sanhedrin and anyone who stands in their way in the process. Everyone is scared. That is why they insist, if they kill Yeshua, the threat will go away and everyone is safe."

"What about Yeshua's claim to be the Meshiah?" Diana asked. "Do they think He is?"

"I tried to tell them He might be, but they would not listen to me, because they cannot imagine He has the power to defeat the Romans in spite of the miracles He has performed. If He was a general they would probably follow Him, but He is only a carpenter from Nazareth with twelve uneducated men as His closest friends. Even I must admit that is not enough to defeat the Romans or anyone else." Nicodemus looked around at everybody with a look of doubt and anxiety. "Let's face it, when He tells His followers that the meek will inherit the earth, it does not inspire great confidence in those of us who are responsible to keep our nation safe from the mighty Caesar. We have no way to defend ourselves against Pontius Pilate and the many legions he can call up from Rome if he feels Yeshua declares Himself King. There is no doubt even in my mind, our nation would cease to exist." He wiped his forehead in a tired gesture of defeat. "I am at a loss as to what to do and feel I have to go along with the Sanhedrin's decision that Yeshua must be stopped. I agree with Caiaphas when he told us that it would be good if one man died for the people. (John 18:14)

Everyone sat stunned, afraid to admit to the logic of what Nicodemus had just shared. Thomas decided he would not say anything. *I cannot change what is going to happen and neither do I want to. This is why the Meshiah came and nothing and no one can do anything to stop it, including God, because He is the One who set it up.*

Chapter 33

It was the next morning. Thomas watched Helena brush Star, Igora's little two-year-old colt. The two had bonded over the last year and pretty soon Star would be ready for her to ride him. So far she had only led him by a halter and allowed him to go wherever he desired. When she was done brushing him, the two slowly made their way down the long driveway toward the road leading to Jerusalem. It was filled with Pilgrims coming down from the Mount of Olives. He was surprised when Helena tied Star to the gate and came running back to the house.

"I forgot to change my sandals. I can't walk in these," she said as she rushed past him. "Watch Star for me, would you, Daddy?"

Thomas decided to walk closer to where the colt was tied up. Before he got to the gate, two men approached the little animal and began to untie it. Some people standing there asked, "What are you doing, untying that colt?"

They answered as Yeshua had told them to, and the people let them go. (Mark 11:5-6)

"Wait a minute, that's my colt," Thomas said before they walked off with Star. "Why are you doing this?"

"Shalom, Thomas," one of the men said, "I am Philip and this is Andrew, don't you remember us?"

"Of course, but that doesn't answer my question. Why are you taking my colt?"

"The Master sent us and said, "Go to the village ahead of you, and just as you enter it you will find a colt tied there, which no one has ever ridden. Untie it and bring it here. "If anyone asks you, 'Why are you doing this?' tell him, "The Lord needs it and will send it back here shortly." (Mark 11:2-3)

Thomas was taken aback. "I guess, if Yeshua needs it, it's alright. I will tell my daughter you will bring it back. Make sure you do, because this little animal is her pet." He didn't know if the two heard him, because they were already walking away toward Bethpage.

"What happened, Daddy?" Helena was out of breath from running. "Where are they taking Star?"

"It seems the Rabbi has need of him, Helena. Maybe we should follow them and see what is going on?" Thomas suggested. "It's not too far, I see a large crowd coming down the mountain. That must be Yeshua and His group. I think I can hear shouting, let's go and see what is going on."

As they got closer, to their astonishment they saw Yeshua sitting on

Star. The little donkey calmly walked down the middle of the road as people threw their outer robes in front of him. The crowd lined the road, shouting and singing, waving and smiling at Yeshua, who sat and smiled back at them with that knowing smile Thomas knew so well.

"Hosanna!"

"Blessed is he who comes in the name of the Lord!"

"Blessed is the coming Kingdom of our father David!"

"Hosanna in the highest!"

Thomas looked at Yeshua and waved with a bright smile and shouted, "You are the Meshiah, the King of Kings and Lord of Lords!"

The Rabbi looked at him with a twinkle in His eyes and Thomas had the feeling He was telling him that He appreciated that Thomas was the only one who knew what was to come and how it would all end. In his heart Thomas felt he and Yeshua were co-conspirators as he took his cloak off and laid it down on the road in front of the little donkey. He looked up at Yeshua and said in a voice filled with emotion only the Master could hear, "I will not forsake You when the time comes."

Yeshua nodded His head in agreement and stretched out his hand in a gesture of blessing.

Thomas fell down on his knees and bowed his head to the ground. He understood he was in the presence of the King of Kings on His way to be crucified for the sins of all these people shouting praise to Him. Thomas had tears in his eyes as he watched the jubilant crowd. Helena touched his shoulder. "Daddy, everybody else is happy. Why are you crying?"

"I'm alright." He blew his nose and got up and took Helena's hand as they followed Yeshua on the road toward Jerusalem. A huge crowd filled the road when they reached the gate of the city. On the way Thomas listened to some of the conversations around him.

"I just know He is the Meshiah," a man told his wife. "You wait and see He is going to get an army together and take the throne of David and drive the Romans out."

"I always knew He was special with all the miracles He did," another said. "I was there when He fed the five thousand and healed a blind man. For that reason alone, He should be our King. He can feed us out of thin air and we don't ever have to worry about going hungry again."

"Does that mean we don't have to work anymore?" a skinny old man asked. "I am too old and wish I could stay home and enjoy free food."

"I'm ready to fight the Romans," a young man said. "I would sign up with Him right away. If I get wounded, the Meshiah would heal me or raise me from the dead like He did Lazarus. I figure He wouldn't need too many men since none of us would ever die." He was excited. "I'm ready to fight now and will stay close to Him so He will choose me for His army."

As they walked on, Thomas found himself in front of a group of religious leaders. He had to strain to hear as they whispered to each other.

"I told you the people want to make Him a King. This is going too far. Caiaphas is not going to like this outpouring one bit. We have to let him know right away what is going on here." The man was dressed like a Pharisee with his robe bordered with many tassels.

"The Sanhedrin will be furious about this," the other said. "Imagine, a lowly carpenter wants to be King. Hmph! We will put a stop to this before the Passover gets here, you wait and see."

"I wonder what Pontius Pilate thinks about this," the third one said, breathless from walking. "I can't imagine he will be too pleased."

"It would even be worse if the Emperor found out," the first whispered. "Israel will be overrun with Roman legions in no time and we could lose everything, including our lives.

Just like Nicodemus said, Thomas thought. *They are trapped in their own politics and fears, with no other way out but to kill Yeshua.*

Before they walked through the gate, Thomas decided to turn around and go home. The crowd was getting so large, he did not think it was safe any longer for Helena. Since he had no idea how the events coming up would go, he thought it would be better to take her home and away from the volatile throngs.

"What was going on out there?" Lucius asked when they got back to the house.

"Yeshua is riding on Star into Jerusalem," Helena cried with excitement. "You should have seen him. My little colt acted like he had done this all his life. I am so proud of him to have the Rabbi be the first one to ride him."

"Why did Yeshua take Star?" Lucius asked.

"There were so many people along the road, putting their cloaks out before the Rabbi and shouting for Him to be King and take the throne of David," Thomas told him. "Some were waving palm fronds and others were throwing flowers on the road. Everyone wanted Yeshua to be their King. The trouble is, their enthusiasm isn't going to last long from what little I know."

"Maybe you are all wrong, Thomas. Could it be Yeshua will be the King of the Jews after all and all your doomsday predictions of His death are wrong," Lucius wondered.

"I think Lucius is right, Daddy," Helena said. "Everybody was so excited today and they all believed He was the Meshiah. Wouldn't it be nice to be friends with a King?"

"Master, the Lady Joanna is here to see you." It was Ruth, one of the servants he had brought from Galilee.

"Joanna, come on in!" Thomas jumped up and rushed out to greet her.

"Thomas, how good to see you," Joanna reached out her hands to take his. "I found out from Cassius where you are staying. Chuza and I arrived yesterday as part of Herod's entourage. He decided to attend the Passover festival in Jerusalem this year."

"Joanna, I heard you were going to be here. I suppose you will spend most of your time following the Rabbi?" Thomas asked.

"I will indeed since Chuza will be busy with Herod's many parties in honor of the occasion. Herod doesn't really care about the Passover or all that religious fervor. He just wants to show the Jews he is one of them. Not that they believe him, but he somehow keeps on trying to ingratiate himself with them." Her voice showed contempt. "Sometimes I wish my husband had a different job, but I shouldn't complain, Herod has been very generous to us over the years."

"I am so glad to see you," Thomas said. "It has been a while."

"You look wonderful Thomas and I see you have fully recovered from your ordeal in The Tombs."

"I have no after-effects from my leprosy whatsoever. Yeshua did a thorough job healing me." Thomas chuckled. "He is definitely a better physician than I will ever be."

"I am afraid I have to agree with you there," Joanna laughed. "However, I think Herod wants to see you while he is here. He heard you were in Jerusalem."

"I am not sure I want to see him," Thomas said. "I don't know that I ever want to be near him again. He is a despicable man. Besides, I am no longer his physician."

"I don't think he knows that, Thomas, and even if he does, it won't make any difference. He will still call for you if he needs you," she said.

"Joanna is right, you may not have a choice, Thomas," Lucius said cautiously. "If he summons you, I think it will be better for you and for all of us if you obey him. Maybe you can even tell Him about Yeshua."

"I doubt he wants to hear from me that I think the Rabbi is the new King of the Jews," Thomas said with a chuckle. "He might put me back into Macheraus and I know for sure I never want to go there again."

"From what I understand, Herod does not want to have anything to do with putting Yeshua on trial," Joanna said. "He is afraid the Rabbi is the reincarnation of John the Baptizer. From what I have gathered from snatches of conversation, he will leave the sentencing to Pontius Pilate and the Sanhedrin."

"So why is he here then?" Thomas asked.

"I don't know exactly, maybe just to watch what's going to happen?" Joanna looked worried. "I am very sure something is up and we are in for a terrible time this Passover. I am so very worried about Yeshua and so are His men. They tried to persuade Him to stay away, but He wouldn't hear of it. He even tried to tell us they will put Him on trial and kill Him, but He still came anyway. Of course none of us believed what He said, because He is the Meshiah and He can't die." She sighed deeply. "But in any case, there is a feeling in all of us that something bad is going to happen."

They sat in silence after she was finished talking.

"Master, a carriage is driving into the courtyard." It was Ruth again. "I think it is Master Cassius."

"Isn't that nice, we are all together, the only one missing is Nicodemus," Thomas said as he got up and went to the door to greet Cassius. "Nicodemus, you are here!" Thomas shouted as he saw the two men walk in.

"I thought I would bring him to tell us what has been going on," Cassius said. "Sorry Diana couldn't come, she had a previous commitment."

"Nicodemus, we were just talking about you," Lucius said, "wishing you were here."

"I just came from a meeting with the Sanhedrin and all the elders and teachers at Caiapha's palace," Nicodemus said as he sat down and took a sip of wine. "It was awful."

"Tell us what happened," Joanna said, sitting on the edge of her seat. "Was it about Yeshua?"

"It was all about Yeshua," he answered. "There was a great discussion about how to find evidence enough to put Him on trial. They were literally plotting in a sly way to find false witnesses to prove He blasphemed Yahweh and disobeyed the Law of Moses. When they couldn't find anyone to testify to that, they tried to coach a few people what they should say, but I don't think that worked too well." Nicodemus took a piece of bread with goat cheese on it from a tray put there by one of the servants. "Finally, they found two witnesses who told that Yeshua said He would tear down the Temple and build it up again in three days," he said between bites. "I'm sorry, but the meeting was early and I have not had anything to eat all day."

"I know He said that," Joanna said. "I am wondering myself what

He meant by it."

"I think we all do," Nicodemus said, "so I really couldn't argue against them in His defense."

"So what are they going to do?" Thomas asked.

"I don't know. They couldn't come up with anything concrete, since the witnesses told different stories or couldn't remember enough detail or a reason to arrest Him." Nicodemus took another piece of bread and carefully spread the goat cheese on it. As he reached for his goblet of wine he said, "But that's not all I came to tell you. There is something worse." He leaned back in his seat with a deep sigh.

"What is it," three voices asked in unison.

"One of Yeshua's disciples has come forward to betray Him."

There was stunned silence.

Joanna jumped up from her seat and shouted," I know all of His men. None of them would ever do such a horrible thing!"

"I know one," Thomas said. "I talked to him a long time ago and he is into money. I would not be surprised if he demanded a lot of it to do this."

"Who?" Joanna asked in a low, almost threatening tone. "Tell me who it is and I will warn Yeshua so He can leave Jerusalem before they can arrest Him."

"It is Judas, the son of Iscariot," Nicodemus said. "He came to the chief priests and the officers of the temple guard and offered his services for thirty pieces of silver just yesterday in the late hours of darkness."

"Have they accepted his offer?" Lucius asked.

"They were delighted and told him to find a good time to do it and then let them know. But even with that they still have to have more evidence for a conviction or Pontius Pilate will have no choice but to let Yeshua go, no matter what the Sanhedrin wants," Nicodemus said.

"Oh my lord," Joanna said. "I traveled with Judas for these many months. He heard and saw all the wonderful signs and miracles Yeshua did, how in the world could he do such a thing?" She started to cry. "I must go and warn Yeshua right now before it is too late." She started to get up from her seat.

"It is too late, Joanna," Nicodemus said in a tired voice. "They will arrest Him, no matter where He goes, if not today then later."

"He has told us all this would happen many times. We just haven't wanted to believe it," Joanna sat back down, close to tears. "How can this be? He is the Meshiah, how can He die?"

No one spoke as they sat, stunned at the turn of events.

"I will go talk to Pontius Pilate and his wife Claudia," Thomas said. "Maybe I can persuade him to let Yeshua go at the prisoner release he usually does each Passover. It won't hurt to try." He stood up. "I will send a messenger and see if they will receive me today. They owe me a big favor and I am ready to collect." Before he could do anything, Ruth came in, "There is a messenger from King Herod, Master. Shall I tell him to come in?"

"You might as well," Thomas said. "Here we go, I have to go and see what that sly old fox wants."

"That is just what Yeshua called him," Joanna said.

"Maybe I can clip his broken toenail and he will tell everyone I saved his life again," Thomas said with disgust. "It looks like my visit to Pontius Pilate will have to wait."

The sleek carriage Herod had sent didn't take long to reach the Royal Palace in the Upper City. The wide road led directly from the Temple across to the opposite side of the city. The palace towered over the other buildings in size second only to the Temple. It was actually part of the wall and the back of it faced the Hinnom Valley with the front looking out toward the city.

The guards waved the carriage through without delay and it stopped at the imposing entrance of the large palatial edifice. Three slaves rushed to help Thomas down. He grabbed his medical bag and followed one of them into the interior of the palace. It was decorated much like the one in Sepphoris with elaborate mosaic tiles on the floor and rich, colorful murals on the wall. Except here he noticed there were no statues of gods of any kind and no images or busts since it was against the Law of Moses to have graven images within the city of Jerusalem. All the pictures were of flowers and landscapes in vivid, bright colors.

"His Majesty is waiting for you, Master," a slave said as Thomas approached a large double door.

"Thomas, my dear friend, how good to see you," Herod shouted as Thomas entered. He was sitting on a plush, red divan with gold pillows across it. "Come sit right over there," he said, pointing to a chair opposite from him. "I want to talk to you about an important matter that has been bothering me."

"Then I gather you are well, Majesty?" Thomas asked.

"Oh yes, I am taking your medicine every day and I feel great. This concerns the Rabbi Yeshua and his followers. I will come right to the point. You are from Galilee and as I understand you have met Him and know something about His philosophy. Pontius Pilate wants to pawn the problem he is having with this man off on me since this Rabbi is a Galilean."

"The procurator is correct, Sir. Yeshua is from Nazareth in Galilee,"

Thomas said. "That would make it indeed your problem."

"I am looking for a way out of this since someone told me that this Yeshua could be John the Baptizer come back to life and that would truly put me in a bind, wouldn't it? Darn it, Herodias really tricked me into having the man beheaded and if I order him killed again, I would really be in a bad fix with the people." He wiped beads of sweat off of his red, pudgy face as his breaths came in labored gasps. He took a large sip of wine and Thomas wondered if he was drunk.

"Have you ever met this Rabbi?" Thomas asked, although he already knew the answer.

"No, I haven't, but I am going to. I have heard so many interesting things about Him. I will love to ask Him some questions and have Him perform a miracle for me."

"I doubt He will do that, but then I don't know Him that well," Thomas said noncommittally, knowing Yeshua would not give this man the time of day, least of all perform miracles for his entertainment.

"I thought you were really close to Him. I have been trying for a while to persuade Him to come before me, but He has ignored my command. Imagine the audacity of the man, Him being only a carpenter." Herod leaned back against his pillow with a big sigh. "So I have spoken with Pontius Pilate about this, although I can't stand the man. He is nothing but an arrogant Roman who doesn't know his place in front of royalty."

Thomas looked at the pathetic man with pity as Herod continued, still gasping for breath.

"Majesty, if I may suggest a little moderation with your intake of rich food and wine. It would help with your breathing and overall health. You may even want to walk every day as I have suggested before. As your physician, I feel I have the responsibility to guide you in these matters." Thomas chuckled inside. *This would go over like a lead balloon.*

"My dear Thomas, why bother with all that when I have you to give me medicine when things go wrong." Herod smiled at Thomas and took another sip of wine. "Life is too short to do without."

"There are some things even I can't fix if you don't listen to my advice."

"I'll deal with that should the time come, Thomas. You worry too much." He leaned back on the couch and waved for a slave to bring in refreshments. "Let's eat and be merry, tomorrow will bring enough trouble of its own." He laughed a mirthless laugh. "Trouble is all I have in this god-forsaken land with riots and men claiming to be the Meshiah." He looked at Thomas with frustration. "There is at least one every year, but I must say, this one is more than the normal rabble rouser. He is dangerous and wants to be King of the Jews. What does that make me, Thomas? This can't go on or I will be out of a job. What do you say to that, Physician?" He was slurring his words now. "This is *my* Kingdom and I'm not going to give it to some upstart carpenter from Galilee."

"I'm sure it won't come to that, Sir. I firmly believe your throne is safe from the Rabbi. The people may want Him to be their King, but Yeshua says His Kingdom is not of this world. That means He is no threat to you." Thomas spoke in a soothing tone as if talking to a child. "You are going to be alright, Sir."

"Do you really think so, Thomas? Herodias keeps bothering me constantly with her fears and gloomy predictions. Sometimes I think it's time I get rid of her. She oversteps her bounds lately and she better bide her tongue if she knows what's good for her."

"Majesty, all is set up in the throne room." An official had entered the room and stood respectfully at the door.

"Come Thomas, I have a surprise for you." Herod got up with a sudden burst of energy and headed to the door. "I think we will be in for a great spectacle." He walked faster than Thomas thought he could. A sizable group of officials made a path for Herod as he entered the throne room. Thomas wondered what was going on when the big doors opened and a man walked in surrounded by six soldiers. It was Yeshua! He was surrounded by a number of chief priests and teachers of the law and other Jewish leaders, arguing and gesticulating among themselves until they realized King Herod was already sitting on the throne. Herod stared at them with disapproval.

"While I am honored to see you here, I nevertheless am astounded at your disrespect for my royal person," he said to them, slurring his words. "After all, I am your King."

After a stunned second of silence they bowed in unison.

"Forgive us, Majesty, we did not realize you were already here," one of them said. "These are trying days and we certainly did not mean to offend you."

Thomas could detect the slightest touch of contempt in the Pharisee's voice.

"We bring greetings from Pontius Pilate. He has decided this Yeshua is a Galilean and therefore under your jurisdiction. We hope you realize this man is a heretic and is stirring the people up with delusional talk of being a king."

Herod sat and stared at Yeshua for a long time with squinted eyes.

"You look like an ordinary man, Rabbi. Are you a King?"

Yeshua did not answer, but looked at Herod with pity.

"If you are a King, where is your army? Where is your Kingdom or your palace? Maybe you want to take over my palace here or at Sepphoris?" He looked at Him with a smile. "I know you don't want to replace me, but how about the Emperor?" Herod chuckled. "How would you do that since you have only twelve men you call your army?" He stopped and waited for Yeshua to answer, but He stood in silence with his head bowed.

Thomas tried to catch His eyes, but Yeshua would not look at him.

"If you won't talk to me, at least perform just one miracle and I will let you go. Come on, if you are the Meshiah let us see what you can do. I heard you have thousands of angels at your disposal. Why don't you call them down so we can see your power?"

"Majesty, we are horrified that you would even consider this man a king or from God. He is a heretic and has incited rebellion against you and Rome." One of the chief priests spoke with great emphasis and his voice was filled with fear and anger. "You are our king and together we all serve the Emperor in Rome."

"I have heard about the miracles this man has performed all over," Herod answered in an obstinate tone. "Why can't He do one here. It would be entertaining." He turned to Yeshua. "If you show us your supernatural power, we will fall down and worship you. Why not? Since you want to be the Meshiah, I will personally give you my throne and let your angels beat the Romans." He raised his voice in a drunken slur. One of his court officials rushed over to his side and whispered something in his ear. Herod stopped for a moment and then smiled. "I just said that about Rome, because even you can't beat them, Rabbi, can you?"

Thomas realized Herod's officials were worried he would say something against the Emperor and they would all be in trouble.

Yeshua remained motionless, with his head bowed.

"Why aren't you saying anything?" Herod was suddenly screaming at Him in frustration. "You are nothing and nobody and I am your king. You are only a miserable carpenter and the son of a carpenter. What makes you think you can treat me with such disrespect?" He rose from his throne and staggered towards Yeshua. "I am your King; you will bow before me do you hear me?" His face was red with anger while drool ran out of his mouth into his beard. You are nobody, nothing and worthless. I hope they kill you, not for wanting to be the Meshiah, but for insulting me, your king." Herod looked around in helpless rage and then waved for the soldiers to come closer. "You give this so-called king one of my robes and put it on Him. We'll pretend He is a king and then spit on Him." The men stood as if unable to comprehend what Herod had said. "Do what I told you. Now!" he screamed.

"Majesty, you cannot treat this man like a king," several of the chief priests shouted. "He is a criminal and doesn't deserve to be called a king. We want you to condemn Him to death. He has profaned our God by declaring Himself to be the Meshiah and is leading our people into rebellion against Rome."

Herod was stunned at their outburst and sat back on his throne, staring at them with contempt. Suddenly he straightened up his shoulders." I am in charge here," he yelled. "I decide what to do with this man and not you. If I want to have some fun with Him I will and there is nothing you can do to stop me." He turned to Yeshua. "Don't you agree, King? You and I are royalty and we will conquer the world." He started to laugh hysterically as he watched the soldiers putting an expensive purple colored robe on Yeshua. "Show me your kingdom, Carpenter. Let me see that you are the Son of God and I will personally bow down and kiss the hem of your royal robe."

By now the soldiers started to mock Him, encouraged by Herod's outburst.

"Hail to the King of the Jews." One of them spit on Him and pushed him toward another of the soldiers. They literally played catch with His body, pushing Him back and forth, yet Yeshua said nothing.

Herod is losing this one-sided argument, Thomas thought when they finally stopped. He watched the Rabbi looking at the pitiful excuse of the drunken man on the throne with compassion. Then his hand reached out to one of the soldiers as if to bless him. *Even now He can forgive and love,* Thomas marveled.

"What are you going to do with Him?" one of the religious leaders asked Herod.

"I am not going to do anything with Him, but send Him back to my good friend Pontius Pilate. This man has committed His crimes here in Jerusalem and so He has to be tried by the Sanhedrin or the Romans, it's up to all of you to decide."

"We are not allowed to condemn anyone to death, only Rome can do that," the Pharisee said.

"Then take Him back to Pilate and good luck, I want nothing to do with this matter. My kingdom is in Galilee, not Judea." He looked at the group with utter contempt. "Now get out and leave me alone and take this man with you. He is no more the Meshiah or a king than my lowest slave. This has been a total waste of time." He wiped his forehead in frustration and slumped into his seat as if exhausted from the ordeal. (taken in part from Luke 23:6-12)

Chapter 34

Thomas decided to go into Jerusalem the next morning and told Andrew to get the carriage ready. Passover was only a few days away. *I don't want to miss these historical events coming up,* he thought.

"Do you want to come with me, Lucius?" he asked.

"I sure would, let's go," Lucius said. "Give me a moment to get ready."

"I wish I had paid more attention or read what exactly is going to happen, Lucius," Thomas said as the carriage carried them toward Jerusalem. "I act like I know, but I really don't, except for the words of my wife's grandmother. Since she realized I wasn't interested, she kept her words to a minimum about this time and concentrated more on the why than the how in the events coming up."

"I guess you will have to wait for things to play out like the rest of us," Lucius said. "Whatever it is, I know it is going to be trouble for Yeshua."

"Right now only He knows what is going to take place and He has no intention to change what is coming," Thomas answered. "I wish I could talk to Him, but I don't think He would listen to me, because His path is set to fulfill the scriptures."

The carriage passed many hundreds of pilgrims streaming into Jerusalem, filling the road to capacity. Andrew had a hard time guiding the horse through the crowd. A short while down the road, Thomas saw Yeshua and a large group of His disciples sitting in a field a few hundred feet away. They were listening in rapt attention to His teaching.

"Andrew, let's go over there to the left and stop just before we get to Yeshua and the group," Thomas said, excited. "I want to hear what He is saying. Maybe He is telling His disciples what is going to happen."

They got there just in time to hear Him say,

"Do not let your hearts be troubled. Trust in God, trust also in me. In my Father's house are many rooms; if it were not so, I would have told you. I am going there to prepare a place for you. And if I go and prepare a place for you, I will come back and take you to be with me that you also may be where I am." (John 14: 1-3)

Didymus said to him, "Lord, we don't know where you are going, so how can we know the way?"

Yeshua answered, "I am the way and the truth and the life. No one comes to the Father except through me." (John 14:5-6)

Thomas looked at Lucius with a smile.

"I told you, you will see Lydia again, didn't I?" They were standing a little to the side of the group, but close enough to hear what was being said.

"I wish I could find the peace in my heart to believe that," Lucius said. "Under the circumstances, it is hard to have the faith that Yeshua is the Son of God when the whole world wants to kill Him. How can I stand strong against such overwhelming odds?"

"All this I have spoken while still with you. But the Counselor, the Holy Spirit, whom the Father will send in my name, will teach you all things and will remind you of everything I have said to you. Peace I leave with you, my peace I give you. I do not give to you as the world gives, do not let your hearts be troubled and do not be afraid." (John 14:25-27)

Yeshua looked at Thomas and nodded with a knowing smile.

"You will all fall away," Yeshua told them, "for it is written, 'I will strike the shepherd, and the sheep will be scattered.' "But after I have risen, I will go ahead of you into Galilee." (Mark 14:27-28)

Thomas cringed. *Surely the Rabbi wasn't talking about him? There's no way, I know what's going to happen and I'm not afraid like the others, no, not me.* He looked at Lucius. "You don't think He was talking about us, do you?"

"No way, I would never run off in the face of danger," Lucius said with confidence.

Thomas suddenly remembered the confrontation with Barabbas and how Lucius had hidden behind the cart when the three robbers threatened them. *That explains it. Yeshua must be talking about his friend, not him.* He felt better.

"It is good to see you again, Thomas."

He knew that voice. It was Judas Iscariot.

"Things don't look so good right now." He looked at Thomas with a smirk. "I have planned ahead, though. No matter what happens, I made sure I'm on the winning side." He reached in his pocket and jiggled a bag of coins. "This is my insurance if things go wrong."

"What have you done, Judas?" Thomas said with anger in his voice. "You have betrayed the Meshiah, the Son of God!"

"My, my, you must have gotten around to joining His followers, Thomas. I thought you were smarter than that." Judas said mockingly. "Let's see which one of us will win out in the end," he added before he walked away and sat back down with the others.

It was at that moment Thomas heard the last of the words of Yeshua, "But woe to the man who betrays the Son of Man! It would be better for him if he had not been born." (Mark 14:21)

Thomas looked at Judas and felt sorry for him.

"I am glad I am not in his shoes, Lucius. I would never betray Yeshua, no matter what."

"Neither would I. After all, we know better," Lucius answered.

Thomas tried to catch Yeshua's eyes, but the Rabbi had gotten up and started walking toward Jerusalem with His men right behind Him. When the crowd recognized Yeshua they shouted with great excitement and tried to ask Him many questions, but He kept silent.

"We might as well follow Him into the city," Thomas said as he turned to the servant. "Let's go, Andrew."

This scene reminded Thomas of the day when Yeshua rode on Star into Jerusalem.

"It was right here when the Rabbi started weeping for Jerusalem," Lucius said. "I will never forget when He said not one stone will be left upon another. Can you remember if that is really going to happen, Thomas?"

"Oh yes, Lucius. History tells that it will happen in seventy years. It is widely believed by the followers of Yeshua of my day that the Temple and all of Jerusalem was destroyed because the Jews rejected their Meshiah."

"It definitely goes along with what He said the other day," Lucius said. "I remember it sent chills through me and the words are etched into my heart. 'They will dash you to the ground, you and the children within your walls. They will not leave one stone on another, because you did not recognize the time of God's coming to you.' (Luke 19:44) Lucius looked at Thomas with great sadness. "I feel like Nicodemus. All these many centuries we have waited for the Meshiah and then, when He comes, we kill Him. It is almost too much to comprehend."

"That is if you only look at it from our human point of view. According to God's plan, everything is exactly the way it's supposed to be." Thomas looked down on the city coming into view. "This is why He came, not to establish a kingdom right here and now, but a kingdom for the entire world that will last forever."

"You are right, Thomas. You Jews have always had such a narrow view that God wants only your people. In light of what you said what happens in the future, God's plan of redemption is not just for the Jews, but for all the people God created. This is what used to make me angry when I was searching for a deity. I liked everything about the God of the Jews, except that He chose only these few people among the whole of mankind. Now it makes sense, knowing that I can be included in His plan."

"Don't tell that to the crowd in the city or they will crucify you for heresy," Thomas laughed. "I always thought if I should ever believe in a

God He would have to be smarter than I was. I think I found Him." He chuckled. "God has shown me beyond a shadow of a doubt that, left to my own devices, I am not good enough on my own, nor will I ever be. Given the right circumstances, we are all capable of the most awful actions, no matter how good we think we are."

"So you think mankind is not going to evolve into something better as time goes on and knowledge increases, like our Greek philosophers seem to think it will."

"From what I see, mankind has a tremendous capacity for outward improvement, like technology and knowledge," Thomas said. "But the basic character of a man does not change, unless He is willing to abide by guidelines and laws for daily living that have been set down by the One who created him. Even then, unless man submits his life to Yeshua, who came to die for his sin, he is incapable of being good without His help. This basic truth has set me free, Lucius. Free from thinking I have to be the best or the smartest in whatever I do. That alone makes me good and smart enough to know that without Him I am nothing and with Him I can do all things."

"Being Greek I like logic, and I like what you are saying," Lucius said. "Thomas, you have come a long way from the arrogant atheist who came to ask me for a job so long ago."

At that point their carriage passed through the gate of Jerusalem. The road was hopelessly clogged with literally thousands of people crowding the streets. It took them a long time to reach the front of the Temple. The horse was snorting nervously as the people pressed in around them.

"I better get down," Andrew said and jumped off the carriage to grab the halter.

"Why don't we walk from here and meet Andrew with the carriage later outside the gate," Lucius suggested. "That way we can make much better headway."

Thomas looked up at the Temple from across the street. The large steps to the entrance were filled with pilgrims having come to buy the Passover lamb. The court of the Gentiles was bursting with vendors offering their goods with loud voices. In the midst of the deafening noise of the crowd, Thomas suddenly heard the wheels of a carriage coming down the road. The people parted as if by magic. When the carriage came closer, he could see it was Pontius Pilate and his wife. To his surprise the procurator leaned over and shouted, "Come, join us Thomas!"

"Stay with me, Lucius and let's see what the mighty Pontius Pilate wants with me," Thomas said. "I wanted to talk to him anyway about

Yeshua. Here is my chance." He bowed before the couple and asked, "May I bring my friend along, Sir?"

"Of course, Thomas," Claudia said. "Please join us, both of you."

"This is a surprise, Procurator," Thomas said, once he and Lucius had settled into their seats. "What is it I can do for you?"

"My wife insists that I talk to you about this Rabbi everybody is so excited about. She is convinced He is more than just a regular trouble maker. What do you think, Thomas?" Pontius Pilate sounded genuinely interested. "The religious leaders want me to condemn Him." He wiped his forehead. "I have no idea what this is all about or what He is supposed to have done. That's why I want to ask you. You are the only one I know who doesn't have a personal stake in this. Everybody else is either with the Sanhedrin and hates Him or with the people who worship Him. As a Roman, I don't care either way, just so He doesn't cause me any trouble with Caesar."

"I told Pontius about my dream, Thomas," Claudia said. "I am certain the Rabbi is a special man sent by God and I don't want my husband to be involved."

"You are right, great Lady, He is a special man," Thomas said as a sudden fear swept over him. "I cannot tell you what to do, Procurator, but I think you should listen to what Yeshua has to say when He is brought before you."

"Do you think He is the long awaited Meshiah, Thomas?" Claudia asked.

"I have no idea, why don't you let your husband ask Him," Thomas said, trying to avoid looking at Pontius Pilate. "After all, I am not an expert on religious matters," he added in a low voice. "I am a physician and have no idea what the Rabbi is trying to do."

"Then you don't think He is a king?" Pontius Pilate asked. "There are many who say He is and from what I have heard He has claimed it." He sounded confused and annoyed. "How am I supposed to make sense out of these ridiculous Jewish beliefs?"

"I don't think I have heard Him claim He is a king, Sir. To me He is just a simple carpenter with a positive message for the people." Thomas looked at Lucius and cringed. The look on his friend's face was one of astonishment, confusion and disappointment.

"Thank you, Thomas. That clears up a few things for me. I will ask this Yeshua and then decide what to do with Him." He bowed to Thomas and added, "I hope I haven't detained you from anything important." He tapped on the side of the carriage and it stopped. "I appreciate your opinion in this matter. Have a great day."

A slave opened the door of the carriage and they got out. Thomas bowed to the Lady Claudia and then to Pontius Pilate. He stood motionless in the midst of a throng of people as the enormity of his action began to dawn on him. HE HAD BETRAYED THE MASTER! At the first sign of danger he had denied the Meshiah!

In the midst of his inner turmoil, he heard Yeshua's words from the steps of the Temple. In spite of the distance they sounded like a trumpet blast in his mind.

"They will deliver you to synagogues and prisons, and you will be brought before kings and governors, and all on account of my name. This will result in your being witnesses to them. But make up your mind not to worry beforehand how you will defend yourselves. For I will give you words and wisdom that none of your adversaries will be able to resist or contradict." (Luke 21:12-15)

The color drained out of Thomas' face and he had to lean on Lucius when he heard those words. Yeshua knew what he had just done! *Oh God!*

"Thomas, what have you done?" Lucius said in a low voice, "you have denied the Meshiah before Pontius Pilate."

Thomas could not answer, but stood motionless. *I have not learned anything. All this was for nothing. I was so sure I would not deny Him when He told His men they all would. Pride! My pride is still there, ready to surface when I least expect it. How can Yeshua still love me? He knows! Oh God!*

Into the turmoil of his heart Jeshua spoke,

'I am the true vine, you are the branches. If a man remains in me and I in him, he will bear much fruit; apart from me you can do nothing. (John 15:5)

"If you remain in me and my words remain in you, ask whatever you wish, and it will be given you. This is to my Father's glory, that you bear much fruit, showing yourselves to be my disciples." (John 15:7-8)

He hasn't given up on me! Forgive me, Lord, for being afraid to speak out for you. I have failed You and I am sorry.

Thomas stood there, staring at Yeshua in the distance. When their eyes met, he felt an overpowering love fill his heart, followed by peace. *Apart from You I can do nothing, Lord. That is never going to change, is it? But then Your love for me will never change either.*

"How could you do that, Thomas?" Lucius asked again.

"I don't know."

It was noon. Thomas and Lucius had gone back to the carriage parked just outside the wall of the city. There was a heavy silence between them as Andrew helped serve a simple meal of bread, cheese and fruit. There was enough wine for all three and they sat in the shade under a tree, watching the multitude go in and out of the gate, each deep in thought. Thomas didn't dare look at Lucius throughout the simple meal. What was there to say, he had failed – again.

After they were finished, Andrew gathered the leftovers and started putting them on the carriage.

"Where to now, Master?" he asked when he was finished.

"I would love to go see my former slave Abraham," Thomas said. "Do you remember where his son lives, Lucius?"

"I sure do, it is in the lower city, not too far from here. It wouldn't take but half an hour to walk."

"That's what we'll do then. I promised him two years ago we would visit and never did," Thomas said. He turned to Andrew. "We won't need you until late afternoon. If you want, you can drive home and come and pick us up in time to get back for the evening meal."

"Yes, Master, I will be here," Andrew said and finished cleaning up.

"I wonder if Abraham is home since we didn't let him know we are coming," Thomas said as they approached the modest little home. A young boy opened the door to the tiny courtyard after they had knocked.

"Shalom, we are here to visit Abraham, is he home?" Thomas asked.

"Shalom, Sir, you wish to see my grandfather? Please enter, I will tell him you are here. Could you tell me who wishes to see him?"

"I am Thomas, his former master and my friend Lucius, the physician from Capernaum in Galilee."

"Oh Sir, he talks about you all the time. He will be so glad to see you. Please wait and I will let him know you are here." The boy ran into the house, leaving Thomas and Lucius standing in the middle of the courtyard.

"Praise be to the God of Abraham, Isaac and Jacob, it is you, Master." The old man walked as fast as he could to greet Thomas. He had aged somewhat, but other than that looked the same.

"Shalom, Abraham, my dear old friend, you're looking wonderful," Thomas said and reached out his hand. "How good to see you are doing well."

"Master, I never thought I would see you again. I will never forget your kindness for giving me my freedom so I could return to my wife and family." He was crying. "Please forgive me my emotional outburst, it is all so unexpected."

"Abraham, we are here to hear Yeshua and to celebrate Passover," Thomas said.

"Welcome to our humble home." The voice belonged to Jesse, Abraham's son. "I tried to get you to stay for a meal the last time when you brought my father, Sir. Now I hope I can invite you to break bread with us properly." Jesse bowed to Thomas and Lucius. "It would be an honor to have you both. My wife and my mother will be glad to prepare a meal for us."

"We just had our noon meal, Jesse," Thomas said. "But a little wine after our walk would be most welcome."

Before long they sat in a small eating area in a circle with cushions on the floor and a low table in the middle.

"You must tell us how things are going in Capernaum, Master," Abraham asked, excitement in his voice. "How are Octavia and Lydia and Issus?"

Thomas cleared his throat before he answered. "Octavia is here with us running the rented house we have in Bethany. Issus stayed home to take care of the barley harvest," Thomas said.

"How is the beautiful Lydia?" Abraham asked.

"She is dead, Abraham," Lucius said. "I married her and we were so happy until she died in childbirth."

"All the slaves have been set free, Abraham," Thomas said into the silence. "Lydia went to work for my friend Lucius and he asked her to marry him." He leaned forward toward Abraham. "You remember the words you spoke to me when we dropped you off two years ago? They came to pass when I was stricken with leprosy and spent many months in the Tombs until Yeshua healed me and I turned my life over to Him."

"Oh Master, I am so glad to hear you belong to Him," Abraham said, his eyes filling with tears. "It must have been terrible to go through that, but the Lord knew you would not turn to Him any other way." He turned to Lucius. "What happened to Lydia?"

"We were so happy," Lucius said with great sadness.

"Oh my goodness, I am so sorry, Master. She was such a beautiful girl. I always thought you would take her as your mistress, Master." He looked at Thomas.

"Father, I don't think you should speak so boldly to the master," Jesse said, worry in his voice. "We should not pry into such private matters."

"It was not to be, Abraham," was all Thomas answered.

After the wine was served, the four men sat and talked about old times for a while until Jesse brought up the name of Yeshua.

"I work in the palace of Caiaphas," he said, "and hear a lot of what is going on."

"Really, that is interesting," Thomas said. "What is the latest news?"

"I am an assistant to the man in charge of the slaves who serve in the household of the Chief Priest," Jesse said. "I get to hear what is going on with the Sanhedrin through conversations Caiaphas has with the members who come to visit him. There has been a lot of activity as of late concerning Yeshua and I can tell you, Caiaphas is upset and worried about the Rabbi and His followers. He is scared to do anything drastic, because he fears the people rising up against him almost as much as upsetting Pontius Pilate and Caesar. From what I can tell, he is in a quandary and doesn't know what to do." Jesse took a piece of bread and spread goat cheese on it. "I almost feel sorry for the man," he added as he took a sip of wine.

"What about Judas, the son of Iscariot," Thomas asked. "Has he been to see Caiaphas?"

"Oh yes, he came last night." Jesse moved uncomfortably in his seat. "I must say I did something I have never done before, I listened in on the conversation with him and the members of the Sanhedrin behind a column of the meeting room." He looked decidedly uncomfortable. "I would be dismissed instantly and punished severely if I had gotten caught."

"What happened?" Thomas and Lucius said almost in unison.

"From what I heard Judas say, he asked them how much they would give him if he betrayed Yeshua. It was then Caiaphas offered him thirty pieces of silver with the instruction to find the right time and place to do it. The others were afraid to let it be done during the Passover because the people might riot. (based on Matthew 26:1-5) There was also a lot of discussion about finding witnesses who could come up with evidence of heresy and such. One of the members, I don't know his name, even suggested they might make up things for them to say so that Pontius Pilate will condemn the Rabbi." Jesse took another sip of wine and went on. "From what I heard, they really had no real evidence at all. One, Nicodemus by name, pointed out the many miracles, signs and wonders Yeshua had done and asked them how they could ignore them. The others dismissed him right away and told him there was no other choice, that no matter how good He is, He has to die to keep the people from making Him a king." Jesse looked at his audience with sadness. "Nicodemus was visibly upset at that and left. He didn't look angry, but rather sad. I think he saw me listening in, but didn't give me away."

"So what did they decide, Jesse?" Thomas asked.

"Judas suggested he would need to wait for a time when there were not too many people around for him to point Yeshua out with a kiss. I found that to be rather odd, but no one else seemed to question it," he said, "because they agreed to it right away."

"Where and when is he going to do it?" Thomas asked.

"Judas said there is an olive grove on the Mount of Olives where Yeshua goes to pray often in the evening when it is almost dark. That would be the best time, because only His men would be with Him then."

"Did he say what day this would be?"

"Not that I heard, but it would have to be soon, because Passover is close and Caiaphas wants this matter out of the way before then to avoid a riot, remember?" Jesse said. "I can let you know if I hear anything if you tell me how I can reach you," he added.

"That would be great, because I really want to be there when it happens," Thomas said. According to his calculation, it was Wednesday and he had till tomorrow evening to find out where they would arrest Yeshua.

"I will come with you," Lucius said. "Just send a messenger if you find out, Jesse," he added.

"I will try my best," Jesse said. "I don't know what you can do about it, but maybe you can be there for the Rabbi when the time comes."

"I definitely will and this time I will not deny knowing Him," Thomas said with a hint of sadness in his voice.

Chapter 35

The next morning was the first day of the eight days of the Feast of Unleavened bread when everyone purchased the lamb to be sacrificed at the Temple.

"How come we do not celebrate Passover, Daddy?" Helena asked.

"The way I see it, it will be the last time it will ever have to be done," Thomas said.

"Why?" Helena asked. "Aren't we supposed to do this every year?"

"Yes, but from now on, it will no longer be necessary, because Yeshua says He is *the* sacrifice, the perfect Lamb of God, given for our sins."

"Does that mean we will no longer celebrate Passover, ever?" She sounded shocked.

"There will always be Passover, but now we will remember it without killing lambs or any other animals and still be in right standing with the Father once and for all. That is the reason He sent His Son to die for us."

"You mean Yeshua is going to die?" She looked stricken. "That can't be, Daddy. He is the Meshiah, He can't die, Joanna says."

"Precisely because He is the Meshiah He has to die for us." Thomas reached over and pulled her close to him. "He will rise again in three days and we will get to see Him." He looked at her with a smile. "So you are right when you say He can't die. He can't and yet He will."

"That is very confusing, Daddy," she said and took another piece of fruit and chewed it thoughtfully.

"I know, but as long as Yahweh is not confused about it, we are safe," he said with a smile.

"Master, there is a man named Jesse here to see you. He says he is the son of Abraham," Octavia said.

"Have him come in, Octavia." Thomas was excited. "I think he will have some news for us about Yeshua."

"Come in, Jesse, how good of you to travel all the way out here." Thomas got up and waved for him to come in. "Bring some refreshment for our friend, Octavia." Thomas waved for Jesse to sit down. "What have you come to tell us?"

"The Rabbi will have the Passover meal with His men today and after that He is coming this way to pray in Gethsemane. They will pass your house coming from Jerusalem." Jesse sounded sad. "Things don't look good. From what I have heard from Caiaphas and the Sanhedrin, they are determined to have him arrested and killed. There is not even one who spoke against it."

"How about Nicodemus?" Thomas asked. "I know he thinks He is the Meshiah."

"I did not see him there. I did hear that he is angry with Caiaphas and the others and is staying away." Jesse took a sip of wine as he spoke. "I am afraid there will be trouble and there is nothing anyone can do. I spoke with some of the Rabbi's followers and they are very afraid and upset, but have no idea what to do. I heard Miriam, Yeshua's mother, is here in Jerusalem. She is staying with Joanna and Mary Magdalene and another woman named Leah."

"Do you know where?" Thomas asked, excited. "I know Leah and Miriam. Maybe I can go and talk to them this afternoon. Why don't you join us for the mid-day meal, Jesse and I will drive you back home in the carriage? After that I will try to find Joanna in Herod's palace. They will let me in since I am still the King's royal physician."

"That sounds great, Master. My father is very concerned that I won't make it back for the Passover meal." Jesse sounded relieved. "He insisted that I bring you the news about Yeshua and told me to rush back."

In spite of taking side streets, it took them a long time to reach Jesse's house. Thomas dropped him off and then made his way to the palace. He had no trouble entering when he told the guard he was Thomas, the royal physician. They directed him to the far right wing of the palace where Chuza and Joanna had an apartment. A slave showed him the way.

"Thomas, how good of you to come," Joanna said, surprised to see him there. "Come in and join our little group. You will be glad to know Leah is here and Miriam." She turned and pointed to a strikingly beautiful young woman. "I want you to meet, Mary Magdalene. She is one of His followers."

Thomas was at a loss for words as he bowed. Her eyes were dark and filled with a depth that penetrated his being. Her full, wavy black hair hung down to her shoulders and surrounded a face with flawless features. It was her smile that took his breath away and all he could do was stammer. "I am very glad to meet you." He felt foolish somehow and didn't know what to do with his hands as he stared at her.

"Thomas, don't worry, everyone feels like that when they meet Mary Magdalene," Joanna said with a chuckle. "The rest of us look like wall flowers next to her."

"Thomas, it has been a long time since you came to my house in

Nazareth." It was Miriam. He recognized her kind, gentle voice. "I am so glad to see you."

Thomas bowed to her with a smile. "I am glad you are here, Miriam. I came to find out what is going on with Yeshua."

"Things don't look good, Thomas," Miriam said with a sad little smile. "I am so very worried about Him and His men. The authorities are intent to arrest Him. I told Him to come back with me to Nazareth just yesterday, but He said He had to be about His Father's business." She looked thoughtful. "He said that once before many years ago when He stayed behind at the Temple, while we had returned home."

"Thomas, how wonderful to see you," Leah rushed up to him with a big smile. "Seeing you brings back some mixed memories." She gave him a big hug.

"It sure does, Leah. You look very beautiful," Thomas said as he held her away from him. "Both of us are quite an improvement from the way we used to look," he added with a chuckle. He felt a bond with her as if they had been in combat together. "Is Yeshua going to have the Passover meal with you today?" he asked as he turned to the others.

"No, He told us He wants to give His men last instructions before His time comes," Joanna said. "Those were His words and we don't really know what He means by that. They are going to have the Passover meal in a room not too far from here. I saw some of His men purchase the things for the meal this morning, the lamb, unleavened bread and bitter herbs. John told me Yeshua gave them instructions to follow a man carrying water to his house and to tell him they needed his room." (Mark 14:13-14)

"It was strange, no man carries water, that is women's work," Leah said. "But I guess this way it is easy to spot him. From what John said, that man was probably one of His followers, but he didn't know him."

"Jesse, the son of my former slave Abraham, told me Yeshua and His men will be going to the Mount of Olives to pray after the meal," Thomas said. "I think I will go with them. I have a strong feeling something is going to happen tonight or tomorrow."

"What do you think it is?" Joanna asked with concern in her voice. "Do you remember anything from your past?"

"No, I don't. All I do know is…" Thomas looked at Miriam. "Oh, it's nothing."

"I remember the prophet Simon talking to my husband and me when we presented Yeshua at the Temple many years ago," Miriam said. "He told me that a sword will pierce my soul. (Luke 2:35) I wonder if this is what he was talking about." She looked at Thomas thoughtfully. "So I know what it is you did not want to finish telling us, Thomas. My Son will be crucified, just as He told us many times He would."

"I don't think I am the one to tell you, Miriam. I know very little about all this." Thomas cringed as he looked at her. *How devastating for a mother to watch her son die on the cross.*

"I knew He was destined for great things, but I had no idea it would be to die, because He has done nothing wrong." She sat down with a sigh. "As always, I accept what the Lord has for me. I am only His handmaiden in all this and trust in Him to fulfill what He has for my life and that of my Son."

There was a heavy silence in the room until Joanna invited everyone to help themselves to the refreshments a slave had brought in.

"We need something to strengthen us in this hour of trial. If Yeshua is the Meshiah, then He knows what He is doing and we will continue to believe in Him," Joanna said with conviction. "There is nothing else we can do anyway," she added with a hint of resignation in her voice.

"I cannot believe Yeshua will be killed," Leah said in a fierce tone. "He healed me and so many others, why would anyone want to punish Him for that? In spite of who I was, He loved me anyway. It is because of Him I am set free from a life of horror in Herod's court and then in The Tombs. One was as much a slime pit as the other. No one else would have ever accepted me but Him. When He touched me, covered by leprosy on the outside and filth of prostitution on the inside, He did not reject me, but healed me inside and out. Why would anyone in their right mind want to kill a wonderful man like that?" She stood in front of them, trembling with indignation. "I will not accept it lying down like you, Miriam. I will go to the Sanhedrin and tell them what He did for me and shout for everyone to hear that Yeshua is the Meshiah we have been waiting for."

"You will do no such thing, Leah," Thomas said. "All these things must come to pass for God's word to be fulfilled. Just like He told you all several times, He will die and rise again on the third day."

"I hope you don't expect me to believe that, Thomas. It is one of your crazy prophesies again, isn't it?" Leah looked at him with a hint of her old scorn. "I cannot believe you would try to tell us such a ridiculous tale and expect us to fall for it," she added with contempt.

"I know it sounds crazy, but that is exactly what's going to happen, you will see," Thomas said and picked up a few grapes from a plate in front of him. "You will see I am right."

"He did tell us this several times, Leah," Miriam said in her quiet voice. "If you don't want to believe Thomas, will you not believe Yeshua? He was born under miraculous circumstances and remembering that, I have decided to accept He will die in an unusual way. I more than anyone else knows that He is the Son of God, because I know my husband Joseph was not His father and neither was any other man. Yeshua was conceived of the Holy Spirit." Miriam stood among them with a forceful, yet quiet assurance. "I am a simple woman from the line of David, yet I am the mother of the Son of God. I do not know how or why, but I do know that what I am telling you is the truth. My soul magnifies the Lord and my spirit rejoices in God my Savior, for he has been mindful of the humble state of his servant. From now on all generations will call me blessed, for the Mighty One has done great things for me – holy is his name." (Luke 1:46-49)

There was an awed silence in the room. Leah sat back down and stared at Miriam with a mixture of wonder, doubt and anger. Mary Magdalene looked down at her hands, folded in her lap and Thomas stood by the window, staring down into the courtyard of the palace.

After a while he turned around and faced the women.

"It is time for me to go home so I can be there when Yeshua and His men walk by my house to the garden of Gethsemane after the Passover meal," he said. "I want to be there with them," he added. "I know something is going to happen tonight in order for the crucifixion to happen tomorrow." A feeling of dread and unease came over everyone as those in the room realized, the time had come for Yeshua to die. *Will He really be resurrected after three days?* Thomas wondered on the way out to his carriage.

The sun sat low on the horizon. Thomas stood on the flat roof of his house, watching for Yeshua and His men to pass by. Lucius had decided he wanted to stay home. It had been a long day for him in Jerusalem and he felt too tired to walk the long way to the lower slopes of the Mount of Olives. His heart was heavy after listening to Thomas and his predictions of the terrible things which were supposed to happen tomorrow.

"I truly hope you are wrong this time," he told Thomas while they were eating the evening meal.

"I hope I'm wrong, too, Lucius," Thomas answered as they continued their meal in silence.

It was not long until he saw a group of men walking along the road, in the opposite direction of the late stragglers on their pilgrimage to Jerusalem. Thomas had put on a heavy woolen robe and a warm head dress. It felt like it would be cold tonight and he hurried to join the group with Yeshua. He caught up with Cephas some little ways down the road.

"Shalom, Cephas," Thomas said. "It is good to see you. I hope you had a good Passover meal."

"I must say it was different, Thomas," Cephas said. He looked thoughtful. "It was very different."

"In what way?" Thomas asked.

"The Rabbi served us the bread and wine and told us that it represented His body and blood which will be poured out for us as a sacrifice. And then He had us drink from a cup, because it represented a new covenant, according to His words. I have no idea what that means. All of us were confused and afraid. The worst thing was when He told us one of us would betray Him." Cephas sounded indignant as he went on. "We knew that could never be and I especially made very sure to tell Him that whatever happens, I would stand by Him. I even showed Him my sword and said I would defend Him even unto death." Cephas looked at Thomas, determined. "Then He said the worst, He told me that tonight I would deny Him three times before the rooster crows. Imagine that, me, Cephas, whom He put in charge of everything. I made sure to let Him know that I would die for Him before I disown Him. The others said the same thing." (taken from Matthew 26:17-35)

Thomas did not answer. He knew Cephas as a man who spoke before he thought, but he also knew Cephas loved Yeshua.

"Did Yeshua ever say who is going to betray Him?" He asked.

"He said it was Judas and told him during the Passover meal to go and do what he must, whatever that means." Cephas sounded angry. "That weasel Judas. I always knew there was something wrong with him. Good riddance, we don't need him."

"Why is Yeshua going to the olive grove at such a late hour?" Thomas asked.

"He says He wants to pray," Cephas said. "This place we're going to is His favorite place to talk to Yahweh. Why He is going there so late I have no idea." He was slightly out of breath, because they were coming closer to the outcrops of the Mount of Olives. "I don't always understand the Master," he went on. "He could call on angels to defend Him and wipe away all His enemies; and here He talks about being betrayed and killed. Those of us close to Him have wondered when He is going to establish His government so we can drive out the Romans." Cephas sounded frustrated. "I think it is about time He does something about it before the Sanhedrin has Him arrested."

"Do you think you are going to get a big position if Yeshua becomes king?" Thomas asked.

"I think so. After all, He said I would be put in charge of His organization when the time comes. I guess I will have to give up being a fisherman for good," he chuckled. "My father is still waiting for me to come back and help him, because he says he's getting old and needs me."

They had arrived at an isolated olive grove. Yeshua waited until Thomas and Cephas joined the group, since they had fallen behind, talking.

He said to them, "Sit here while I go over there and pray." He took Cephas and the two sons of Zebedee along with him, and he began to be sorrowful and troubled. Then he said to them, "My soul is overwhelmed with sorrow to the point of death. Stay here and keep watch with me." (Matthew 26:36-380)

Thomas hesitated for a moment, but then decided to follow Yeshua, Peter, James and John to a spot just a stone's throw away. He stayed in the shadows of the light of the full moon, behind a group of olive trees, undetected. Yeshua told the men to sit down and pray while He walked on a few steps further. Thomas crept closer so he could hear as Yeshua knelt down with His head low to the ground and his body shaking by heavy sobs.

"Abba, Father," he said, "everything is possible for you. Take this cup from me. Yet not what I will, but what you will." (Mark 14:36)

Thomas never thought Yeshua would be so scared. It shook him to the core. *Yeshua is the Meshiah, He knows what's going to happen. Why would He be so upset and shaken? What if He was just a man and not the Son of God? What if He died and would never rise again?* All of a sudden, Thomas was filled with doubt. *What if this is only a dream and not real? Could it be that he was wrong and there was no Meshiah and he had been following an illusion?* His mind was suddenly filled with misgivings as he crouched behind the tree and continued to listen to Yeshua as He returned to where His men were sleeping.

"Simon," he said to Cephas, "are you asleep? Could you not keep watch for one hour? Watch and pray so that you will not fall into temptation. The spirit is willing, but the body is weak." (Mark 14:36-38)

Thomas was ready to walk over to where the men were, when Yeshua returned to the same spot, knelt again in sorrow and anguish and said,

"My Father, if it is not possible for this cup to be taken away unless I drink it, may your will be done." (Matthew 26:42) He sat in silence and then sobbed in despair.

Thomas felt deeply sorry for Him and wanted to go and comfort Him, but it was as if he was held back. Again he wondered how the Son of God could be so scared when all He had to do was refuse what was to come. God would still love Him, wouldn't He? After all, He hadn't done anything wrong. And if He was just an ordinary man, what would be the point to stay and be killed for nothing? He could never be King with these few men who slept through this whole thing, when they should have supported Him.

Thomas was overwhelmed with doubt and confusion. *I hate religion. It is all about faith and nothing is ever certain. Why can't God make things easier to believe? What if there is no God and I am a fool for sitting here in the dark, in a dream and thinking I am looking at the Son of God come to earth. I am a man of science, not a philosopher or a Rabbi. I wish I could wake up and go back to my old life of being so sure about everything, but mostly about myself. This cannot possibly be real, can it?*

Yeshua had gotten up and walked back to where Cephas, John and James were lying sound asleep. This time He didn't even wake them up, but came back to the same spot and prayed a third time, saying the same thing. (Matthew 26:44)

Thomas watched again with a heavy, confused heart. He wished he hadn't seen Yeshua like this, scared and crying. It didn't seem right. He had figured the Meshiah would be strong and full of faith at all times, knowing what He had to do without fear. How could He be God and feel that way?

When he looked up He saw Yeshua walk over to him. As He laid both hands on Thomas' shoulders He smiled His familiar, knowing smile. Thomas had the feeling the Master was glad he had stayed awake with Him. Before he could say anything, Yeshua walked on to where the others were, still sleeping and said with sorrow in His voice,

"Are you still sleeping and resting? Look the hour is near and the Son of Man is betrayed into the hands of sinners. Rise, let us go! Here comes my betrayer!" (Matthew 26:45-46)

Chapter 36

Thomas saw the torch lights before he heard the many voices through the thick olive grove. His heart raced when a large crowd, made up of Caiaphas's guards, religious leaders and elders of the people, appeared with clubs and swords like evil shadows out of the darkness. As they drew nearer, he noticed Judas at the head of the throng. This is it! They are going to arrest Yeshua. *Oh God!* Thomas moved back into the shadows of the grove and watched as Judas stepped toward Yeshua. Thomas wanted to run and hide deeper in the woods, but again, it was as if someone held him to the spot behind a large tree. The Rabbi stood perfectly calm, waiting for them. Thomas saw none of the agony or fear on His face from before.

Walking up to Yeshua, Judas said, "Greetings, Rabbi!" and kissed him. Yeshua replied, "Friend, do what you came for." (Matthew 26:49-50)

Thomas watched as the guards stepped forward and grabbed Yeshua from behind and bound His hands together with a rope. As they pushed Him forward in a rough manner, Thomas saw Cephas rush into the middle of the guards in a burst of anger, his sword drawn. He swung it at one of them, and in a single, smooth motion sliced the man's ear off, screaming at the same time, "You will not lay hands on the Master. Get away from Him!"

"Put your sword back in its place," Yeshua said to him, "for all who draw the sword will die by the sword. Do you think I cannot call on my Father and he will at once put at my disposal more than twelve legions of angels? But how then would the Scriptures be fulfilled that say it must happen this way?" (Matthew 26:52-54)

Thomas watched the man whose ear had been severed by Cephas hold the side of his head, blood streaming down through his fingers. Before Thomas could run and see what he could do to help stop the bleeding, Yeshua stepped up and laid His hand on the place where the ear was and said, "No more of this!" When He took His hand away, the ear was restored with no sign of bleeding.

Then He said to the chief priests, the officers of the temple guard, and the elders, who had come for him, "Am I leading a rebellion, that you have come with swords and clubs? Every day I was with you in the temple courts, and you did not lay a hand on me. But this is your hour – when darkness reins." (Luke 22:52-53)

When Thomas looked for the disciples, he realized every one of them had run off! He hid behind a large olive tree, trembling in fear and anger. It had begun! He waited until they led Yeshua away with a small crowd following close behind. The full moon shed enough light for him to find his way back to Jerusalem by staying on the road that led right by his house. While wondering whether to go home or follow the crowd, Cephas, John and Mark stepped out of the shadows and joined him.

"Thomas, it is you!" Cephas whispered when he drew closer. "They have arrested the Master."

"I know, Cephas, I was there," Thomas said. "It was terrible, but then how would you know, you all ran off."

"I am so mad at Judas, I could tear him to shreds," Cephas hissed. "He betrayed the Master with a kiss. How dare he?"

"I always knew there was something wrong with him," Mark said. "I can't say I ever trusted him," he added with sadness and anger in his voice.

"Didn't the Master tell us at our last Supper that it would be him?" John said. "He knew all the time Judas would do it; why didn't He try to stop the weasel." John was near tears. "I can't understand any of this. When is Yeshua going to become King? He is running out of time. Instead, He told us again He would be killed when we were eating supper. He's been talking about that a lot lately. How can He be the Meshiah and die? That is not what is supposed to happen, is it?" He looked at the others with a bewildered look.

"I tried to defend Him," Cephas said. "Nobody else did," he added as he looked at John and Mark.

"I didn't see you sticking around when they arrested Him though," Mark said. "You ran just like the rest of us."

"Didn't the Master tell you, Cephas, you would betray Him before the cock crows twice?" John asked.

"I have no idea why He would say such a thing," Cephas said with indignation. "I would never betray Him. You saw me take out my sword and take off the ear of Malchus. You watch me, I will do it again and this time Yeshua won't be there to put it back on." He was shouting by now. "I ran because I was taken by surprise. I guarantee you I will not run the next time, but fight for Him even unto death, you will see!" Cephas raised himself up to his full height. "I will be there for the Master, if it is the last thing I do."

"Maybe Yahweh will send a bunch of angels to help us," John said. He was always the spiritual one of the group. "Yeshua said He could ask for them if He wanted to," he added with a slight waver in his voice. "I don't think He can beat the Romans on His own, can He?" He looked at the others, doubt written across his face.

They followed the crowd into the city to the palace of the high priest.

"I think they are taking Yeshua to the house of Caiaphas," John said. "I know the high priest. I am sure his servants will let me into the courtyard, if that is where they plan to question Him."

"Can you get all of us inside?" Thomas asked.

"I'm pretty sure I can. With this much commotion, the servants will not care who comes with me." John sounded sure.

The moon was hidden by a cloud when they reached the palace. There was no one to stop them from entering and they joined a group of people warming themselves around a large fire in the middle of the courtyard. It had gotten chilly by now and Thomas was glad he wore his wool coat. In the dim light of the fire he could make out some of the people. They were several guards of the high priest, while others seemed to be slaves and bystanders from the crowd, who had made their way into the courtyard.

"It's about time they do something about this rabble-rouser Yeshua," one of the guards said to the one standing next to him. "I've been saying it since last year at Passover, they should arrest Him for claiming to be the Meshiah."

"I don't understand how so many people can believe the things He says about being the Son of God or even being a king," another guard said. "Everybody knows the Meshiah will be a great general and free our people once and for all from all outsiders. Not like this carpenter from Nazareth, who says He will tear down the Temple and build it up again in three days." His laugh was loud and rough. He was joined by others standing around the fire.

"We don't need a new Temple, we need a new King," a man said under his breath as he cast glances over at a group of Roman soldiers on the other side of the large courtyard.

"You better be careful with that kind of talk, Joseph, or you will hang next to Yeshua on the cross tomorrow," the leader of the guards said as he looked around in fear.

"Are they going to crucify Him?" Thomas asked no one in particular.

"That is what I heard the Sanhedrin discuss yesterday. A lot of them want this trouble-maker gone for good, because they are afraid of Him." The man looked at the other people around the fire. "Let's face it, anyone who feeds five thousand people with only a few fish and loaves of bread like this guy has done twice, could be crowned King in no time. And you know what that would mean for the Sanhedrin, they would be in deep trouble with the Romans. Even I would vote for Him if He gives me bread and fish every day," he added with a chuckle. "Why, I could stay home and take it easy."

"I can just see you staying home with your wife every day, Philip," a guard next to him said laughing as he punched him on the shoulder. "She would nag you day and night and you would beg to come back to work after a few days." The entire group broke out in raucous laughter.

"Maybe they better put Him on the cross, now that you mention it, Caleb," Philip answered with a good-natured chuckle. "You do have a point there, my friend. And while they're at it, they might include His disciples as well. In my opinion they are as bad as He is."

"That is true," a third guard pointed out, "look what one of them did to Malchus, he cut off his ear. That alone should land him in prison for a while."

"They are a bunch of low-life Galileans who come here to Jerusalem thinking they are big stuff, because their Rabbi heals a few people," another added with scorn. "I don't trust Galileans if you ask me and that includes Herod. He is nothing but a cursed Idomean who thinks he can be King of the Jews."

"He is better than this so-called King," the guard named Philip said. "At least Herod lives in a palace. This Yeshua we arrested tonight doesn't even have a home and calls twelve ignorant, backward guys from Galilee His army." He laughed out loud and the others joined in.

"I wonder what Caesar thinks about Him when he hears who his rival is," a tall, muscled guard said as he walked up to the fire. "Our Sanhedrin better do something or all of them will be hanging on a cross," he added as he rubbed his hands over the flames. "From what I can tell, Caiaphas is pretty worried and so are the rest of them. I think for once the Sadducees and Pharisees agree on something. All of them want this guy Yeshua gone for good." He turned to the people around the fire. "There will be a crucifixion, you mark my words." Suddenly he fastened his eyes on Cephas. "Hey, aren't you one of His followers?"

"Yeah, he is," another agreed. "I think I saw him with the Rabbi yesterday." He stepped toward Cephas to have a closer look. "Yes, he definitely is one of them."

"I have no idea what you are talking about," Cephas said with great emphasis. "I do not know this man Yeshua." He looked at both guards with defiance and then tuned back to warm his hands over the fire.

Thomas was amazed at his words, but kept silent. This was not the time to make waves. He knew the guards might arrest all of them if they knew who they were. He looked at Mark and John. They did not dare say anything either and stared intently into the fire.

"I have seen this man before, he is one of them," a female voice said. "He is definitely one of the followers of Yeshua." She was a young slave girl who had walked up to the group to warm herself.

"Are you sure?" one of the guards asked.

"I am very sure, I never forget a face," she said as she pointed toward Cephas.

"I'm telling you, I do not know the man, you have to believe me." Cephas sounded even more emphatic. "Do I look like one of those crazy followers of this man to you?" He straightened up his shoulders and looked the guard in the eye. "I am just a pilgrim for Passover, here to see the action." He looked at the girl with a threatening look. "You go and do your chores instead of standing around and making false accusations."

Thomas cringed. How typical of Cephas, all mouth and good intentions, but no courage when it counted. He looked at him with disdain and then suddenly remembered how he had denied the Master not too long ago. He tried to catch John's and Mark's eyes, but they were still staring into the fire. Thomas could see Cephas' hands shake as he held them out over the flames. Even in the dim light of the fire, he could see beads of sweat on his forehead. Poor Cephas, Thomas did not blame him and was glad it wasn't him who stood accused of knowing Yeshua.

"Well, look at that, the man who cut my ear off," Malchus said as he stepped out of the dark into the light. "You are the one who cut my ear off, aren't you? You are lucky your Master put it back on or I would arrest you right here and now."

Cephas whirled around and shouted in anger, "I have no idea what you're talking about. It is dark, how can you tell a man's face. You are mistaken. I'm telling you I do not know the Rabbi."

At that moment a rooster crowed twice and Thomas watched Cephas' face fall. With a look of utter despair, he turned and walked into the dark and away from the group. Thomas followed him to a lone corner of the courtyard and listened as he cried bitterly. (taken from Luke 22:54-62)

"It happened exactly as the Rabbi had foretold it would. I denied Him three times before the rooster crowed twice," Cephas managed to whisper between sobs. Thomas knew he loved Yeshua, but as usual his boasting had gotten him into trouble.

"You know the Master will forgive you, Cephas," Thomas said as he put his hand on his shoulder.

"That is exactly what makes me feel so bad. He knew and He loves me anyway!"

Before Thomas could answer, he heard a great commotion coming from the entrance to the main house. When he looked to see what was going on, he saw six guards pushing Yeshua out into the courtyard, closer to the fire.

"Here He is, the King of the Jews!" one of them shouted. "Come and worship Him the way He deserves." With that he slapped Yeshua's face and spit on him.

"Hail, King Nobody, send your angels to get me!" another shouted. "Maybe you can multiply some more bread and fish for us, we are hungry. Here," he shouted and shoved a piece of stale bread at Yeshua. "Just make sure it is fresh out of the oven," he laughed. "Oh, I forgot, you don't even have a house, least of all an oven." The crowd roared with laughter.

"How about preaching to us, Rabbi? We want to hear about your army in heaven coming to save us all. Where are they?" The guard stepped closer to Yeshua and slapped His face violently. "Maybe if I hit you often enough, your angels will come and defend you, King of the Jews." The crowd was delighted with the spectacle and urged the other guards to join in.

"Ask Him to prophesy, Nathan," someone shouted.

"An excellent idea," the leader of the guard detail laughed. "Blindfold Him James, and see if He knows who strikes Him."

One of the guards covered Yeshua's eyes with a cloth and tied it at the back of His head. When he was done, the man named Nathan slapped His face hard on both sides.

"Well, who was it, your Majesty, tell me?"

"I know what you need, King of the Jews," another guard said as he broke several twigs off a thorny bush nearby and wrought them into a circle. "You need a crown." With that he pressed them on Yeshua's head until the thorny spikes caused the blood to trickle down in bright, red lines around the Rabbi's head and face.

The crowd was delighted and cheered him on with more shouts and laughter. Yeshua stood in silence. He looked at Thomas with a fleeting expression of pain and love. A feeling of utter helplessness swept over Thomas and he realized the Master wanted him to know He did it all for him. The love Thomas felt at that moment was so overwhelming, he could barely stand up as tears of gratitude ran down his cheeks.

As the raucous jeering and laughter continued, Thomas couldn't take any more of this and decided he would walk home. It was very late at night and he wanted to come back early in the morning. He realized it would be difficult to find his way in the dark, but just then the moon had come out. He was certain the dim light was enough for him to make it home.

Chapter 37

It was very early the next morning and the sun had not yet risen. Thomas felt tired and depressed. He knew this would be the worst day of his life, watching Yeshua being crucified. Before he went to sleep last night, he had decided he would try to talk to Pontius Pilate to see if he could be allowed to stand nearby for the trial.

"I want to go with you today, Thomas," Lucius said. "I think there will be trouble and I don't want you to be on your own. Joanna sent a messenger to let us know her group of women will be at the house of Caiaphas. We may want to meet them there."

"That's great. You go ahead, I have decided to go talk to Pontius Pilate and let him know what I think about Yeshua. It won't leave me alone that I denied Him the last time we met. I know what I have to say will not affect the outcome of the trial, but it will change how I feel about myself. I will never deny my Meshiah again as long as I live," he added with great emphasis.

After a light breakfast, they set out for Jerusalem. The roads were not yet clogged and it didn't take long until their carriage reached the courtyard at the palace of the high priest. The sun had barely risen over the horizon.

"I will let you out here, Lucius and will drive on to the palace of Pontius Pilate. Maybe I can catch him this morning before the chief priests get there with Yeshua," Thomas said as Lucius got out of the carriage.

It took Thomas only a short while until he reached the gate of the palace and he was admitted without delay after he was recognized by the guard. A slave escorted him into the interior of the large, ornate building into a receiving chamber. It was lavishly decorated in red and gold, the colors of the Roman army's armor.

"Thomas, I am surprised to see you at this early hour," Pontius Pilate said as he entered a short time later. He looked tired, with deep lines etched in his otherwise handsome face. "What can I do for you?"

"I come here on behalf of Yeshua, the Nazarene carpenter," Thomas answered. "I know I told you I did not know Him very well the last time you asked me, but I must confess I was not entirely honest with you. While I don't know Him as well as I would like, I have had dealings with Him."

"Why are you telling me this now, Thomas?" Pontius Pilate sounded irritated.

"Because I am sorry I did not share with you that He healed me of leprosy and cured many people in my presence. As a physician, I can assure you He did not fake these miracles, but healed many people from diseases from which there is no cure. I was dying of leprosy, so I know first-hand." Thomas shifted uneasily as he looked straight into Pilate's eyes. "I think I came here to make you aware that this Yeshua is not a criminal and does not deserve to die for crimes He did not commit."

"You sound like my wife, Thomas. She has been badgering me about this man for many days because of a dream and wants me to let Him go." Pontius Pilate looked at Thomas with a steely glare. "If you did not tell me the truth before, why would you tell me now?"

"He is the King of the Jews, but not in the way that would oppose Caesar. His Kingdom is not of this world, but of a spiritual nature. He is the long awaited Meshiah of the Jews and has come to save them, not from Caesar, but from their sins." Thomas felt beads of sweat on his forehead as he went on. "I would encourage you, Procurator, to examine Him very carefully and not listen to what the religious leaders say. They don't understand any of this and feel threatened by Him for many reasons, some religious, some out of fear of Roman reprisal. It is up to you to stop them from condemning this innocent man to death. Listen to your wife. God sent her a warning to give to you. Do not ignore it or you will be held accountable for committing the greatest injustice in human history," Thomas was breathing hard, trying to hold his emotions in check.

"Why did you not tell me this when I asked you before?" Pilate asked, still irritated.

"I was scared you would think me crazy," Thomas answered without fear.

"And now you're not?" There was astonishment in Pilate's voice. "What has changed?"

"I have changed. I am no longer afraid, but have decided I will follow Yeshua no matter what happens, without ever denying Him again."

"You give me something to think about, Physician. I am sure they will bring this carpenter to me later on. I will question Him carefully and try my best to find out if He is guilty or not."

"That is all I ask," Thomas said as he rose from his seat. "There is one more thing, Procurator, before I go. Should you decide to condemn Him to death like I know you will, He will still forgive you if you ask Him to, even after He has died on the cross. Remember, He will die for your sins and so give you a chance to live with Him for all eternity."

"I'm a Roman, what does He care about me?" Pilate asked, puzzled at Thomas' words.

"He came even for the Romans, Sir, even for you, the one who sends Him to the cross." Thomas looked at Pilate with assurance. "It will never be too late for you to reach out to Him, even after He has died, because He will rise again after three days. Remember my words, Pontius Pilate, in the days to come when you are sorry for what you have done to the Son of God." Before Pilate could answer, Thomas turned and left.

By the time he reached the outer court of the palace, a large crowd of people, among them the Chief Priests, Scribes, Pharisees and many others were leading Yeshua through the gate. Thomas was appalled to see them push and shove Him as they led Him into the middle of the courtyard. He noticed a crusty layer of dried blood covering the Master's face. The fancy robe Herod had put on Him was hanging in shreds, stained with large blotches of blood on His back from repeated beatings.

"This is far enough," Caiaphas, the High Priest shouted to the soldiers. "We don't want to go any further, because we cannot defile ourselves by entering into the home of a gentile if we want to eat the Passover meal tonight." He turned to one of the men and ordered him to go and get Pontius Pilate to come out to where they stood. Yeshua stood silent with His head down.

"I am glad to find you here," a voice said next to Thomas. It was Lucius. "Did you get to talk to Pontius Pilate?"

"I did. I think it went well."

"Maybe he will let Yeshua go," Lucius asked.

"No, he won't, he can't. It all has to play out in order to fulfill the plan of God. How else would He be able to save us, Lucius?" Thomas asked. "It will happen, but through me Yeshua reached out to the man to let him know there is salvation even for him."

At that moment Pontius Pilate appeared in the entrance of the courtyard. He looked decidedly uncomfortable as he approached the Chief Priests. His snow white linen garment was partially covered by a vivid red stole draped gracefully over one shoulder and wrapped around one arm.

"What charges are you bringing against this man?"

"If he were not a criminal," they replied, "we would not have handed him over to you."

Pilate said, "Take him yourselves and judge him by your own law."

"But we have no right to execute anyone," the Jews objected. (John 18:29-31)

Thomas watched Pilate's face and saw indecision mixed with fear in his eyes as he looked at Yeshua first and then at Thomas. "You haven't even tried Him and yet you already want Him crucified. I do not see anything He has done that warrants such harsh punishment." His eyes scanned the crowd with a scowl. "You are supposed to be a religious people. I have it on good authority that this carpenter has done nothing but heal people and preach a peaceful message of love and forgiveness. Which one of these do you object to?" His remark dripped with sarcasm.

But they insisted, "He stirs up the people all over Judea by his teaching. He started in Galilee and has come all the way here." (Luke 23:5)

"I will decide what to do with Him after I have spoken to Him myself," Pilate finally said. He turned to the Roman guards. "Bring Him so I may talk to Him in private." He waved for Thomas to follow him. Once inside, Pilate asked Thomas to sit next to him as Yeshua stood at a distance.

"Come closer," Pilate said to Him. "I have no idea what to do with You, but there is one thing I am certain about and that is that you have done nothing to deserve to be crucified."

The guards pushed Yeshua forward forcefully so that He almost fell. With His face covered in dried blood from the crown of thorns on his head and His shoulders hunched over, He presented a pitiful picture.

"Are you the King of the Jews?" Pilate asked Him.

"Is that your own idea or did others talk to you about me?"

"Am I a Jew?" Pilate replied. "It was your people and your Chief Priests who handed you over to me. What is it you have done?"

Yeshua said, "My kingdom is not of this world. If it were, my servants would fight to prevent my arrest by the Jews. But now my kingdom is from another place."

"You are a king then!" said Pilate.

Yeshua answered, "You are right in saying I am a king. In fact, for this reason I was born, and for this I came into the world, to testify to the truth. Everyone on the side of truth listens to me."

What is truth?" Pilate asked. (John 18:33-38)

"I don't understand You," he added in frustration and turned to Thomas. "Do you have any idea what He is talking about?"

"I do in a way, but not to the point of explaining it all to you. All I know for sure is that He is innocent and that He has maintained that the Father in heaven has sent Him for this purpose," Thomas said.

"What is His purpose?" Pilate thundered. "I do not understand why He does not defend Himself or explain to me further what He means by all this religious talk. I am a Roman. We serve many gods, but none of them would lay down their lives for me or anyone else. They would rather strike us dead for doing wrong instead of dying for us like you tell me He will." He was still shouting as he pointed to Yeshua. "How am I supposed to make a ruling on His guilt or innocence since I have no idea what He has done wrong? All I can do is keep the peace and do what that wild crowd outside wants from me, condemn an innocent man to death." Pilate was breathing hard as he stared at Yeshua. There was real fear in his eyes. "What if He is a God and gets even with me? I don't want to do this, but for some reason the crowd outside is hell-bent on having Him killed. I can't risk a riot if I don't give them what they want." He sighed in frustration as he looked at Yeshua. "Why don't You say anything? Why won't You help me make a decision if You are indeed the Meshiah?" He looked at Yeshua for a long time, waiting for an answer, but there was only silence. Finally, Pilate stood up and gestured to the guards to take Yeshua back outside.

Pilate called together the chief priests, the rulers and the people, and said to them," You brought me this man as one who was inciting the people to rebellion. I have examined Him in your presence and have found no basis for your charges against Him. Neither has Herod, for he sent him back to us. You can see, He has done nothing to deserve death. Therefore, I will punish Him and then release him."

"With one voice they cried out, "Away with this man! Release Barabbas to us! (Barabbas had been thrown into prison for an insurrection in the city and for murder.)

Wanting to release Yeshua, Pilate appealed to them again, but they kept shouting, "Crucify him! Crucify him!"
For a third time he spoke to them: "Why? What crime has this man committed? I have found in him no grounds for the death penalty. Therefore, I will have him punished and then release him."

But with loud shouts they insistently demanded that he be crucified, and their shouts prevailed. (Luke 23:13-23)

"I find no basis for a charge against him. But it is your custom for me to release to you one prisoner at the time of the Passover. Do you want me to release the king of the Jews?"

They shouted back, "No, not him! Give us Barabbas!" (John 18:38-40)

Thomas stood mesmerized as he watched Pilate's face. The man was clearly torn between listening to the crowd and doing what he knew was right. If the people started a riot, his position as Governor was in peril with Caesar, because his relationship with the Emperor was already on shaky grounds. After all, that is why he was banished to this god-forsaken place on the edge of the Roman Empire in the first place. On the other hand, there was the dream his wife had and the words Thomas had spoken to him about this prisoner, as well as his own impression of this man who might be the Son of God.

With sadness Thomas realized the terrible spot Pilate was in and the inevitability of the choice he would have to make. He also remembered Barabbas and his encounters with him. It was incredible to watch the religious leaders choose this murderous thief over their Meshiah. But that is what they did.

It was then Thomas heard Pilate's words through the uproar of the crowd.

"I am innocent of this man's blood," he said. "He is your responsibility."

All the people answered, "Let his blood be on us and on our children!"

Then he released Barabbas to them. But he had Yeshua flogged and handed him over to be crucified. (Matthew 27:4-26)

Thomas stood motionless amidst the jubilant crowd. They had brought in Barabbas. His heart sank as he watched the burly criminal raise his arms high with his fists over his head and a big smile on his face. Thomas turned to Pontius Pilate who was washing his hands, his face flushed with anger, fear and disgust. He thought the Governor said something, but Thomas couldn't hear what it was. He stepped closer to hear, but after drying his hands on a towel, handed to him by a servant, Pilate turned around and without another word, walked into the palace.

"It is time for us to leave," Lucius shouted above the noise of the crowd. "We don't want to cross paths with Barabbas right now. Who knows what he would do to us."

"You are right. I've had enough of this disgusting spectacle anyway," Thomas said and followed his friend out of the courtyard. As he looked back, he saw the Roman soldiers beat Yeshua with sticks on the face and head as blood spurted from His nose. He could hear them taunting and cursing Him, spitting in His face while striking Him with a leather whip on the back, legs and torso. Yeshua's hands were tied up over His head on a long pole. Thomas' stomach lurched in revulsion at the cruelty and barbarism, but knew this was the normal way of the Romans to treat a criminal before execution from what Lucius had told him earlier. According to his friend, crucifixion had been practiced for centuries, but the Romans had developed it into a cruel art.

Before they reached the carriage, they met Miriam, Mary Magdalene, Joanna, Leah and John. Miriam was leaning her head on John's shoulder, sobbing uncontrollably.

"I don't understand any of this. Why would they want to kill my wonderful Son? He has done nothing but good all His life." Mary Magdalene, Leah and Joanna stood by helplessly as she held on to John with her head on his shoulder. Thomas cringed when he realized how much more Miriam would have to suffer before it was all over. He looked at Leah. There was nothing left of her resolve earlier to defend the Rabbi, just fear. Her face was filled with shame as she looked at Thomas.

"Where do we go from here?" he asked Lucius. "What is the custom in cases like this? Tonight is the beginning of Passover, are they going to wait until it is over and then crucify Yeshua?"

"I'm afraid not. He will be led to a place called Golgotha or the Place of the Skull as it is also called. It is where hardened criminals are executed, mostly by crucifixion. As a physician, you know it is one of the most cruel punishments there is. And now that Pontius Pilate has given in to the Chief Priests, his soldiers will take Him to Golgotha without delay, so that His crucifixion will not interfere with the Passover meal."

"Are you saying He will be killed today?" Thomas sounded incredulous.

"That is right. It will be all over by this afternoon."

"How does Yeshua get there?"

"He will have to carry the cross Himself, or at least one beam of it. It depends on what the authorities decide. I imagine a big crowd will line the streets along the way." Lucius sounded sad as he went on. "It reminds me of the games in the Roman amphitheater. Like there, the crowds love a gory spectacle, and this definitely qualifies."

"We better wait right here then until they lead Yeshua out," Thomas said. "I don't want to miss this, because twenty-one centuries later this event is still known as the most infamous crucifixion in the history of mankind. We should leave the carriage at the palace and follow on foot to where they are leading Yeshua." They walked through the gate of the palace out into the street in the midst of a throng of people, pouring out with Yeshua in their midst. Thomas watched in horror as the soldiers taunted, beat and pushed the Rabbi, encouraged by the jeering, laughing crowd on each side of the road.

"Here is the king of the Jews, bow down and worship him," they shouted. "Come and see how many of his servants are ready to help him, folks," one of the Roman soldiers yelled into the crowd as his lash landed on Yeshua's back with each word. Thomas shuddered at the sound coming from the whip finding its target. He could see the face of the Rabbi cringe in pain as He stumbled along in silence.

Suddenly, the group stopped as two soldiers carried a large cross and put it in front of Him.

"This is for you, your Majesty," they said with sarcasm in their voice. "Let's see how well You do with it." They laughed as they put it on His back, right on top of His wounds oozing with blood. Yeshua flinched and then groaned from the pain as He stumbled on.

Thomas looked around to see if there was anyone who was upset about this cruel spectacle, aside from him, in the midst of this frenzied crowd. That's when he saw the group of Yeshua's men gathered just outside the gate. He walked over to join them.

"I always knew this would happen," he heard Didymus say. "The Master just wouldn't listen when I told Him we should go back to Galilee."

"What does this mean, Cephas?" Philip asked, his voice filled with fear. "He is supposed to be the Meshiah who will never die. Well, He is going to be crucified today. What do you say to that?" His tone had turned to anger.

"I have no idea, Philip," Cephas said as he stared at Yeshua. "I can't believe what I'm seeing. If He is the Son of God, why isn't He doing something?" he added in a low voice, "If He leaves us, we are doomed. How can He be the Meshiah if He dies and we are left behind with the authorities coming after us next?"

"I heard Judas has killed himself," James said. "One of the guards told me. He tried to give the money back he took for betraying the Master, but the Chief Priest laughed at him and told him to get lost. That's when he went to the Potter's field and hanged himself."

"He deserves nothing less," Cephas said with venom in his voice. "Look at what he's done! This is truly his fault," he added, pointing to the throng of people lining the streets, staring at Yeshua carrying the cross toward Golgotha.

"Oh my God, the Master looks terrible," another disciple said. Thomas looked over to where John, Miriam, Mary Magdalene, Leah and Joanna stood. He could hear the women's pitiful crying and wailing. Miriam reached her hands out to Yeshua in a pleading gesture as He walked by. He looked at her and said something, but Thomas couldn't hear what it was. Miriam swayed as if she was going to faint, but John caught her at the last minute.

Suddenly, there was a loud thump as the cross Yeshua was carrying hit the ground, His body crumpled underneath. Loud cries emanated from the many women who had gathered along both sides of the street. With dismay Thomas watched as the soldiers beat Him unmercifully until He managed to get up with slow, painful movements. He groaned and then picked up the cross and stumbled on.

Thomas stood mesmerized by the horrible spectacle, when a voice behind him said in a mournful tone, "This is not a man who could possibly be the Meshiah. He might be a prophet and a good man, but He is not the One we have been waiting for." It was Didymus with his usual doubting attitude. He sounded close to tears.

"I agree, we have been wrong thinking Yeshua would bring a new kingdom to Israel. Instead, He will be dead in a few hours and, like Didymus says, we will be in danger of being arrested for being His disciples," Matthew said in a low tone. "I think I better go back to Galilee collecting taxes. It is safer than staying here waiting for the soldiers to arrest me." Matthew was barely able to hide his terror.

"You could at least wait until they have crucified Him," Cephas said almost with a growl. "Maybe His angels could still come and save Him."

"Good luck with that." Didymus' sarcasm struck a chord with the rest of them.

Thomas turned around and looked at the group. He could see the fear in their faces as they slowly followed the procession. His heart was heavy since he had to admit, he agreed with every word they had said. It suddenly dawned on him that this might only be a dream and nothing about it was real. *Why would he think this actually happened two thousand years ago? How could anyone possibly rise from the dead like Yeshua claimed He would? I am a physician, a man of science! No one comes back to life once they are dead, except in a dream. I must be crazy to believe this stuff. There is no God, there is no Meshiah, no reality but science.* Thomas looked at Yeshua. He had fallen underneath the cross again. The soldiers were beating Him repeatedly to make Him get back up, but it seemed He no longer had the strength. *If Yeshua was indeed the Son of God, He should be able to carry His cross like other prisoners had before Him. Let's face it, He was a weak, beaten man who had bragged He was sent by God to be the Meshiah. Well, where was God now? Why didn't He send angels to help Him?* A feeling of dread spread over Thomas. *None of this was real and he would wake up in his house in Philadelphia on his birthday and find out again Melissa forgot!* Walking in the middle of the shouting, cheering crowd, Thomas was overcome with a feeling of utter despair. Not because Yeshua was going to die, but because He was not real. None of this was, not Lucius, not Helena, his little girl, or anything else he had experienced. And then the crushing realization came to him: there was no God, no afterlife, just his miserable existence with a wife who hated him, no children and what felt like a career that did not sound near as important as he once thought it was. For the first time he thought it would be nice if he could stay in this dream and live out his life in the land of Israel in the year AD 30. That way Yeshua would be real and His death would give him a new life that included faith, the love of real friends and a little girl to call his own. But it wasn't real and he would wake up and face his world in the future, which was almost alien to him by now.

His thoughts were interrupted by loud shouting as two of the Roman soldiers grabbed a man a few feet away from Thomas and dragged him to where Yeshua lay on the ground.

"You will help Him carry this," they shouted, threatening to beat him if he resisted. Without a word and with little effort, the man picked up the cross and put it on his shoulders.

Yeshua looked up with gratitude and then turned toward Thomas. As His eyes fastened on him, it was as if the tide of doubt, discouragement and fear left his heart. Thomas stood bolted to the ground. *Yeshua knows! He knows about my doubts, fears and discouragement even in His present horrible circumstances. How was that possible? Was it because it was only a dream or because He really was the Meshiah and would willingly die for me?* Thomas' mind, while still filled with a lot of confusion, slowly began to give way to a measure of peace and determination. *No matter what, I will stick it out and follow Him on the long road to the cross.*

When Thomas walked on, he noticed two more prisoners who carried not an entire cross, but a single beam. They had not been beaten like Yeshua and therefore were not weakened like Him. The crowd had significantly increased as they moved along toward the hill of Golgotha, just outside of the city. Thomas guessed it was maybe a mile from Pontius Pilate's palace to the Place of the Skull.

He tried to ignore the jeering, taunting and shouting of the many hundreds of people lining the street as he caught up with Yeshua. He realized the Rabbi was weakened to the point of passing out from the heavy blood loss sustained from the wounds over His entire body. Thomas knew it would not take long for Him to die once nailed to the cross.

He looked back and saw John and the women following the crowd. He could only imagine the agony Miriam was going through, seeing her Son's suffering like this. He did not have the stomach to wait for them, but continued on with Lucius at his side. He realized the physician had not said a word during all this time.

"Are you alright, Lucius?" he asked.

"No, I'm not, but I will not leave the Rabbi. This is a nightmare, something I never thought could've happened. All the good He has done, all the miracles He performed, the many thousands of people He fed, where are those people now? I don't understand how they can hail Him as the Meshiah one day and crucify Him the next?" He sounded discouraged and tired.

"I'm afraid the worst is yet to come, my friend," Thomas said. "Yet in all this, Yeshua looked at me a while ago and I knew He understood my thoughts of doubt and despair. He was thinking about me instead of what He was going through."

"Only the son of God could do that," Lucius said with hope in his voice. "I was beginning to have my doubts as well, but this helps me realize He is who He says He is, the Meshiah who cares enough to die for us, just as He said He would."

Suddenly Thomas felt a hand tap on his shoulder. It was Nicodemus.

"What a sad day for all of us," he said in a low voice. "I was there when they condemned Him and I didn't speak against it, because I was scared. I am as much to blame as any of the members of the Sanhedrin. It is something I will have to live with for the rest of my life." Tears streamed down his face as he added, "I have killed my Meshiah and I am sure He will never forgive me." Nicodemus was so overcome by emotion, he would have collapsed, had Thomas and Lucius not held him up.

"You know better, Nicodemus," Thomas said. "You are the one who told us Yeshua had to go through this in order to fulfill the scriptures."

"I know, but why did it have to be me who realized fully who He is and yet did not speak out, even if it meant risking my place in the Sanhedrin or even my life. The others didn't know, but I did. I have no excuse, don't you see?" People stared at him as he shouted out the words, but soon they lost interest and continued yelling insults at the man walking behind the cross.

"Come, Nicodemus, Lucius and I will stay with you throughout and then we can talk some more after it is over," Thomas shouted above the noise. "There is nothing you could have done to change the outcome, you know that. How else can Yeshua die for your sins, yes, even the one you have committed, if He does not die on the cross?"

Nicodemus looked at Thomas and shrugged his shoulders in resignation and then continued to walk on until they finally reached the Place of the Skull. They stopped and watched as the soldiers arranged three crosses on the ground on top of the hill. They were soon joined by John and the women with him, followed by the rest of the disciples.

Some of the onlookers recognized Nicodemus and were astounded to see him with the group of Yeshua's followers.

"Since when are you one of them?" a man scowled at him. "Aren't you one of the Sanhedrin who condemned Him to death?"

"I did and I am sorry," Nicodemus said as he looked at the man with deep sorrow. "This Yeshua is a good man, but more than that, He is the promised One and we are getting ready to kill Him. May He forgive me for what I have done," he added. "I am guilty of His death and I wish I could stop this, but it is too late."

The man looked at Nicodemus with confusion and then lowered his eyes. All conversation stopped when Yeshua, together with the other two criminals, was led in front of their individual crosses. A strange silence hung over the crowd, except for the shouting of the soldiers as they threw Yeshua on the ground first and then lifted his body onto the beams. Thomas could only imagine the pain as the Rabbi's raw, bloody back hit the hard surface of the wood. He heard Him cry out in agony and then closed his eyes. Thomas saw His lips moving as if in silent prayer.

"Markus, did you bring the nails?" one of the soldiers yelled to another standing a few feet away.

"I got them right here," he said and handed them over.

Thomas shuddered at the size of the long nails and watched in horror as the soldier took first one of Yeshua's hands and then the other and pounded the nails through the flesh onto the beam underneath. With the women screaming, it made it impossible for him to hear Yeshua cry out in pain again.

As a physician, Thomas knew the medical results of flesh and ligaments being torn, which causes unimaginable, searing pain. He also understood the torture of the human body hanging on a cross as the person tries to hold the body up on a tiny wooden ledge with his feet. After a short time, this causes shooting agony, not only in the legs, but throughout the body. He knew, that after a while, the lungs would not have enough room to expand when the body finally gives way and sags down and breathing becomes impossible. For the first time in his life Thomas wished he wasn't a physician with the full knowledge of what was happening to this poor man.

The soldiers acted as if in a frenzy of hate during this time as one drove a nail through both of His feet arranged on top of each other. Throughout they continued to hit Yeshua, kicked Him and spat in His face, while taunting Him to save Himself if He was the King of the Jews. One of them stepped forward and fastened a sign on the very top of the vertical beam of the cross. On it was written "YESHUA OF NAZARETH, KING OF THE JEWS" in three languages, Aramaic, Latin and Greek. When it was fastened securely, the soldiers and the crowd started laughing and jeering once more.

Thomas stood in silent horror as the spectacle continued. His mind was too numb to think or act as he could not take his eyes off the scene. He held his breath as several soldiers finally raised the cross with Yeshua up so that it slid into the permanent hole in the ground, especially designed for this purpose. It settled in with a thud and as it did, it almost ripped Yeshua's hands loose from the nails. Thomas realized the other two criminals had their arms held by ropes around the beams instead of fastened with nails, which was not nearly as painful. They were raised up next with one on each side of the Rabbi. The crowd clapped when all three crosses stood in place each with their unfortunate occupants hanging until death would end their agony.

As if drawn by an unknown force, Thomas stepped closer to the three crosses and looked up at Yeshua. The Master had His eyes closed and His breathing was labored, while blood poured out of the nail wounds of His hands and feet. As Thomas stood and stared into His face, Yeshua opened His eyes and looked at him with such love, he began to tremble under the powerful gaze. He had never experienced such intense emotions of peace, faith, compassion and belonging before. Overriding all else was a total assurance that His Meshiah was doing this for him, because He wanted Thomas to follow Him, not just here on earth but for all eternity. There was no doubt left, no wondering if this was only a dream. Thomas knew if it was, it was designed to bring him home to the One who came to give His life so that he could tell others about the love the Father has for those who accept it. Thomas held out his hands as if to take Yeshua's love and put them on his chest over his heart.

At that moment, he heard voices belonging to the chief priests, the teachers of the law and the elders as they mocked Yeshua.

"He saved others, they said, "but he can't save himself! If he is the King of Israel, let him come down now from the cross, and we will believe in him. He trusts in God. Let God rescue him now if he wants him, for he said, "I am the Son of God." (Matthew 27:42-43)

Nicodemus had joined Thomas in front of the cross.

"Those fools! If the Father would get His Son down now all this would be for nothing," he whispered to Thomas. "All this," and he waved his hand towards Yeshua, "all this was told to us by the prophet Isaiah four hundred years ago.

"Just as there were many who were appalled at him – his appearance was so disfigured beyond that of any man and his form marred beyond human likeness – so will he sprinkle many nations." (Isaiah 52:14-15)

"Now I finally understand what the prophet was talking about," Nicodemus added. "In spite of what I did, I am still honored to stand in the presence of the One who came to give His life for mankind, that all who accept His sacrificed, will be able to come to Him, cleansed from sin and free to follow Him." Nicodemus looked at Thomas with a smile. "And I want to be one of those who do, if He will have me, because in the words of Isaiah, "for he bore the sin of many, and made intercession for the transgressors." (Isaiah 53:12)

"I can truthfully say, I qualify after what I have done," he added with a broad smile as he gazed up at Yeshua.

At that moment Thomas heard the voice of one of the criminals on the cross mocking Yeshua.

"Aren't you the Christ? Save yourself and us!"

But the other criminal rebuked him. "Don't you fear God," he said, "since you are under the same sentence? We are punished justly, for we are getting what our deeds deserve. But this man has done nothing wrong."

Then he said, "Yeshua, remember me when you come into your kingdom."

Yeshua answered him, "I tell you the truth, today you will be with me in paradise." (Luke 23:39-43)

Thomas looked at Nicodemus with a smile.

"I think you have your answer. If the Master accepts this criminal, I know He will accept you, a leader of the people of Israel."

As he was still speaking, suddenly, the sky slowly darkened. Thomas looked around to see if anyone else saw it. After all, it was only noon and the sun was high in the sky. He realized something extraordinary was happening. Fear descended over the crowd standing nearby. It was a strange and eerie darkness and Thomas could see the stars, yet they seemed fainter than at night. Neither was it pitch black, but rather a grayish black that seemed to come from the earth below. Thomas wondered whether it could be an eclipse, but he knew Passover fell on the full moon, so it couldn't be. The crowd was uneasy, since there was not a cloud in the sky and yet the sun did not shine.

Miriam pulled John by the hand and moved closer to the cross in order to see Yeshua in the dim light. They had to pass by the soldiers who were dividing Yeshua's clothes among themselves, one was seamless and therefore expensive, they cast lots for it. Miriam had given it to her Son the day before He left for Jerusalem. She stopped right in front of the cross and started to cry as she held John's hand.

When Yeshua saw his mother there, and the disciple whom he loved, standing nearby, he said to his mother, "Dear woman, here is your son," and to the disciple, "Here is your mother." (John 19:26-27)

Thomas felt deeply sorry for Miriam and wished he could make her understand why all this had to happen. He watched as one of the soldiers came and took a sponge and dipped it in wine mixed with vinegar and held it up to Yeshua's lips, but He refused to drink it. It was close to three o'clock in the afternoon by now and the Place of the Skull was still covered in eerie darkness. Suddenly, a low rumble shook the earth like an earthquake and the three crosses swayed slightly as a gust of wind swept over the hill. The people were terrified and Thomas could hear women cry out in fear.

He stood close enough so he could see clearly as Yeshua lifted His head and looked out over the crowd. As His eyes rested on the religious leaders and the Roman soldiers, He said, "Father forgive them, for they do not know what they are doing." (Luke 23:14)

After that Yeshua cried out in a loud voice. "My God, my God, why have you forsaken me?" (Mark 15:34)

Thomas trembled and fell to his knees as He heard Yeshua say in a clear voice, "It is finished. (John 19:30) Father, into your hands I commit my spirit." (Luke 23:46)

The centurion who stood close to Thomas in front of the cross, heard Yeshua's words. He turned to Thomas and said, "I truly believe this was the Son of God and a righteous man."

And then the earth trembled again. It was only for a few minutes, but it seemed to last for an eternity. The crowd stood in awed silence as the darkness covered the scene. Some wept openly and beat their breasts, while others trembled in fear. After a long time, the sun appeared in the clear sky overhead. Where had it been for three hours? There were no clouds, no eclipse and no explanation for what had happened.

Thomas had no idea what to make of it and decided it was an act of God. Nothing else made sense. Relieved the ordeal was over, he turned to Nicodemus and said, "At least Yeshua doesn't suffer anymore. It was the most horrifying and cruel thing I have ever seen."

"This was much more than a normal death on the cross, Thomas," Nicodemus said. "According to Isaiah, there is still one thing missing. For it says," He was pierced for our transgressions, he was crushed for our iniquities; the punishment that brought us peace was upon him, and by his wounds we are healed. We all, like sheep, have gone astray, each of us has turned to his own way; and the Lord has laid on him the iniquity of us all." (Isaiah 53:5-7)

"You see, Thomas, He has not been pierced yet. I don't understand. Everything else fits perfectly." Before Nicodemus could go on, one of the soldiers walked up to Yeshua, raised his lance and pierced His side with the words, "To make sure He is dead." Since the other two criminals were still alive, several soldiers broke their legs.

"Why are they doing that?" Thomas asked Nicodemus.

"It is not lawful to allow them to stay on the cross over Passover. Since Yeshua is already dead, they did not have to do that so that the scripture might be fulfilled that not one of His bones might be broken."

Thomas looked at Nicodemus with amazement. "You were right, now everything is as scripture has foretold it."

As they walked down the hill with the rest of the crowd, Nicodemus said, "Thomas, you might ask if this crucifixion was worse than all others. It was much worse. Outwardly, Yeshua went through what all other criminals suffer when they are punished in this fashion. The real agony He faced however, the one that really counts, was not the physical torture, but the one that took place in the spiritual realm. As Isaiah said, He suffered for all our sins and in the process became sin. As the Son of God, that was a supreme sacrifice. That was the real death, not just the one on the cross. In becoming sin for us, He set us free from the bondage of our transgression. The enemy has no more hold over us from now on."

"Does that mean the whole world is included automatically and all will be set free?" Thomas asked.

"The opportunity to accept His sacrifice is there for everyone, but that does not mean everyone will take it. It is a gift and like any other gift, it must be accepted in order to be received. For those who reject the Son of God and His gift, they are still under the curse of sin and will not see eternal life in the presence of God."

"In other words, to become a follower of the Meshiah, a person has to agree to it," Thomas said.

"That is right, Thomas. It is a freely offered decision and available to everyone who chooses it."

Nicodemus was out of breath when they reached the bottom of the hill. He turned to Thomas with a smile and said, "How fortunate I was to have witnessed what the prophets foretold four hundred years earlier. Our God never forgets a promise, even if it takes a long time to fulfill it. What remains now is the resurrection Yeshua says will happen in three days. I can't wait; until then, shalom my friends." With that he turned into the street that led to the Temple, while Thomas and Lucius walked on to the palace of Pontius Pilate, where their carriage waited for them.

Chapter 38

A strange, subdued silence hung over the city as they drove home through Jerusalem that afternoon. Somehow, eating the Passover meal in a few hours did not seem appealing to Thomas. His heart was filled with the events of the day and all he wanted to do was hide in his room with the shades drawn. He did not feel like sharing with anyone at the house about what happened. It was all too much and his mind felt numb. Yeshua was dead. Would He really rise again? Suddenly, doubt began to gnaw at his heart and depression swept over him like a cloud. He sighed deeply. *Would he ever be able to believe without questioning or be tossed by circumstances? After all, this might only be a dream and until he woke up, it would never be truly reality. And even after he woke up, all this will still have been only a dream.* He looked at Lucius and realized, when this was over, his friend and all the people he had come to love, might no longer be there. *There would only be Melissa. Would she still be mad at him or forgive him? If not, he faced a life alone with just his colleagues at the hospital.* His stomach tightened. *Work. There was a time when he thought surgery was his life and to be Chief of Thoracic Surgery was everything he ever wanted. How would he cope with his new faith, new attitudes and his old ways? Would he forget about all this the way he had forgotten about his life there? If Yeshua did not rise from the dead, he knew he would forget in time, because then he was certain He was not the Meshiah. What if He did come back to life, what then?* Thomas shifted uncomfortably in his seat as the carriage rumbled on. *What if he woke up as a Christian? He could imagine the snickering and even disdain at work and the rejection and condemnation of his family. His grandmother would be devastated and his parents would probably disown him, embarrassed by his religious emotionalism. Melissa and her family would love the whole thing and expect him to preach the Gospel. I will never be a preacher. In spite of all this, I am still a physician and always will be!* Uncertainty swept over him as the carriage turned into the driveway of his villa. *His little girl Helena would be there with her beautiful smile and deep love for him, but she might not be real either. Nothing in his life right now was real.* The thought hit home with such force he felt sick to his stomach. *Please Yeshua, don't let me wake up! I like my life here. It is more real than Philadelphia, because I don't like the person I was there, the arrogant, prideful surgeon who thinks he is in control of his life. What a joke! I don't have people there who love me like the ones here. But then again, I don't have You now either. You were always there with me with Your knowing smile which let me feel You knew who I really was and still accepted me. But You are dead, gone forever and I am left with nothing.*

Thomas jumped off the carriage before it stopped and ran into the house straight to his room, trying to hide the tears filling his eyes. He threw himself on his pallet. *There is no reality anywhere, whether here in this life or the one in the future! There is only an alternate reality of what could have been and a future I no longer want. I am without hope!*

"Yeshua, I want to believe in You, but I don't know how, because I can't figure out what is real and what is not. Please, show me You are real, because I can't do it on my own." Without realizing he was talking out loud, he said, "I can't do anything without You, please don't leave me. Show me what to do."

There was only silence.

"Daddy, there are two men who have come to see you," Helena said, standing in the doorway. "One of them is Nicodemus, the other says his name is Joseph of Arimathea. They want to talk to you."

"I will be there in a minute, Angel."

"Are you alright, Daddy? You have been crying, what's wrong?" She leaned over him and kissed his cheek. "I have never seen you cry."

"I am fine. It's just that Yeshua was killed today and it has upset me greatly," he said as he wiped his eyes. "Go tell them I will be with them in a moment," he said as he got up.

"Thomas, I brought a friend, a fellow member of the Sanhedrin," Nicodemus said when Thomas walked into the atrium. "This is Joseph of Arimathea. He is, or rather was, a follower of Yeshua."

Joseph was a man in his fifties, dressed in an expensive blue outer garment over a white linen piece of clothing. His brown eyes accentuated a strong face, covered by a well-groomed beard with curly brown hair to match. He was of medium height and slender built and exuded a high degree of wealth, culture and education.

"It is a great pleasure to meet the royal physician of Herod," he said with a smile as he bowed to Thomas. I have heard a lot about you."

"I am glad to meet a friend of Nicodemus any time," Thomas said. "Welcome to my house. What can I do for you?"

"We know you have the ear of Pontius Pilate," Nicodemus said without preamble. "Joseph wants to ask the Prefect if he can take possession of the body of Yeshua for burial."

"I have a newly hewn grave near Golgotha that I bought not too long ago and wish to bury Yeshua in it. It is the least I can do for Him after what He suffered today. In order to do that, I need Pilate's permission and wondered if you can come with me to get it."

"It is true I have had some dealings with Pilate, but I don't know how far it extends in getting favors of this magnitude," Thomas answered. "This is a pretty explosive political deal and my word may not mean much, but I will be most happy to come with you. Yeshua healed me when I was dying, it is the least I can do for Him." He waved to Helena. "I will be gone for a while. Please, tell Lucius where I am." He leaned down and kissed her on the head. "We will talk when I get back and I will tell you all about what happened today."

The carriage made its way through the dense crowd toward Jerusalem. It was late afternoon and time was of the essence. Today was the Day of Preparation and they had only a few hours to bury Yeshua until Passover started.

"Did you say you are a member of the Sanhedrin?" Thomas asked Joseph.

"I am and this is a sad day for our people," Joseph answered.

"I must tell you that Joseph was not present when the Sanhedrin voted to crucify Yeshua," Nicodemus said with sadness and regret in his voice. "He is not guilty of killing the Meshiah like I am."

"Do not be too hard on yourself, Nicodemus," Joseph said in a kind tone. "You really had no choice. I don't know what I would have done had I been there," he added thoughtfully. "I am so grateful I didn't have to make that choice. If I had really loved Yeshua, I would not have kept my belief in Him a secret."

"Do you think Yeshua was the One Israel has been waiting for?" Thomas asked. "Now that He is dead, I mean."

"He will rise in three days just as He told us, you will see," Joseph said emphatically. "You will see."

"I believe that as well," Nicodemus said. "According to the scriptures, His body will not decay, but come back to life."

"I hope you are right," Thomas said. "It was a terrible sight to see Him bleeding and bruised beyond recognition. It would be a miracle if He rises from that kind of trauma, speaking as a physician."

"He has healed so many from incurable diseases, why wouldn't He be able to renew His own body since He is the Son of God?" Joseph said. "I know His eleven disciples do not have the faith to believe that, but I do. I talked to Cephas after the crucifixion and he was in a state of utter despair, ready to go back to being a fisherman," he added.

"It is the same with the others," Nicodemus said. "All of them were devastated when the Master died and are without hope. When I tried to tell them Yeshua will rise again, they looked at me like I was mad. I can't say as I blame them, but I also know He told them many times this would happen."

When the carriage finally stopped at the gate to Pilate's palace,

Thomas looked out and the guard waved them through without delay. When a slave approached, he asked to speak to Pilate and they were shown inside immediately.

"Are you sure the carpenter is already dead?" Pilate asked, astonished. "It usually takes more than a day or two to die with this form of punishment." He turned to one of the servants nearby. "Get me the centurion in charge so he can verify this." Pontius Pilate turned to Thomas with a half-smile. "You turn up everywhere, Physician. I'm sure you witnessed His death as well."

"I did, Sir," Thomas said, "it was terrible. I have never seen a more gruesome spectacle."

Pilate sounded weary as he wiped his forehead and sat down with a deep sigh. "I still don't think the man was guilty, but what could I do. These people are fanatics and would rather let a dangerous criminal go free and instead condemn, from what I could see, a harmless religious preacher. In the end, I had to give in to keep the peace and stay out of trouble with Caesar." He looked at Thomas and Joseph with a frown as he went on, "I will never hear the end of it with my wife. She has been riding me about this endlessly and even told me, the Carpenter will rise again after three days. What do you think, Thomas, is that possible medically speaking?"

"No, Sir, it is not, but spiritually speaking it might be."

"That would be just what I need to start this circus all over again with a guy who comes back from the dead." Pilate laughed a short, mirthless laugh. "I truly hope not; I'm tired of dealing with this Passover crowd. It gets worse every year."

At that moment, the centurion walked in and stopped in front of Pilate with a smart salute.

"Tell me, Centurion, is the man called Yeshua of Nazareth dead?" Pilate asked.

"Yes, Sir, He is. One of my men made sure and took a lance and opened up His side. There can be no doubt, He is dead. I was there and watched him."

"Just for the heck of it, Centurion, do you think this Yeshua was guilty?"

"No, Sir, He wasn't. As a matter of fact, the way He died and the way it got dark for three hours and then the earthquake, I'm sure He was the Son of God. I even heard that the veil of the Temple was miraculously torn in two at the precise time He breathed His last. The way it is told, many dead came out of their graves right then and walked around and talked to people."

"That does sound strange, but then everything about this has been unusual," Pilate added thoughtfully and turned to Joseph, Nicodemus and Thomas. "You can have the body. Do with it what you want, it doesn't matter to me. Just so long this whole business is behind me." He turned and left abruptly.

"There is a man who is clearly in turmoil," Nicodemus said. "I don't blame him, he has a lot to answer for," he added on the way back to the carriage.

"We need to hurry, because it is late and we have much to do," Joseph said.

"I have brought enough spices for a royal burial," Nicodemus said, pointing to several baskets in the back. "Yeshua is a King and He deserves a King's burial."

There were no people on the road as soon as they drove through the gate leading to Golgotha. It took the three of them only a few minutes to lower the body of Yeshua off the cross and to the ground.

"My tomb is only a few feet over to the left, in a garden nearby," Joseph said as he pointed to a rock formation close by in an area where several burial chambers had been carved out from the stone. A flat, heavy, disk-shaped bolder leaned to the side, rounded to fit the opening perfectly. The inside of the tomb consisted of a small room hewn out of the rock with a niche carved out where Joseph and Nicodemus gently laid the body of the Master. Thomas stood and watched in silence as the two men prepared the body according to the law and customs with the spices Nicodemus had brought. When they were done, they wrapped it in clean, white linen cloth, including His head, until it was completely covered. Finally, they stood in silence, not knowing what to say until Joseph spoke softly, "Let's go, there is nothing more we can do for the Lord. It is up to Him now to show us where to go from here."

As they emerged from the interior, Thomas saw Mary Magdalene and several other women standing at a distance, watching where they had buried Yeshua. By now the sun was setting and it was time to stop all work because of the beginning of Shabbat. They would barely make it home for the Passover meal.

Chapter 39

"How does one wait for someone to rise from the dead?" Thomas looked around the table the next morning. "It sounds ridiculous."

"Yet that is what we are all doing, isn't it?" Lucius answered as he put fruit, wheat bread and goat cheese on his plate. "What else can we do but wait. The Master said He would rise after three days. It has been two since He died. I guess we just sit here and wait and go crazy," he added with obvious frustration.

"We could go and check on the grave site," Helena said as she spread cheese on her slice of bread. "There would be no one there, I'm sure. Maybe we could see something unusual."

"The messenger from Joanna yesterday asked that we go see the group of followers at the house of a wealthy follower of Yeshua named Simon of Bethany. Joanna has organized a meeting with the disciples to discuss and plan what to do next," Thomas said. "I think we better go there and not upset things with the Romans. Pilate ordered that the entrance be sealed with a special seal and guarded by several soldiers. They may not take kindly to us showing up snooping around."

"You are right, Thomas," Lucius said. "With the rumors of Yeshua rising from the dead, everyone is pretty touchy about the place. I bet the members of the Sanhedrin are holding their breath."

"I hope Nicodemus has been invited by Joanna," Thomas said. "He and Joseph of Arimathea were the last ones to see the body. They can verify that they put Him into the tomb."

There were over thirty people gathered in the upper room of the large house in Bethany by the time Thomas and Lucius arrived. They were standing in groups of four or five, discussing the events of the past few days. Thomas noticed the disciples huddled in a group by themselves way over in a corner, talking in low tones as not to draw attention.

"The question is and has always been, was Yeshua the Meshiah or should we wait for another?" The man's voice was loud enough for Thomas to hear above the noise. "Let's face it, the man died and we are left with nothing."

"We may even get arrested if we are caught meeting like this," another voice said. It belonged to the leader of the local synagogue in Bethany. "I am not willing to put my position and reputation on the line for a dead man. Are we sure Yeshua meant He would rise again now or at the time of the end when all shall rise again?"

"I don't remember, Caleb," an old man, bent over with age, answered. "At my age, my memory isn't as good as it once was. "Did the Master even say He would come back from the dead?"

"Yes, He did, I heard Him tell us many times." It was Joanna. Her voice was calm and confident. "He promised He would rise again on the third day, which is tomorrow. As a matter of fact, some of us women will go early in the morning and see if we need to prepare the body some more."

"Why would you do that, if you tell us He will rise from the dead?" a man by the name of Josephus said with a short laugh. "You are not making any sense, Joanna."

"I know," she answered. "I can't explain it, but we are going, no matter what you say. It is the least we can do for the Master," she added, suddenly less confident.

"Cephas, what do you think we should do? You are the one in charge now, aren't you?" Josephus said as he turned toward the group of Yeshua's men. "Surely you know what is going to happen since you were with Him all the time."

Cephas presented a picture of helplessness, mixed with sadness as he pulled on his robe. "I don't know what to think." He looked at the other disciples, his face filled with confusion. "We were so sure He was going to throw out the Romans and establish His Kingdom. Now we don't know what to think. Most of us have decided to return to Galilee and take up our old jobs. There is no sense waiting around here to get arrested by the Sanhedrin." A sudden silence followed his words as a heavy spirit of discouragement settled over the gathering.

"Nobody would listen to me when I tried to tell all of you it wouldn't go well," Didymus said, adding to the gloom.

"According to you nothing was ever going to work out," Andrew, the brother of Cephas said. "I still think the Master will rise again, you wait and see. He said He would and I believe Him."

Thomas did not know what to think at this point. *After all, if this was only a dream, it didn't matter, since nothing was real. No matter what Christians believed two thousand years later, no human had ever come back from the dead. All this had to do with faith and faith does not depend on fact, but what someone wants to believe.* Once again, the old frustration and anger rose up in him. How could he possibly make a decision based on that?

"It is not what we believe right now, but what the scriptures have foretold so long ago," Nicodemus said with a strong, confidant voice. "I have spent many days over the last year to search the ancient prophesies and I am telling you, Yeshua has fulfilled them all. He will rise again and we will see Him just as He has told us He would. Do not let doubt overwhelm you, but believe in the One who came to set us free from sin. The moment He is raised from the dead tomorrow, His victory over sin and death is complete." Nicodemus stood, his face shining with joy as he raised his arms. "Praise be to the God of Abraham, Isaac and Jacob who has sent His Son to die for us in order to gather His people to Himself. Blessed are we who have beheld the Son of God and walked with Him. Many who will come after us will wish they could have seen what we have seen, yet still they will believe, even into the far distant future."

Nicodemus sounds like a prophet, Thomas thought.

Slowly, the atmosphere changed as joy took the place of doom and hope cast out doubt and fear in many. Thomas stood to the side as he watched the group change, and just like he, those present were filled with an intense desire to believe what Nicodemus said was true.

As it got late, no one wanted to go home, but finally, at around midnight, He and Lucius made it back to the villa. Thomas had a hard time falling asleep. Tomorrow was the day when Yeshua was supposed to rise from the dead. Would He?

In spite of his anxiety the night before, Thomas was jolted out of his sleep at mid-morning by a loud rap on the door and shouting. He threw on his clothes and hurried to the atrium, where he found Joanna and Leah gesticulating frantically.

"He has risen! Thomas, the Lord has risen just like He said He would! We have seen Him with our own eyes!"

"What are you saying? Where have you seen Him?" Thomas tried to calm the women down. "Take a deep breath so we can understand what you are saying."

Joanna was the first one to speak. "Mary Magdalene and the other Mary went to the tomb early this morning like they said they would. Leah and I got there shortly after. We were wondering who would roll away the heavy stone to the entrance as we got close. Mary was also worried about the guards, if they would let us take care of the Master's body, but when we walked up to the tomb, there were no guards and the stone was already rolled away." Joanna tried to catch her breath before she went on. "Mary Magdalene was the first one to go inside. She came right back out, her face as white as a sheet. 'The Lord is not here. Someone has taken Him.' She was shaking and started to cry. 'His clothes are still there, neatly folded,' she told us. The rest of us went inside and confirmed what she had said. The Master's body was gone."

"What happened to it?" Lucius had come out to the atrium. "Did the Sanhedrin take it?"

"I don't think so," Leah said with confidence. "The reason is, when we were wondering what happened to the body, two men in gleaming white clothes suddenly appeared before us. Their appearance was like lightening and we were frightened and bowed low to the ground. One of them said these words,

'Why do you look for the living among the dead? He is not here; he has risen! Remember how he told you while he was still with you in Galilee, 'The Son of Man must be delivered into the hands of sinful men, be crucified and on the third day be raised again.'

"I am certain they were angels and I will never forget their words," Leah added with great emphasis. "The Lord has indeed risen!" She was shouting by now.

"Did you tell the apostles?" Thomas asked.

"Of course we did, but like typical men they did not believe us," Leah said with disdain. "Peter was the only one who at least ran out to the tomb, followed by John. We didn't wait for them to come back, but came here to let you know what happened."

"Where is Mary Magdalene?" Lucius asked.

"She stayed behind, because she was too upset and kept saying someone stole the body."

"Didn't she see the angels?" Thomas asked.

"She did, but she was so distraught to find the Lord's body gone, she just stood there, crying when we left."

"Where are the apostles now?" Lucius inquired.

"We don't know, but I imagine they are all together in the room where they had their last supper with Yeshua. The last time I spoke to them, they were scared they might be arrested and told me they would lock the doors so no one could find them," Leah said. "They are not exactly the mighty warriors standing by their leader, are they?" Her voice was dripping with sarcasm.

"I think we should go to the place where the apostles are hiding out," Thomas said. "They will let us in. I would really like to find out more about what has happened at the tomb."

"Well, let's all go together in your carriage, Thomas. It is faster that way," Leah said, always the practical one.

"Can I come along, Daddy?" Helena begged as she tugged on Thomas' robe.

"Sure, Angel," he answered as he smiled at her. "Andrew, get the carriage ready. I will do the driving so we can all fit in," he added.

The upper room was on the other side of Jerusalem and it took them over an hour to get there. The gate to the house was locked tight and they had to shout until Philip came to see who it was.

"Come on, Philip, let us in," Thomas said as he banged on the gate.

"Why not let the whole world know we are here," Philip said with fear in his voice. "We are trying very hard not to get arrested by the authorities," he added in a grumpy tone as he opened the gate.

They found a large group of people in the room, sitting or standing in small groups, talking in whispers. Before Thomas could say anything, there was another knock on the door. It was Mary Magdalene. She was out of breath from running. It was the first time Thomas had seen her disheveled. Her usual, peaceful demeanor was replaced by unrestrained excitement as she shouted to everyone,

"I have seen the Lord!" (John 20:18)

"What do you mean, you have seen the Lord," Cephas said as he stepped forward. "You mean you have found His body?"

"No, Cephas, I talked to Him! He spoke to me. It was Him, I know it."

"Calm down and tell us about it," John said as he led her to a seat up front, "why don't you tell us exactly what happened."

The moment she began to speak, the room became silent as everyone hung on to her every word.

"When the women and I came to the tomb this morning, I saw the angels and the clothes left in the tomb, but I was too upset to leave with them and stood there crying in front of the place where the Lord had been laid. That's when two angels stood, one at the head and the other at the foot. They asked me why I was crying and I told them that someone had taken my Lord and I didn't know where they had put Him." Mary Magdalene paused for a moment before she went on. "Suddenly, there was a man standing there. I thought it was the gardener. He also asked me why I was crying and I asked him to tell me where he had taken my Lord so I could get Him." She looked around the room and in a triumphant voice went on.

"That's when the man called me by name and I ran toward Him and cried 'Rabboni', because I knew it was the Master. But He said, 'Do not hold on to me, for I have not yet returned to the Father. Go instead to my brothers and tell them, 'I am returning to my Father and your Father, to my God and your God.' (taken from John 20:10-17)

There was silence in the room. No one knew what to say. They loved Mary Magdalene and knew how much she loved the Master. Thomas studied the faces around him and saw the doubt, hope and confusion on each one of them. He felt a great excitement rise within him and realized, Yeshua had indeed risen from the dead. There was no doubt in his heart that Mary Magdalene had spoken the truth.

"I believe you, Mary," he said in a voice filled with faith and confidence. "I know the Meshiah has come back to claim His people like the scripture says. "He has indeed risen and we will all see Him in the days to come."

At that moment a light appeared at the door and out of it Yeshua stepped into the room. "Peace be with you!" (John 20:19)

Before anyone could make a sound, He showed them His hands and His side with the wounds clearly visible. Thomas saw that His garments were as white as snow and of an almost translucent material. There were no scars on His face, no marks where the crown of thorns had been. His eyes had that same gentle, yet powerful look in them as He looked directly at Thomas with His wonderful knowing smile. "As the Father has sent me, I am sending you." And with that he breathed on him and said, "Receive the Holy Spirit." (John 20:21-22) Thomas closed his eyes as a feeling of power went through him. He couldn't explain it, but all doubt, confusion and fear left him as he suddenly understood what would be expected of him in the days to come. The Master had selected him to go to the people of Israel in the end times and share with them about their Meshiah. When he opened his eyes, Yeshua had turned to the rest of the people in the room. Amidst shouts of joy and laughter, He touched each person with His wonderful, loving and reassuring smile and then breathed the Holy Spirit on them. After an hour or so, He suddenly disappeared as mysteriously as He had come.

No one knew what to do after He was gone, until Cephas stepped up to the front and addressed the group.

"The Lord has risen just as He said He would! I am certain He is going to gather His forces to throw the Romans out now and establish His kingdom and we are the ones who will reign with Him. Prepare yourselves to be endued with power to defeat our enemies, the very ones who killed the Master. I am sure we will be fighting alongside the host of angels in the days to come until Israel is free of the Roman scourge." He was getting fired up as he continued and every man in the room was ready to do battle by the time he was finished.

They will find out this is not going to happen. Poor Cephas, as usual he was running his mouth before thinking things through. Thomas pulled Lucius aside. "It's time we should leave. This gathering is going to go on all night."

"You don't agree with Cephas, do you?" Lucius asked on the ride home. "What does your future tell you will happen?"

Thomas made sure Helena was inside the carriage sleeping before he answered.

"I have no idea about details. All I know is that the Romans will not be thrown out by Yeshua. Instead His followers, called Christians, will form what will be called the Church. It will spread across the known world by the disciples in spite of opposition by the Jewish religious leaders. In time there will be a great persecution of all believers by Rome and many will die horrible deaths in the arena. Yet in spite of it, Christianity will survive and thrive into the 21st century and be counted as one of the major religions of the world. The amazing thing is, it will replace the Roman Empire, not with weapons, but with faith in Yeshua."

"So what you are saying, He did come to defeat the Romans, just not the way Cephas thinks," Lucius said.

"You could say that. The sad thing is, the Jews never will accept their Meshiah even in my time. From what Yeshua told me at the meeting today, He wants me to go and tell them what I have seen and heard before He returns. It must be very sad for Him to know that most will refuse to believe Him for twenty-one centuries, while still waiting for His coming in my day. In seventy years from now Jerusalem and the Temple will be destroyed by the Romans and the Jewish nation will cease to exist for almost two thousand years."

"Is that in punishment for killing the Meshiah?" Lucius asked.

"Some say it is, but I don't know. In the year 1948 the nation of Israel is re-born and becomes a powerful force in this region with the help of my country America. So the God of the Jews does not forget about His favorite people in the end," Thomas added thoughtfully. "To remain Jewish after all that time, without having been integrated within the many nations they fled to, is a miracle in itself. We were and are still His chosen people."

"Does that mean you will go back soon since Yeshua's purpose for coming has been accomplished?" Lucius asked.

"I think so, although it makes me feel sad, since I will never see you or Helena or any of my friends again." Thomas leaned over and looked at Lucius with sadness. "Remember, all of this has only been some sort of vision and when I return, I will be back in Philadelphia in the year 2016."

"That also means I am not real, doesn't it?" Lucius said with sudden fear in his voice. "Following that logic, and as you know I do like logic, none of this, our friendship, your villa, Helena and everything else other than Yeshua, does not really exist."

"Yes."

Thomas lifted Helena out of the carriage when they arrived at the villa and carried her to her room. He gently lowered her onto her pallet and leaned over to kiss her forehead. She opened her eyes and smiled at him.

"I love you, Daddy," she said as a sleepy smile crossed her face.

"I love you, too, Angel."

He was exhausted from the long, dramatic day and collapsed on his pallet. The last thing he felt was an unusual, soothing heaviness spreading gently throughout his body.

Chapter 40

"Thomas, I'm home."

He had a hard time focusing his eyes as he woke up and was afraid to move. The voice belonged to Melissa!

"You didn't eat the food I left for you," she shouted from the kitchen. "I will heat it up and bring it to you. You must have had a hard day at work to sleep till now."

Thomas felt as if he was paralyzed. He was home!

"Happy Birthday, Sweetheart." Melissa stood in front of him with a card and a box wrapped in birthday paper. "Here, this is for you. I didn't forget like you probably thought I did."

"What time is it?" he finally managed to say.

"It is six-thirty. I came home early because it is your birthday," she said with a shy smile. "I thought maybe that leaves us enough time to celebrate a little, just the two of us."

He looked at her, trying desperately to find something to say that made any sense.

"What is wrong, did I do something to offend you?" Melissa's smile faded as she turned to go back into the kitchen to put dinner on.

Thomas realized he had only been asleep for one hour! He looked down at his Armani clothes and brown leather shoes and felt for his wallet. It was still there. He sat up in his chair and took in the familiar, yet strange surroundings of his house.

"I am really home," was all he could say when Melissa came in to let him know dinner was on the table.

"What do you mean you're really home?" she asked. "Where else would you be?"

"You cannot possibly imagine where I have been for the past three years," he said as he sat down at the table opposite from her.

"You mean for the last three hours?" Melissa said with a puzzled look on her face.

"No, I mean years."

"Thomas, what are you talking about?" She frowned at him. "You look as if you have been miles away."

"You have no idea." He looked at her with a strange smile. "Before I tell you where I've been, could you please bring me your Bible? I want to verify something."

"Can it wait until we have finished eating?" She sounded even more puzzled. "I have never known you to read the Bible."

"Maybe you can answer me some questions then," he said as he cut into the grilled salmon, one of his favorite dishes.

"Of course, what do you want to know?" Melissa asked, totally astonished by his request.

"Do you know a man named Lucius the physician during Jesus' time?"

"Yes, of course, that would be Luke who wrote the book of Luke and Acts in the New Testament."

"Can you tell me if he ever met Jesus?"

"I don't know about that, but what I do know he travelled extensively with the apostle Paul on many of his missionary journeys during the early church. He is also known for writing the most accurate account of what happened during Jesus' ministry."

"Is there anything in the Bible about Joanna, the wife of Chuza, King Herod's head steward?"

"Yes, she is mentioned as being one of the early followers of Jesus and traveled with Him extensively."

"Now, what do you know about an incident where a paraplegic was lowered down through the roof of a house for Jesus to heal him?"

"That is also recorded in the Bible. I don't know exactly where right now, but it is in there."

"Did Jesus ever heal ten lepers?"

"Yes, He did."

"What about a man called Nicodemus, a member of the Sanhedrin? Did he and a man name Joseph of Arimathea bury Jesus in his tomb?"

"Yes."

"I have one more question. Who did Jesus appear to first after He was resurrected?"

"There were several women, I don't know exactly all of them, but one was Mary Magdalene and Mary, the mother of James, referred to as the other Mary. What is this all about, Thomas? How do you know all these details out of the Gospels?" Melissa sounded confused.

"Because I was there."

"What do you mean, you were there. Where?"

"I have just returned from three years in the land of Israel in A.D. 27 through 30."

Melissa looked at him with a blank look. "You're kidding, right?"

"No, I'm not. That's why I want to read the New Testament to see if the things I experienced really happened or if it was just a dream."

"Thomas, you're not making any sense."

"Melissa," he said and took her hands. "I have become a follower of Yeshua, my Meshiah."

"Oh, my God," she said in a whisper, "oh, my God."

"I have given my life to Him and will serve Him in whatever way He wants to use me."

"Thomas, I can't believe it. How did this happen?" She jumped up and flung her arms around him, laughing and crying at the same time. "I love you."

"I love you, too, Sweetheart."

They stood and looked at each other with a love that had not been there for a long time.

"I don't understand any of this, but I am so happy I can't stand it," Melissa said as she leaned her head against his chest. "I never stopped loving you, Thomas. I just didn't know how to reach you."

"Before I share with you what happened, I want to ask your forgiveness for having been such an unmitigated, arrogant and prideful jerk. Yeshua showed me what horrible things I am capable of, given the right circumstances. I found out that without Him I am nothing and cannot ever be good, no matter how hard I try. But come, let's sit down and I will tell you what happened. It will take hours, even days to share what I have been shown in a dream that only lasted for an hour this afternoon."

"A dream?"

"Yes, during one hour this afternoon, the Lord allowed me to live for three years in the land of Israel during the time of Jesus' ministry. I didn't know anything about the New Testament other than what your grandmother told me, yet I experienced things I could have never known. That's why I asked you the questions of what's in the Bible. I am pretty sure I experienced most of the things in there as an eyewitness. Yeshua told me twice how blessed I was to see what I did, since many great scholars would give anything to have been there."

"You talked to Jesus?"

"Yes, many times."

"What was He like?" Melissa said with awe in her voice.

"He was a very nice, normal looking man with the most wonderfully kind, gentle eyes and a knowing smile He used each time He knew I was doing something wrong."

"Was it a dream or a vision?" Melissa asked.

"I don't know the difference between the two, but all throughout it felt like a dream. I met the most wonderful people of that time and they are as real to me as you are. The last person I saw before I woke up was a little girl named Helena. She was only thirteen years old and was my slave until I set her free and adopted her as my daughter."

"Your slave?" Melissa sounded incredulous. "You owned a slave?"

"I owned a hundred slaves, a fabulous villa and a lot of land."

Thomas looked at Melissa with a sheepish grin. "I was also the royal physician to King Herod and a good friend to Lucius, the physician."

"Thomas, are you sure this really happened or are you making it up?"

"Sweetheart, there is no way I could make up something as incredible as this," he said, laughing. "It was as real to me as you are now, although I doubted many times whether I could believe any of it. That is why I have to read the New Testament to know for sure."

"Maybe tomorrow you can get started on that. For now, I think the two of us should celebrate your birthday the way it deserves." She blushed as she pulled him into the bedroom.

An hour later, they lay together, holding onto each other with a love that felt new and exciting.

"I never thought we could be this happy again," Melissa said as she snuggled up to him. "I still can't believe you are a Christian."

"Let's wait on that until I get a chance to read your Bible. If it confirms what I experienced, it proves my dream was real and not just my imagination." He stuck his foot out from under the cover the way he always did.

"Thomas," Melissa whispered. "Look at your foot."

"What's the matter with it?" he asked.

"It has five toes."

They stared in wonder. Both of his feet had five toes!

"Your dream was real, Thomas! The Lord gave you the missing toe." Melissa was crying. "It was real!"

Thomas jumped up and fell on his knees beside the bed.

"My Lord and my God," he whispered as tears streamed down his face. "You are truly Yeshua, my Meshiah."

The End

Here is the first chapter of the sequel to this story. If you want to follow Thomas into the land of Israel and into the tumultuous end times, read on and then go to Amazon to find it on Kindle or in paperback.

COUNTDOWN TO THE FUTURE

Chapter 1

Thomas Peterson, MD entered the surgical suite with an uneasy feeling. It felt as if he had been gone for three years as he looked around the gleaming, sterile environment with a mixture of awe and a certain feeling of nostalgia. What a difference a day makes! It had only been yesterday since he had walked the crowded streets of Jerusalem and watched the most famous trial and crucifixion in the history of the world.

There was a lump in his throat when he thought about his little girl Helena, his friend Lucius and the many people he encountered on his treacherous journey through ancient Israel. He would never see them again.

His heart took an extra beat when the picture of Yeshua appeared in his mind with crystal clarity. His warm, brown eyes and knowing, wonderful smile of unconditional love would always be with him. His last words were seared into his mind as if etched in stone. "As the Father has sent me, I am sending you." And with that he breathed on him and said, "Receive the Holy Spirit." (John 20:21-22)

The words of the old man Jonah at the wedding at Cana appeared with equal power. "You are a stranger in this land and are filled with unbelief. And yet the Lord Jehovah shows me that you will see the Glory of His coming and be touched by Him in a special way. Turn from your doubts and prepare your heart for He will anoint you to take His message into a distant land and time."

The words of John the Baptist in the prison fortress of Machaerus were even more specific.

"You have seen the Meshiah, Thomas, I am sure of it. You have been sent by the God of Abraham, Isaac and Jacob to behold His Son and believe, for He will use you greatly in the far distant future. Do not resist Him, but repent for He has chosen you to serve Him in a different age."

How would he tell his family, his colleagues and especially his grandmother? They would mock him and Nana would be heartbroken that he left the Jewish faith to become a Christian.

Thomas suddenly realized everyone was looking at him with a strange look, because he was standing motionless, staring at nowhere in particular with a scalpel in his hand. He cleared his throat with an embarrassed little cough and held out his hand to the surgical nurse next to him.

"Scalpel, please."

The nurse looked at him with obvious surprise.

"You already have it, Doctor."

"Of course, thank you Brenda."

With a certain amount of bewilderment, he noticed the absence of the adrenaline rush he usually felt as he guided the scalpel with steady, sure hands. He had no doubt he was still an excellent surgeon, but there was not the sense of accomplishment or pride connected with it that had been there only yesterday. A little smile crossed his face, hidden by the mask. He realized his priorities had changed dramatically since he accepted the Carpenter of Nazareth as his Meshiah during his dramatic dream.

"Brenda, you did a good job," he turned to the nurse when he was finished. "Thank you."

"I am surprised you noticed, Dr. Peterson," she said as they walked out of the surgical suite. "I have been assisting you for two years and you have never mentioned it before."

"I know and I am sorry." He looked at her with a warm smile. "It's time I do, don't you think?"

"What happened to you, Doctor? You are different; did you get religion?" She chuckled as she walked off without waiting for an answer.

It was late afternoon when his shiny, black BMW turned into the driveway of his large home surrounded by manicured landscaping in an upscale neighborhood. It was hard to imagine it had only been yesterday since he had come home to an empty house to find that his wife Melissa seemed to have forgotten his birthday. He had fixed himself a glass of wine and gone to sleep in his chair only to wake up in the market place of Nazareth in the year 27 A.D. Today, he still had difficulties separating the dream from reality and felt like he was in limbo between the past and the present. Nothing felt the same and he yearned for his life back then instead of living in the present in the year 2016. He had not shared his experience with anyone except Melissa.

As he got out of the car, he found himself wishing it was his horse-drawn carriage and shook his head in confusion. It had taken only an hour-long dream for his life to be turned upside down and shake everything he had ever believed in. He was still in shock over the appearance of the missing toe on his left foot when he woke up. It was a birth defect and it's miraculous appearance proved beyond a shadow of a doubt, that what he had experienced was real. Still, it felt like the Twilight Zone.

"We are invited to your parents' house for dinner, honey. I guess they want to celebrate your birthday," Melissa said as she kissed him with great affection. "Are you going to share with them about what happened?"

He looked at his wife with a deep love he had not felt for several years. Their love for each other had returned when he returned and it was still a wonder to him.

"I don't know. It's all still so new to me. I was actually going to read the Bible tonight to see if the things I experienced are really in there."

"Trust me, from what you told me, they are. Every single one of them." Melissa smiled at him. "You are an eyewitness to what happened during Jesus' ministry here on this earth. I don't think I will ever get used to that." She looked at Thomas with sudden concern. "What do you think your parents are going to say?"

"I have some idea and that's why I dread telling them. I wouldn't blame them if they thought I have lost my mind; if it wasn't for my toe." He suddenly laughed. "Imagine, Yeshua wants me to use a toe to share about Him."

"I think this miracle is undeniable, especially for your parents. They will not be able to doubt your experience," Melissa said with conviction. "Let's face it, your father has the same birth defect and your mother definitely knows about both of you. So how can they not believe you?"

"You don't know my parents. They scoff at anything religious and take great pride in science to dispel faith of any kind," he answered as he got a glass of milk out of the fridge.

"And how in the world can they explain your toe with their precious science; answer me that?"

"I don't know, but trust me, they will manage." His voice took on a hint of confusion as he went on. "How am I supposed to explain it to them or to the rest of the world when I don't even understand it? The great Chief of Thoracic Surgery at Philadelphia Mercy Hospital suddenly believes in God and miracles, because he went back to 27 A.D. and met Jesus, the Messiah." He looked at Melissa with a look of doubt. "Even I find that hard to believe; and I was there."

"The Lord will be there with you, Thomas. He will give you the words, don't you worry." Melissa hugged him and then kissed him on the cheek. "It will be alright, honey. You are not the one who has to convince people of what happened. All you have to do is share your experience and then let the Holy Spirit do the rest." She took his hand and led him to the couch in the living room. "That is why God gave you the dream, so you can "go into all the world and preach the Gospel"."

"So you think Jesus wants me to be a preacher?" He cringed at the thought. "I have no intention of ever doing that."

"Then what do you think He wants you to do with what happened?" Melissa looked at him with astonishment and disappointment.

"I don't know. In a way I wish I was back there, because everyone believed what happened and didn't expect me to become religious." He leaned back with a sigh. "This is all too new and confusing and I really don't want to talk about it to anyone until I have gotten used to the whole idea of being a Christian." He looked at Melissa with pleading eyes. "Can you understand that?"

"I can, honey. The Lord will show you what to say and when to say it. If you don't want to go tonight, I will call and tell your parents we can't make it. It was short notice anyway."

"No, I somehow feel I haven't seen them in a long time." He smiled. "Like for three years maybe?"

"I will admit that sounds pretty crazy." She got up, "Let's get ready then."

Dear Reader,

If you have enjoyed this book, please consider writing a review on Amazon to let other potential readers know your opinions and thoughts. Reviews are the lifeline of any writer and will help to spread the "Word" in more ways than one.

The sequel, called 'Countdown To The Future', is available on Amazon.

Please go to my website at **www.barbarahmartin.com** for my other six books or find out how to schedule a **speaking engagement** for your event. I have been a motivational speaker and teacher for many years with my books or any subject suitable for your organization.

Here is a description of my other six books which you can find on Amazon or on my website.

#1 BESTSELLING novel WHEN THE EAST WIND BLOWS (4.5-star rating on Amazon) deals with my mother's story during the last six months of WWII in Nazi Germany. It tells of her heroic flight from the incoming Russian front into the carpet bombing of the Allies with her four children and a maid. On the way they meet up with an escaped Jewish concentration camp prisoner who then travels with them dressed as a girl. (available on Kindle. In paperback **only** through my website)

THE LITTLE BOOK OF MIRACLES shares 16 inspirational stories of real, astounding miracles which happened over the many years since I came from atheism to finding the Lord in a dramatic way. (available on Kindle. In paperback **only** through my website)

WALKING IN POWER deals with a deeper walk in the spiritual realm with personal experiences and comparisons between today's Christianity and the early church. It can be used as a study guide for Bible studies, using Scripture as back up. (Available on Kindle. In paperback **only** through my website)

If you like good, clean, suspenseful Christian murder mysteries you will love the **PERFECT CRIME TRILOGY**. (All three are available on Kindle and paperback)

SILK SHEETS AND OTHER THINGS THAT DON'T WORK

A parody on getting old together with all the changes and pitfalls, wrinkles and quirks that come with being married for a long time. In reading this book, you will find yourself and your spouse with amusing clarity and realize, all things considered, getting old together is not so bad after all.

If you wish to get in touch with me or have any questions, please go to my website at **www.barbarahmartin.com** and click on 'Contact'. I will answer all correspondence promptly if at all possible. May God bless you.

Made in the USA
Charleston, SC
04 February 2017